A DIFFERENCE IN TIMES

David Thurlow's interviews with British international athletes – from the 1920s to the 1970s

National Union of Track Statisticians

A Difference In Times
Copyright © 2017 David Thurlow

All Rights Reserved

ISBN 978-0-904612-25-7

Published in 2017 by the National Union of Track Statisticians, web site www.nuts.org.uk

The National Union of Track Statisticians (NUTS) was formed in 1958 and since then has published every year an annual listing the leading British athletics performances and has also produced a series of booklets detailing the history of individual events.

Editors of "A Difference In Times": Bob Phillips and Stuart Mazdon. **Introduction:** Peter Lovesey. With thanks for photographs to Kevin Kelly, Neil Shuttleworth and Clive Williams.

Front cover illustration. Athletics in the 1930s. The celebration of a world record. Sydney Wooderson is carried shoulder-high in triumph away from the Motspur Park track after running a mile in 4min 6.4sec on the afternoon of 28 August 1937. Among the excited crowd are Sydney's brother, Stanley, to the left, also wearing the all-black vest and shorts of their club, Blackheath Harriers, who was one of the pace-makers, and Albert Hill, to the right, dressed in an immaculate three-piece suit (and smoking a cigarette!), who had been the Olympic champion at 800 and 1500 metres in 1920 and was Sydney Wooderson's coach. This performance is one of the many described by David Thurlow in the collection of the interviews which he has conducted from the 1990s onwards for the quarterly journal of the National Union of Track Statisticians, "Track Stats", and which have now been gathered together in book form.

Back cover illustration. Jack Holden is introduced to Queen Elizabeth (later the Queen Mother) before the start of the Polytechnic Marathon at Windsor Castle on 19 June 1948. To Holden's left are Dick Tobin (No. 14) and George Chantler (looking at Holden), both of Belgrave Harriers. Facing the camera, and with his own camera, is Sir Eric Studd, President of Polytechnic Harriers and far right, with hand in pocket, is the race organiser Arthur Winter.

Contents

Introduction *by Peter Lovesey*

A journalist's life, and so many enjoyable interviews with the ageing champions

In January 1998 "Track Stats" published an article about the veteran athlete Arthur Collyer, aged 88. It was based in large part on an interview conducted by the writer, David Thurlow. Later that year David interviewed Sir Arthur Marshall and Sydney Wooderson. Thus began a series of profiles and interviews collected here for the first time. They form a precious record of the experience and opinions of outstanding athletes from five decades, spoken with the perspective that great age brings. Sadly, many of them have since died, and it is worth reflecting that if David Thurlow hadn't taken the trouble to record their words, numerous previously unknown stories and insights would have died with them.

We thought that the best way of introducing this book would be to turn the tables on David and interview him. He is 85 himself now and recovering from a stroke and we are grateful to his daughter Fiona Barton for going through the questions with him and typing the answers.

The spark that lit David's enthusiasm for athletics was Sydney Wooderson taking on Arne Andersson, of Sweden, in the one mile at the White City Stadium, in London, in 1945. "I was 13 and on my school holidays", David recalls; "I remember listening to it on the radio, but the race attracted a record-breaking crowd for the White City. Lots of people couldn't get in. Wooderson had recently recovered from rheumatic fever, but he was only just beaten by the Swede. What inspired me was the courageous way Wooderson ran against one of the two top milers of that era. He was a tremendous runner".

Born in Wisbech, Cambridgeshire, in February 1932, David was given a combined 16th birthday and Christmas present which most of us would have coveted – tickets for each day of the track and field programme for the 1948 Olympics. A year later came another treat. "I was given a lift by the 1924 Olympic gold-medallist, Harold Abrahams. We'd both been at a White City meeting, and my father, a friend of Harold's, arranged for him to bring me home. He was very pleasant company and I remember chatting to him about my running."

Was David's father an athlete? "No, he wasn't sporty at all. I certainly didn't get my interest in athletics from him. That came from a great-uncle who won the Essex quarter-mile before the turn of the century and became part of my family history". As for his own running: "I never wanted to be a sprinter. I was never much good at it. I was better at middle-distance and I got lots of fun out of it. My best performance was winning the London AC three miles at Motspur Park in South London in 1952". Most of all, he enjoyed cross-country: "I always felt there was more to it than just running round a track. My last race was an evening road race in 1953, which I won. The year-and-a-bit that I was racing was a very inspiring time. I was silly really because I stopped just when I was getting good when I got a job up north on the 'Northern Echo' newspaper. There was no chance of doing any running at all when I was doing that job. I just didn't have time".

His career was entirely in journalism, which had begun in the traditional way on a local newspaper, the "Leicester Evening Mail", and later with some of the great national papers in Fleet Street. He was with the "Welwyn Times", the "Northern Echo", the "Yorkshire Evening News", the "Daily Herald", "Daily Mirror", Anglia Television, the "Daily Express" for 26 years and finally "The Times". He says, "It is strange, but I never covered sport during my journalistic career. I was more interested in reporting news".

While still working as a reporter, David wrote more than a dozen books, working in several genres, including science fiction, crime fiction and accounts of real crime. "I always preferred real crime because it is so much more interesting to write about", he says, "When you are writing fictional crime, you know what's going to happen. You know all the answers in fiction because you are creating it, whereas in real crime there are occasions when it is impossible to discover who did it".

An outstanding example is "The Essex Triangle: Four Decades of Murder" (1990), in which he wrote of a remarkable concentration of crimes in Essex confined to an area between Colchester, Great Dunmow and Tolleshunt D'Arcy, of which the most notorious was the murder of five members of the Bamber family in 1985. David reported for his newspaper on the trial of Jeremy Bamber, who continues to protest his innocence from prison. However, David is in no doubt that the correct verdict was reached.

In another book he broke new ground, firstly by writing about politics and secondly by proving that a long-accepted theory was untrue. In "Profumo: the Hate Factor" (1992) he showed that instead of the osteopath Dr Stephen Ward being the man who exposed Profumo's affair with Christine Keeler and took the blame for the downfall of the Macmillan Government in 1963, the real instigator was a former MP, businessman and socialite called John Lewis, driven by the paranoid belief that Ward once had an affair with his wife. It was Lewis who fed information about Ward to George Wigg MP that brought the scandal to light.

With such a spread of themes it would be surprising if David had not at some point written about athletics. It is not widely known that under a pseudonym, as Jonathan MacGowan, he published a suspense thriller in 1980 called "Death at the Games". 'The inspiration came when I was watching the finish of the marathon on television. I think it was the 1980 Moscow Olympics, and I thought how simple – and shocking – it would be to kill someone in those final minutes. There is so much open space as the leading athletes enter the stadium and it is being shown on live television. All I had to do was choose the most impressive way of killing the runner!"

David's best-known work on athletics is, of course, non-fiction. For "Track Stats" he has penned numerous articles. It is almost invidious to pick any out, but one in which his research skills were put to strong purpose was the story behind the choice of the Cambridge University runner, John Mark, to carry the Olympic flame into Wembley stadium in 1948. As always, there had been speculation who the last runner would be, and many had expected Wooderson to be the choice. "But what a pity they didn't get dear little Sydney to do it," the Queen was said to have remarked.

The story is touched on again in David's much-praised biography, "Sydney Wooderson: Forgotten Champion". He won't mind the book being described as a labour of love, because it's about a man who loved to run. "I saw Sydney run in the Nationals in 1949. He was in his 30s and in the senior cross-country. He was just running for the love of it. For fun. I never saw him run seriously, which is a big regret, but I met him in the late 1980s. He was the runner who first got me interested in athletics, and he was a very unlikely athlete at that. There was more meat on a butcher's pencil than Sydney. In America they said he looked like he couldn't run round the corner, but he was very, very fast. And so self-effacing and honourable. He was a complete amateur, an ordinary man who happened to be able to run very fast. He was fantastic, a fantastic runner. No other word for him. He held the world record for the one mile for almost five years. Typically, Sydney didn't understand why a book was being written about him. He loved the running, but not the attention".

Later, in 2000, David wrote about a hero in another sport. "I have always loved cricket, but I love athletics more. I wrote "Ken Farnes: Diary of an Essex Master" at the suggestion of a friend. I knew a bit about Ken Farnes and what a marvellous fast bowler he was. But I was interested in what made him such a great sportsman. I also knew there were obstacles he had to overcome – he couldn't always bowl because of his job as a schoolteacher. He volunteered as soon as war started and became a bomber pilot, He was so tall it was difficult to fit into the cockpit. Sadly, he was killed during his service".

This question of what makes a great sportsman is one that David has often pondered as he carried out the interviews for the present book. Several of those he met were world record holders: Dorothy Tyler, Sheila Lerwill, Wooderson, Chris Chataway and Freddie Green. Did he notice anything different about them? "It is an intriguing thing, but these are ordinary people who happened to have been the best in the world. You wouldn't spot it if you met someone like Wooderson or Freddie Green, but it was there. But not revealed until they got on the track and led the field. You cannot put your finger on what it was that made them great, but perhaps they recognised it in each other. Chris Chataway, when he was a government minister, broke all the schedules on a visit to a factory when he stopped to chat to Stan Cox, who happened to be a minor cog in the company but was one of the top marathon runners of his day".

David summarised his method in setting up the interviews. "I used to contact the ex-athletes first and then go and see them. The major difficulty was finding interviewees who could remember what they had done. I was talking to quite elderly people and there were some who couldn't remember anything. Only one declined, saying he didn't think it was worthwhile. At one interview, I used the athlete's scrapbook to get the information. And at another, the athlete couldn't remember anything after the moment he got on a train to go to the Empire Games in 1930.

"I took notes in shorthand, or sometimes longhand. I varied my method – sometimes doing the interview on the phone, sometimes over lunch. But I always preferred to go to people's homes to talk to them. They were more relaxed and there were fewer distractions. Also you got a glimpse of the sort of people they were off the track. I was amazed that some of the athletes were quite affluent, while others were just ordinary folk. They were all so very pleasant, which is why I enjoyed doing the interviews so much."

One distance-runner and fellow journalist became a close friend. "I used to meet Doug Wilson for years on a weekly basis at a pub just outside Winchester where he lived, and it only ended the weekend before he died. We met so often that the bar staff used to pull the drinks and start making the sandwiches before we ordered them. We talked of many things, not always athletics. But one memory that always upset him was his loyalty, or stupidity, in travelling to Glasgow and back for the Rangers meeting on the August Bank Holiday weekend, 1945, when he was due to face Gunder Hägg at White City on the Monday. He couldn't get a seat on the train and stood the whole way. After a 36-hour round-trip he lost to the great Swede by 120 yards. He was a great friend and I miss him". For a fuller account see the interview with Wilson.

David's enjoyment of the interviews shines through, which is why we were keen to collect the articles in this book. When asked if his own opinions – for example, on amateurism and its effects – had been altered by the experience of hearing so many accounts, David said, "My views never changed because the athletes were so varied. Some trained desperately hard and there were others who didn't. Some were naturally brilliant and didn't need the hard training. I remember Sydney Wooderson trained very hard indeed and rarely spoke of it or boasted of all the hard work."

Finally he was asked to name three British athletes and three from other countries he would have dearly loved to have met and interviewed. "This is very hard, but I'm going for Alfred Shrubb (1879-1964), a distance-runner who won about 1000 races from 1800 starts; Willie Applegarth

David Thurlow on his way to 2nd place in a race at Peterborough, Easter 1953.

(1890-1958), the gold-medallist sprinter; Cyril Ellis (1904-1973), the middle-distance runner who couldn't afford to go to the Olympics; then Paavo Nurmi (1897-1973), the Flying Finn; Jack Lovelock (1910-1949), the Olympic Champion middle-distance runner from New Zealand; and Otto Peltzer (1900-1970), the German middle-distance runner who set records in the 1920s. They were all outstanding in their field, but I would love to ask them what made them outstanding".

Peter Lovesey, May 2017

Note: Peter Lovesey is the author of more than 30 books, including the centenary history of the Amateur Athletic Association and a collection of biographies of athletes, "Kings of Distance", and is regarded as one of the leading authorities on Victorian-era athletics. He is further renowned as an internationally-acclaimed award-winning crime novelist.

Sir Arthur Marshall, Olympic Games 4 x 400 metres relay reserve 1924

Carrying the baton onwards: the last survivor of the wonderful "Chariots of Fire" team

On the morning of 23 March 1923 Harold Abrahams, the Cambridge University athletics president, took his young freshman 440 yards champion, A.G.G. Marshall, for a walk in London's Kensington Gardens. Abrahams wanted to know what his 19-year-old team member – always referred to by his initials as a tribute to his speed because they stood for "a gee-gee" – thought of his chances against Oxford's American, William Stevenson.

Marshall, who had been named as first string for the Oxford-v-Cambridge match, knew no one else had been selected even though Stan Nelson, son of the university's legendary professional coach, Alec Nelson, had finished a good 2nd in the university sports, Marshall thought this a bit strange, but being a new boy he did not ask, and a week later he learnt that Abrahams himself was to be the second string. He thought little more of it until the morning of the match.

Then Abrahams, who had rarely run a 440 yards in his life, started questioning him again about his chances, Marshall replied: "I know I'm going to be up against it because Stevenson has a much better record, but I'm full of confidence and will have a jolly good go and do my best". To Marshall's surprise Abrahams said: "Will you give up every chance if we get a plan out in which I might have a chance of winning?" AGG – now Sir Arthur Marshall, doyen of the British aircraft industry – recalled the conversation with perfect clarity and unhesitatingly 75 years later: "I said 'no' and he told me the plan".

Sir Arthur was in his office overlooking the Cambridge airport and hangars which he and his father had set up in 1929. Sir Arthur was born on 4 December 1903, and in his 95th year he remains an amazing man, erect at his racing height of 5ft 10½in (1.79m), silver-haired, as articulate as he was as a young man and a Jesus College undergraduate, and only his very poor eyesight giving a clue to his age. Four days after I went to see him in the company of fellow NUTS member Dave Terry, Sir Arthur memorised a 10-page speech which he gave on acceptance of the 1998 Masefield Gold Medal for services to the aircraft industry.

He is the last remaining member of that wonderful British Olympic team of 1924 – the "Chariots Of Fire" gang – which won three gold medals and four bronzes. AGG was reserve for the 4 x 400 metres relay after being run out of a qualifying place for the final of the AAA Championships 440 yards behind Liddell and Stevenson (gold in the Olympic 4 x 400) in a blanket finish. The two qualifiers both ran 49.6 and Marshall just failed in a lifetime best of 49.8. Canada's Dave Johnson (4th in the Olympic 400 final) was even faster in another semi-final with 49.4.

Sir Arthur's recollection of Abrahams's plan for the 1923 Inter-Varsity match is also vivid; "Harold said that if we could achieve a very slow race he might have enough speed left to pip the Oxford man at the post. He said that as the second-string pacemaker he should set off at a fast pace with me making no attempt to keep up with him. He would then continue at a slower pace until the finishing straight when he would run wide to let me through.

"But I should not put any pressure on Stevenson, Harold said. Stevenson would be watching me as the first string and would believe he could beat me on the run-in regardless of the speed of the race. He would never consider Harold as a possible winner, and if I made no attempt to increase the speed Harold might be able to keep up and have the speed for the final burst."

The 1924 Inter-Varsity 440 yards. Above, left to right - Dave Johnson, A.G.G. Marshall, William Stevenson and Stan Nelson. Spectators crowd enthusiastically round the start on the Queen's Club cinder track. No lanes, no starting-blocks. As Sir Arthur so graphically recalls, a different era. Below, the finish with Johnson winning from Marshall.

AGG agreed to the plan and it worked perfectly. The 440 was not run in lanes, and as the three went round the last bend of the Queen's Club track, in London, with AGG on Stevenson's shoulder, Abrahams came up on the other side and shot off to a lead of five or six yards, holding on by three yards to win in a lifetime best of 50.8. Oxford won the match, anyway, by seven events to four. Abrahams never forgot Marshall's sacrifice. In 1974 Abrahams wrote to congratulate Sir Arthur on his knighthood, starting his letter "As your second string".

In the 1924 Inter-Varsity match AGG beat Stevenson but lost to Dave Johnson, with Stan Nelson rightfully completing the field as Marshall's second string. The reason for Nelson's omission the previous year was only found out many years later by AGG at a lunch with Abrahams, who was by then NUTS President, too, in 1970, and it provides an historical note of snobbery and prejudice which is shameful even today. Nelson was not selected because, as Abrahams explained, the university committee of the time would not have the son of the club's professional trainer as a member of the team. AGG was himself the son of a Cambridge tradesman.

The runners selected for the Olympic 4 x 400 metres relay were Edward Toms (Queen's Park Harriers), George Renwick (Achilles Club), Richard Ripley (Polytechnic Harriers) and Guy Butler (also Achilles Club). Great Britain's medallists at those Games were as follows: Harold Abrahams, gold 100 metres; Eric Liddell, bronze 200 metres & gold 400 metres; Douglas Lowe, gold 800 metres; Hyla Stallard, bronze 1500 metres; Bertram McDonald, Herbert ("Johnny") Johnston & George Webber, silver 3000 metres team; Gordon Goodwin, silver 10,000 metres walk; Malcolm Nokes, bronze hammer. Abrahams, Walter Rangeley, Lancelot Royle & William Nichol, silver 4 x 100 metres relay; Toms, Renwick, Ripley & Butler, bronze 4 x 400 metres relay.

A leg injury suffered playing rugby football largely ended AGG's track career soon after, but he was in the Achilles team which won the AAA 4 x 440 yards relay in 1925, and uniquely for a quarter-miler – until Derek Johnson came along 30 years later – ran in the 7½ miles (12km) Inter-Varsity cross-country match at Roehampton in December, finishing 7th of the 12 runners as Cambridge won by 23pts to 32.

Much has changed in the sport since those days, and Sir Arthur, still involved in athletics and particularly the annual "Chariots Of Fire" charity relay race in Cambridge, expresses some fascinating views: "Everyone then was an amateur. Oxford and Cambridge provided most of the British team, and those working for a living had limited time for training. I well remember a good miler from Manchester, who was a welder standing all day at his job, saying to me, 'You know, I believe I could do so much better if I had your easier life'. It is difficult to understand now, but in my day we always worried about running too much and getting stale. Douglas Lowe used to try and plan that he did not have more than two or three hard races a year, whereas today they seem to go on running and running with longer seasons and more races with major competitions worldwide.

"There is a tremendous difference in times, but part of that is the shoes and the tracks. I remember Harold Abrahams saying that one thing was for sure – he would not be 10 yards behind the winner of any sprint race today!"

Note: this article was first published in "Track Stats", Volume 36, No.3, July 1998. When Sir Arthur Marshall died on 16 March 2007, a week before his 104th birthday, he was the oldest surviving Olympian from all countries and all sports.

Kemeys Bagnall-Oakeley, Long jump versus France 1926 & 1927

At the Attleborough sports – let's move the coconut shy and the competition can begin!

Henry Kemeys Bagnall-Oakeley was born in Norwich on 2 July 1904. He was educated at Gresham's School, Holt, and Clare College, Cambridge. He ran for the Achilles club and for Great Yarmouth AC and was 6ft (1.83m) tall and weighed 10½st (66kg).

On a summer's afternoon in 1925 young "Kem" was on the verge of achieving a tremendous double, having already won the 100 yards in 10.3 in a close finish with his regular college and university rival, John Rinkel, who would three years later place 4th in the Olympic 400 metres final. Kem went over to the long jump where the groundsman would not allow competitors to practise in the pit, insisting that they measured their run-ups beside it. "We thought he was proud of it and wanted the spectators to see it, so we willingly did as he asked", Kem recalled. "It was customary in those days to jump in alphabetical order, so I was first – to find that there was no pit at all".

The idle groundsman had covered some hard ground with sand and gravel to avoid having to dig it up in the hot weather, and when Kem landed he all but broke his ankle. Yet he still set a lifetime best of 23ft 3in (7.07m) with his only jump before being taken off to hospital. The severely swollen ankle kept him out of the Oxford & Cambridge Universities tour to the USA for matches against Harvard & Yale and Princeton & Cornell.

This did not upset him too much because he came from the small Norfolk village of Hemsby, where his father was vicar, and he was not used to the sort of celebration which would have been held for his 21st birthday during the ocean crossing on the liner, "Mauretania". The Hemsby villagers had been astonished to learn that the newspaper headline, "Famous Varsity Athlete Injured", referred to their Mr Kem junior.

Kem encountered several weird long-jump pits during his top-level career which went on to 1938. He had been an outstanding and unexpected 2nd in the inaugural indoor AAA Championships in 1935 when he and other veterans entered in case the youngsters were not attracted by the novel idea of indoor competition. Many were not and stayed away! The meeting was held on the Wembley Ice Rink and the track was covered with canvas, but the long-jump run-up was on boards raised on supports to bring it to the level of the box of wood-chips which formed the landing-area. Kem said: "The supports were too far apart and the board sagged between them. We ran as though we were lame, and as there was nothing to check us on landing we slid along the ice at least as far again as the jump". He managed 21ft 1in (6.43m) on ice!

In an England-v-Scotland match at Belle Vue, Manchester, there was a trench across the run-up that was not properly filled in. Harold Abrahams, who was reporting on the meeting, assessed the situation and gave his verdict: "Aim for the right-hand edge of the board so you will land in the left-hand corner of the pit". Kem did, and won with 22-4 (6.80).

Then at a Norfolk sports meeting at Attleborough the run-up was only 10 yards long because of the stalls which had been set up for fete day. So the jumpers had to move the coconut-shy temporarily for the event to go ahead. It was at a subsequent meeting at Attleborough that Kem ran his first official 10-flat for 100 yards, causing the timekeepers to leap up in the air and the local newspaper to dub him "Fastest Man in Britain".

On another occasion a meeting was held on the Wellington pier at Yarmouth. "The run-up was

11

on the wooden deck, and so we couldn't use spikes, and the pit was a wide box of sawdust which looked like a coffin. On landing, I skidded along the deck, pushing most of the sawdust in front of me. The spectators loved it, and I won, but with less than 20ft".

There was a purpose to him competing in Norfolk. The AAA officials wanted to keep an eye on his progress during 1927 when he could not get to the major meetings, and after his pier fiasco they selected him for a match against the Army where he jumped 23-0 (7.01), and he was also in the team against France at Stamford Bridge when he finished equal 2nd with 23-1¼ (7.04) behind Charles Alzieu, of France. Kem said: "There had to be a jump-off. My opponent went first and did a great jump, but I did even better – over 23ft 6in, I think, the best I ever did, but it did not count officially". Alzieu's official winning leap was less than that – 23-2¾ (7.08).

Growing up in rural Norfolk, and discovering early on that he could run and jump well, one of Bagnall-Oakeley's earliest memories is of being taken to see the Olympic marathon in 1908. "I was actually there at the finish as a small boy aged four in a sailor suit, having been a page at a wedding earlier in the day. One of the ushers reckoned they ought to take little Kem to see the finish, so he could tell his grandchildren that he had been there. He thought it was unlikely that the marathon would be held again in London in my lifetime – wrong by over 50 years!

"I have a vivid recollection of the circumstances, but how much of that is genuine memory I am doubtful, as I've seen the photographs and heard the descriptions so many times. Dorando arrived at the stadium in a state of collapse, and the runners had been told to turn right so they could run round the track and pass the Royal party in the stands – the extra 385 yards. Dorando evidently did not hear the announcement, or didn't understand it, and tried to go the wrong way round, whereupon he was impeded by groups of officials.

"He struggled with them, thinking they were supporters of Hayes, the American, who was running 2nd, and eventually these officials frog-marched him round with the result that he was disqualified for receiving outside assistance. I have a vivid recollection of the scene, but I doubt whether it is genuine memory".

Quick off the mark as a Zeppelin airship flies overhead

Kem's school athletics at Gresham's was curtailed by World War I and by a headmaster who thought that competitive sport was unpatriotic, but he kept in training by having to run the quarter-mile or so from his boarding-house and back three times a day. On one occasion he had to run flat out because a German Zeppelin airship started its engine right above him, having followed the usual practice of drifting over the North Sea on its way to bomb London.

When athletics resumed, it was all crammed into one day during the hockey season. This was a game at which he excelled and he would have won his Blue at Cambridge but for the shortage of cash. The players had to pay their own expenses to take part in the Varsity match. He continued to play at a high level until the age of 54.

Of the school sports he recalled: "The 100 was run between strings that made a series of curves in a side wind. I carried rope burns on my legs for years afterwards, and I was once asked if they were war wounds! The long jumpers had a pit but no take-off board. There was a piece of wood on the edge to prevent the run-up from crumbling. I was credited with the school record at over 21ft, but I kept quiet about it as the pit was quite a bit lower than the take-off."

Another problem was that of infectious diseases, and pneumonia was a particular ever-present risk before the days of antibiotics, although the vicarage gardener grew his own kind of penicillin in a mould on a rotting piece of leather which worked wonders on grazed knees and other cycling injuries. There were deaths, and boys who ran a temperature of 102°F or more were automatically banned from sports for the rest of the term as a precaution.

In his last year at school Kem ran 100 yards in 10.1, but he doubted the time because the watches came from the physics laboratory and ticked in half-seconds, though marked in one-fifths. In later years, when competing for Cambridge University against RAF Cranwell, he set another doubtful record with a wind of 50 knots at his back, running either 9.4 or 9.6 for 100 yards (he cannot remember exactly which) and suffering more rope marks because the tape as real rope and he was all but garrotted at the finish. Later in the afternoon, when he ran in the relay against the wind, he could only manage 11 seconds.

He went up to Cambridge in 1923 but did not make the team in the first of his four years because of the glittering array of talent around. While he was there the university could call on Douglas Lowe, Lord Burghley, John Rinkel, Guy Butler (who Kem once paced in a successful 300 yards record attempt) and Bob Tisdall. In the long jump Villiers Powell and Christopher Mackintosh, who were also both GB internationals, were Bagnall-Oakeley's great rivals. Powell won in the match against France in 1926.

At Cambridge he was a consistent 22ft "sail" long jumper with occasional flashes that took him over 23ft to make him one of the best in Britain in 1925-26. He was also a good 10.1 man for 100 yards under the watchful eye of coach Sam Mussabini and ran 22.8 for 220 yards. At the Varsity Match Kem was 2nd and 3rd in the long jump in 1925 and 1926 and lost the 100 by inches to John Rinkel, who did 10.0sec in 1927. Kem also regularly competed for the university in outside matches and went on his first tour to the USA for the combined Oxford & Cambridge team.

Twice 2nd in international matches against the French

He represented the AAA in some of their fixtures and he appeared twice in internationals, against France in 1926, when he was 2nd by three-quarters of an inch to Powell with 22-3¾, (6.80), and again in 1927 when he was involved in the previously mentioned jump-off. In one of these encounters a French sprinter was sent away by the starter for wearing shorts which were too brief, and after changing behind a blanket he reappeared with them on back-to-front and was given the starter's approval!

He also went on a tour to Greece and found that the ideal way to run round the very sharp bend at the end of the tight track was to hold on to the statue to provide impetus. The team manager, Evan Hunter, gave him a tip about starting, saying, 'Don't wait for the pistol, go when the first Greek moves', and it was at the same meeting that Lord Burghley took part in the javelin and caused some havoc. Kem recalls, "It was a small stadium and although the throw was the winner it went off line into the crowd, hitting one of the marble benches. Everyone stood up like a modern Mexican wave as the javelin skidded underneath them, and then the judges solemnly searched for the spot where the javelin first hit and measured it".

Kem had a lot of fun with Burghley and recalls one night when he and several others were witnesses to a car accident. The police constable taking particulars was not amused as first Kem, then Burghley, then hurdler George Weightman-Smith, and finally the great England cricketer, K.S. Duleepsinjhi, who threw the shot for Clare College, all provided the extremely long full names demanded of them.

Then Kem's university career ended with a shock as the family was short of money and he had to find work. He obtained a teaching post at Eastbourne College which was to last until his retirement in 1964, but his headmaster would not permit him to compete or to take part in special training sessions on a Saturday as a 1928 Olympic "possible". Other schools had allowed masters in line for the Amsterdam Games to exchange their work with others, but one master at Eastbourne College had already been refused permission to play cricket for Yorkshire on a Saturday in a game in which his brother was captain and another was not allowed to take part in an important rugby match at Twickenham.

Matters changed when a new headmaster arrived in 1929 and Kem found himself on a boat to South Africa for an Achilles tour, with training on the voyage consisting of regularly heaving three tons of coal in a wheelbarrow from the bunkers. He set a Basutoland (now Lesotho) long-jump record and was given a statue of Paavo Nurmi which he still has by his bedside at Guildford, in Surrey.

This was almost the end of his athletics career apart from some running in Norfolk, his appearance at the 1935 AAA indoor championships, and a 1945 Eastbourne sports meeting in which he took part in the hop step and jump and remembers the official lining up the competitors in the impression that they hopped, skipped and jumped for 100 yards. Kem demonstrated the event properly and was promptly appointed judge. As sports master at Eastbourne College Kem remembers two good stories about athletics meetings with which he was involved.

On one occasion the Queen Mother came with her two daughters, Princess Elizabeth (now Queen) and Princess Margaret Rose. The family was in mourning because of the death of King George V in 1935 and was making no public appearances. However, they were staying nearby and so came to the sports. One of the boys competing was Woodrow Wyatt, later Lord Wyatt, and he made such a noise in the long jump, snorting as he ran up and took off, that it alarmed the Princesses, who hid behind one of the masters, cautiously peering round his legs when the noise had stopped.

There was also a match against Westminster School for which there was a rule that no boy could compete in both the colts' (16-year-olds) and senior events, and Westminster's team included a boy named von Ribbentrop, whose father, Joachim, was German Ambassador (and later executed as a war criminal). "Westminster readily agreed that the young von Ribbentrop should be dropped from one event, but the Ambassador was annoyed and protested before finally accepting the decision with bad grace. My headmaster had warned me that if the Ambassador came to the match he would make himself scarce, and he did so, saying, 'I am not prepared to stand on the same field as that man'."

Von Ribbentrop's place was taken by a cosmopolitan young man named Peter Ustinov!

Note:. this article was first published in "Track Stats", Volume 40, No.2, March 2002. Henry Kemeys Bagnall-Oakeley died on 23 January 2005, aged 100.

This graphic photograph illustrates the simple "sail" technique which took H.K. Bagnall-Oakeley to success in the long jump in the 1920s.

This photograph comes from the collection of the late H.K. Bagnall-Oakeley.

Reginald Revans, Empire Games silver-medallist Long jump & Triple jump 1930

Action learning: taking the mathematician's approach to the three-part athletics equation

Reginald William Revans was born in Portsmouth on 14 May 1907 and was a member of Polytechnic Harriers, the Achilles club and Chelmsford AC. His most notable achievement was his silver-medal-winning double in the horizontal jumps at the inaugural British Empire Games of 1930 in Hamilton, Ontario. Many and varied are the ways in which people become interested in athletics, and few can equal his manner of introduction. Now, at the age of 95, he is one of the last survivors from those Games and internationally-renowned as one of the great management thinkers with his "Action Learning" concept of the 20th century.

Revans was an academic, and while at the University of London, where he was studying maths and physics, he became interested in the long jump and in the distance which athletes could reach from the take-off board. This depended on the square of the speed from the board to the point of landing, and he later gave a lecture on his findings at Cambridge University, where he went as a research student, studying for his doctorate in maths.

At his home in Shropshire, and looking back more than 70 years, he told me: "I discovered that a good jumper used to do 21 or 22 feet, and I thought I could perhaps do a little better than this and found that I could". He had not been much interested in sport while at Battersea Grammar School, in London, but within 18 months of his starting long jumping he was in the 1928 Olympic team at Amsterdam – where he finished a disappointing 32nd with 6.58m after placing 4th at the AAA Championships. Then, having watched the Americans using the hitch-kick technique, with Ed Hamm winning the Olympic gold medal at 7.70, Revans improved a year later to a lifetime best of 23ft 7½in (7.20).

He recalled: "I watched them doing it and this justified my entry. I was just a novice. I enjoyed doing the hitch-kick with its movement of the legs in the air, swinging them backwards and forwards, and I improved because of it". At 5ft 10½in (1.79m) tall, and weighing 10st (63kg), he had a build of short legs on a long body, and he had a cat-like walk and balance, with a great deal of spring in his jumping. His father was a naval officer who became HM Principal Surveyor of Mercantile Ships, and one of his tasks had been to examine the circumstances of the sinking of the "Titanic" liner.

Although Revans continued to compete regularly until 1936, he was never to win the AAA title, nor even to finish in the first three, and the situation in the event was even more acute in British terms than in the hop step and jump (as the triple jump was then called), with the AAA title going abroad in all but five of the 21 meetings held between the wars. To be fair to the home competitors, it should be pointed out that the AAA Championships were regarded then (and for many years after World War II) as a meeting of major international status, and long-jump winners included Wilhelm Björnemann, of Sweden, who was the Olympic champion in 1920, and Luz Long, of Germany, who was the silver-medallist behind Jesse Owens in 1936.

Revans did win the event in the Kinnaird Trophy inter-club competition which was domestically so important in those days, and he was to do so on five occasions in all between 1927 and 1933, His best leap was 23-1 (7.03) on the first occasion when he beat his great friend and rival, Kemeys Bagnall-Oakeley.

In his three international matches, all against France, Revans placed 6th in 1927 with 22-6¾ (6.87), 4th in 1930 with 22-11¾ (7.00) and 4th again in 1933 with 22-0¾ (6.72). Only in 1927, when Bagnall-Oakeley was 3rd, were the French prevented from taking the first three places in the event, but that was not an unusual experience for British long jumpers between the wars. Of the total of 25 international matches which were held from 1921 to 1939 (13 against France, six against Germany, and two each against Finland, Italy and Norway), Britons won only four 1st places and their opponents took maximum points on 15 occasions.

Having discovered the event at meetings organised by London University and by Polytechnic Harriers, and then taken part in the Olympics, Revans began his athletics career at Emanuel College, Cambridge, by winning an inter-college event with 22-3½ (6.79), and also did a 5ft 6in (1.68m) high jump and 17.6 for the 120 yards hurdles. He cleared exactly 22ft (6.70) in the Freshmen's Sports, then improved to 22-3 (6.78) and to 22-5 (6.83) in the 1929 Cambridge University Sports in the cold weather of February and March. Then against Oxford he was 2nd to his Cambridge team-mate, Wilfred Sartain, with 22-6¼ (6.86), and Sartain later beat him again at Aldershot in June when they both set personal bests of 23-9½ (7.25) and 23-3¼ (7.09) respectively. Coincidentally, Sartain had also been born in Portsmouth in 1907.

Revans cleared 22-10¼ (6.96) for Achilles in a match against Berliner SC and Deutscher SC and won the Kinnaird at 23-1¾ (7.05). His best-ever jump of 23-7½ (7.20) was achieved in the Polytechnic Harriers club championships at Battersea Park, near to where he had been to school, and he was close to 23ft again in the match with Harvard & Yale when he went to the USA with an Oxford/Cambridge team which included future Olympic champions Tom Hampson and Bob Tisdall.

Rare appearances in the hop step and jump – but an English record, nevertheless

Another overseas Achilles tour was to South Africa in 1929, with Bagnall-Oakeley and Tisdall also in the party, and Revans started with a 23-2½ (7.07) win in Cape Town, and was consistently around that distance throughout the visit, as well as high jumping 5-9 (1.75) in Kimberley and clearing 44-10½ (13.67) in the hop step and jump in Pretoria. He remembered: "I tried the triple jump only when it was on the programme and necessary, but I thought I would have a go and I enjoyed it". In fact it was a pity that he did not try it more often because he excelled at the technicalities of the event and was to improve more than two feet the next year when he won his silver medals in Canada. His distance of 46-10¾ (14.29) at the Games beat Jack Higginson's English native record of four years before, and it was to still rank as the 10th best British performance of all-time 21 years later in 1951!

Before then Revans had run in the 4 x 220 yards at the annual Inter-Varsity relays in the cold of autumn, having previously set a 100 yards best of 10.0, and he won the University Sports long jump at 22-6 (6.85) and then turned the tables on Sartain in the match against Oxford, winning with 23-3¼ (7.09) to 22-3¼ (6.78) and also placing 3rd in the high jump at 5-7 (1.70). In the summer of 1930 he won against Princeton & Cornell at Stamford Bridge with 23-2¾ (7.08) and was very close to 23ft again when he cleared 22-11 (6.98) to win the Kinnaird, 22-10½ (6.97) for another 1st place in the Cambridge University-v-AAA match, and then 22-11¾ (7.00) against France. He had the seven longest jumps of the year by a Briton.

At the Empire Games Revans maintained the same consistency, clearing 22-10 (6.96) for his 2nd place in the long jump, and though his memory is understandably fading now he recalls the visits to North America and South Africa as being great fun. After the Empire Games he competed in the USA-v-British Empire match in Chicago (4th behind the three Americans) and was so impressed with what he saw that he became a Rhodes Scholar in the USA for the next two years.

It was during the universities' tour of 1929 that he foresaw international financial disaster. He remembers: "I was in the USA a couple of months before the Wall Street Crash, and the lavish extravagance of the American institutions was so irresponsible that I was absolutely convinced that things could not last. Having made a lot of friends in New York, I was soon sent lots of stories about how the experts in economic theory were committing suicide. The management consultants made a packet by advising stockbrokers which were the best windows to jump out of!

"So I asked for a Commonwealth Fellowship so that I could spend a couple of years near Detroit and see what effect the recession would have on the richest and most prosperous manufacturing cities of the world. So I had these two experiences – before the disaster with economic and financial experts, and then after the disaster in Wall Street, and deaths from starvation in Michigan. What may encourage others than myself is the approach I now get from US universities to suggest to them how such contrasts may be stopped from threatening our next generations".

Until he returned to Cambridge University in 1933, Revans was out of athletics. He resumed his academic career as a physicist at the Cavendish Laboratories under Ernest Rutherford and J.J. Thompson as they were splitting the atom, and he took up his long jumping again with 4th place at the AAA Championships, as he had been in 1928. He won the Southern title that year at Southend-on-Sea with 22-9½ (6.94) and the Kinnaird at 21-11¼ (6.68) and was again 4th in the match with France.

He did not compete again until 1935 when he moved to Chelmsford to become Director of Education, which was a post he was to hold until after the end of the World War II, during which he had organised the evacuation of children from London to the safety of the countryside and then helped R.A. Butler with the Government's 1944 Education Act.

Revans won a standard medal at the 1935 AAA Championships and also came 3rd in a major meeting in Hanover, where he recalls that "the Germans were very keen to be involved in athletics in asserting their superiority and were very interested indeed in occupying top position". In his new job, he joined Chelmsford AC and competed for them occasionally. He won the Southern hop step and jump in 1936 with 42-6½ (12.96) and was 2nd in 1937 in what was to be his last competition with 42-2 (12.85). He gained AAA standards again in that event and in the long jump in 1936 and was 2nd in the Essex county long-jump the next year with just over 20ft.

Having narrowly survived death during the war when a bomb made a direct hit on his car just after he had stepped out of it, he was asked in 1946 by the newly-formed National Coal Board to create an education plan for them as the world's largest employer, and it was as their Director of Education that he began to develop his "Action learning" management and industrial concept of basing the way forward on what was not known. This became a universally-recognised system which brought him international acclaim as a great 20th century thinker.

He used his theory in the 1960s to turn round Belgium's poor economic performance and take them to the top of the league in terms of annual improvement. He was a friend of many of the world's great achievers, including Einstein, and was Professor of Industrial Management in Brussels for many years, lecturing in Sweden and the USA. He is still internationally feted for his ideas.

Note: this article was first published in "Track Stats", Volume 40, No.4, November 2002. Reginald Revans died on 8 January 2003, aged 95.

Reginald Revans in action. This photograph appeared in the book, "Athletics", written by members of the Achilles Club and published in 1938. The chapter on long jumping was contributed by Kenneth ("Sandy") Duncan, himself a long-jump international, and Revans was described as "showing fine landing position, the body is leaning back and the hips have been brought well forward, giving a big leg-shoot".

Stuart Townend, British Empire Games 4 x 440 yards relay gold-medallist 1930

At 92, looking back to the days when the fire was first kindled for the Colonel's life of adventure

British Empire Games gold-medallist Stuart Townend does not run any more. He skis and climbs mountains instead above his home overlooking Lake Geneva, where he has established the Swiss part of the 1000-pupil international school for 4-to-14-year-olds which he owns in "Top People's" Knightsbridge, in London, just a javelin throw away from Harrods.

He commutes between the two schools every week, with over 4000 return flights on Swissair so far, and spends each weekend in Switzerland. He recently had a fall, not on the slopes but climbing the steps to see his accountant. He nearly missed a day's work, which would have broken his lifelong record of never having any time off for ill-health.

Even shrapnel from a German shell in Holland during the post-D-Day push in World War II, when he was a career officer in the Royal Artillery, did not put him off. He was back from the hospital before the telegram had arrived to inform his wife, Beatrice, that he had been injured in action. It was his wife with whom he founded Hill House School 51 years ago, and the Prince of Wales leads the star-studded list of pupils.

In fact, Stuart Townend is almost as active as he ever was and is extremely fit, which is not bad for a 92-year-old! I met him at the school after athletics historian Ian Buchanan had spotted him appearing in Harry Secombe's edition of "Songs Of Praise" on BBC television. Townend, known to everyone as "The Colonel", is a sprightly, silver-haired but balding, extremely with-it, immaculate-looking man. He was wearing a spotted bow tie and white shirt, and is 5ft 9in (1.75m) tall but less than the 10st 7lb (66kg) in weight which is the same as he used to be at the peak of his athletic prowess.

His life is very much that of a hero in a John Buchan novel: a double blue for athletics and soccer at Oxford; a degree in science and maths; Colonel in the Royal Artillery; wartime hero under Churchill and the War Cabinet, organising worldwide air cover against artillery fire; then commanding a gunnery battery through the last days of World War II and being mentioned in despatches.

He failed in his bid for Parliament as he left the Army after the war, wrote on athletics for "The Observer" newspaper, and was the chap who arranged the housing for the 6000 competitors and officials at the 1948 Olympic Games under the overall leadership of his friend, David Burghley (the Marquess of Exeter), before opening his school. He is an OBE but turned down a knighthood in the late 1940s because he thought he was far too young and did not want one anyway. He is also the man who introduced into British athletics the wearing of sleeveless vests and the idea of running 440 yards races in lanes after his first trip to the USA in 1929.

His gold medal was won at the 1930 British Empire Games in Hamilton, Ontario, for the 4 x 440 yards relay, with Roger Leigh-Wood the leadoff, Townend on the second leg, Burghley on the third, and Kenneth Brangwin on the last leg. They clocked 3:19.4, only four-tenths ahead of the Canadian team anchored by Alex Wilson, whom Tom Hampson was to just beat in the great first sub-1:50 800 metres at the 1932 Olympics.

Hampson, who had been Townend's second string for Oxford against Cambridge in 1929, won the 880 yards at the 1930 Empire Games with Townend 6th. This was at the height of Britain's Golden Age of half-miling during which Albert Hill, Douglas Lowe (twice) and Hampson won four successive Olympic 800 metres titles.

In the AAA Championships of 1931 it was one-two for Hampson and Townend, and it was with a twinkle in his eye that Townend told me that Hampson had not been a very good runner but then in 1930 had suddenly "woken up" – for reasons no one was really able to fathom – and became unbeatable. Hampson, said Townend, was a serious-minded man who had suddenly found powers of concentration but was still not able to overcome the nervousness that made him physically sick before every race.

Townend continued running as he went up the Army career ladder, having been sent straight from Oxford to Switzerland for two years to learn foreign languages, but mixed athletics with skiing and mountaineering, building his strength and stamina so that by the spring of Olympic year he was ready to take on all-comers, including Hampson.

That Olympic season of 1932 was supposed to have been Townend's year, and he began by beating Paul Martin, of Switzerland, who had been runner-up to Douglas Lowe in the 1924 Olympics, in an international 800 metres race in Berne on 4 June in 1:55.0. Townend was feeling full of running, and made it a double with a lifetime best of 49.8 for 400 metres the same day. He was improving all the time, but he damaged an Achilles tendon in the heats of the AAA Championships, and although he achieved standard times in both that event and the 440 it was the end of all his Olympic dreams. Townend remembers: "I think old Tom might have been worried because, although I had not beaten him since 1929, I was in the form of my life. I have never trained so hard and never been so fit".

He won an international ski race in Austria in 1934 but still achieved the AAA standard time at the AAA Championships of that year and the next. He also ran in Achilles matches in Norway and Sweden and in Army events, mixing athletics with soccer, and was secretary and organiser for the Milocarian athletics club, the military equivalent of Oxbridge's Achilles Club.

He won the Army half-mile title in 1935 in 1:57.6 as a Lieutenant in the Royal Artillery. That followed a morning's gunnery practice while flying an old Tiger Moth aeroplane over Salisbury Plain, then flying up to Farnborough, taking a car to the track at Aldershot, and after his victory flying back to his base in Wiltshire and having a celebration dinner in the mess! But by this stage of his running career the spring in his stride, and the times he had achieved earlier in the decade, had sadly gone.

However, let's go back to the beginning of his fascinating life story ...

Stuart Townend was born in Tiverton, in Devon, on 24 September 1909. He was a vicar's son but orphaned when he was five years old and then sent to St Edmund's, Canterbury, which was a public school which provided education for such boys. It was there that he came under the influence of the sports master, Carol Powers, who found that young Townend was a natural runner and all-round sportsman. He played soccer for the school at outside-right and he was also a junior hockey international. He remembers Powers's methods vividly: "He drove me on to run like hell round the track. Then he would say, 'That's no good, do it better', and after a little rest I would do it again and I would do it better. It was a wonderful way to learn".

The regime worked. Townend won every race from 100 yards to cross-country, though he was to abandon the latter, as well as the mile and three miles, because it bored him running so far. At 17 he entered the Public Schools Championships in 1927 and won both the 880 and the mile – the first boy to do so since a future double Olympian, Wilfred Tatham, 10 years before – with the half-mile in 2:01.6, which broke the meeting record of 20 years before, and the mile in 4:37.4. The record for the latter event comfortably evaded him and still stood at 4:32.6 by B.T. Ward in

1898 and H.W. Gregson in 1900.

Townend retained the mile title the next year in slightly slower time, 4:39.8, but failed in the half because he tried to become the first British schoolboy to go under two minutes and ran out of steam in the home straight after setting a blistering pace with 58.6 for the first lap. He finished 2nd in an estimated 2:04.6 to 2:04.4 by T.B.L. Bryan , whose son, Tom, would be a Great Britain 400 metres hurdles international in the 1960s. The two-minute barrier was not beaten by a British junior until the hugely talented Ralph Scott ran 1:59.2 in 1935 – and then produced 1:53.9 to just lose in the AAA Championships that year before suffering poor health and disappearing into oblivion. Even Godfrey Brown, who won the Public Schools 880 yards title three times in succession, had not beaten two minutes.

Townend went up to Oxford and lived life to the full in both the sporting and social senses at Brasenose College. He won his blue in 1929 but lost the mile against Cambridge by just two yards, running an estimated 4:22.6 to C.E.G. Green's 4:22.2. This was Townend's best time, and it was enough to take him on a magnificent athletics tour to Canada and the USA before coming back to England for two days and then going off again to South Africa. He finally returned to Oxford in time for the new term in October. Tom Hampson was lucky to be selected for the 880 in that Inter-Varsity match in his final year, and the reason was obvious when he trailed in last in over two minutes. Townend recalls "I could always beat him, and then one day it all changed".

Hampson's transformation from "plodder" to Olympic champion

Hampson came in as a reserve for the US tour in which the Oxford & Cambridge combined team met Harvard & Yale and then Princeton & Cornell, and on the Transatlantic voyage in the "Mauretania", the fastest of the ocean liners in those days, he was transformed from plodder to champion supreme and never lost again. In the USA he won both races in 1:57 and 1:56. Townend was 3rd in the mile against Harvard & Yale and had to wait until the following year to have a crack at his former cabin-mate.

Then Townend joined the 1929 Achilles club tour to South Africa – lasting two months, including voyages there and back – and the young man from Canterbury, who trained twice a day under the watchful eye of the university coach, Bill Thomas, had more opportunities to race and was consistently under two minutes for the half-mile. In one match at Kimberley on 28 August, the future Empire Games finalist, John Chandler, was the home winner at 880 yards in 1:54.8, which would rank 11th in the world for the year. There Townend was 3rd in a hard-run race in a time of around 1:56-1:57. He was also 2nd in Cape Town in just over 1:58 and 3rd in a slow mile at Bloemfontein.

He remembers the visit well: "There was a lot of socialising on those trips. Everyone was very friendly, and it didn't matter who you were because it was what you could do that counted. Our team manager was Evan Hunter, who did great work for our Olympic teams later, and he was a wonderful chap. He looked after us very well and made sure we didn't go too far socially and make a fool of ourselves and get thrown in jail!

"There were a lot of banquets and laying of wreaths because it was not that long after the First World War. We all had a marvellous time travelling around and competing. We were all amateurs and there was no money in it. You toured free. They gave you expenses and your clothes were free. There was no question of money like today where there are huge sums and things are becoming far too serious. We used to joke about it and it was all good fun. There was plenty of training on board and lots of parties and lots of eating and drinking."

By that time Townend had great hopes for his athletics future. "I was really a 440/880 man. I was a natural with an athlete's balance, which is useful for anything, but they kept putting me in the mile and I would get bored! I used to train twice a day – not too strenuous, no distance work – during the week and then there would be a race on Saturday, and on Saturday night there would be a dinner and we would get drunk and let our hair down and then have a rest on Sunday.

"There was no gym training like there is now. You might do press-ups and skip in your room. The big thing in the sport was that everyone was very friendly. When you were beaten, you were beaten, perhaps because you were a bit off colour or because the other chap was faster, anyway. There were no dirty tricks. It was a clean and highly enjoyable sport."

In 1930 he was 3rd in both the 880 and the mile in the Inter-Varsity match, with Mike Gutteridge and Jerry Cornes the respective winners, but he then ran Hampson to a stride in the Southern Championships on the Iffley Road track at Oxford, recording his lifetime best of an estimated 1:55.6 to Hampson's 1:55.4. He was a disappointed 5th in his only international match appearance against France at Stamford Bridge when Hampson won at 800 metres in 1:53.8, and was then a member of the winning Achilles team in the 4 x 1 mile Victory Cup race. This gained him selection in the England team for another long sea trip to the inaugural Empire Games and after his 6th place in the 880 came the relay and his gold medal. It was the most satisfying race of his life.

As he explained: "I loved relay racing because it was a team event. You did your best and you were determined not to let the team down. There was a great spirit among the four of us, as there always was in a relay team, and each contributed to a great win. We changed the baton in a different way. You handed the baton down into the hand outstretched by the man taking over. He automatically gripped and then the hand came up. We never dropped the baton – unlike some today."

On to Chicago and the USA-v-British Empire match alongside Hampson

Townend then had an excellent run at Soldier's Field, in Chicago, when the USA took on the British Empire. He was leadoff man in the 4 x 880, handing over level with Orval Martin. The next two runners were Chandler, of South Africa, and the legendary British Guiana-born Canadian, Phil Edwards, and they held their own to give Hampson every chance on the final stage against Edwin Genung, who was to finish 4th in the Los Angeles Olympic 800 metres, but it was not to be. Tired after his efforts at the Empire Games, Hampson could not match his opponent and the Americans won.

In 1931 Townend became President of Oxford University Athletics Club, doubling the membership and organising the matches in his usual efficient manner. He also had the rules for the Inter-Varsity match changed to raise the maximum age limit of 24 so that he could use his best sprinter, who was an American, E.W. Goodwillie, but he unfortunately lost. Townend won the 880 against the old enemy in 1:59.8 to become the first Oxford winner of the event since Bevil Rudd in his Olympic 400 metres winning year of 1920 – and ran his best ever 440 yards with an estimated 49.8 in 3rd place to the future Olympic relay gold-medallist, Godfrey Rampling, and John Hanlon, of Polytechnic Harriers, in the match against the AAA on 28 May, where he was also 2nd in the half-mile to Hampson, 1:56.2 to 1:56.6e.

Townend continued his good form with a 1:56.0 for the AAA against Cambridge University on 12 June. His running made the newspapers wonder how he would do against the champion, Hampson, in the AAA final on 4 July, but after leading at the bell Townend was taken in the straight by Hampson, who won with 1:54.8 to 1:56.4. This, incidentally, was the last AAA Championships ever to be held at Stamford Bridge. A fortnight later, again at Stamford Bridge, he achieved another 1:56.4 when running 2nd to David Cobb, of Harvard & Yale, after leading at the bell in 57. He also had a good 1500 metres behind Jerry Cornes – 4:01.2 for the winner – in Antwerp and was again in the winning Achilles 4 x 1 mile team in the Victory Cup. The great German, Otto Peltzer, who had beaten Douglas Lowe and the world record in the same race in 1926, was 3rd.

Although his interest in athletics had begun to wane as his Army career and involvement in other sports took over, Townend now regrets not continuing running seriously. "I don't know why I gave it up. I should not have done so, looking back, but there were so many other things to do, like horse-riding, where you wore heavy boots which did not help running, and there were other sports, the mountaineering, skiing and my career."

He has instant recall of his running days and remembers meeting Paavo Nurmi at Stamford Bridge and learning from him the secret of sleeping before a race. "Nurmi said that we should go and have a sleep and a rest on the sand under the stands. So we did, and from then on I would warm up and relax completely. This is what you should do: have a sleep for 30 minutes before the race. Complete relaxation. It makes a difference".

He also remembers the crowds at Stamford Bridge: "They were so close that they used to talk to you, make rude remarks, ask what you were going to do. I always used to start my finishing burst at the Oxo sign. They would say, 'What are you going to do today?' and I would tell them I was going to have a rest! We did not know anything about our foreign rivals. We used to ask Joe Binks, the former mile champion and then "News of the World" athletics man, and he would let us know what they had done and how they ran their races. There was a good atmosphere with the press in those days".

Almost 70 years on Townend still follows sport, mainly because his pupils take part in an astonishing number of sporting activities on some of the finest venues in London such as the Oval for cricket and the Duke of York's ground for their annual sports day. The school motto reads: "A child's mind is not a vessel to be filled but a fire to be kindled".

The individual style of education practised by cigar-smoking Townend, whose wife died in 1984, attracts children from all over the world and he keeps photographs of himself when he was running and of the teams that he was in so that his pupils will know that "the old fogey could do something". He regards any age beyond 80 as a bonus which he takes with open arms, and as he points out: "You don't need money when you are old, but you do need fitness. If you haven't got it, what can you do with your life? If you haven't got your health, you have nothing. Being with 1000 young children certainly keeps you fit!"

Note: this article was first published in "Track Stats", Volume 39, No.2, June 2001. Stuart Townend died on 26 October 2002, aged 92.

Photograph opposite, above: The 1930 British Empire Games 880 yards final. Of the eight contestants four were from England – Tom Hampson, Stuart Townend, Reg Thomas (actually Welsh) and Mike Gutteridge. The others were Alex Wilson and Percy Pickard (both of Canada), Phil Edwards (British Guiana) and John Chandler (South Africa). In this rare photograph, showing a false start as the runners prepare for the rush to the nearby first bend, Hampson is in lane three and Townend in lane six. Hampson was the winner of the race and Townend was 6th.

Photograph opposite, below: Oxford University v AAA at Iffley Road, 1931. Hampson wins the 880 in 1:56.2 with Townend 2nd in an estimated 1:56.6. As can be seen, races were held in a clockwise direction

Jerry Cornes, Olympic Games silver-medallist 1500 metres 1932, British Empire Games bronze-medallist One mile 1934

On leave from the Colonial Office and off to the Games after four months' training

Jerry Cornes, the Olympic 1500 metres silver-medallist of 1932, was born in India on 23 March 1910 and was a man of great natural athletic talent. He abandoned the sport completely while working for the Colonial Office in Nigeria and twice came back to England on leave to start from scratch after a break of 18 months or so. Training from March through to high summer, he won a bronze medal in the 1934 Empire Games mile on the first occasion and then finished 6th in his second Olympic 1500 metres final in Berlin in 1936.

He was a good enough schoolboy cricketer at Clifton College to open the batting for the Young Amateurs of Essex v Surrey, and he followed in his father's footsteps by winning the school's distance run, the "Long Race". He was much encouraged when he beat the double Olympic 800 metres champion, Douglas Lowe, from a handicap start in a match between the school and Achilles, and when he went up to Oxford in 1928 he ran cross-country to increase his stamina. Tall (6ft/1.83m), barrel-chested (10st 8lb/67kg) and always cheerful, he came under the eye of the legendary coach, Bill Thomas, at the immortal Iffley Road track, and Thomas had him build on his stamina with speed sessions over 600 yards three times a week.

Jack Lovelock arrived at Oxford in the winter of 1931 and Cornes deliberately staged a dead-heat with him in the Inter-Varsity match so that Lovelock would also get a full blue. At the AAA Championships Cornes won in 4:14.2 – his favourite race – ahead of Lovelock and Cyril Ellis, of Birchfield Harriers, who had placed 5th in the 1928 Olympic 1500 metres, had run a sub-4:13 relay leg for the British Empire against the USA in the post-Olympic match the same year, and had won the AAA mile three times. Cornes still expresses strong views about the circumstances of that amateur era:

"There is absolutely no comparison between then and now. In 1932 there were three places available for the Olympic 1500 metres after the AAA Championships. The RAF allowed Reg Thomas, the 1930 Empire mile champion, paid leave, and I had just left Oxford and had been appointed to the colonial administrative service, and they allowed me unpaid time off so that I could join a month later in Nigeria. But Ellis was a married man who earned his money as a miner by piecework. If he did not work, he didn't get paid, and he could not afford to lose the money. Nurmi, perhaps the greatest runner of all time, was entered for the Olympic marathon but was refused permission to compete because he had a small shop in Helsinki and was therefore not regarded as an amateur. What an extraordinary story! Right from the beginning when I started running I believed that Baron de Coubertin had made a mistake by insisting that we should all be amateurs. Now amateur status has completely gone, but all that time ago I thought it was wrong that Ellis should miss out.

"Everything was different then. Travelling by boat and train to the Olympics took a tremendous time longer than it would now. Very few countries competed. There were no Russians and there were no Africans. Athletics was not nearly as important to the media, and anybody who got a medal then did not get the same attention as someone who gets one nowadays. I liked Los Angeles a lot and my race was a good one. I remember Beccali coming past me like a thunderbolt to my astonishment. I was disappointed I didn't win. You were never satisfied if you were 2nd."

After that Cornes went off to Nigeria with his silver medal and as a co-holder of a world record by an Achilles team of mixed nationalities at 4 x 1 mile which he regarded as very bogus, and of which no note exists in any progressive world or British records lists. While abroad he played polo and did no running, but when he returned for a five-month leave he ran two-to-three miles a day, mixed with speed sessions. After the 1934 Empire Games bronze he again did not think about running until he returned to England in March of 1936 and began four months' training which brought him his fastest ever time in the Olympic final. A striking recollection from Berlin is of meeting a German fencer, Helen Meier, whom he had also met at the 1932 Games. She told him that she had been expelled from her club because she was Jewish and had only started competing again to avoid difficulties for her family. That was the first knowledge Cornes had of Hitler's anti-Jewish policies.

Cornes did not compete again at that level after 1936. He married in 1938 and concentrated on his colonial service career which took him to Palestine, and it was there in 1945 that he met up again with fellow-Olympian Crew Stoneley, who was in command of a signals regiment. After retirement Cornes set up a preparatory school in Winchester and kept on running, always enjoying the experience even when finishing 20 minutes behind the winner in the Southern cross-country one year.

Note: first published in "Track Stats", Volume 37, No.4, December 1999. Jerry Cornes died on 19 June 2001, aged 90.

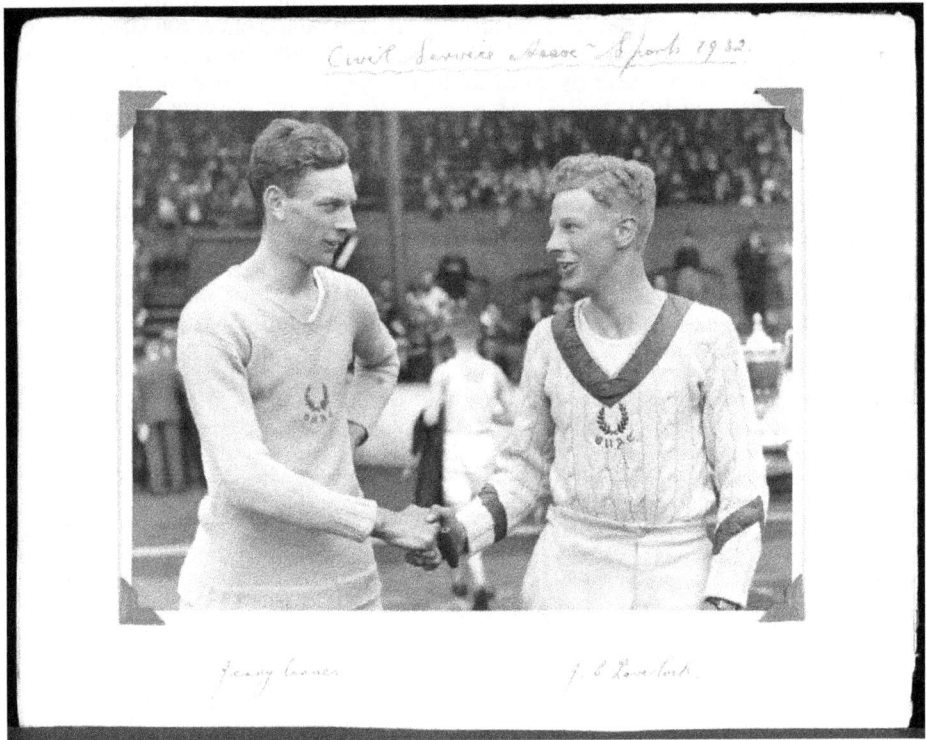

Olympic silver, Olympic gold. Jerry Cornes (left) and Jack Lovelock at the Civil Service Sports in 1932. This photograph appeared in this stylised form in the collection of Lovelock's diaries edited by David Colquhoun and published in 2008.

Crew Stoneley, Olympic Games 4 x 400 metres relay silver-medallist 1932, British Empire Games 4 x 440 yards relay gold-medallist 1934

A soldier's duty calls away Second Lieutenant Stoneley of the "Silver Class"

In the Californian sunshine of the summer of 1932 Britain did well at the Olympic Games, winning two gold medals, four silvers and a bronze. Almost 70 years on, and three of those silver-medallists were still alive – old men now, but with great memories of August days when they all ran faster than ever before.

The "Silver Class" of 1932 still with us in 1999 were Jerry (John Frederick) Cornes, born 23 March 1910, and living in Winchester, in Hampshire; Lt. Col. Godfrey Rampling, born 14 May 1909, and living in South London; and Brigadier Crew Stoneley O.B.E., born 9 May 1911, and living near Blandford Forum, in Dorset. I spoke to two of them – Cornes and Stoneley – who both had short and disrupted running careers because of their professions but who retained clear recollections of those days and whose lives crossed at various stages.

All three travelled out together by ship and across the USA and back by train to produce some of the best individual performances of their lives in the rarified atmosphere of the Los Angeles Olympics. Rampling and Stoneley were eliminated in the semi-finals of the 400 metres, but the former ran 48.0 to equal his best time set in Paris a year before (though a mystery blood virus had sapped his strength and severely curtailed his training after relay legs of 47.0 and 46.7 against Germany, also in 1931), and the latter achieved a lifetime best of 48.3. Then the two young Army officers made amends in the 4 x 400 relay, beating the old world record with 3:11.2 but still a full three seconds behind the USA.

For the British team Stoneley ran 48.8 and was followed by the 800 metres winner, Tom Hampson, with 47.6, and David Burghley, who had failed to retain his 1928 400 metres hurdles title but ran his stage in 46.7. Rampling's 48.1 on the final leg might have been better but for his running flat out against the fastest 400 metres runner of all time, Bill Carr, who had won the Olympic individual title from his great rival, Ben Eastman. Rampling cut Carr's lead from 12 metres to six but could not hold the pace that brought Carr home in 46.2.

Cornes won the silver at 1500 metres in 3:52.6 a few strides behind Luigi Beccali, of Italy, who finished faster than anyone ever had before in a race at that distance in a time of 3:51.2.

All three Britons went on to further triumphs, though Stoneley did not ran in 1933 due to suffering appendicitis and then a broken wrist playing rugby, while Cornes went to Nigeria as a district officer in the colonial service and Rampling did little racing. In 1934 at the British Empire Games at the White City Stadium, Rampling won the 440 yards in 48.0 with Stoneley 3rd in 48.7, and Cornes was 3rd in the mile in his lifetime best of 4:13.6 behind Jack Lovelock (4:12.8) and Sydney Wooderson (4:13.4). Rampling and Stoneley were also in England's winning 4 x 440 team.

Stoneley also went on a posting with the Colonial Office to Nigeria in 1935 because the Army was determined that he should go abroad, but Rampling and Cornes were still around for the Berlin Olympics in 1936. Rampling again went out at the semi-final stage of the 400 metres but was in the winning 4 x 400 team with individual silver-medallist Godfrey Brown, Bill Roberts and Freddy Wolff. Cornes managed 6th place behind Lovelock at 1500 metres in a time of 3:51.4 which was more than a second faster than four years previously.

Those, indeed, were the days, and Crew Stoneley remembers them as if they were yesterday. His main memories are of fun, good friendships, and great relay races in the Army with nothing taken too seriously until the race itself. He and Rampling were both members of the team representing Milocarian, which won the AAA 4 x 440 title in 1934. Milocarian was the services' equivalent of the Achilles club, and both men were founder-members. The club tie was coloured yellow for "The Shop" (the nickname for the Army college at Woolwich where they had first met), red for Sandhurst, pale blue for Cranwell and dark blue for the Navy.

Stoneley first found that he could run when he was at school at Blundells, in his native Devon, with a range from 100 yards to 880, and he almost won the Public Schools half-mile in 1929 but was nipped at the tape by W.G. Bannister, of Eton, in 2:04.8. At "The Shop", which was a great rival to the other Royal Military Academy at Sandhurst, Stoneley developed his running by training three times a week, mixing speed and distance, and Rampling, who was his senior at the college by six months, was already doing great things.

Rampling won the Army 440 in 1930 and Stoneley did so the following year, when Rampling won the 220. Rampling was also AAA 440 champion for the first time in 48.6, and he ran 48.8 at Oxford and in London as well as his 48-flat for 400 metres in Paris and his two great relay legs against Germany in which he each time saw off their champion, Adolf Metzner. At his racing peak Stoneley weighed 8st (51kg), was 5ft 7in (1.70m) tall, and was very light on his feet, which also made him an excellent dancer, and he particularly recalls one meeting in his early Army career:

"I remember the triangular match in 1930, The Shop v Sandhurst v RAF College Cranwell, in which I won the 440 yards and was in the 880, the last event of the day which we had to win. I was so 'fluttered' by the 440 that there was some doubt if I could ever stand up, but I recovered and we were 1st and 2nd, me winning. It was a great achievement for we Officer Cadets. When I had to train hard I was laid off riding because riding developed the wrong muscles.

"I trained fairly regularly, three times a week, at the Woolwich track, and the officer in charge, Roger Ames, got W.G. George to come down periodically to give us his views and his coaching ideas. We ran round the track for three or four laps on a training evening, finishing up with sprints. He took us in starting, digging holes in the track, and one did what one felt inclined for training. There was no pattern to it. When the season was coming on we did three or four miles on the road for stamina at the best speed for you. I had my natural speed and by 1932 had decided that the 440 yards was my best event."

Stoneley beats Hampson and becomes Britain's No. 1

Because Rampling was unwell in the early part of the 1932 season he was never fully fit, and he told me recently at the age of 90 that he felt he really should not have gone to the Olympics that year. So Stoneley was Britain's top man and in the run-up to the AAA Championships he surprisingly beat Tom Hampson on the last leg of the AAA 4 x 440 relay, held at Stamford Bridge during the AAA junior championships. Hampson ran a 49.2 for Achilles after setting a lifetime relay best of 48.8 for 400 metres in Antwerp the previous Sunday, but Stoneley ran his fastest of 48.8. At this same meeting Cornes and Lovelock both recorded times of 4:21 as the mainstays of the Achilles team which won the 4 x 1 mile Victory Cup.

At the AAA Championships Hampson was the 880 winner in 1:56.4 and also dearly wanted to win the 440, but Stoneley beat him by two yards in 49.8 to take his only national title. Cornes also won his solitary AAA mile title at those championships in 4:14.2 from Lovelock. The two of them had dead-heated to win for Oxford against Cambridge in the Inter-Varsity match earlier in the year in 4:22.4, and in the interim Lovelock had run a British record 4:12.0 at Oxford and had just beaten Cornes by a stride at ¾ mile in 3:02.

When they all set off for the Los Angeles Olympics Stoneley was a newly-commissioned £20-a-month Second Lieutenant in the Royal Corps of Signals and was stationed at Catterick, in Yorkshire, where he often ran in regimental and inter-services relays. Again his reminiscences of this era are graphically clear:

"I smoked slightly in those days, but when in training I gave it up, and I did not drink more than the odd glass of beer. When it became known that I had been picked for the Olympic team several dozen of the soldiery gave sixpence from their next pay towards the Olympic Fund. I got the details of the arrangements but no programme, and when we knew that the teams had to gather to embark on the "Empress of Britain" at Southampton, Rampling invited me to stay at his parents' house in Roehampton, in south-west London, and catch the boat train the next morning. When we got to his home I discovered that one of my nice new pigskin suitcases had gone and it must have been taken by somebody while I was buying a paper. The suitcases had all my civilian clothes in it and £100 in travellers' cheques, which was a very large amount of money then, but my snakeskin hand-made-to-measure running shoes (two pairs from J.T. Law for 25 shillings) and my track suit were safely in the other case.

"Rampling's mother said that there was just time for her son to run me to Austin Reed's in Piccadilly to get some clothes, and she gave me some money. There was a sequel because Joe Binks, the former mile record-holder and then "News of the World" correspondent who came with us to the USA, knew me well, heard about the story, and wrote it up in the paper. When we were in the camp at Los Angeles an envelope arrived and in it was the book of travellers' cheques and a note wishing me good luck. The thief must have read about it and sent the money but nothing else".

Training on deck on the transatlantic crossing to Canada

During the sea crossing the British team, led by their captain, David Burghley, had asked for coconut matting to be laid on the promenade deck and the athletes ran round it every morning and kept reasonably fit. On one occasion Crew Stoneley recalls that David – the future Marquess of Exeter – was spotted by J.H. Thomas, a Labour Party minister who was leading a parliamentary delegation to Ottawa and was travelling in the upper class, and was invited to join him. David Burghley replied that he couldn't because he was a tourist-class passenger, to which the minister responded, "Come on up, there's no class distinction here".

The ship docked in Quebec and the team went by train to Chicago. The rail journey across the USA lasted five days, with a stop-off for bathing in Salt Lake City and regular halts to take on blocks of ice because of the heat and the absence of air-conditioning. When they finally arrived in Los Angeles Stoneley was impressed.

"It was a great place and the first to have an Olympic 'city'. There were little chalets built by an entrepreneur with an eye to the future, and Tom Hampson and I shared one of them. I had got to know him reasonably well by that time. He was a schoolmaster and a curious character with very established views on all sorts of things. He used to smoke one cigarette a day at lunchtime and I said to him one day, 'Why don't you knock it on the head when you're in training?' But he gave me a reasoned argument in reply, saying that he had thought about it but had come to the conclusion that giving it up might have an adverse affect on his metabolism. So he went on smoking and broke the world record!

"We went out for a walk when we arrived to see the lie of the land. There was a very high chain-link fence all round with a cowboy patrolling on a horse. We stopped and asked, 'Do you think

Crew Stoneley in action at the White City Stadium, in London, where so many of the major meetings in Britain were held from the early 1930s onwards. Stoneley trained no more than three times a week, but he was still talented enough to win Games medals.

we're going to escape?' 'No sir', he said. 'It's to keep the dames out'. We did not realise we were in such peril".

For the British team, the Los Angeles Olympics were a revelation. Stoneley takes up the tale again: "It was an absolutely different class of running. The surface of the track was entirely different to anything anyone had run on before. Not crunching cinders but smooth, flat and firm like an En-Tout-Cas tennis court. Running on it was so much easier, and the weather was wonderful. I ran though several heats – one of them against Bill Carr – and I made it to the semi-final, but there I was outclassed, even though running my lifetime best. Rampling went out in the other semi, but he was not fully fit. Then the relay came up and we broke the world record and lost by three seconds.

"In the 1500 metres final Jerry, who I knew very well from student days in London, was leading coming round the final bend. As he came into the straight the crowd rose and shouted madly, and he thought it was for him because he was winning, but they were applauding the Italian, Beccali, who was coming with a tremendous run from behind. As they came into the straight they were almost level and the crowd could see Beccali but Jerry could not, and Beccali just got to the front and Jerry never knew he was there. Afterwards Jerry was furious. He said, 'If only I could have seen him and knew he was there I could have done something about him'."

In 1933 Stoneley did very little running, as previously indicated. His right wrist was broken when a scrum collapsed on him in an Army rugby match and his arm remained in plaster for some months. Then he was diagnosed as suffering from appendicitis, and that meant that he could not run for the rest of the year because in those days appendicitis patients were kept in bed for long periods. The illness could have had far worse consequences, though, because when it occurred the Army surgeons were away playing golf and the duty medical officer was not keen to operate until the hospital sister insisted that if he didn't his patient would be dead by the morning.

Stoneley was abroad during the winter of 1933-34 but started training again in readiness for the 1934 season. Rampling was in the form of a lifetime, fully fit and almost unbeatable. He won the AAA title in 49.6 with Stoneley 2nd in an estimated 50.0, the Empire Games in 48.0, and the Kinnaird Trophy in 49.2 from Stoneley and the future athletics writer, Roy Moor. But it was also a good year for Stoneley, who ran 48.8 for 400 metres in Paris in June and was in the winning medley relay team against France in Paris in July. At that latter meeting Rampling ran 48.2 and Cornes 3:53.8 for 1500 metres, both winning. Stoneley recalls:

"I started training again as soon as I was able that year. Many were a bit disappointed that the Empire Games were in London because they fancied a trip abroad, but running was just fun then. It wasn't the main part of life. There was no money, no pressure, no drugs. I won the Army 440 and was 2nd to Rampling in the AAA, and so was picked for the team, but I have a slight blur about the Games because it was all so very casual. I travelled up and down from Aldershot by car when needed and met my team-mates when I got to the start. We were not living together and one did just what one was asked to do, running to the best of your ability and just getting on with it. I knew Rampling, but I didn't know Bill Roberts, other than he was in the individual race but not the relay, and I have no idea why not. He was a nice chap when I met him and did very well".

In 1935 Stoneley won the Kinnaird Trophy 440 in 50.2 and received a letter from the Great Britain team manager, Arthur Turk, telling him he was on the list of possibles for the 1936 Olympics in Berlin. There were two problems with this for Stoneley: the first being that he was suffering some Achilles tendon trouble; and the second, and far more important, was the question of where the Army would post him. Despite being assured by his adjutant that he "would speak to the War Office and fix it", orders came indicating postings to Palestine, to India, and then to Egypt before Stoneley saw a notice that there was a vacancy for a signals officer with the King's African Rifles in Nairobi. He applied, was accepted, and sailed for Mombasa in December. This was the start of 10 years' service abroad, and it brought his athletics career to an end.

He eventually retired from the Army with the rank of Brigadier. Years later he had hip operations and they were performed by a Dorset surgeon, John Wrighton, who was European gold-medallist at 400 metres and 4 x 400 metres relay in 1958.

Note: first published in "Track Stats", Volume 37, No.4, December 1999. Crew Stoneley died on 27 August 2002, aged 90.

George Bailey, British Empire Games Two miles steeplechase gold-medallist 1930, 5th Olympic Games 3000 metres steeplechase 1932

A lap too far: as the bell sounded there was a furious shout of "We're bloody well finished!"

To my delight I found in the course of my research into the career of George Bailey, the British Empire Games steeplechase champion of 1930, that he was still alive and well, living in a small Suffolk village with his wife, Irene, to whom he has been married for 57 years. They moved there 27 years ago from George's native Buxton, in Derbyshire, to be near some of their five children, five grandchildren and five great-grandchildren. George, aged 93 this year (born 29 April 1906), now has a good head of silver hair, and if his legs and his memory are understandably not as sharp as they used to be he still does some gardening and he has a twinkle and a sharpness about him that makes him seem young for his years.

Although he is a bit hazy in recalling his Empire triumph, his Olympic 5th place two years later and his International Cross-Country Championships team wins, including the great English 1-2-3-4-5-6 sweep in Brussels in 1932, he remembers how he started in athletics, how the King of the Belgians told him he was the best runner he had ever seen, and how he enjoyed his happy days with Salford Harriers. He had been a capable local footballer in the Buxton area but found he was short-winded and so at the age of 20 started running to cure the problem. It showed him that he was a natural long-distance man.

"A former Salford chap who had 'The Duke of York' pub at Burbage got up a little sports meeting", George recollects. "I ran in the mile and finished 2nd, and then there were four open meetings in the area where anyone could have a run, and I think I might have won one or two, but I ended up joining Salford Harriers". He was Empire Champion within three years and an international for seven years. In the International Cross-Country Championships he was in England's winning team in 1930, 1932 and 1933, placing 6th, 5th and 6th respectively, and was a non-scoring 23rd in 1935 and 26th in 1937 when England won again.

His only memory of the Los Angeles Olympics is that of someone giving him a push in the back at the water-jump first time round, and then of being told as he thought that he was finishing that he had to run on for another lap. The runners covered 3460 metres in all, and Volmari Iso-Hollo, of Finland, won easily in 10:33.4, with Bailey's Salford Harriers club-mate, Tom Evenson, 2nd in 10:46.0. Bailey also remembers with pleasure the great team-spirit during his many years with the Salford club and his close rivalry and friendship with Evenson (born 9 January 1910), with whom he travelled abroad regularly for both track and cross-country races. Those appearances cost him money that he had earned because in those days, as he puts it, "No work. No pay. So we just had to make do to be able to run. I was always happy while running".

In the 1930s British athletes found gold medals hard to come by at the Olympic Games, though silver was more common and there were a few bronzes. In Los Angeles in 1932 Britain's only winners were Tom Hampson, with his world record first sub-1:50 for 800 metres, and little Tommy Green in the 50 kilometres walk, even though he had been unable to walk at all until the age of five because of rickets and had been wounded and gassed in World War I. In Berlin in 1936 there was success for the 4 x 400 metres relay team and another walk win for Harold Whitlock.

There might conceivably have been a further gold in the 1932 steeplechase because the Finn, Iso-Hollo, was not as invincible then as he was to become later. As it was, Tom Evenson was in

3rd place 40 metres down and Bailey was just behind him when the proper distance of 3000 metres was completed. However, the lap-checker, who was substituting for the regular man who was ill, had forgotten to change the board when the runners went by for the first time, and they were sent round again for a further 460 metres. In the confusion and exhaustion of the extra lap Evenson managed to beat the American, Joe McCluskey, for the silver medal and Bailey finished a very tired 5th. When the bell had sounded Bailey roared at the officials, "We're bloody finished!", but they shouted back, "One more lap!" Evenson and McCluskey, who sportingly refused to protest, were offered a re-run but declined, saying they were quite happy with the medals which they had already won.

Comparison with performances almost 70 years later is intriguing because the times of the two Salford men were really only marginally slower than that for the 10th ranked Briton in 1998! Evenson won the first heat in Los Angeles in 9:18.8 and Bailey ran an estimated 9:16.0 behind Iso-Hollo's 9:14.6 in the second heat. What the two of them would have done in the final without the extra lap is obviously conjecture, but the form they were in suggests around 9:10, with the Finn three or four seconds faster. With the benefit of modern tracks and equipment they would have given Britain's No.10 of 1998 (who actually ran 8:55.74) a very good race!

By contrast with the majority of the British team of the 1930s, who were either members of Achilles or were in the services, Evenson and Bailey were ordinary working men: Evenson was a carpenter in Manchester, while Bailey was a quarryman in Buxton, where he trained on the local golf course. When they travelled by ship to the 1932 Olympics they were in steerage class and much inferior accommodation to the Achilles men. They were the regular British choice for the steeplechase during the 1930s, swapping national titles, and they were even joined by a third Salford Harriers steeplechase international, Thomas ("Pat") Campbell, who was a dye-worker. In the English cross-country team of that decade there was yet another Salford Harrier, Bill Eaton, who was an electrician.

Eaton, born 20 April 1909, was 7th in the International championship in 1933, 3rd in 1935, and then the winner in 1936. Within a couple of weeks of that success he broke Alfred Shrubb's 32-year-old 10 miles track record with 50:30.8 and then Shrubb's six miles record with 29:51.4. Unfortunately, he was poorly advised before the 1936 Olympic 10,000 metres and told to rest, and when he resumed to training he never regained his form. Upset by his Olympic failure he retired, but he then changed his mind and ran in the Manchester-to-Blackpool relay and won the Manchester Business Houses' cross-country title for the fifth time. Tragically, he caught a chill after training one night in vest and shorts and contracted pneumonia and died in April 1938.

For one club to have such talent at the same time was quite extraordinary, and among the four of them there were complete differences in style. Bailey was compared to a Greek god – a lithe and bronzed figure eating up the ground with his effortless stride. Evenson was a gritty, solid runner who never gave up. Campbell and Eaton were stocky types. Bailey had two supreme runs at long distances. The first of them was when he took over for the final stage of the 1932 Manchester-to-Blackpool road relay 1min 12sec behind F. Quinn, of Birchfield Harriers, and in a thunderstorm and an icy wind along the seafront covered the 6 miles 1,056 yards in 32:17 for victory by 15 seconds. The structure of the race was subsequently changed and the only comparable time is the 32:39 for 6½ miles in 1960 by Fred Norris, who had improved the UK 10 miles track record to 48:32.4 in 1959 and had placed 8th in the 1952 Olympic Games 10,000 metres and 4th in the 1958 European Championships marathon.

Bailey's other great race was in the AAA 10 miles in 1933 when he won in 50:51, passing six miles in 30:03.8 and beating Ernie Harper. Yet, although the three watches recorded the exact finishing time, and the track measurement was correct, there was a failure to comply precisely with the rules regarding a string barrier on the inside of the grass track and the record was disallowed. It was typical of Bailey's luck because he also never won the National cross-country title, suffering a leg injury in 1931 and mistaking the finish by 80 yards in 1932 when in a winning position on both occasions. He was still active after World War II, running a leg in the Manchester-to-Blackpool relay in the late 1950s.

The first outstanding run by Bailey's long-time colleague, Evenson, was in the 1930 International Cross-country Championship as a 20-year-old, and he won again in 1932 and the National in 1933. At the inaugural 1930 British Empire Games in Hamilton, Ontario, he was 5th at three miles and 3rd at six miles and then won over the former distance in 14:34.0 in the post-Games USA-v-British Empire match in Chicago. In 1931 he became the first Briton to run under 15 minutes for 5000 metres, recording 14:54.8 in winning in the Germany-v-GB match in Cologne, He got his preparation for the 1936 Olympics wrong and was 5th in his heat after practising sprints the night before and suffering from stiffness.

Note: this article was first published in "Track Stats", Volume 37, No.2, June 1999. George Bailey died in August 2000, aged 94. He outlived his clubmate, Tom Evenson, by three years. Evenson died on 28 November 1997, aged 87.

Even for George Bailey, with his effortless stride, the White City steeple-chase water jump was a formidable obstacle. He won the AAA title there in 1930 and 1935.

Bill Land, the youngest ever British international, aged 16 in 1931

Hope and Glory – high jump, discus, javelin, but a pity about those missing decathlon chances

All-rounders in athletics go for the decathlon nowadays. Back in the 1930s they had to make do with competing in as many events as possible, and Bill Land took the opportunity to become the only Briton to represent his country individually in the high jump, discus and javelin. He also put the shot for the AAA and once won four Kent county titles in an afternoon.

A strapping 6ft 3in tall (1.90m) and weighing 12½st (80kg), Land was that rare being – a natural-born athlete whose dilemma was not knowing which of the seven sports that he excelled in should be left out. His prowess as an athlete brought an approach from Harvard and Yale Universities in the USA. His skill as a footballer attracted Chelsea and Huddersfield Town. His promise as a hard-hitting batsman and medium-fast bowler caught the eye of the Kent selectors. But his father told him to stay in the Army. Not only that, but Bill Land was an excellent centre-half at hockey, a very high standard club tennis player (still active until into his 60s), a fine swimmer and water-polo player and an Army skier! He was a war hero, too, winning the Military Cross for continuing to build a bridge over the Rhine in 1944 under heavy enemy fire.

William Anthony Land was born on 24 November 1914 in Enfield into a "Sapper" family. His father was a Warrant Officer in the Royal Engineers and his grandfather a Captain. He joined the Army as a Royal Engineers boy bugler in 1929 and trained for four years as an architectural draughtsman, entering the ranks in 1933. He was an all-round sportsman from his schooldays, winning the Inter-Counties Schools high jump for Kent at Stamford Bridge and receiving a special cricket award from the newspaper, "News of the World", for scoring centuries.

So far as his athletics is concerned, let us start by saying that he was a precocious self-taught talent with a brilliant natural spring, literally leaping on to the scene in 1931 with a 6ft 1in (1.85m) high jump at the age of 16½ as a boy soldier in the Inter-Services Championships. This feat brought him instant international selection, and as the youngest ever for Britain, against Italy and Germany, and so full of adrenaline and youthful confidence was he that he won against Italy at Stamford Bridge on 22 August with another 6ft 1in clearance and tied with the leading Briton, Geoffrey Turner, and the Germans in Cologne on 30 August at 6-2¾ (1.90). That was to remain his lifetime best in a career that went on until he was almost 40 years of age, and it lasted as a British junior record until Alan Paterson came along in the 1940s.

It was in his second year as an apprentice that Land had started taking the high jump seriously, winning both the Kent senior and junior titles on the same afternoon at 5-8 (1.73) and 5-9 (1.75), placing 3rd in the Southern championships at 5-9¾ (1.77) with a split shoe, and then clearing 6-0 (1.83) to be Army champion and 6-1 (1.85) in the Inter-Services, where he met up with the great hurdler, Don Finlay, for the first time and they became firm friends. Then followed Land's international appearances against Italy and Germany when others in the team included Finlay, Jack London, Jerry Cornes, Godfrey Rampling, Lord Burghley, Tom Hampson and Tom Evenson.

Land remembers clearly the thrill of being selected as a novice 16-year-old amongst seasoned internationals who treated him with fatherly kindness and always made sure that he was included in the many social activities. He recalls Lord Burghley inviting him to breakfast, and his memory is of a great team spirit with none of the class distinction – Oxford and Cambridge athletes in one camp, the workers in another – that some recall.

He never encountered that sort of feeling and in fact says: "The builders, the prime movers, of athletics in this country were Oxford and Cambridge. Their athletes used to give up their holidays to go all over the country teaching and lecturing on athletics in order to get it going. Achilles had matches everywhere, going to remote places in Devon and Cornwall, over to Ireland, and competing against schools and Army and RAF teams anywhere. There was never any class distinction, and when we had matches there they were very hospitable with no barriers".

In its review of the year 1930 the writer for "The Times" said: "In spite of much exhortation English athletics has hardly improved on the field since 1924. The one bright feature is the discovery of Sgt Bill Land, who with Turner jumped against Germany. His method of landing on his back after a half-scissors must be very painful for himself, but the heights he reached are a joy to the spectator."

Land jumped with a flat "scissors" style, which had been suggested by a leading British high jumper of the day, Edward Bradbrooke, who had seven international appearances between 1929 and 1933, and it entailed him landing hard on his back in the heavy sand pits which were provided. Bradbrooke had told him not to bother with the extremely intricate eastern cut-off technique and stick to a modified scissors. Land was also encouraged by the legendary England goalkeeper, Benjamin Howard Baker, who was the British high-jump record-holder at 6ft 5in (1.95m) from 1921 to 1946 and was also 6th in the 1920 Olympics. Howard Baker was another brilliant multi-sports all-rounder, and one of his abilities was to kick a football the length of the ground with his bare feet!

Land had hoped to make the Olympic team in 1932, having been officially told that he would probably be selected, and many experts at the time thought that at the age of 17 he should have been sent to Los Angeles for the experience. After a successful season in which he won the Army title at Aldershot at a record 6-2¼ (1.89), his only AAA title at 6-1 (1.85), and the AAA matches against both Oxford and Cambridge at 6-2 (1.88) he was actually measured for the official kit, only to be told shortly before departure that he would not be in the team because there was money available only for a fixed number and as he was the youngest the selectors had decided not to take him.

The Olympic high jump competition on 31 July was held as a straight final, with 14 competitors – one each from Canada, Finland, France, Italy, Japan, Norway, Philippines, Poland and Switzerland, two from Japan and three from the USA. The Californian-trained Canadian, Duncan McNaughton, won at 1.97, and at his best Land would have been in a tie for 9th place. He ranked 14th in Europe for the year. The world record still stood from 1924 to the Olympic champion of that year, Harold Osborn, of the USA, who used the western roll technique, clearing the bar on his side.

A cartilage injury to Land's right knee in a football match kept him out of athletics for the whole of the 1933 season, and this was to afflict him for the rest of his life and certainly curtail his high jumping, but he made up for it in the next two years. By early 1934 he had enlarged his repertoire by learning to throw the discus and javelin so successfully that he set English native records in both. He competed in the high jump and discus for England at the 1934 British Empire Games at the White City Stadium, in London, placing 6th in the former at 6-1 (1.85) and 5th in the latter at 129-1 (39.36).

His method of throwing the javelin was similar to that advocated by the sprinter and author, W.R. Loader, after the Czech international, Josef Klein, had tried to teach novice Cambridge University athletes the basics of the event. Klein demonstrated the highly technical action used by the leading Finns of the time, but Loader thought that he would have done better simply to run up to the line and hurl the thing as far as possible! Land had no real coaching, but he was fascinated by the event and modelled himself on the athletes he faced such as the Finnish world record-holders and Olympic champions. His attitude towards shot-putting, in which he achieved over 42ft (12.80m), was much the same.

In one of his first javelin competition, at the 1935 Kent championships at Gillingham on 1 June, he threw 185-9 (56.62), and he then set an English native record of 191-7¼ (58.40) in the match against Finland which was held at Hampden Park, Glasgow, on 29 June. The Finnish winner, Hugo Vainio, was not all that far ahead at 210-2½ (64.07), but he was only his country's 4th-ranked thrower, and his compatriot, Matti Järvinen, would set the ninth of his 10 official world records at 76.66 in winning the European title in September. There were 11 Finns over 64 metres during 1935, though even they could not match the USA's 12. Other countries with throwers of that calibre were Estonia, Germany, Holland, Hungary, Italy, Japan, Poland and Sweden. No thrower from the British Empire ranked in the world's top 50.

Land also won the Kent high jump and discus, and in the Army championships he took the high jump/discus/javelin treble, now serving as a Sapper in the Royal Engineers, and was 2nd in the shot. He was equal 3rd in the AAA high jump and competed in that event and the discus against France. He was in line for a place in the 1936 Olympic Games team when the Army posted him to Hong Kong – as was the way with the armed services in those days. That untimely decision by the Army came straight after Land had won three titles at the Kent county championships and had finished 2nd in both the discus and the javelin at the early-season Inter-Counties meeting. It also prevented happening a tantalising possible meeting in the decathlon with the great RAF all-rounder, Don Finlay, who won bronze and silver medals in the Olympic 110 metres hurdles of 1932 and 1936. Land had entered the AAA decathlon that year but was unable to take part. The AAA decathlon had been held only once before, in 1928, and the winner on its revival eight years later was a Scotsman, Ronald Walker, of Shettleston Harriers, at 5,291pts (1934 tables). He later became honorary secretary, treasurer and then president of the Scottish AAA when the Commonwealth Games were held in Edinburgh in 1970.

Neither Land nor Finlay were ever to try the 10 events, but on the evidence which is available to us the clash could have produced a British record – which would be set at 5,513pts on the 1934 scoring tables by Tom Lockton in 1938 and would last until 1947 – and might even have put them in line for a medal at the 1938 European Championships. The individual performances at Loughborough on 5-6 August by Lockton, who had represented Oxford University at the 120 yards hurdles, 220 yards hurdles and long jump, were as follows: 100 metres, 11.6; long jump, 6.54; shot, 9.49; high jump, 1.67, 400 metres, 53.4; 110 metres hurdles, 15.5; discus, 25.70; pole vault, 2.43; javelin, 38.19; 1500 metres, 4:43.8.

During his career Finlay ran 110 metres hurdles in 14.1, 100 yards in 10.0, long jumped 22ft 4¼in (6.81m), high jumped 6ft (1.83m), threw the javelin 141ft 5in (43.10m), and was over 40ft (12.19m) with the shot. I think Finlay would have done as well as Lockton in the discus and would have run a good 400 metres, staggered round the 1500 metres, and made quite a good attempt at the pole vault. Land could point to 6ft 2¾in (1.90m) in the high jump, 191ft 7¼in (58.40m) in the javelin, 145ft 9½in (44.45m) in the discus, 42ft 7in(12.98m) in the shot, 21ft (6.40m) in the long jump and 10-flat for the 100 yards. He tried the hurdles once or twice, with times of around 16 seconds, and he certainly had the stamina from his other sports of cricket, soccer and hockey for the 400 and 1500 metres.

If they had met at their peak (that wonderful "if"!), what a contest it would have made! The airman would have won the sprint and the long jump. The shot would have been close. The soldier would have regained points in the high jump. As to the 400, who knows? But I would guess that Finlay would have won and been ahead at the end of the first day.

His lead would have increased considerably over the hurdles, but Land would have the discus and the javelin to make up much of the deficit, and so the intriguing question is 'what would have happened in the pole vault and the 1500 metres?' Both were men without an ounce of waste on their finely-tuned bodies, and both were good gymnasts. They were extremely determined and competitive, and if Land had beaten Finlay by 50ft in the javelin and 20-to-30ft in the discus he might have been back on terms, and the will to win in both cases would have driven them on.

What a pity it never happened! Yet we can play 'make believe'. We can guess at the 400 and 1500 times, and taking a conservative view of these, and make the calculations based on the 1934 scoring tables, the contest could be visualised thus:

First day: 100 metres, Finlay 11.2 (787pts), Land 11.4 (735). **Long jump,** Finlay 6.81 (754), Land 6.55 (688). **Shot,** Land 12.98 (714), Finlay 12.19 (638). **High jump,** Land 1.88 (884), inlay 1.83 (822). **400 metres,** Finlay 51.0 (818), Land 52.0 (765).

At the end of the first day Finlay would have led by 33pts – 3,819 to 3,786.

Second day: 110 metres hurdles, Finlay 14.1 (1099), Land 16.0 (766). **Discus,** Land 44.20 (840), Finlay 36.58 (613). **Pole vault,** Land 3.20 (575), Finlay 2.90 (466). **Javelin,** Land 58.22 (746), Finlay 43.00 (464). **1500 metres,** Finlay and Land both 4:45.0 (509).

Final scores –- Land 7,232pts, Finlay 6,970. So on this basis Land would win by 262pts!

Land's hypothetical score would not be beaten by another Briton until Derek Clarke achieved 7,002pts (1962 tables, on which Land scores 6,903) in Berlin in 1965, helped by a strongly wind-assisted 100 metres. More immediately, Land and Finlay would have finished 4th and 9th in the 1936 Olympics, won by Glenn Morris of the USA, with 7,900pts, and 1st and 4th in the 1938 European Championships, won by Olle Bexell, of Sweden, with 7,214. Finlay, of course, went on to greater things in the hurdles, while Land took part in cricket, football, tennis, water polo, swimming and the annual athletics sports with the Army in Hong Kong and turned down a tentative approach by team manager Arthur Turk to go to Sydney for the 1938 British Empire Games because he knew that he was not at all championship-fit. Both Land and Finlay then went off to war, serving their country in outstanding fashion.

Land's recollections of pre-war internationals are invariably happy ones. On one occasion the distance-runners, Jack Potts and Wally Beavers, were arrested in Paris for "larking around" and ended up in the cells overnight with no one in the team management knowing where they were. The two athletes still managed to arrive in time for the match, explaining that they had bought their freedom by teaching the Paris policemen how to play pontoon and winning all their money off them. On another tour one of the athletes changed round all the shoes outside the doors in a five-storey hotel, much to the anger of the staff and the amusement of the team. One distance runner told Land that he trained every lunch-time by running round and round the top of the gasometer on which he was working.

Army service interrupted Land's athletics career for nine years until he restarted after the war – and continued on until 1954. During six years of war service with the Royal Engineers he reached the rank of Captain, having been a "Desert Rat", fought at the Battle of El Alamein, taken part in the Sicily and D-Day invasions, and then gone right through Germany to link up with the Red Army. Even without any training or practice throughout that time, he slung the discus so far in his first competition for seven years in Cologne in 1945 that he was promptly picked for the British team in the first post-war international against France in Paris, and hitchhiked his way to Paris by air in a Lysander and a US shuttle Dakota to compete.

After the war Land left the Royal Engineers and became a civilian and engineer technician, building bridges and surveying motorways. He married the girl next door, Avice, who was a tennis player and came from a sporting family. An uncle had refereed an FA Cup semi-final and Avice gave her new husband a discus for a wedding present.

Bill Land competed for Britain against France again in 1947 and won the Southern and Inter-Counties titles. As an Olympic Games "possible" he received food parcels to supplement his diet. His "Olympic" training included a visit to in-laws in North Wales where he threw the discus in a local field, and his wife retrieved it for him, but he did not get into the team at the age of 34 because there were now younger and better throwers around. Yet he threw a personal best 145-9½ (44.45) the following year and was 2nd in the Inter-Counties and 3rd in the Southern. He won the Middlesex title each year from 1949 to 1952, beating Mark Pharaoh (who was to be 4th in the 1956 Olympics) and John Savidge (6th in the 1952 Olympic shot put) in 1951, and he completed his career with 2nd places in 1953 and 1954. One of his last appearances was as a member of the AAA team against Oxford on the evening that Roger Bannister broke four minutes for the mile.

Knee trouble had been aggravated by an injury during an "international" rugby union tournament in the desert in 1943 when he was snapped up for the Irish team because his mother had been born in Ireland. This put an end to his throwing and tennis took over. I met him recently: an erect, smart, very sharp old soldier who had become a great-grandfather and still played two hours of table-tennis twice a week with his wife in a winning partnership in retirement near the front at Bexhill-on-Sea.

Note: this article was first published in "Track Stats", Volume 38, No.1, April 2000. Bill Land died in May 2006, aged 91.

Bill Land strikes an impressive pose with the javelin, and he was equally adept at many other events. What a pity, then, that he never had the chance to contest a decathlon.

It didn't matter who won, just so long as the Union Jack went up the flag-pole

Time has that awful habit of overtaking everything in its path, and athletes are no exception, but I have found one more to add to the pre-World War II collection of survivors, and he competed at the highest level and still retains clear memories of those days. He talked avidly when recalling his triumphs and his low spots, with anecdotes from a past which we all know was so different to the sport of today. Exceptional athletic talent was discovered very early in life by Alec Burns, at the age of 12, making certain that he had clean bath-water at the YMCA as he raced down Byker Bank, in Newcastle, ahead of the other boys and the harriers.

Burns was self-taught, with a strong Christian background, and became sales distributor supervisor for a major oil company which allowed him paid time off, which was so unusual in those days of the 1930s for those in the Great Britain team who were neither university students nor serving in the armed forces. By such benevolent means Burns was able to compete in the Olympic Games of both 1932 and 1936, though this often entailed hurrying from work on a Friday evening to take a train (often overnight) to get to the continent and then be back at work by 0800 on Monday morning. Yet he revelled in it, being a good social mixer and able to fit athletics into his everyday life without fuss, basking in the fun without bothering too much about training. He continued to finish high up in strong North-Eastern cross-country races until 1950.

James Alexander Burns – familiarly known as "Alec", though often referred to as "Alex" – was born in Newcastle on 5 November 1907. At his athletic peak he was almost 6ft (1.83m) tall and weighed 11½st (73kg). He first built on his natural ability by helping to pull the mat which levelled the cinder track used for professional sprint racing at the Victoria Grounds near his home. Then he joined Elswick Harriers, and once he had overcome his inclination not to leave the others behind in his races because he was not sure of the way he began to win, and win well. This was in the Northern cauldron of cross-country running where his opponents were Olympians or internationals such as Jack Potts, Bill Eaton, George Bailey, Tom Evenson, Ernie Harper, Sam Dodd, and his perpetual rival, the erratic Wally Beavers.

It was a toss-up as to whether Burns joined Elswick or moved to Birmingham where he had a cousin, Harry Houghton, who had finished 9th in the 1924 Olympic 800 metres behind Douglas Lowe and had competed again in the 1928 Games. Burns decided to stay in the North-East and build up a sound cross-country pedigree before trying his luck further afield.

He won the Northern cross-country title at his first attempt in 1930, though it was his only win in that event, and the next year he tried the Northern AAA track four miles. He won that and was automatically entered for the AAA Championships. In the last championship race at that distance before it was replaced by the three miles in 1932 he won in 19:49.4, considered a slow time by the pundits, but he was greeted as "dropping from the blue" by Sir Adolphe Abrahams, brother of HMA.

It was his only AAA title, as he was to finish 2nd on eight further occasions: at three miles in 1932, at six miles in 1935-36-37, and at 10 miles in 1932 and 1935-36-1937. That lone AAA success brought him three international caps in 1931, and he won at three miles against Italy in 14:36.0 and was 2nd against France and 3rd against Germany at 5000 metres in his first trips abroad. In the match against Germany the first three home were not only British but all broke 15 minutes for the first time by British athletes – Tom Evenson 14:54.8, Jack Winfield 14:55.0, Burns 14:56.0.

Burns was mixing long working hours with night study to improve his position and with twice-a-week training on club nights, running seven miles and more on the roads, and racing at the weekend. He said: "I was lucky. When I was growing up the dole queues were a mile long and the best of our young men had been killed in the war. I knew a driver/salesman for the Anglo-American Oil Company (later Esso, and his lifetime employers) with a cart and two horses, and I started with him. I made my way up to sales representative, and my work was everything, my life. I was in a reserved occupation with them during the Second World War. They were very good to me, giving me paid leave to go to Los Angeles in 1932 and Berlin in 1936".

The same chance was not available to others. Walter Beavers would have been the first string in Los Angeles, having beaten Burns in the AAA three miles, but he would have had to pay for himself and lose wages if he had gone.

By that time Alec's long raking stride – some called it mechanical – that ate up the ground was being noticed. "I found I had this natural ability, but it never made me big-headed or egotistical. That way you could lose your talent. I enjoyed cross-country more than the track, even though the tracks were soft and the running easy. The country could be boggy, and the shorter men like Evenson and Beavers found it easier. It was too heavy for me as the bigger man, and I didn't want to fall and break my collar-bone or arm leaping a five-bar gate. The elements didn't matter, but sometimes you didn't know what you were going to put your foot on, and I remember one race in Belgium where the hills were so steep that the Belgians were pushing each other up as we struggled. We soon caught on".

Despite his concerns, regularly in the winning England cross-country team

Burns's worries about his ability over the country were unnecessary. He represented the all-conquering England team six times between 1932 and 1938, and in his first appearance after winning the National that year England finished 1-2-3-4-5-6 in Brussels. His highest position was 2nd to Jack Holden in 1934, when he captained the team, and in return they gave him a clock as a wedding present which still ticks over the mantle-piece of his Newcastle home. The clock is one of his few prizes left, as thieves took almost all of them.

In 1932 he ran a 14:22.0 for three miles against Oxford University at Iffley Road, smashing the ground record by 23 seconds in one of the fastest times by a British athlete. He loved that track and regarded tracks in the South as "money for old rope", acknowledging that the North was a good two years behind in terms of training, meetings and facilities. He was in top form that year but still lost out to Beavers in the AAA Championships. Beavers ran a typical race, leading by 40 yards at one stage, dropping back looking exhausted, and then producing a dramatic last lap which in the words of "The Times" was "far too fast for Burns who looked all over the winner. The turn of speed Beavers produced almost jocularly was enough to disconcert anyone". The times were 14:23.2 to 14:31.2.

So off to Los Angeles went Alec as a member of the small British team, and he had a tremendous time. The cliché "trip of a lifetime" is now dragged out daily, but to a young man from the hard north-east of England it was just that: five days at sea on the "Empress of Britain", where he trained round the deck under the eye of his captain, Lord Burghley, and meeting the Prime Minister, Stanley Baldwin, en route to an international conference. The ocean crossing was followed by five days on the train from east to west of the USA, using stops for some running, and the sunshine of Los Angeles where he met and partied with stars like Charlie Chaplin.

The athletics team was a mixture of Achilles (Oxford and Cambridge Universities), Milocarian (Army, Navy and RAF officers) and ordinary working chaps. They all got on very well, as they always seemed to on the long trips. On the shorter international-match weekends there was not time to make real friendships, but again there was never any bother. Burns particularly remembers one train journey to Germany during which "Bonzo" Howland (the perennial 20-match shot-putter who never won and was 2nd in the AAA on eight occasions) used the luggage straps for strengthening exercises for most of the journey.

At the Los Angeles Olympics Burns was unfortunately not quite in the same form as earlier in the season, but he did not do badly, winning his 5000 metres heat and then finishing 7th in the final in 15:04.4 as Lauri Lehtinen, of Finland, controversially won from the USA's Ralph Hill. Burns said: "It was a wonderful experience. The track was magnificent. When my spikes went in it, it was like a sponge, and I thought it was pennies from heaven. While there I was offered a medical scholarship at one of the colleges, and as I was interested in medicine I thought about it, but it was too close to professionalism, and although they showed me around I decided not to stay there. For one thing, I was engaged to be married!"

Before the trip he had been offered money to write articles from Los Angeles but had turned that down, too. He felt strongly – and still does – about taking money for running. He knew that it happened, and it was obvious to him at the Games that some competitors were professionals, but he never took a penny. On the occasion that a bookmaker offered him money to fall in a race his response was to run harder than usual and win easily. He always raced to the best of his ability because the competition in the North and in the national championships was fierce, with the same men racing against each other all year round. No quarter was given; none was expected; and they all remained friends, although only a few of them are left alive at the time of writing, including Jack Holden.

Missing the Empire Games six miles – that would have meant time off work

Burns was ill in 1933 after a successful season over the country and married early in 1934 [Note: he now has two daughters and a son and two grandchildren, one of whom, Richard, is one of the world's leading car rally drivers]. He ran 14:30.0 for three miles on his favourite Oxford track and was then 6th at the AAA and selected for the Empire Games in London. He would have preferred the six miles, but that was on the Friday and he could not get time off work. So he went down overnight. He led the three-mile race most of the way, and this is how "The Times" reported the closing stages:

"Next came a remarkable effort and no less remarkable collapse of Burns, and finally a well-earned victory for the faithful and lion-hearted Beavers who, to his infinite relief, discovered that Burns was no Finn in English clothing. Perhaps he knew it all along because he never hurried until Burns's lead and mechanical stride proved a complete snare and delusion. Burns was beginning to stop before the bell sounded and he was all but standing still when first Beavers and then Allen, another English runner, raced by him."

Beavers won in 14:32.6, with Burns nearly 13 seconds adrift, and just why he blew up – as he was to do in the match against Germany in 1935 when he was leading Max Syring by 80 yards with 200 yards to go – he still cannot explain so long after. He thinks that it might have been the rush of travelling, but two such setbacks in dozens of races is not uncommon even now. He had another international race that year in Paris, where he lost by 12.8 seconds to the Frenchman, Roger Rochard, who had won the European Championships 5000 metres. British officialdom decided against sending a team to that inaugural meeting because they thought that the Empire Games provided quite enough competition for one year.

In 1935 Burns suffered leg problems for part of the year after placing 9th in the International cross-country but had two good races, losing a three miles at the White City to the RAF star,

Reggie Thomas (1930 British Empire Games mile champion), by a second in 14:34.0, and then still getting the points for 2nd place against Germany despite his collapse on the last lap in Munich.

He had a great year in 1936. He was 5th in the International cross-country, and he then had his customary season of road relays, club matches, two-mile team events and regional championships, including losing to Bill Eaton, of Salford Harriers, in the AAA track 10 miles and then again when the latter finally removed Alfred Shrubb's 32-year-old record for six miles with 29:51.4 on a lousy April day in Birmingham, before going to the AAA Championships. There Burns gained revenge by comfortably beating Eaton, who was well over his early-season peak, at six miles. After leading most of the way, Burns was run out of it by Józef Noji, of Poland, 29:43.4 to 29:45.0, but his time was a new British record which lasted until Frank Aaron broke it in 1950.

At the Berlin Games Burns dined with Jesse Owens, met Göring and Hitler, and recalled: "I was very impressed with the way they were developing the youth and getting them involved in sport. Of course, I had no idea of what was to come, which was terrible, but at the Games those I met were decent ordinary people".

Another British record and 5th place behind the Finns and Murakoso.

In the 10,000 metres Burns was with the leaders at halfway in 15:09 but fell back towards the end. He ran in well behind the Finns, who finished 1-2-3, led by Ilmari Salminen, and the Japanese, Kohei Murakoso, and placed 5th in 30:58.2, which set another British record. He was 23 seconds behind Murakoso and 23 ahead of Juan Zabala, the Argentinian who had won the 1932 Olympic marathon. Burns's last race of the track season was a 5000 metres in Luxemburg which he won in 15:08.0.

That was to be his closing international appearance, although he continued racing for many more years. He nearly won the AAA six miles in 1937 in a tremendous battle with the Hungarian, János Kelen, who tried to run the legs off his British rivals. In the end only Burns was left, and they fought stride-for-stride round the White City track until it was Kelen who had the finish and the tall Tynesider, who was excellent at a fast even pace, who did not: 30:07.8 to 30:10.5.

The last two years before the war showed the same pattern as before with a lot of racing, but age taking the edge off, so that in the AAA 10 miles he was only 6th in 1938 and in the six miles he was 5th in 1939. He took up coaching after he finished his racing career and has kept his interest in the sport over the years, attending the 2001 National Cross-Country Championships and still a regular when celebrations are held for the champions of today. One of his successors in glory from the Elswick Harriers club was Mike McLeod, who was 2nd in the Olympic 10,000 metres in 1984.

Like us all, Alec Burns has strong views about the differences in athletics between now and then. He did not run further than 10 miles because he would have been bored stiff by doing so. His training, he considered, was enough for his racing. He said: "Every post was a winning-post to me. I did not want to be the best in the world, just to do the best I can. Perhaps if I had not had to travel to and fro in such a short space of time I might have been better. I don't know. The diet we had in those days was better. We ate a lot of meat and we drank a lot of milk. Training every day would have driven me mad. You would get too fit. I could not do that like they do now. They amuse me, strutting around like peacocks flapping their wings before a race! It was all low-key in my day, and more fun, I think."

"I was captain of the England cross-country team and would help the lads along. It didn't matter

23 August 1936, Luxemburg, an international 5000 metres race. Alec Burns leads Max Syring, of Germany, and went on to win in 15:08.0.

who won as long as the Union Jack went up the pole after the race. Now all this money is spoiling it. There's too much of it. It's taking the cream off the top. There was no holding back when we raced each other. No avoiding each other. We met often and gave of our best every time, always aiming to win.

"That's how I liked it."

Note: this article was first published in "Track Stats", Volume 40, No.1, March 2002. Alec Burns died in May 2003, aged 95.

Ken Harris, British Empire Games One mile finalist 1934

You're selected for Wales to run in Paris, and that will be £1 each, please

On 7 August 1934 Ken Harris lined up for the final of the British Empire Games one mile at the White City. He was the first Welsh representative to qualify, although his friend and fellow-countryman, Reg Thomas, had won the inaugural race in 1930 wearing the vest of England. Harris was first and foremost a clubman, as he was to remain throughout his long and varied career, and now, at the age of 93, he has served Welsh athletics in almost every post at club, regional and national level.

He was not overawed by the competition that Saturday of almost 70 years ago, even though it contained such world-class athletes as Jack Lovelock, Sydney Wooderson, Jerry Cornes and, Aubrey Reeve, plus Bobby Graham, of Scotland, and Les Wade, of Canada. The lightweight from Wales thought that he would do well, having won his heat from Horace Craske (England), Cornes and Graham in 4:35.4, seven seconds slower than his time in unexpectedly winning at the Welsh championships, where his 4:28.2 was his first sub-4:30 performance.

As part of his training he had taken a tip from his club secretary and lengthened his stride by an inch, using kerbstones as markers, on his five-mile walk each day to work and back. So he went with the pace as Craske (who had been 6th in the AAA Championships behind Lovelock, Wooderson and Cornes) took the pack through the first lap in a suicidal 59.5. The second lap slowed to 66 but still gave a half-mile time of 2:06, and Harris was with them – just.

Now a great-grandfather, but as bright as a man of 60, he remembered all this when we met in his home near Hereford: "I was absolutely knackered. Instead of using my head and running to my ability, I tried to go with them, and when it came to the third lap I'd had it! It was almost as fast at halfway as I ran for the half-mile! I had to keep going out of shame, not letting my country down. So I could not not finish, and I was last by a long way. I suppose I did 4:30, or probably a bit over, but I kept going. I was lucky to be on my feet. Afterwards, I was as sick as a dog. I had taken the hiding of my life, and I have never forgotten it".

Lovelock had won the race in 4:12.8 from Wooderson and Cornes, and Harris's biggest impression had been Lovelock's peerless power. "He was the finest athlete of them all in my book. He ran with his head. He knew when to go. He planned his races and won the ones he wanted to. The only thing that mattered to him was getting to a tape first".

Harris's account of the race solves one mystery because all previous reports gave Harris and Craske as the last two finishers, but now we know that it was Harris who was last with an estimated time of 4:35. It was his one big-occasion race on the track, and the only cinders he had ever previously run on were at Cardiff's speedway stadium. The Empire Games humiliation did not stop Harris competing, as he was always available for his club, and he got down to a best mile time of 4:22.8 when finishing 3rd to Reg Thomas in the 1936 Welsh Championships, but he never represented Wales on the track again.

At cross-country Harris was a staunch member of the Welsh team, taking part in the International Championship on five occasions between 1935 and 1950. He never won the Welsh title, and his highest pacing was 4th in 1946, when he was made captain of the national team, but he was in the first 10 every year but one and his club won the team title six times.

Harris happily admits that at the International "I was never in the top men's class and always at

Stalwart Welsh cross-country runners of the 1930s from the Roath Harriers club in Cardiff. Ken Harris is No.4 and Jim Alford, the 1938 Empire Games mile champion, is No.1. *Thanks to Clive Williams for supplying this photograph.*

the back of the field". In fact, the only year in which he was in the Welsh scoring six was at Ayr, in Scotland, in 1946 when the team was last, as usual, including in its ranks Tom Richards, who was to be 2nd in the 1948 Olympic marathon and who had been one of several of Harris's team-mates who had moved to London to find work before World War II. Harris swapped his Welsh vest after the race with the winner, Raphaël Pujazon, who was also European steeplechase champion for France that year.

Harris's first appearance in 1935 had been in Paris, when the Welsh team members had to contribute £1 each (a lot of money then) just to go on the trip, and in Blackpool the next year he finished in his highest position of 47th. Back in Paris in 1947 Pujazon won again, and Harris, who was a lifelong sales representative by profession, had heard beforehand that the French were short of coffee and bicycle inner-tubes, and so he took a supply, sold them at a profit, and paid for his trip.

His final appearance was in Brussels in 1950, when 10 teams took part and Wales were not last, but he was very near the back in 78th position. He recalls: "I took a terrible hiding. I was so far back that I decided that no one was ever going to do that to me again. So I packed up and became a starter instead". He continued running with his club but passed all his officials' grades quickly to become an international-standard starter and a regular at the White City and all over the country for 45 years.

He was renowned for his remark of "Small gun today – so no false starts" and for his polite instructions to runners, which included, "Gentlemen, fingers to the line but not on it". He added: "It always annoyed me when one athlete who was always difficult in getting to the start and difficult to handle became a commentator and said things like, 'What's an inch or two?' when runners were going to their marks and might have their fingers over the line. With modern technology, an inch or two could win a gold medal! Having been a runner was a great advantage to me as a starter. I knew that they were all a bundle of nerves. The only man I have always seen cool was Colin Jackson, who always followed the same routine".

Harris believes that the new rule of disqualification for competitors following one false start in the race is wrong because it takes no consideration of the highly-strung state of athletes. Ironically, a few days after Harris had made this observation Jackson was caught out by the new rule at an indoor meeting in Karlsruhe.

Harris, 5ft 8in (1.73m) tall and weighing 10st 7lb (66kg), was born on 20 July 1910 in Bristol of Welsh parents and started running in the traditional way, winning a 1000 yards race at school and with it a rose bowl delightfully named the "Mirror of Gems", but he took no further part in sport until a friend suggested he train with Roath Harriers, in Cardiff. Before his first club competitions he ran in Whitsun races at his church, but this meeting brought forth a rebuke from the AAA, saying that the event should be registered and requiring all athletes to fill in an official form that included a declaration that they had never run for money.

"We didn't run for money", Harris reflected. "We were all amateurs, and I couldn't fill in the part of the form that asked for my last three competitions because I had not competed anywhere. But, oh, how different it is today where money rules everything! I don't mind that, but I just wish that they put money into the sport to encourage people and provide the amenities. Money has ruined club life. In my day we were like a family in the club. We trained twice a week and we raced on Saturdays. On Sundays I would go for a long walk because I considered walking was the basis of training for running.

"We would travel many miles at our own expense to compete against each other. That's how it was, and I'm not complaining, but not everyone has the means to do this, and some should be state-assisted nowadays and parents helped if necessary so their children can make a start. When you get youngsters in the club, you want to keep them, but they disappear because of lack of money".

There were no financial rewards in Ken Harris's competitive days, and no more than expenses when he became a starter. Once, during World War II, he was given a guinea (£1 5p) as his share of a relay first prize and he was so conscience-stricken that he could not stop worrying about it until he bought a coffee percolator, which he still has in his possession. He and his club-mates won a lot of furniture and clocks, and he still has many of them, along with his collection of medals and trophies.

"We always used to look at the prize-list first whenever we went to compete, and one day at a small meeting Jim Alford, who won the Empire Games mile in 1938 and is a great friend, and I saw that the prize for the mile was a china clock and two china vases. The second prize of an oak clock was much better. Jim was in the half-mile, so it was up to me and I didn't want the vase. Though there was a good local boy running, up the straight I knew I could get to the tape first, but at the tape I pulled back and he won. When they handed out the prizes, he went up and they gave him the oak clock, and then me the vase. They had twigged and thought, 'He's not getting away with it!'".

Harris only won the Welsh mile on a single occasion, in 1934, although 2nd to Alford in 1935 and 3rd in the half-mile in 1933, but towards the end of his running career he won the first two miles steeplechase title event. "I'd competed in a steeplechase at the White City, and before that race I met an army sergeant who was a steeplechaser and I asked him how to run it because I'd never done one before. He said, 'Don't worry about it. Can you jump? Yes? Well, increase your speed before a hurdle, and that will do it. And don't be afraid of the water-jump. You'll be alright as long as you take it in your stride'. There was no jumping from the top of the hurdle in those days.

"I enjoyed it so much that I asked the Welsh AAA if they would include it in their Championships. They agreed, but the organiser wasn't best pleased because he said, 'How am I going to dig a water-jump in the speedway track?'." Harris became champion in a Welsh record time of 11:31 that was quickly beaten by one of the greatest of Welsh athletes, John Disley.

Later in his running career Harris joined the Cardiff club and is a man who still loves running and everything to do with the sport. His enthusiasm has never waned and two nights after our meeting he was off to the annual club dinner.

Note: this article was first published in "Track Stats", Volume 41, No.2, June 2003. Ken Harris died in November 2008, aged 98.

Harold Whitlock, Olympic Games & European Championships 50 kilometres walk gold-medallist 1936 & 1938

The "guardsman" who conquered Berlin. Then, to celebrate, kippers for tea

Unfortunately, Harold Whitlock died in 1985 before I had found the opportunity to interview him, but one of his three sons, Terry, who was himself a very capable race-walker, reminisced about his father's achievements at length when we met up almost 30 years later.

Like old soldiers, old walkers simply fade away and then are fondly remembered for their great achievements. Few events have brought more Olympic gold medals to Britain than the 50 kilometres walk (three, and another to a British-born New Zealander), and none of the winners has a higher reputation than Harold Whitlock. He was a tall man, just over 6ft (1.83m), of perfect style and ability, whether it was marching the roads like a guardsman or working as a motor mechanic with world-record-breaking cars on the 2¾ miles (4.43 kilometres) race-track at Brooklands, near Weybridge, in Surrey, which was in existence from 1907 to 1939. And now, rightly, he has been inducted into the UK Athletics Hall of Fame.

His career was one of winning, and between 1935 and the outbreak of World War II this highly respected – and in some cases revered – man was without doubt the best in the world. But for the war he might well have added not one but two Olympic gold medals over the 50 kilometres distance. He was so good and fit that after missing the 1948 Games, in which his brother, Rex, competed, he came back in 1952 aged 48 and finished 11th in Helsinki. He was still competing at the age of 71when he walked 50 kilometres in a charity event an hour slower than his gold-medal effort.

He was everything an athletics idol should be: fair, honest, hard-working, and then after finishing top-level competition going into the administration of the sport. He was head judge at the 1960 Olympic Games, and he wrote books on walking and lectured and coached. The only blemish on his very long career came in 1938 in the National (Race Walking Association) 20 miles championship when he was disqualified. Shock horror! It really was. No one could believe it, and no one is sure just how it happened. Some think he might just have been trying that extra bit too hard in a long hard-fought race with his great rival, Joe Hopkins, for the title.

Whatever it was, it caused one journalist at the event to write: "I watched Whitlock closely, particularly in the early stages where speedy walking was expected. In fact, I missed him only for a short way at the half distance and in the 14th mile. He appeared to be enjoying his tussle with Hopkins. Certainly nothing appeared to me to be in any way doubtful at that point. Indeed, I remarked to several people about me on the remarkably fine and fast walking both men were showing. Yet Whitlock was ruled out shortly afterwards. Here we had disqualified a very conscientious man who made race walking a real study. Guardsman-like in action and stride, Whitlock does not wriggle or 'jump' his body. It did, in fact, seem that Whitlock has shown us what walking was. He had always been accepted as a fine example not only by the road walking officials and competitors but by clubs all over the world. So just when we believed that the tricky question of race walking had definitely been settled we see one club official able to smash the whole theory in one short moment by ruling Whitlock out".

The writer ended by posing the question that has never been satisfactorily resolved: "I find myself wondering if the decision is correct".

It never happened again, and in his heyday Whitlock was only beaten once. In 1935 his great rival and friend, Tebbs Lloyd Johnson, who by finishing 3rd in the 1948 50 kilometres was to become the oldest person ever to win an Olympic medal, won by a few yards to gain the National title, only to be disqualified after he had broken the tape. The next year, 1936, Whitlock, who – shock horror again! – enjoyed smoking a cigarette and a pipe, went to the Games in Berlin and showed just how brilliant he was. He had won the British championships and trial in a world best time of 4:30:38, with the Olympic title-holder, Tommy Green, who suffered rickets and was gassed in World War I after lying about his age to join up at 16, finishing 4th in a time that would have beaten all previous winners. Britain had tremendous depth at the distance in those days when walking was a very popular sport.

There were 31 competitors for the Olympic race, with all the world's best there. The official report said the course was sufficiently difficult to provide a real test of pace and endurance. It did not mention that the weather was poor – cold and miserable, with a whirling wind and squally showers.

"Sensing his weakness, I drove him hard for another five kilometres"

Harold Whitlock saw it rather differently. He later said: "My own event only started and finished within the stadium, being conducted on closed roads outside. Every conceivable type of surface made up the course, whether by accident or design I don't know, but it was certainly strange to find a path through woods and parkland included. Last out of the stadium I began to get through the field by quarter distance until just after the turn I was 3rd to Jaroslav Stork, of Czechoslovakia, and Janis Dalins, of Latvia. In another five kilometres Dalins was alongside, and sensing his weakness I drove him hard for another five kilometres before going ahead.

"Victory seemed in sight, but a bout of sickness – probably food poisoning of some kind – caused me some concern, with the added knowledge that Arthur Schwab, of Switzerland, was closing my lead. Fortunately my recovery soon afterwards allowed me to increase my advantage again, to arrive in the stadium – there were 100,000 packed into it – a very tired but very proud man, having accomplished what I set out to do three years before. Win an Olympic title."

The British Olympic Association's official report tells how Whitlock overcame his sickness and "along the rise towards the stadium the Britisher displayed excellent style and walking very fast he increased his lead. Amidst tremendous enthusiasm he entered the stadium and a few seconds later had broken the tape to give GB her first win in the 1936 Olympic Games – her only individual track and field win – and to set up a new Olympic record time for the event". Whitlock won by 88 seconds. His great friend, Lloyd Johnson, was 17th and 24 minutes behind Whitlock's 4:30:41.4 and Joe Hopkins had to retire at 40 kilometres. In 1948 the title was won in a time 11 seconds slower.

To put Whitlock's performance in a social context, he took a fortnight's unpaid leave, granted very reluctantly by his boss, to compete, leaving his wife and three young sons – a daughter came later – at home in Greenford, in Middlesex, listening to the race on the wireless. One of those sons, Terry, remembers three-quarters of a century later: "I was at home with the rest of the family sitting around the radio as we cheered Dad on. Things were different in those days and my mother would no sooner have thought of taking us all the way to Berlin than she would have thought of flying to the moon. Dad's boss at the garage where he was foreman reluctantly gave him two weeks' unpaid lead to go to Berlin. He was none too pleased at him taking time off, although after dad's medal success he did soften somewhat. In the meantime mum had to struggle for a while to make ends meet".

Terry remembers the race and says, "He cruised into the stadium for the final lap with not a rival in sight, greeted by the roar of cheers echoing around the arena from the 100,000 strong crowd.

According to a newspaper report at the time Hitler rose impulsively and applauded again and again. My father smashed the old record by nearly 20 minutes – Tommy Green's time in 1932, the first time the race had been held. He had covered the 50k at an average of nearly seven miles an hour, which was not bad for a course that was for the most part over cobblestones. Instead of being cocooned in a foil blanket, checked over by medical people and whisked away by officials, as competitors would be today, Dad was left to find his own way off the track. He wandered for some time in a labyrinth of underground tunnels before he eventually found his way back to the dressing-room where he no doubt lit up his usual post-race cigarette. I still have the telegram my aunt sent him to congratulate him. It read, 'Well done Harold. See you in a few days. Kippers for tea' ".

Saying "no" – reluctantly – to a lifetime's supply of Shredded Wheat

No great welcome for the smart moustached gold-medallist on his return home; instead straight back to work after a reception in his honour when he was greeted by the local mayor. Terry adds, "There were no celebrity appearances or lucrative advertising deals in those days. One story, in particular, highlights this. After a reporter asked him the secret of his success he put it down to the Shredded Wheat he ate for breakfast every morning. The Shredded Wheat company promptly offered him a lifetime's supply of the breakfast cereal, but reluctantly he had to turn it down or risk losing his amateur status".

Those were the days! Or were they? Nowadays, the winner would be an hour or so faster and a wealthy man. But there was no doping in those days. There was a mixed life of work and play. There was probably more time because modern technology had not provided all those things that take up so much of the day. All of these factors very much make for a talking point more than 80 years after those Berlin Olympics.

Whitlock did not lose his amateur status and went on to win the European title in 1938. This was the first European Championships in which Britain competed, having missed the inaugural meeting in 1934 because officialdom thought that the Empire Games that year provided quite enough top-class competition for one summer. Ironically, there were no race walks at the Empire Games, and the European title was won by Whitlock's Berlin rival-to-be from Latvia, Janis Dalins, in 4:49:52.6. The following year Whitlock was to set a world record for 30 miles of 4:29:31.8 which was worth more than 10 minutes faster than Dalins for the 50 kilometres distance (31 miles 120 yards).

The course for the 1938 European title race in Paris was difficult and testing and the weather was poor. The event was dubbed a veterans' race because nine of the 16 competitors were over 30. Whitlock, who was then 34 years old, won in 4:41:51, more than two minutes ahead of Herbert Dill, of Germany, and the unofficial world record-holder, Edgar Bruun, of Norway. The oldest men in the race were Evald Segerstrom, of Sweden (38 and 6th), and Dutchman Antonius Toscani (37 and 8th).

It was not Whitlock's last major championship race. He did not compete in the 1948 Olympics because work and family stopped him training sufficiently – he would do an hour or so three times a week and then a long walk at the weekend when not racing – but was an official as his brother, Rex, a possible for a medal, unfortunately had to retire. But Harold was back in 1952 aged 48. The old urge that had started him walking had merely lain dormant. He was itching to keep on. He started in June in the Bradford walk, which he had won five times already and had kept the cup. This time he dead-heated with Charles Colman for a sixth win.

The next month he competed for the Race Walking Association 50 kilometres title – he had won it six times out of seven before World War II – and finished 3rd behind Don Tunbridge and

Welcome refreshment for Harold Whitlock during an eight-hour time-trial walk on the White City track in 1935. He set a world record for 30 miles and British records for 40 and 50 miles. In this era he was almost unbeatable.

brother Rex. He was picked for Helsinki. "Athletics Weekly" commented, "This old soldier does not even seem to fade away".

He did well at the Games – and even better than that when you consider his age. He finished 11th out of 28 in a time only a little slower than his winning effort in Berlin, 4:45:12. Brother Rex was 4th and nearly 13 minutes quicker. Harold, one of eight children, who had carried the British team flag into the stadium at the opening ceremony, had the misfortune when he returned at the end of the race to see on the giant scoreboard that the winner, Giuseppe Dordoni, of Italy, had smashed his record time with a fine 4:28:07.8.

Whitlock, who was born in Hendon, North London, on 16 December 1903, started race-walking late at the age of 25. He, like his brother, Rex, was a superb engineer and worked at the racing circuit at Brooklands where he not only tuned cars to break world records but was a passenger when they did so. It was because of the achievements of one of his drivers, Sir Henry Segrave, who was the first man to hold the land and water speed records simultaneously, that after initial success Whitlock dropped out of the walking scene for a while. It was in 1933, three years after Segrave was killed on Lake Windermere, that Whitlock became a real name in the walking world by winning the first of his six RWA 50 kilometres championships in seven years. It came a year after his first major success when he won the Hastings-to-Brighton tough 37-mile walk in 5:56:03, beating Tommy Green's record by four minutes.

At a pinnacle with the first of four London-to-Brighton victories

After that he was practically unbeatable over anything further than 20 miles, although he never became a Centurion. He set world records for distances up to 50 miles and for eight hours' walking, but he never covered 100 miles. His other great love was the London-to-Brighton 52-mile annual race, the pinnacle of the year for all top walkers. The first time he competed was in 1934 when he won in one of the fastest times on record – 8:17:23. It was the first of his four victories. His son has a marvellous photograph of him, seconds after winning, with a lit cigarette in his mouth, his favourite relaxation immediately after eight hours of fast walking. What would the experts say today?

That year he regained his Hastings-to-Brighton title, beating by five minutes Green's new record set the year before. Green was undisputed champion of the world after his Olympic win in Los Angeles, but Whitlock was the new man on the block, and he soon proved that he was the best. In 1935 he had a magnificent year. He won the Bradford 32½-mile walk, beating Green's record by five minutes, and then had a tremendous battle with Green for the RWA 50 kilometres title, with the new man finally breaking away to win by just 29 seconds. In September Whitlock won his second London-to-Brighton. His time was the first ever under eight hours, a scintillating 7:53:50, which stood until the man he helped train to win the 1960 Olympic 50km walk, Don Thompson ("The little mouse"), did 7:45:32. Thompson's gold medal was the fourth by a British-born athlete in this event in just six Olympics, though only three are credited to Britain because Sussex-born Norman Read competed in 1956 for New Zealand, to where he had emigrated because he could not gain selection in his homeland.

Late in 1935 Whitlock competed in a special long-distance track time-trial at the White City Stadium in London. He set a batch of records; the best being a world one for 30 miles (4:29:31.8) and British records for 40 miles (6:07:07), 50 miles (7:44:47.2), six hours (39 miles 473 yards), seven hours (45 miles 803 yards) and eight hours (51 miles 1042 yards). There was one blot on the year: as mentioned previously, he was disqualified for the only time in Birmingham.

In 1936 the one target was the Olympic gold. He timed his season to perfection, starting with a win in Bradford in June, then the RWA title in 4:30:38 (his fastest time ever), with Green 4th and thus not picked for the Berlin team. It was a tremendous race, with Whitlock and Lloyd Johnson battling it out every yard of the road until the latter got away in the last quarter mile only to be disqualified for lifting, after he had gone through the tape. Then came Berlin and the gold, but even that was not enough. Whitlock returned to win his third straight London-to-Brighton walk in just over eight hours, 8:01:35.

Over the next four years until World War II he was unbeatable. He had three more wins in the Bradford walk (1937, 1938 and 1940), a fourth win in the London-to-Brighton in 1937 with 8:02:38, the RWA 20 kilometres in 1939 and the RWA 50 kilometres in 1937-38-39. In the 1937 race his brother, Rex, competed for the first time and finished 3rd to start another great Whitlock era. Harold set his lifetime fastest 20 kilometres in Stockholm on 1 August 1937 of 1:33:31 on a short course, with a 1:36:02 in Hamburg in 1938 – the year that he won the European 50 kilometres. Then came the war, and after it Whitlock, a lifelong member of the Metropolitan Walking Club in London, continued his interest mainly with coaching rather than competing. It was not until 1950 that he started top racing again and then in 1952 he was back in the RWA 50 kilometres field, as related before.

After he finished at the top he moved into coaching, officiating and administration. He was secretary and then president of the RWA. He went on to be a member of the IAAF Walking Commission and chief judge of many other major competitions in addition to the 1960 Olympic 50 kilometres The immaculately turned out gold-medallist was always easily recognised; smart, tall and pleasant.

Colin Young, a long-time member of the National Union of Track Statisticians and a great fan who walked against Whitlock as a young man, says, "He was such a gentleman and he commanded respect wherever he went. He influenced me and all walkers around that time. He was immaculate in everything he did. He was one of the giants of his age, like Shrubb, George, Abrahams or Mussabini in theirs. When I was a teenager I wrote to him and he wrote back saying, 'You may never win that Olympic medal you so desire. But you will be a wonderful race walker because of your dedication' ". Colin, an international walker himself, was 19 when he raced against Whitlock, then 50, in April 1954. The field of 133 in the Metropolitan Walking Club's 15-mile event round Regent's Park in London contained major international walkers, but Colin finished a fine 12th in 2:08:59, just over a minute behind his hero.

It was not just as an administrator that Whitlock continued to involve himself. He coached and wrote a definitive book, "Race Walking", which covered every aspect of the sport and provided the basic principles from which many countries produced world-class walkers. He became English national walking coach in the 1960s and played a major part in the introduction of a 20 kilometres team race into the international programme and in the introduction of the Lugano Cup competition which preceded the World Cup. He was awarded the MBE for his services to walking.

Note: this article was first published in "Track Stats", Volume 51, No.2, April 2013. Harold Whitlock died on 27 December 1985, aged 82.

Richard Webster, equal 6th Olympic Games Pole vault 1936

From family fun athletics at bracing Bacton-on-Sea to the flawed Berlin Olympics of 1936

Frederick Richard Webster was born on 31 December 1914 in Harpenden, in Hertfordshire. He was 6ft 2in (1.88m) and 12 stone (76kg) when competing and was a member of London Athletic Club, Achilles and Milocarian. He was 6th equal in the 1936 Olympic Games pole vault with 13ft 1½in (4.00m), which was his lifetime best, and it was – until 2012 – the best ever achievement by a British athlete in this event in the Games. He held the British record for 15 years after improving it four times, was twice more over 13ft in the USA in 1937, and was consistently the best Briton in the late 1930s, always over 12ft. He was AAA champion in 1936, in 1939 and in 1948, when he decided to try again after a break of nine years because of World War II and regular Army service. He was the inaugural AAA indoor champion in 1935, and during the next three years he was International (later World) Student Games champion in 1937 and winner at each Oxford-v-Cambridge match.

He had been Public Schools champion from 1931 to 1933, first competing while still a preparatory school boy aged 12, and he was record-holder for the meeting for more than 20 years. He was also AAA junior pole-vault and discus-throw champion in 1932 and 1933. After the Berlin Olympics he went on to place 4th in the British Empire Games in Sydney in 1938 and 7th in the European Championships that year. He took part in four head-on internationals v France and Germany, with the last of them being the match in Cologne in 1939 on the eve of the war. One setback was that he failed to qualify for the final pool in the 1948 Olympics at Wembley.

Dick Webster was aged six when his father went on a visit to Sweden and came back with an unusual present – a small bamboo vaulting pole. His father was Lieutenant-Colonel F.A.M. (Frederick Annesley Michael) Webster, the most prolific athletics author of all time, whose list of 50-plus published books on the sport started in 1913 and ended in 1948, most of them lavishly illustrated with dozens of action photos. Lt-Col. Webster died in 1949, aged 62. His son, who was to become one of the best pole vaulters in Europe and the Empire, had taken to the event with great enthusiasm, and in Berlin, where there were 25 finalists, his 6th place was shared with 10 others, only tiredness stopped him clearing 13ft 7¼in (4.15m) as his weary leg brushed the bar on the way down. The five who placed ahead of him represented only two different countries: three Americans (Earle Meadows 1st, Bill Sefton 4th, Bill Graber 5th) and two Japanese (Shuhei Nishida 2nd, Sueo Oe 3rd).

Webster had made annual progress in the event of a foot a year until 12ft became a commonplace accomplishment for him, and 13ft was always possible when the competition was right. His father had learnt to vault in order to coach his son and managed 11ft, but the lack of paternal coaching when Dick Webster went into the Army, where he eventually reached the rank of Brigadier in the Royal Artillery, and then the outbreak of war when he was 24, largely ended (as with so many others) a very promising career.

At Bedford School his father coached the athletics team to many wins in the London area during prewar years, and athletics for the Webster children, Dick and his younger sisters, Joan and Peggy, was a game of fun. Some fathers lay out cricket pitches, or erect soccer and rugby goalposts, but "FAM" (a leading discus and javelin thrower in the 1910s and 1920s and still competing well into the 1930s for Bedfordshire) built a cinder run-up for the pole vault and the high and long jumps and a shot-put circle, and set up a few hurdles in the garden of their home near Bedford where young Dick was a Public Schools champion. The children loved to play athletics all the time in the garden. As well as local meetings, they had their own with friends at Bacton-on-Sea, on the bracing Norfolk coast, where the winds blow in direct from Siberia. There, seven or eight families who knew each other well would meet for a fortnight in August and the fathers would organise a full sports meeting on the sands.

Among them were the Moll bothers, who both also went to Bedford School: Gerry Moll won the discus at the Public Schools Championships in 1929 and high jumped 5-11¼ (1.81) that year. Jack Moll succeeded him as the Public Schools discus winner in 1930 and 1931 and would also be a member of South London Harriers and a fine rugby footballer, captaining the Bedford School 1st XV in 1931-32 and playing for the Barbarians invitation side against the East Midlands in 1938. Thus the seaside competition was fierce. Events included the shot, discus and pole vault, and at 13 Webster won the pole vault on the heavy sand with 7-10½ (2.40). As he soared over each new height it gave him a great thrill, he recalls, and he still has the records in a family diary – sadly, his father's scrapbooks were lost long ago in an Army move. He showed me the diary at his home in Mere, in Wiltshire, which he shares with his wife, Beryl, whom he met on the Oxford and Cambridge tour to South Africa in 1935 and married in 1940. She arrived by boat from Africa at the same time as he was getting a lift back from France after the evacuation from Dunkirk.

He remembers his athletic days as if they were yesterday.

From the beach Games to Cambridge University was a tale of progress and yearly improvement. He was not just a schoolboy champion, but at the same time a county and regional champion, breaking records as he went. In those days crowds were regularly in five figures at the main meetings, but the fans did not consider that pole vaulting and all the field events were worth watching. There was some justification for that viewpoint. The standards in the jumps and throws were, to use a neutral word, pathetic, and even 70 years later they are not a great deal better, with a few rare exceptions such as Edwards, Davies, Backley, Hill and Smith.

The Websters, father and son, set about improving British field-event standards

Their coaching relationship made the Websters seem like brothers, rather than father and son, and they wanted to alter the poor state of affairs in British athletics and provide a field-events man who could challenge the very best.

Young Dick began to grow and the heights which he cleared increased simultaneously. He vaulted 9ft (2.74) for the first time aged 14 to win the junior county championships, was over 10ft (3.05) in a county match in 1930, pushed it up six inches to be 2nd in the Midlands Championships in 1931, and managed 11ft (3.35) in the British Games at the White City in May of Olympic year, when he did three inches more to come equal 3rd in the AAA Championships with a future coach of renown, Fred Housden. The title was won by Patrick Ogilvie, of the Achilles Club, at 12ft (3.66). Of course, no British pole-vaulter was sent to the Los Angeles Olympics – nor, for that matter, was anyone else in the field events – but the 17-year-old Webster made his international debut the next year against Germany at the White City, finishing 4th with 11-7½ (3.54). He won the Public Schools pole vault for three successive years, 1931 to 1933, adding more than 14 inches to the previous meeting record, and was also 2nd in the discus in the last of those years to a visitor from Salem, in Germany, named T. Henning.

Internationally, Sabin Carr of the USA was the first man over 14ft (4.27) in 1927 and fellow countryman Bill Graber took it up to 14-4⅜ (4.37) in 1932. Two more Americans, Bill Sefton and Earle Meadows, known as "The Heavenly Twins" because they shared so many titles, took it to within an inch of 15ft (4.57). Then Cornelius ("Dutch") Warmerdam was first over the magic height, moving up to 4.77 in 1942 before the steel pole came in to replace bamboo, and

Don Bragg, who later played Tarzan in the movies, took it up to 4.80 in 1960 and then the next year George Davies moved higher to 4.83 for the first world record with a fibre-glass pole. All of them were Americans. Needless to say, neither the bamboo nor steel poles had any flexibility in them compared with fibre-glass, and this list of performances serves to put Webster into perspective in his era. In the United States there were hundreds of pole vaulters at hundreds of colleges, all with coaches, all determined to be the best. In Great Britain there were hardly any.

Under his father's ever enthusiastic eye, Dick Webster continued to go higher in 1933, mixing his vaulting with jumping and throwing on a two-days-a-week training programme in the summer and rope and bar work in the gym in the winter. He said: "It was not all-absorbing like it is today. Right from my childhood it was part of my life. It was fun rather than a way of life. But I loved the sport and I loved to win".

In 1933 he set a Midlands record in his school sports and gained five standards altogether in the Public Schools Championships. He qualified for the final of the AAA Championships but was unplaced and ended the year just a tantalising inch below 12ft with 11-11 for 1st place in the Bedfordshire-v-London University match at RAF Henlow on 10 June. The leading British vaulter of the year was a reinstated ex-professional, Frank Phillipson, of Salford Harriers, who was not much higher at 12-1½ (3.70) for 3rd place in the White City match against France. Though the series of matches against the French had begun in 1921, this was only the second time in 10 encounters that a pole vault had been included.

The Empire Games season of 1934 and over 12 feet at last

Webster at last got over 12ft early in 1934, and by 2½in in the March cold in one of those club-v-school matches so popular in those days, raising standards in schools and encouraging the boys to go on into senior athletics. Webster was competing for the now defunct London Athletic Club, founded in 1864 and the oldest club in Britain, and on 24 March, against Oundle School, in Northamptonshire, he improved enormously to 12-6 (3.81). This would rank him a respectable 23rd in Europe at the year's end, though 12 other countries – Bulgaria, Denmark, Finland, France, Germany, Holland, Hungary, Italy, Norway, Poland, Sweden and the USSR – had vaulters at 3.82 or better, led by Gustav Wegner, of Germany, at 4.11.

Webster continued as an LAC member before going up to Cambridge University late in the year and competing for them and becoming a member of Achilles, another club which took on the schools all over the British Isles. He won for Cambridge University against the AAA on 5 June at 12-3 (3.73), but his clearance against the no doubt impressed Oundle public schoolboys remained his best for the year, and he was beaten for 2nd place in a jump-off with Patrick Ogilvie at 12ft (3.66) in the AAA Championships on 14 July, as Frank Phillipson won at 12-3 (3.73). The Scots-born Ogilvie was to be one of the casualties of World War II, missing in action after a bombing mission with the RAF over Germany in 1944.

At the British Empire Games at the White City on 6 August Webster could clear only 11ft (3.50) for equal 6th place. The winner here at 12-9 (3.88) was a Canadian, Sylvanus Apps, who came to be rather better known in his home country as an outstanding ice-hockey player for the Toronto Maple Leafs. Apps also, coincidentally, was one of those fellow-competitors who would share 6th place with Webster at the Olympics two years later.

Webster won his favourite two events, pole vault and discus, in the Freshman's sports in the icy winds at Fenner's in October and November of 1934, and he then won the University handicaps and University sports with record vaults in the following February and March before also winning the event against Oxford with an English native record of 12-6½ (3.82), which was one-eighth of an inch better than Laurence Bond, a Cambridge graduate, had done five years before.

Britain's most successful Olympic pole vaulter for more than half-a-century, Dick Webster was also a pioneer of indoor athletics, winning the AAA title every year from 1935 to 1938.

Competing that spring of 1935 in matches he had a 5-7 (1.70) high jump, tying in 2nd place with a chance of a half Blue, but as he already had one they gave it to the other man. Webster also threw 161-6 (49.22) in in the javelin and 112-10 (34.40) in the discus, and had a 37-2½ (11.34) shot put, all good grounding for a decathlon later in the year.

He was injured in the summer, missing the AAA championships and the Oxford & Cambridge match against Harvard & Yale. He was fit again to go on a spectacular tour to South Africa in September with a team that included Godfrey Brown (1936 Olympic 400 metres silver and 4x400 metres gold, 1938 European 400 metres gold) and a guest, Arthur Sweeney (1934 Empire Games gold at 100 and 220 yards), who was brought in because they had no real sprinters. Sweeney, an RAF officer who died in World War II, had a wind-assisted 9.7 for only 3rd in Johannesburg and an estimated 21.2 for 2nd at 220 yards in the same meeting, plus 21.8 in another match, while Brown ran 100 yards in an estimated 9.9 for 2nd in Pretoria.

Webster apparently cleared a personal best vault of 12-7½ (3.85) in Johannesburg on 14 September 1935, but the marks recorded in his personal diary of the tour often differ from those reported in the UK press. Research by Gert le Roux, a South African member of the Association of Track & Field Statisticians, indicates that Webster actually finished 3rd in this meeting with

12-5½ (3.80). Surprisingly, F.A.M. Webster makes no mention at all of this in his copious writing about his son's achievements, and no trace of what would have been a British record in retrospect has ever been found by the National Union of Track Statisticians. In Webster's era British records were, in effect, British all-comers' records, and there were no UK national records as such, whether set at home or abroad.

Webster also had a 171-3 (52.20) javelin throw in one match, though a local press report stated that "he was unable to cover more than 170 feet", and he ran his fastest ever 440 yards relay leg (although he was never much of a runner) against Orange Free State when an Alsatian dog slipped its lead and bounded out of the crowd after him. This was just one of his amusing anecdotes from those far-off days when everything was much more relaxed and easy going in athletics.

He recalls his prolific author father, who wrote in all 100 books on different subjects and who was a Captain who was wounded in the First World War and then rejoined in World War II, taking him to the 1928 Olympics in Amsterdam and the International (later World) Student Games in Darmstadt in Germany. Dick Webster remembers with glee: "After the Games we went to a beer garden, and I will always remember Pat Ogilvie, who we had met there, and, who was a short, squat gymnast type, climbing onto the roof of the stadium afterwards and round to where all the national flags were flying. He climbed up the poles and began pulling all the flags down. After the third or fourth flag he was caught by the German police who arrested him and put him in prison for the night. He was brought up into the charge-room in the morning, but when the policeman went out of the room Pat tried to find his charge-sheet but couldn't. So he grabbed all of them, pushed them down the lavatory, pulled the plug, and escaped through the window. The Germans couldn't see the funny side of this at all, but to avoid an international incident he was released".

Another character he recalled in this thread was Walter Beavers, a Northerner who won the 1934 British Empire Games three miles and had the reputation of being 'a rough number'. Webster said: "He was competing in Yorkshire and was approached by a bookmaker and agreed to lose the race. He then won the race comfortably and escaped in a taxi, leaving a friend to pick up his winnings. There were a lot of bookmakers around in those days, but amateurism was frightfully strict and I remember my father keeping me out of a children's race because first prize was half-a-crown (12½ pence), saying, 'You'll lose your amateur status'. And you would have done in those days".

Webster would carry his 16ft vaulting-pole strapped to the side of his tiny car as if he was a duelling mediaeval horseman with lances, and he recalled another time when he and a team-mate carried the pole outside the window of the top deck of a London bus because it would not fit inside! He said: "Of course, it's a different world nowadays. Athletes all have coaches going everywhere with them. They have the training and strength, and the scientific knowledge which far outstrips what we did. They also have the fibre-glass poles which at the critical point lift them three or four feet and catapult them over the bar. We had bamboo poles which replaced the ash after one vaulter had his pole snap and was impaled. I had my bamboo break seven times, but it broke as you were going upwards so you were more or less upside down and there was not much danger of falling on it. Even so, you landed pretty heavily on your back. The pits were just sand and occasionally forked over, but it was just like landing on a flower bed, and that was the cause of my back trouble later on".

He went on: "And the money helps as well. Look at Bubka, inching the record up time after time for new world records and more and more money". Reverting to the story of his career, Webster recalls returning to Cambridge in 1935 to meet the Czech, Josef Klein, in a December decathlon.

Webster won with 4632 points (1934 tables), which included a 12ft 4¾in (3.78) pole vault. Klein turned the tables in May 1936, scoring a UK all-comers' record of 6237 points to Webster's 5161 which was still a British national record.

The Olympic year of 1936 was his best. He won against Oxford and took the AAA title with a new English native record of 12-8 (3.86) at Enfield on 4 July, to which he added an inch a week later in winning his first AAA title at the White City before going on to the Olympics in Berlin. The atmosphere there that worried some did not bother him and he had a great time, particularly in his event. He remembered: "It took a hell of a long time. The pole vault always did, and so you hardly saw your team-mates in normal international events. There was a great number of competitors and we were divided into two pools, split between two pits in the morning. Those who qualified were brought together in one pit in the afternoon and it went on and on and ended under floodlights".

It was pouring with rain, too, but he does not remember that. He cleared 4.00 (13-1½) for a lifetime best and thus become the first Briton over four metres, with the performances of the Americans and Japanese acting as a spur to push him higher than ever before. At the next height of 13-7¼ (4.15) he almost made it. His father wrote in confirmation: "He had cleared all his previous heights at the first time of asking. At 4.15 metres he took the bar off with his chest on the first vault, was well clear with his second but took the bar with his arm, and at the third, when he looked to be almost a foot clear, dropped his knee and removed the bar with that. By this time, with the rain falling, it was so late that the vaulting had to be continued by floodlight".

It is inexplicable as to why the bar, having been previously set at 4.00 metres, should then be raised all the way to 4.15. Of the 11 vaulters who cleared 4.00 none had a season's best higher than 4.10, and eight of them were at 4.05 or lower. So to ask them to attempt a height so much beyond their current form had no logic to it. According to the results meticulously compiled by the German statistician, Ekkehard zur Megede, for his book, "The Modern Olympic Century 1896-1996", it would seem that the bar had been raised at even greater 20-centimetre intervals earlier in the competition (3.40, 3.60, 3.80), and this is confirmed by the British Olympic Association's Official Report of the Games, edited by Harold Abrahams, who knew as much as anybody in those days about the rules, procedures and statistics of athletics.

Seven men tied for 17th place at 3.80, all having failed three times at 4.00. In the closing stages the differences in height were still much greater than we have come to expect in the 21st century, with a sequence of 4.15, 4.25, 4.35 and 4.45. There were 31 vaults alone by the leading five competitors at 4.15 or higher, of which 21 were failures, and there were at least 80 vaults in the entire competition, for which the qualifying round on Wednesday 6 August had begun at 10:30am The final, starting at 4pm, eventually ended in darkness. There had been 36 entrants originally, but fortunately only 25 of them actually appeared.

Even so, Dick Webster revelled in the occasion: "It gives you a tremendous lift competing in the Olympic Games, a tremendous boost, and when you see them sailing over you think, 'I am blooming well going to do that'. It's a boost to your belief that you can do it too". He had the same feeling when competing on tour the next year against the Americans in the Oxford & Cambridge v Harvard & Yale match and then against Princeton & Cornell, with his opponents inspiring him to get over 13ft in each meet. But he never reached their fine heights. He explained: "They had wonderful coaching, many more vaulters, and they took it more seriously than we did and had excellent facilities. If I had been at university in the States I could have got the extra height. I think my potential might have been an extra foot with the bamboo – I never liked the aluminium poles – but I don't really know. On my trip there it was competing against people who were pushing you along that made me go higher. No one was pushing me at home. I would have gone higher but for the war, and after I went up to Cambridge I did not have a coach except my father in the vacation, and then once I was in the Army there was no one. You must have a coach".

He had not maintained his Berlin Olympic achievement in the post-Games match between the USA and the British Empire, this time at the White City, because as he ran in for his first try at 13ft his pole snapped and he fell very heavily. In 1937 he won again for Cambridge, but his visit to the USA meant that he missed the AAA Championships. He won the International Student Games in Paris on his return. He was selected for the 1938 British Empire Games, but the Army, which he had recently joined as a regular officer, was at first not keen to give him leave, though later changing its mind, and he joined the ship at Toulon, in France, for the long sea journey to Sydney.

It was a mix of a team with students, military officers, policemen and working people living together. Webster said: "We mixed fairly well. You naturally tend to go with the people with whom you were friendly. We all got on well together. I shared a cabin with a policeman and we got on very well. I remember I got horribly drunk one night when they spiked my drink and was put to bed. I was bloody ill!" After the long trip he was 4th with 12-9 (3.89), and he also did 12-6¾ (3.83) in Melbourne and 12-7½ (3.85) in Perth during February behind the South African, Andries du Plessis, who later in the year managed 13-6¾ (4.13) in Johannesburg, ranking equal 20th in the world for the year after 15 men from the USA, three from Japan and one from the USSR. Webster's best was 12-9½ (3.90), finishing 2nd to the Italian, Mario Romeo, in the AAA Championships, and the same height of 3.90 for 7th in the European Championships in Paris behind Karl Sutter, of Germany.

1939 was very much a quiet season because of the threat of war, but he won the AAA title and was finally given late permission by the Army to compete against Germany on August 20, days before war broke out between the two countries. He served in France, Italy and Egypt and did not vault again until 1948 when he was struck by a sudden whim that he would like to try and see if he could make the Olympic team. He said: "I thought I would have one more shot at it. I was stationed at Larkhill, on Salisbury Plain, and there were no facilities. So I practised on the cricket field. My wife, Beryl, brought down my son, Michael, who was aged six, to watch, but I missed on my first jump and he walked away in disgust!

"Because I was a 'possible' for the Games I got extra meat ration and my local butcher was delighted. I had not touched a pole for the duration of the war and it was quite a tough job. I don't know what motivated my decision, but I was delighted with what I did". What he did do was to clear 11-6 (3.50) from the start of his comeback as if it was a natural thing to do without training, like riding a bicycle. He became Army champion, reached 12ft (3.66) for the AAA against London University and then 12-3 (3.73) in the trials to win the AAA title for the third time, with a pulled muscle, but he failed to qualify for the Olympic final at Wembley, clearing only 3.60 as the leading 12 went through at four metres.

He cleared 12-6 (3.81) for 4th place in the British Empire-v-USA match at the White City on 12 August ... and that was the end of his athletics career. Apart from a bit of throwing in regimental sports, he did not compete again, and when he left the Army as a Brigadier (including peace-keeping duties in Korea) in 1967 he and Beryl went back to her native land and they farmed 12,000 acres near Natal before retiring to Wiltshire in 1987. All his medals are under glass on specially made tables to pass on to his three children – just as his father handed on his medals.

Note: this article was first published in "Track Stats", Volume 39, No.1, March 2001. Richard Webster died on 28 September 2009, aged 94. His British record had lasted 14 years until 1951.

"Time went pleasantly by and I remember emerging from a good stretch of plough with only one man ahead of me – Jack Holden"

Carl Allun John (known as Jack) Emery was born on 27 December 1913 in Stoke-on-Trent and was educated at Newcastle-under-Lyme High School and Emmanuel College, Cambridge. A member of the Achilles Club and North Staffs Harriers, he was 5ft 11½in (1.82m) tall, weighed 10½st (66kg) and on the track he was 4th in the European Championships 5000 metres in 1938 and was AAA three miles champion in 1938 and 1939. He was 2nd in the International Student Games 1500 metres of 1937 to Jim Alford, who would be the Empire mile champion the following year. In head-to-head international matches Emery was 1st v France at three miles, 2nd v Norway at 1500 metres and 2nd= v Germany at 5000 metres. His personal best performances were as follows: 880 yards 1:56.4, 1500 metres 3:53.4, 1 mile 4:13.8, 2 miles 9:03.4, 3 miles 14:08.0, 5000 metres 14:40.4 in his last race on 20 August 1939, on the eve of World War II.

A week before the International cross-country championship race in Belfast in 1938, Jack Emery, who had won his place by finishing 2nd to the great Jack Holden in the National, ran in a nine-mile handicap organised by Liverpool Harriers. He is now a sprightly 93 (the oldest international still alive except for Godfrey Rampling, I believe) but still remembers the day: "Of all the competitive races in my career, this was the one in which I felt completely at ease, strong, dominant, flowing and tireless – a wonderful feeling. I felt wonderful, and I felt much the same in the International cross-country which I won. I never felt the same on the track. It was hard graft, and you were wondering what time you hit for the first lap time in a mile, and then that horrible third lap. I don't know whether other milers found it difficult and hated it as much as I did".

His feelings did not stop him from becoming a successful miler and three miler in the two years before World War II which ended his career. He was in Monaco for the International Student Games again in September 1939, where he stood an excellent chance of gold in either the 1500 or 5000 metres, but never ran as the Germans invaded Poland and war was declared, and he came home before his first race. He did not run seriously in competition again but had a great career as a schoolmaster at King Edward VI School, Lichfield, in Staffordshire, as coach for dozens of schoolboys (and world three miles record-holder Freddie Green, of Birchfield) and organiser of athletics and cross country. His own career had started as a schoolboy in the Midlands with the crowning moment being 3rd place in 4:35.0 (an improvement of 10 seconds) behind Sydney Wooderson and Dennis Pell (whose last race would also be in the 1939 match against Germany) as the little Blackheath Harrier became the first schoolboy to run under 4:30 with 4:29.8.

Emery, who lives in Ambleside, Cumbria, said: "Some talent for running was first discovered when I was a junior against seniors in a school cross-country. But how to run, how to train for the track? I was fortunate to have the advice and company of a school old boy called E.I. Ackroyd, two or three years my senior, with a Cambridge cross-country half-blue, who came to train on the school track – grass, five laps to the mile – and he taught me the basics for half-mile and mile training such as times to aim for, lap-timings and even race-pacing. Consequently, there were school records of 2:08 and 4:45. Otherwise, one would have just run in training and racing with the hope of coming first".

He was not a natural ball player but was able to play rugby to school-team level and found that his sporting prowess "gave me that amount of self-esteem and confidence necessary for the happiness of a shy teenager. And so it was throughout the rest of my running career and life. The self-doubts one always lives with are much lightened by moderate success in any field of human endeavour which society accepts as worthwhile. I consider myself fortunate that success at pedestrianism in one form or another is possible to that end".

He went up to Cambridge University and ran as a freshman in the Inter-Varsity cross-country where he came up against another future British international and record-holder, Peter Ward, for the first of their races against each other over six years. Neither was particularly good at the time. Emery remembers: "I was undistinguished but keen for the first year or two in university athletics. There was no training advice and no ex-university aspirations. My best performance was 3rd in the Inter-Varsity cross-country in 1936". He and Ward raced against each other twice in those clashes: Ward 8th and Emery 11th in 1933, 5th and 9th in 1934.

Emery's best mile was around 4:28 in 1936, which was the year when Ward improved by 40 seconds at three miles to set a British record with 14:15.6 and then finished 11th in the Olympic 5000 metres. Things changed for Emery in 1937: "Then came my *annus mirabilis*. The Oxbridge tour to America in July was stimulating bait. I won the Cambridge mile trial in about 4:25 and the match against Oxford in 4:22.2 in March and continued to train, and I remember doing a 3:09 ¾-mile trial with Peter Ward at Fenner's, 63, 63, 63. He thought it too good to be true! A day or two before embarking for the States the team had a match with the Army and I brought my mile time down to 4:18."

Hanging on desperately but the reward is a personal best time

It came down even more across the Atlantic, and what would today's pundits have made about the sensational improvements of both men in one season? "In the first match v Harvard & Yale luck was with me. My second string took us through the half in 2:07, leaving me leaden into the dreaded third quarter. I have to say that I could neither front run nor sprint finish, an unhappy combination. The American first string, Northrop, was a half-miler and therefore with a good finish. Ill-advisedly he took on the third lap maintaining the pace. I just hung on desperately, and just as desperately made the end of the back straight my finish and broke the half-miler with my cross-country background. The final bend and straight were a matter of struggling on without the need to face the final sprint, and my opponent had knocked himself out".

Emery's time was a lifetime best (and one of the world's leading times for the year) of 4:13.8. He recalls: "Peter Ward told me he thought the report in the paper was a misprint". A few days later against Princeton & Cornell it was a different story. Emery said: "It didn't go my way because I was forced to take on the third lap and the Princeton man, Bradley, easily passed me in the final straight and I was just under 4:15".

By this time he was developing his own finish to combat the lack of sprint: "My secret was to make your finish the end of the back straight – and then just hold on. You started your finish round the first bend of the last lap and finished at the end of the straight, and you just had to hang on for the rest of the way. You surprise people and open up a gap of a few yards before they sprint with their dash in the final straight. Freddie Green used it like the time he beat Chataway for the world three miles record in 1954. Freddie was a wonderful pupil who used to visit me once a week, and I would give him a schedule and he would carry it out to the 'T' – a very very good man".

The Oxbridge team moved on to Canada where Emery tried two miles for the first time and set a Canadian record of 9:20.0 in Hamilton. "So having begun the year as a 4:28 miler I arrived back in England a potential international athlete and very pleased with myself. I was soon asked to run as the great Sydney's second string in Norway where I was 3rd in the 1500 metres in a time I think was a little faster than the mile at Harvard. That was on the Wednesday. On Thursday I finished 2nd in a 3000 metres, and on the Friday I won my first 5000 metres in terrible conditions".

1937 was Peter Ward's great year – not that Emery had any idea. He knew nothing of his friend and rival's performances until they met up in 1938 for the AAA three miles. Ward had run Taisto Mäki, of Finland, who was then clearly the best man in the world, to a few yards at 5000 metres in the match against Finland in Helsinki, 14:31.0 to 14.31.6 (14:02 for three miles), and then in the Empire Games in February 1938 Ward just lost to Cecil Matthews, of New Zealand, who became the first Empire athlete under 14 minutes (13:59.6), with Ward running 14:05.0.

Emery said: "My professional duties as a schoolmaster prevented me accepting the invitation to run in the Empire Games in Australia where Peter did so well. Could I have done better?" For Emery 1938 was the year of continued success after a move up to two miles and three miles. The reason? "I never ran a quarter faster than 55. I once ran a half-mile in 1:56 (58, 58), leading all the way until Godfrey Brown, who was not in great fettle at the time, passed me about three yards out. But as you know Sydney was a 49-second quarter-miler and Pell was not much slower. How could I compete?" Emery was one of the pacemakers off 40 yards when Sydney broke the world 800 metres/880 yards records in late August, and says, "Following that the winter of 1937-38 was to be used just for running plenty of short and long fartlek over the country to build up strength for the forthcoming 1938 track season".

But that was not quite how it worked out

He explained: "I ran an occasional Saturday club race with North Staffs Harriers or Wirral Athletic Club, with no serious intent but piling up the miles for the beginning of the 1938 track season. Dear old Edgar Sandbach, the honorary secretary of North Staffs, suggested I might run for the club in the National, and the offer of an all-expenses paid trip to Reading persuaded me. I remember a fine warm day with no particular onus on my shoulders and a pair of Dunlop tennis shoes on my feet. Time went pleasantly by and I remember emerging from a good stretch of plough with only one man ahead of me – Jack Holden". So, in an illustrious field of an almost unbeatable group of regulars who kept taking the International individual and team titles, Emery finished 2nd.

Then came the Liverpool race with that "wonderful feeling" that Emery experienced, and the euphoria spread into the International where England were defending a record of having won the team race every year since 1930. Emery recalls: "A Belgian, Jean Chapelle, went off fast and I, the least experienced of the English team, stayed with Holden, Alec Burns and Potts and co. Chapelle led by 150 yards. It was about two miles to go when no one else had made a move that I decided to go after him and found it surprisingly easy to catch him about a mile from home. We came to a stile with perhaps half-a-mile to go. He climbed it, I leapt it, left him, and sailed easily enough home by 39 seconds". England packed 1, 4, 6, 9, 11, and 12 for 43 points to win by 53 (France 96, Belgium 117, then Wales, Scotland, Northern Ireland and Eire).

Emery remembered, "Track loomed. Wooderson and Pell were unbeatable in the mile. Peter Ward had won the three miles championship the year before, but I had no idea when I moved up that he had had such prestigious performances in the years before. 'What about the steeplechase?' I thought. I entered all three in the championships, but common-sense prevailed and thankfully I avoided making a fool of myself in the steeplechase". He won a tight battle with Ward (in all races they had on track and country they ended up three-all) and went to Paris for the European Championships 5000 metres, where he finished 4th to Mäki.

"I remember warming up under the stands and the two Finns were there, round and round and round, and I was very impressed just on my own and rather overwhelmed. How casual things were in those days. I ran the five and the team manager, Jack Crump, came and asked if I would like to run the 10,000 metres. I had no suggestion of anything like that before. I had just had a night out and thought I had better not".

Just after the Games he ran 3:53.6 for 1500 metres behind Wooderson's world's best for the year of 3:48.7 in Oslo and ran a British record for two miles with 9:07.6 to beat Shrubb's 33-year-old record. Even so, he did not retain his cross-country title: "I am not a terribly confident person, but if the Gods had not been against me I would have won. I had been training very well, but about three weeks before the National I had a frightful heavy, heavy cold and was taking nasal sprays to clear my nose. So when I could run I ran very badly. But then there was a good gap of three weeks between the National and the International to recover, and I started running extremely well and thought 'Oh good, I will be all right', and then a week before I had one of those awful heel bruises and that stopped me from finishing what would have been three weeks training and stopped me retaining my title".

He finished 19th nearly two minutes behind Holden, who won the individual title, but England lost the team event to a superb French team who had 36 points, 59 less than the holders.

Another AAA title and then Lovelock's record is broken

1939 was Jack Emery's best year on the track. He retained his Midlands mile title but lost the three miles later in the afternoon by inches when trying to complete the double. The AAA three miles was run in the rain and was a great race in which Emery just had the edge, thanks to his finishing style. "The Times" commented, "He is a much faster finisher than his running suggests", and he won in 14:08.0, with Ward a stride back in 14:08.6. Nearly three weeks later they met again in Manchester, and in an epic struggle the bespectacled Emery just beat his stylish rival, 9:03.4 to 9:04.0, to break Jack Lovelock's British record.

A few days later Ward had his revenge in Glasgow where he strode away by 150 yards in 9:10.8 to take Alfred Shrubb's 35-year-old Scottish record. Emery reminisced: "I was pathetic. Indeed, I was foolish. It was not typical of me in my way of life, but four days before the race a friend had a stag party to which I went and stayed up very late and drank quite a lot of beer, and so by Saturday I was suffering the effect of poisoning and an almighty hangover. Peter and I got on very well, but we never talked about our running, You didn't in those days. What I remember is his lovely flowing style that everyone remembers. A very handsome runner indeed, handsome".

Emery's season was not over. He went to the Lakes on holiday and then his calf muscle was injured while training. But he said: "I ran in Germany in spite of that, and ran well, and from Cologne I went down to Monte Carlo for the World Student Games, but we were caught out when Germany invaded Poland". So he and Godfrey Brown and Alan Pennington, among others, came home before the Games ended. If he had stayed on he could have won either the 1500 metres (Blaine Rideout, of the USA, 4:01.1) or the 5000 metres (Morrison Carstairs, of Scotland, 15:20.2).

He said: "I do look back on those years, 1937 to 40, as indeed halcyon days. Apart from the pleasure of moderate athletic success I was given the experience of a little foreign travel out of reach of a comparatively impoverished schoolmaster. So far as the ending of such frivolities as athletics with the outbreak of the war were concerned, in the great scheme of things it was of no importance at all, but I might have felt disappointed and thwarted as an athlete only halfway through a possibly illustrious career, or at least an Olympic Games. In fact, I have to tell you that my predominant feeling was one of relief, the weight been lifted from my shoulders! One aspect,

I suppose, of the difference between a dedicated amateur and a professional."

He never raced again at a serious level, returning to coaching and organising when he went back to teaching after the war, which was an occupation he stayed with until retirement. He did not race again until he was his late 60s and living in the Lake District, when he was tempted to run in the Windermere marathon as the worldwide marathon craze started. He was first in the 70-plus section and twice ran the London Marathon (4hr 30min) and remembers: "My aim was merely to maintain a running gait the whole distance. This I did, but I shall never forget a tall young lady walking briskly past me as a lady spectator called out to me, 'What a beautiful pair of legs you have, young man!' In my early 70s I continued to enjoy running more or less daily on the fells and rocks, with an occasional half-marathon and other distances, but knee and Achilles tendon trouble in my mid-70s limited me to walking".

And that included Nepal, the Pyrenees, the Dolomites, and dozens of Scottish climbs, including the Cuillin Inaccessible Pinnacle at the age of 78 and the Welsh 15 Peaks round Snowdonia (4am to 10pm) when a mere lad in his 60s. He added: "Now at 93 as a four-legged animal – two poles – I manage a couple of flat miles with the beautiful ever-changing Langdale Pikes as an inspirational backcloth". Thus proving once again that like old soldiers old athletes never lose their fitness.

Author's footnote: My thanks to Chris Thorne and Harold Ogden for their help.

Note: this article was first published in "Track Stats", Volume 45, No.4, November 2007. Jack Emery died in February 2013, aged 99. David Thurlow's interview with Freddie Green, who was coached by Jack Emery, also appears in this book.

This photograph shows Jack Emery beating Peter Ward for the AAA three miles title in 1939. They raced each other regularly and between them set 10 British records at distances from 2000 metres to 5000 metres.

The sort of tale that Hollywood loves: running for the fun of it even under ominously dark skies

Following the retirement of the Los Angeles Olympic champion and world record-holder, Tom Hampson, there were a number of 880 yards runners in Britain battling against each other for international honours during the 1930s, Those were the innocent cash-free days when progression was through the traditional route of county, district and national championships.

The AAA title changed hands regularly, and prominent among the internationals, to take them in alphabetical order, were Jim Alford, 4th in the 1938 British Empire Games; Alfred Baldwin, who ran in the European Championships that year; Jack Cooper, 1:52.2 for 800 metres in 1934 and 6th in that year's Empire Games; Mike Gutteridge, who also ran in the 1934 Empire Games before going on active service to India where he died of typhoid within a year; Frank Handley, 2nd in the 1938 Empire Games and a best of 1:52.9 for 880 yards in 1937; Austin Littler, 1:51.4 metric in 1939; John Moreton, 1:54.4 for yards the same year; Brian MacCabe, 1:53.1 yards in 1938 and an Olympic finalist in 1936; his London Athletic Club colleague, John Powell, 1:50.8 metric in 1936 and 7th in the 1932 Olympic final; Tom Scrimshaw, 1:54.6 yards in 1933; James Stothard, 1:53.3 yards in 1935 and 3rd in the 1934 Empire Games; Clifford Whitehead, 1:54.0 yards in 1933; and, of course, Sydney Wooderson, world records of 1:48.4 metric /1:49.2 yards in 1938.

Then add Godfrey Brown, who won the AAA 880 yards in 1939 but never ran an individual half-mile in an international; Ralph Scott, the 19-year-old prodigy who ran 1:53.9y in the 1935 AAA final but nothing after; and Guy Wethered, the exciting new find of 1939 with 1:52.4y. Yet the only man to win the AAA 880 yards title twice in those pre-war years following Hampson's retirement was Arthur Collyer, a railway clerk from Watford.

Arthur Collyer's story is real "Alf Tupper and Wilson" stuff – the sort of tale that Hollywood loves. It started, like epics of this kind, on a beautiful mid-summer evening in 1931 when Collyer went to meet his friend, Bill Beaumont, with neither of the alternatives of the cinema or the pub seeming to appeal. Bill had other ideas. He had joined the small local club, Watford Harriers, in Hertfordshire, and that Wednesday night was training night. So Arthur, who had never had any interest in sport whatsoever, went along, liked what he saw, and thought he would have a try.

Sprinting and 440 yards seemed to need speed which he did not have when he took his first nervous strides. The mile was too far and the half-mile just about right. The truth was quickly revealed: Arthur Collyer was a natural, and being a very determined young man who liked to do whatever he tackled to the best of his ability, and on his own, he set out to be very good indeed.

He gave up smoking 40 cigarettes a day and within a year he was in the winning Hertfordshire medley relay team at the Inter-Counties championships, running the anchor 880. He won the railways championship in 2:02.2 and then for the English railways team against France in 2:02.4. Within two years he was the county 880 champion in record time, and he also won a Bank Holiday Inter-Counties match in 2:01.4 and the first of a stream of London Business Houses and Charity titles.

At 6ft tall (1.83m), and with a racing weight of 10½st (66kg), born on 9 November 1909 in Watford, he reached the AAA final in 1934 within three years of taking up the sport. He ran 1:56.9 in his heat and remembers that he was 4th in the final, won by Cooper from Powell and

Gutteridge. This earned him his first Great Britain vest and he achieved a wonderful 1:53.4 for 800 metres against France in Paris behind Cooper and Powell, both 1:52.2. He qualified again for the 1935 AAA final, finishing 5th in 1:54.4.

He was injured while an Olympic 800 metres prospect in 1936 but came back to win the AAA 880 yards title in 1937, having set an English native record of 1:53.1 in the Southern championships on an undulating grass track in Brighton. He also ran 2nd to the future world record-holder, Rudolf Harbig, in the GB-v-Germany match at the White City that year (1:54.4 to 1:55.3). Collyer retained his AAA title in 1938 and set a lifetime best of 1:52.9 for 880 yards in Glasgow in front of a crowd of 60,000.

He qualified again for the 1939 AAA final but chose the mile instead, for which he had also got through in the Friday evening heats, because he believed he could beat Wooderson, then the world No.1. Wooderson won in 4:11.8 from Dennis Pell (4:12.0) and Collyer (4:15.0), but it brought Collyer his final international vest. He was 4th at 1500 metres in the Germany-GB match in Cologne just a fortnight before World War II began with a time of 3:55.0 behind Ludwig Kaindl, Pell and Herbert Jacob. Collyer had also run Wooderson reasonably close when the latter became the first man to cover three-quarters of a mile in under three minutes, 2:59.5 to 3:03.6.

Then war came, and it was the biggest disappointment of his career that he never ran in the Olympics.

Now that the cricket has finished training can begin

By today's standards the facilities in which his career flowered were primitive indeed. The club headquarters when he started running were at a cricket ground, and no training could be undertaken until the nets practice or game finished around dusk and the athletes could run round the boundary. Shortly afterwards they were asked to leave permanently and moved to a new training ground provided by the council.

It was a field where Collyer and a friend painted a 200-yard diameter track with a six-inch brush and a tin of white distemper before training and changed in a disused hut, with permission to use a barrel of the water which came off the corrugated roof when it rained. Saturday training in winter was based at "The Dog" public house when it was closed in the afternoon, with the landlady providing an old zinc bath filled with hot water. After that there was a move to a room under the Watford public swimming baths and the luxury of having hot water on tap all the time. Now Watford boasts an eight-lane all-weather track of its own which attracts middle-distance runners from all over Britain and from continental Europe for its numerous open meetings.

So it was that Arthur Collyer had begun a career at the age of 22 when many had been running for years, and this was to take him to international level, through wartime service as a Flight Lieutenant physical fitness officer with the RAF Pathfinders squadron, and on until well after peace was declared.

Athletics in Britain was divided in those days between the university athletes from Oxford and Cambridge and the working-men who fitted in their running with their jobs and used their holidays (usually only two weeks a year) for any international selection. Collyer, for example, ran to the railway station in Watford in his city-suit to commute to London and trained during his lunch-hour or in the evening. This entailed about 90 minutes of mixed speed and stamina work three times a week with a race on as many Saturdays as he could find them.

The two camps did not really mix. The university men enjoyed long holidays and had a different outlook on life. For men like Collyer, who regarded athletics almost as a religion and delayed marrying his sweetheart, Hilda, because his sport came before everything, the need to work and the restrictions caused by it were major problems. He was a prime candidate for both the British Empire Games in Sydney in February 1938 and the European Championships at Colombes the following September, but he could not go to either. The Empire Games meant being away for at least three months because of the sea journey involved, and he was told that he could go unpaid and his job might not be there when he came back. When autumn came he had already used his holiday allowance for competing.

He bore no grudge. That was the way things were then. When I met him last year he told me: "The university chaps had preferential treatment. We all knew that. If there were two of you with about the same record, they would always pick the university man. Once after competing I was hauled from my bath to run a relay leg in the heavy rain because one of them didn't fancy it! One year, early in my career, the AAA turned me down for the championships because they said I was not good enough. But I had run faster than one of the university chaps who was accepted. So the editor of the railway magazine rang them. They reinstated me, and I had the fastest heat time! But once you were number one – and I was very determined to be that – you were always selected on merit.

"On tour the Oxford and Cambridge blokes ganged together and did not mix with us. Really, we did not speak the same language. I did not mind a bit. You stayed with athletes of your own level. The trips were great fun and you made the most of them. There were no expenses in those days, and I did not have a holiday for five years because of my running, but I did not mind. Money was very tight, and you ran for the fun, the love, and the glory of it. It was not like today when they are all professionals, I could not afford a car, just a bike. I earned £225 a year before the War and the detached house I still live in cost £850 without a garage".

The injury which deprived him of his one chance of Olympic success happened in late May of 1936. During a training session in his lunch-break on the heavy cinder track at the Duke of York's regimental headquarters in Chelsea he was hopping on one foot as part of his strengthening when it twisted over. He was able to get back to his office at Euston, but an x-ray showed that the fifth metatarsus bone in his right foot was broken. That was the end of racing until late August, though even on crutches and with his foot in plaster he still went to work every day.

Advice from a double Olympic champion

He reckons that he would have been in the Olympic final because of the way he was progressing in training, and although he would not have beaten the USA's Johnny Woodruff he would have kept with the pack, judging by the way the race was run, and his finish could have taken him close. Woodruff won in 1:52.9 from Mario Lanzi, of Italy (1:53.3), and Phil Edwards, of Canada (1:53.6). Had 1940 been an Olympic year, matters would have been altogether different as he would then have been 31 and he had already taken the decision to move up to the mile.

His training sessions of three-quarter-mile runs for stamina, interspersed with 100s, 220s, 440s and a few half-miles were paying off. He had listened to Albert Hill, the Olympic 800 metres and 1500 metres champion of 1920, who was coaching Sydney Wooderson, and to Ted Vowles, a veteran AAA starter of over 40 years' experience and founder-president of Surrey Athletic Club, who wrote letters with plenty of ideas and tips in them. Collyer had fine pace judgment, with an upright style and a stride of 8ft-to-9ft in length.

In Collyer's absence it was John Powell, Frank Handley and Brian MacCabe who went to the Berlin Olympics, but only MacCabe reached the final where he was 9th and last, Collyer did come back at the season's end to win the railways' championships at 880 yards and one mile and continued running during the winter, finishing 4th in the North of the Thames cross-country and 2nd in the Hertfordshire championship over 7½ miles.

He started the 1937 track season with his Southern championships win at Brighton, leading at the bell in 55.1 and then re-passing MacCabe 15 yards from the line to beat Tom Hampson's English record. A week later Collyer ran 3:05.6 for three-quarters of a mile, just 0.6 outside the British record held by Reggie Thomas, the AAA mile champion of 1930-31-33. Then on 17 July, at the White City, Collyer produced what he believes was the greatest performance of his career to win his first AAA title. After a 1:56.5 heat he led through 26.0, 55.1 and 1:23.4 and was then passed by four of the field but came again in the straight to win a desperate battle in 1:53.3, followed by Handley, Alford, MacCabe, Stothard and Powell.

The following week Collyer lost to Handley at 800 metres in the match against France in Paris, 1:52.5 to 1:53.2, but then beat him in Glasgow over 880 yards, 1:53.7 to an estimated 1:53.9. By then all the travel which had to be fitted into a long working and commuting day was taking its toll, and at the August Bank Holiday meeting before a White City crowd of 63,000 Collyer had nothing left on the last lap. The Pole, Kucharski, won at 880 yards in 1:52.8 from Handley (1:52.9), with Collyer trailing in 1:55.7.

Still, this did not stop him from making the long train journey up to Glasgow again the following Saturday where he ran 3rd in an estimated 1:55 behind Alford in a handicap event. He again beat Handley but not the future European champion and world record-holder, Rudolf Harbig, over 880 yards (1:54.8 to 1:55.3) in the GB-Germany match at the White City on 14 August, and he then went off on a Scandinavian tour. During that he beat Stothard over 800 metres (1:53.5) in the match against Norway in Oslo, was in the winning 4 x 800 relay team against Finland in Helsinki, and ran a 1:53.6 for 800 metres in Stockholm. He averaged 1:54.5 in the seven races he contested, plus a 49.5 400 metres relay leg.

Missing the Empire Games but another AAA success

During the following winter he was again 2nd in the Hertfordshire cross-country championship but could only read the reports of the 1938 Empire Games in Sydney. It is difficult for people now to understand that while the university and services athletes were allowed time off, others could not take the risk of losing their jobs to represent their country. The Empire 880 yards title was won in an impressive 1:51.2 by Pat Boot, of New Zealand, with Handley 2nd in an estimated 1:53.5.

Collyer started the 1938 track season in fine form, setting a record 1:56.0 in the City & Hospitals meeting, winning the Inter-Counties title in 1:57.1 with an out-of-sorts Handley 3rd, and running 1:54.6 for 800 metres on a flooded Antwerp track in early July. He was a distant 2nd to Wooderson in the Southern (1:54.4 to 1:57.7 after a 56.5 first lap) and he lost to Hoel, of Norway, over 800 metres (1:54.9 to 1:55.2) in the return match at the White City a week before the AAA Championships. But he retained his AAA title after a 1:55.1 heat, leading all the way in the rain through a first lap of 55.4 to win in 1:53.7 from the Army champion, Alfred Baldwin (1:54.9), and MacCabe (1:55.2), with Handley nowhere.

On 1 August, again at the White City, Collyer's class was tested as Wooderson ran the fastest 880 yards time yet achieved on that heavy track, 1:50.9, just ahead of Lanzi (1:51.1), with Sjabbe Bouman, of Holland, 3rd in 1:53.0 and Collyer 4th in 1:53.7. "The Times" commented regarding Collyer: "Beautiful runner as he was he could not go such a pace". Yet he could go faster, as he proved five days later in Glasgow where he ran the full distance in a handicap race against his old enemy, Handley, who was off six yards, and Dick Littlejohn, the Scots champion off 12 yards. Handley won by a yard in 1:52.4 from Littlejohn, with Collyer holding on for 3rd in

71

a lifetime best of 1:52.9 which broke Stothard's Scottish all-comers' record by 0.8.

The next weekend, against France at the White City, Collyer was a shadow of himself after having teeth extracted and ran a poor 3rd to Wooderson. It did not do his chances of selection for the European Championships in Paris much good, but that was academic as he was not allowed the time off anyway, and he stayed at home to listen to the broadcasts and read the newspapers. Harbig won the title comfortably in 1:50.6 and Handley and Baldwin failed miserably in the heats with 1:55.0 and 1:56.6 respectively. Jacques Leveque, of France, was 2nd in 1:51.8, Lanzi 3rd in 1:52.0, and Bouman 4th in 1:52.3.

During the winter Collyer thought about retirement as he was now coming up to 30 and he had set his wedding date for October 1939, but his enthusiasm for competing was too much and he started his 1939 season with 3rd place in the AAA indoor championships at Wembley to George Morris (2:00.4). Collyer then won his county 880 yards and mile titles in record times, but he was still not racing fit and was beaten by inches by new boy Guy Wethered in the annual Oxford University-v-AAA match in 1:57.0 and was 2nd in 1:55.9 to another newcomer, John Moreton, in the Inter-Counties meeting.

Then came a race which was to change the course of his athletics ambitions for the future. Invited to take part in Wooderson's attack on the three-quarter-mile record in Manchester on 7 June, Collyer found the pace just right. Together with Wooderson at 880 yards in exactly two minutes, he hung on grimly over the last lap for a time of 3:03.6 behind Wooderson's record 2:59.5. The reporter from the now defunct "Daily Sketch" wrote: "This illustrates perfectly the difference in speed of the world-beater compared with the ordinary international-class performer such as Collyer undoubtedly is".

Confident in the belief that Wooderson could be beaten

But Collyer thought otherwise, and when Wooderson lost to the Americans in the famous mile at Princeton on 17 June he became even more sure that the little Blackheath Harrier was beatable. In the Southern championships Collyer was run out of it in his 880 heat after suffering food poisoning during the week, and he then concentrated on building up for the mile at the AAA Championships, winning the London Business Houses title in 4:23.8 in the meantime.

In the AAA he ran in both the 880 and one mile heats, with times of 1:57.1 and 4:25 about an hour apart, and then chose the mile for the Saturday. Collyer told me in our interview: "It was my ego. I thought I could beat Sydney Wooderson. I thought that surely somebody could beat him, and I was getting older and thought I could do better in the mile". But Wooderson, as previously related, won with Collyer a strong 3rd in 4:15.0, much to the surprise of the press.

To show it was no fluke, Collyer recorded 4:18.4 in the Metropolitan Police Sports a week later, and he followed this by running very well in a 1000 yards short-limit handicap race at the Ibrox Sports in Glasgow won by the American, Charlie Beetham, in a British all-comers' record of 2:11.0, with Collyer just beating another leading US runner, Blaine Rideout, to the tape in 2:13.1.

Then came his last race before the war, running as second string at 1500 metres in place of the injured Wooderson against Germany in Cologne on 20 August and finishing 4th in 3:55.0. The skies were ominously dark, with thunder crashing, and there was a heavy feeling of doom as army recruits poured into the city. The AAA president, Lord Burghley, correctly warned of war within a fortnight.

Collyer joined up in the ranks of the Royal Air Force shortly after marrying Hilda. As a physical fitness officer he ran as often as he could, and in 1942 he won the 880 at the White City Games

A study in white – the "desperate battle" in the 1937 AAA 880 yards final. Left to right, Frank Handley (2nd), Arthur Collyer (1st), John Powell (6th), Jim Alford (3rd), James Stothard (5th) and Brian MacCabe (4th).

in 1:59.0 and had a great battle with Harry Fox in front of a 40,000 crowd in Glasgow, with Fox winning in 1:56.0 after a 53 first lap and Collyer close behind in 1:57.1. In 1943 he ran 1:57.4 for 880 yards at the White City but did not compete again until 1947.

He took up where he had left off as Hertfordshire county mile champion in 4:31.6, and a month later regaining his City & Hospitals mile title in 4:26.8 and then the railways championship in 4:44.8. He kept going for a while, even running in the AAA one mile heats and for Hertfordshire in the Inter-Counties cross-country at Leicester in 1950 at the age of 40, having finished 6th in the county championships. After retirement he kept in close contact with Watford Harriers, officiating and coaching.

In October 1952, by which time he was assistant to the British Rail industrial relations officer, he was on the local train which was hit by the Perth-to-London express at Harrow, killing 112 people. Knocked unconscious, he came to as someone stepped on his leg, and he then walked away and caught a bus back to a Watford hospital to seek treatment!

Even at the age of 87, when I met him, he still maintained a training programme: 120 hops when he got up at 5.30 in the morning, followed by a four-mile cycle ride and another 150 hops at night.

Note: this article was first published in "Track Stats", Volume 36, No.1, January 1998. Arthur Collyer died on 18 November 2006, nine days after his 97th birthday.

A £20 loan from the club president pays dividends in gold for the active Welsh manager

On 12 February 1938 Jim Alford lined up for the start of the British Empire Games mile final on the grass track at the Sydney cricket ground. As was to be the case with Sebastian Coe more than 40 years later at the 1980 Olympics, Alford had been odds-on favourite earlier in the Games, at 880 yards, and like Coe he had been beaten, lacking sharpness, commitment and confidence. Again like Coe, Alford was to regain everything in the race he was not expected to win, defeating his conqueror at the shorter distance.

It had been Pat Boot, of New Zealand, who had nailed Alford to the track in the Empire Games 880 yards, leaving him in such desperation that he wrote (but did not post) a letter of apology to his coach, Sid Virgin, saying that he had let him down. But in the heats of the mile Alford ran 4:17.3, only 0.2sec slower than the Welsh record he had set the previous year in Pontypridd when beating the holder and 1930 Empire Games champion, Reg Thomas. In the Sydney final Alford let fly on the last lap with a 61, after 59, 65.5 and 66, to win by 10 yards in his lifetime best and break Jack Lovelock's Games record from four years earlier in London.

James William Llewellyn Alford had been born on 15 October 1913. He had run in the heats of the 1934 Empire Games 880 yards. He won the International (later World) Student Games 800 and 1500 in 1937 in 1:54.1 and 3:56.0. At the 1938 Empire Games he had been 4th at 880 yards before winning the mile. He was a finalist in the 1938 European Championships 1500 metres, placing 6th. He ran in four international matches for Great Britain, including the 800 metres in 1945 against France after serving as a Squadron Leader pilot during World War II. He won nine Welsh titles between 1934 and 1948: once at 440, four times at 880, and twice each at the mile and three miles. He was also Welsh cross-country champion in 1948 and finished 40th in the International championship.

He became the first National Coach for Wales in 1948 and was in charge of the Welsh team for the 1958 British Empire & Commonwealth Games in his home town of Cardiff. He was then appointed coach for Rhodesia & Nyasaland but resigned when he was not invited to go with the team to the 1962 Games in Australia, where his athletes did well. He taught in the London area up to his retirement, continuing to run until a recent hip operation. At 85 he was still coaching runners and javelin-throwers at the Tooting Bec track, and some of his many successes over the years include Peter Driver, the 1954 Empire Games six miles champion; middle-distance runner Phyllis Perkins; Welsh sprinters Ken Jones, Ron Jones and Nick Whitehead; Ann Farquhar-Kinch, the 1970 Commonwealth Games javelin silver-medallist; and Gowry Retchakan, also winning a Commonwealth silver, at 400 hurdles at the end of her career in 1998.

Alford lives near the Tooting Bec track and is as articulate and bright as ever. He talked with tremendous enthusiasm and recall about the 1938 Empire Games and about his athletics career, which had started by chance when a shoulder injury prevented him from playing his favourite sport, rugby union football, while at university in Cardiff. A couple of years earlier he had found that he had natural running talent, and with time to train he became Welsh champion almost immediately. Then came his wonderful 1937 season which included the Student Games double and the only blot on which was his 3rd place to Arthur Collyer in the AAA Championships 880, though in a personal best 1:54.3.

Alford was due to start at Loughborough College in the autumn on 1937 after obtaining degrees at the University of Cardiff and Bristol University, and the only reason he went to the Empire

Games was that Loughborough was still awaiting official recognition by the Ministry of Education and he was left with nothing to do. The Welsh AAA had approached his grandfather, who was a motor mechanic (Jim's father had been killed in World War I), about Alford going to the Games, but he had said he was not sure because "where was the money coming from?" In those far-off days of pure amateurism, Wales had been given just £200 by the Central Council for Physical Recreation and was able to send only six competitors – an athlete, a boxer, a cyclist and three swimmers – for the four-month trip.

Alford borrowed £20, which was an amount equivalent to four times the average weekly wage, from Cyril Howells, the president of Roath Harriers, as pocket-money and trained like mad, warming up on the old cinder speedway track in Cardiff by hauling the roller round and round on the inside lane. He then set off for the long voyage in early December aboard the "S.S. Ormonde" as captain and manager of the Welsh squad, together with members of the English and Scottish teams in a party of 30 or so. England had left behind some very hot favourites for gold such as Sydney Wooderson, Godfrey Brown and Don Finlay who could not afford the time away. Only those who could get paid time off work such as miler Bernard Eeles, who was a schoolteacher, or who had wealthy parents or independent means, like distance-runner Peter Ward, or owned their own business, like half-miler Brian MacCabe, were able to go. Quarter-miler Bill Roberts resigned as a manager of a Manchester timber-yard in order to compete in Sydney and had promptly been offered a similar job with another company in London which had business interests in Australia.

A month on the high seas … but training on deck every day

For more than a month on the ship, which was small enough to be classless, the athletes lived a very pleasant life, training for an hour a day on the large deck which provided a lap of 400 metres, and then another hour of exercises, plus deck quoits and tennis, and eating very well – so well that Alford put on half-a-stone (three kilogrammes) in weight. There were also dances and bingo sessions, but no drinking except for a glass of wine on Christmas Day. There were four stops en route for the happy group, at Gibraltar, Rome, Bombay and Colombo, and on each occasion tracks were provided so that the athletes could train again on dry land and get rid of that peculiar leggy feeling from being on the high seas.

Once they had arrived in Australia Alford ran a 1:56.0 for 880 and a 50.4 for 440 under floodlights in handicap races which showed that he was in good shape. When the Games began he qualified with ease in his heat of the 880, comfortably running an estimated 1:53.7 lifetime best, and allowing Pat Boot to have what was expected to be his moment of glory as he set a new Games record of 1:52.3. Then, after a sleepless night in his tiny cubicle at the Agricultural Showground as a speedway meeting was held yards away, everything went wrong for Alford.

He warmed up for the race as he did at home, with his track-suit on, but the temperature was 85-to-90°F and it was very humid. He takes up the story: "I was so certain to win that one of the judges came up to me as we lined up for the start, shook me by the hand and said, "You've got it!" I took the lead early at the first bend and then I relaxed and the whole lot went by before I could realise what had happened. After 250 yards I was running tight on the shoulder of the Australian, Backhouse, who was a fidgety sort of runner. He decided he did not want to be boxed and came straight out in front of me. I had to push him on the shoulder and he went forwards and I went back and was last.

"It was a nightmare. He was not impeded and he just went forward and was lying 2nd. At the bell I went up to 2nd, and then with 300 yards to go I thought I should take the lead although I did not feel very good. I had not been there very long when Pat Boot, of New Zealand, went by so fast I dropped back, and then I tried to go after him and tied up completely. On the last bend my legs were heavy like lead and I could not think why no one was coming up to go past. I was trying to drive and drive but was not relaxed. Dale and Handley passed me in a blanket finish and I was 4th in 1:53.8. I knew I could run 1:52, but there it was. I was very disappointed." The result was 1st Pat Boot (New Zealand) 1:51.2, 2nd Frank Handley (England) 1:53.3, 3rd Bill Dale (Canada) 1:53.5, 4th Jim Alford (Wales) 1:53.8. Only Boot's time was officially recorded and the other times are estimates.

The next day Alford ran three-quarters-of-a-mile in training in 3:12¾ and knew he could do a 60sec last lap. The mile heats were the day after that, and he recalls, "After my heat I was feeling strong and confident, particularly when Boot and Backhouse made a race of it in theirs but in a slower time than me. An odd thing happened, though, as we travelled in a tram down to the stadium for the final. There was a chap from New Zealand and he asked me how I thought I would do. I said that they'd have to run 4:12 to beat me, and he replied, "That's no good! Boot will do 4:04!" I just dismissed it by saying he couldn't do that.

"When the race started I did not think of Boot at all. I just ran my own race, and it turned out pretty much as I had planned it – following the pace until the bell and then going – except for one thing. There was no struggling or fighting. I stayed at the back for a while and gradually made my way through until I was at the shoulder of the leader, Graham, at about the middle of the third lap, but he had set too fast a pace and now began to slow right up. As we entered the finishing straight on the third lap he dropped out, leaving me with the lead which I did not want with about 500 yards to go.

"Then at the bell (3:10.6) Backhouse and Boot came past me very fast indeed. This was the worst point of the race for me, and I remember thinking that if I relaxed and stuck to them at least I would get some sort of medal this time. Then I felt the pace slowing and I began to feel strong again. As Backhouse went to pass Boot I passed both of them and at the last bend I was in the lead.

"Then the spectators on 'The Hill' began to cheer wildly, and I knew it was not for me but for their man, Backhouse, who was trying to catch me. I could feel the hairs on the back of my neck standing up out of nervousness. It was the first time I had experienced anything like it, and the result was that it made me go again and I won by 10 yards. The time was a lifetime best 4:11.5, and I could have done half-a-second faster. When I went through the tape and knew that I had done it, I had this feeling of euphoria. It was my best race and the most satisfying." The result was 1st Alford 4:11.5, 2nd Backhouse (Australia) 4:12.2, 3rd Pat Boot (New Zealand) 4:12.6, 4th Art Clarke (Canada) 4:14.4. All times after Alford's are estimated.

Alford's vivid description of his races in Sydney explains exactly why he knew how Sebastian Coe felt in 1980. Coe repeated his 1500 metres win in the 1984 Olympics in Los Angeles, but Alford did not have the same chance because of World War II, and by the time the Empire Games were held again in 1950 he was National Coach and his racing days were over.

After the celebrations in Sydney and the winding down, including a mile win in Tasmania, came the long journey home on a new liner, the "Stratheden", where those who could afford it enjoyed first-class while others like Alford and the high-jump winner, Dorothy Odam (later Dorothy Tyler), travelled in the ordinary part of the ship. Once back home Alford was a stone overweight, and he was lacking both the cross-country background to build his stamina and the same motivation he had before Sydney. Even so, he now thought of himself as a miler and after beating Jack Emery in the Bourneville mile in the Midlands he finished 3rd behind Sydney Wooderson and Dennis Pell in the AAA Championships and as Pell was getting married was selected for the European Championships instead. He qualified for the final in Paris, but his legs were not up to running a first lap in 58sec to put Wooderson in line for Jack Lovelock's world

The 1938 Empire Games mile final. The Scotsman, Bobby Graham, leads on the third lap from Alford and the Australian, Gerald Backhouse.

record 3:47.8, as had been requested of him by the British team manager, Jack Crump – and he finished way back to Wooderson's mediocre winning time of 3:53.6. In his last full year of competition in 1939 Alford was at Carnegie College of Physical Education, in Leeds, and despite finding little time for specialised training, and suffering injuries while playing rugby again, he managed to finish 2nd to Wooderson in the Inter-Counties mile and then 4th in the AAA Championships in an estimated 4:15.8. Even as an operational pilot throughout the war he ran a mile in 4:17.0 in 1942 and in 4:15.0 behind Wooderson's 4:13.8 in 1943.

In 1945 Alford ran 4:19.2 in the famous mile race at the White City when Arne Andersson, of Sweden, beat Wooderson in 4:08.8 to 4:09.2, and was 2nd to Robert Chef d'Hotel, of France, in a 1:54.2 800 metres in the first post-war international match in Paris. Back in civilian life and teaching in Wanstead, where one of his pupils was Geoff Elliott, who was to be Empire Games pole-vault champion in 1954 and 1958, he was invited by Geoff Dyson, the National Coach, to address a conference on middle-distance running, and so his coaching career began.

Author's footnote: "I only saw Jim race once, in the 1947 match between Cambridge University and the AAA in front of a crowd that was so big that people could not get into the ground. He won a slow mile and then stood talking to a group of people. Jim told me during our conversation that among them was Paavo Nurmi. I would have been furious if for 50 years I had known the great Nurmi was there and I hadn't met him!" **Note:** this article was first published in "Track Stats", Volume 37, No.3, November 1999. Jim Alford died on 5 August 2004, aged 90.

"Have a look at this number on my back. You'll be looking at it the rest of the way"

When the competitors lined up for the 1948 Olympic marathon at Wembley Stadium in London the clear favourite was 41-year-old Jack Holden, whose international career had started at cross-country in 1929 and whose first track appearance for Great Britain had been in 1933. After a flirtation with the marathon in 1946, when he had won the Midlands title in 2:46:34 but had not been selected for the European Championships, he had turned to the event full-time the following year.

The change had taken place earlier than he had anticipated, and it came about because he missed running in the National cross-country championships. Competitors from the Midlands had been trapped in the snow which caused havoc throughout Britain in the spring of 1947 and could not get to the National course at Apsley, in Hertfordshire. Even though Holden had won the title on three occasions, including the previous year, the selectors did not consider him for the International championships in accordance with their draconian rules that a man had to run and finish in the top nine in the National to be picked.

Holden was extremely angry and said that he would never run cross-country again – and he never did. He was a man of strong principles and still is at the age of 93. He remains very articulate, with an excellent memory of his international athletics career which lasted from 1929 to 1950. He is a Christian man who went to Communion before every race. He is a family man with two daughters. His honesty and integrity was well-known and respected. A great man to meet!

When he made the decision to take up marathon-running seriously he changed his training routine from twice a week with his club-mates – a hard six miles or so "bash" on grass or on the road – to five days a week. The exceptions were Saturdays, which were days for the family unless he was racing, and Sundays, which were for church-going, and on which he only ever competed once and that was because he had confused the dates of a race and was committed to it.

In those five weekdays he still averaged 100 miles a week, and he was the first marathon runner to take on such a heavy schedule. All this running was done after five o'clock in the evening at the end of a working day at the Palethorpe sausage-making firm in Staffordshire, where he was employed as a groundsman but described as a general labourer in case the nature of his job broke the AAA rules!

It meant that his way of life had to fit in with family, church and work. With the agreement of his wife, he went straight out running as soon as he got home from work. He told his wife how long he would be, and she had his bath running as he got back and then prepared his evening meal. Holden fondly recalls that on one occasion when he was out running, a cyclist came alongside him on a steep hill and asked him why he did it. Holden told him it was because he didn't have the threepence for the bus fare, and the cyclist stopped and offered him the money!

Holden ate 100 eggs a week, plus mussels and oysters which he kept to supplement his diet, and he did all this on very small wages. When he ran abroad he lost pay, except for the major events, but he took his holidays with the family, so that they wouldn't go without, rather than use them for running. Holden now has three grandchildren, and since his wife died 15 years ago after 50 years of marriage, he has lived at the home of his daughter, Joan, in Cumbria, where we met for our discussion about his career. She remembers that "our household was regimented to his training programme. He used to train and then go to bed at 9:30 to 10 o'clock or even earlier. Sunday was for church. We did not have much money and no car, but we lived well, and I always remember my father as a handsome, smart, well-dressed man".

His first AAA marathon victory was achieved in 2:33:20.2 in 1947, and he was 2nd to Charles Heirendt, of Luxemburg, in the annual Kosice race in Czechoslovakia in 2:37:10.6. In the following Olympic year he ran a 2:36:44.6 and was going so well that the first British Olympic marathon gold looked almost a certainty. During his final preparations for the Olympic race he trained from the home in North London of the father of Doug Wilson, who ran the 1500 metres at those Games and later became a national newspaper athletics correspondent. Holden ran in the company of one of his Olympic team-mates, Tommy Richards, of South London Harriers, who was a nurse by profession, and – as always before a marathon – Holden pickled his feet in permanganate of potash to harden the skin. The trouble was that on this occasion he increased the treatment and his Olympic bid was ruined.

As Holden explains: "I had the lead in the race and was the favourite. I was almost a certainty. I knew I could win it. But then I blistered badly and had to come out. I'd had blisters many times before. They would burst and sting, but I carried on. This time I'd overdone the hardening and made the skin like leather and I couldn't carry on. It had blistered under the skin and at 17 miles I had to drop out". Richards, who never before or after was close to Holden in road races, finished 2nd to the Argentinian, Delfo Cabrera, and Holden has never really got over the memory of that day. "I was so disappointed that I had let everybody down," he reflects. "I could not run any more after the Olympics because of letting them down. I thought I was going to die, I was so upset about it. I felt really ill. I kept on training but not racing".

Jack Crump says, "Hang on! We haven't got anyone else"

It was Holden's religious beliefs that helped him to work it out. He recalls, "After considering it all I realised I was not meant to win. It was an act of God. I had been so sure of winning that I'd packed my clothes to take my wife and the two little girls on holiday, and there I met a woman who told me I'd been stopped from winning by God. But I replied that it was definitely not so, and that all I'd ever asked Him for was to reproduce the form I had shown in training, and that in a race I would force myself to do better. Then it was Jack Crump, the British team manager, who worked on me to start racing again. He said to me, 'Hang on until we have someone to take your place. We haven't got anyone'."

Later in the year Holden's wife – "behind every great man is a wonderful woman, and she was", he says – timed him on some of his occasional training runs and discovered that he was, in fact, running very fast. "I didn't feel that I was," Holden says, "but the next week I timed myself and found I was running even faster when I was dying emotionally".

He had run the South London Harriers 30 miles race again after the Olympics and had won by over 20 minutes, but his recovery really began with the annual Morpeth-to-Newcastle race on New Year's Day 1949 when "still smarting over the Olympics, vowing I wouldn't run any more and thinking that I didn't care if I died on the course" he ran right away from the field, including Richards, and smashed the course record in one of his four consecutive wins in the event. He also won the 1949 AAA marathon comfortably in 2:34:10.6 and the next year his hard training brought him another AAA title win by almost six minutes in a lifetime best of 2:31:03.4. The second man home was Edward Denison, of the Milocarian club and the Army, with whom Holden had shared his first track international at three miles against France 17 years previously in 1933. Holden also went to Enschede, in Holland, for the annual marathon in September, but for some reason the course was only 40km that year. Inspired by the music which was played to competitors in the last 800 metres to lift their spirits, Holden ran 2:20:52, which was worth about 2:29 for the full distance.

The year of 1950 was his great one, erasing the shame of the Olympics. Holden was favourite for the British Empire title in Auckland in February, and he made no mistake, leading all the way and winning by over four minutes from Syd Luyt, of South Africa, in 2:32:57, but the race was not without its mishaps.

"Everything was in my favour," Holden explains. "I was favourite and fit enough to win it, and then everything went wrong. I knew that I should have had a new pair of shoes, but you can't run a marathon in new shoes. There was a cloud-burst at the start and the water came over the kerbs of the road. My old plimsoll shoes burst, and because I couldn't stop and ask someone for a couple of handkerchiefs to wrap round my feet I threw the shoes away and ran the last nine miles barefoot. It was then that a dog leapt out of the crowd. It was a Great Dane and it didn't attack me, but people thought that it had because there was blood on my back from my feet. When I finished I ran straight across to the microphone to ask that whoever had found my shoes should bring them back to me. I gave them to an old couple who'd been helpful to me".

Such confidence! Holden spies out the European Championships course

Back in England Holden ran in the "Sheffield Telegraph" marathon which he had twice won before but pulled out when leading into rain and a headwind at 18 miles. Then Jack Crump got to work on Holden again, telling him he could win the European title, too, and after wins in the Polytechnic and AAA races Holden duly went off to Brussels for the championships. He got on well with Denison, the Army officer who had also been selected for Great Britain, and they shared a car-ride of reconnaisance round the course. They spotted a long and winding hill, and Holden told his companion, "If I win this race I'll win it here". Denison, amazed, had never seen such confidence.

In the dressing-room the Britons came across the two competitors from the Soviet Union, and Holden, who has a sharp sense of humour, recalls their encounter: "Denison said he had never seen anyone so sly and we watched them looking around. So I went up to one of them and asked how Stalin was getting on. He grunted, and so did the other. So I pointed to my number over the Union Jack on my chest and then to my number on my back and said, 'Here, have a look at this because you'll be looking at it for the rest of the way'.

"I never took a drink during a race because I'd found that if I took a drink in training it took 20 to 30 minutes to settle down again, but I always made up some lemonade and sugar in a small brandy bottle just in case I needed it. Somehow, the British coach, Geoff Dyson, dropped it, and Jack Crump told him to tell the people helping out on the course that if I asked for a drink they should ignore me!

"I was ahead, but when I came to the hill the Russian, Vanin, came up to my shoulder. He obviously had the same theory as me that if you catch someone up you don't stay with them. I believe in psychology, and I guessed he thought I was a little chap with plenty of guts. He came up to me again, but when we came to a drinks station and I saw his hand go out for his bottle I decided that was when I was going to go – it was either Joe Stalin or King George – and I did".

Holden won by 32 seconds from Veikko Karvonen, of Finland, with the other Soviet runner, Filin, 3rd, and when he was congratulated by Prince Baudouin of Belgium he told him that he had met his grandfather and father after winning a pre-war International cross-country title. "You couldn't arrange to meet three Belgian kings, not even in a pack of cards", Holden says.

It was typical of the way of life even for champions in those days that when Holden arrived back in his home town at 6 o'clock in the morning, having travelled overnight by rail and sea, and called into work to say that he had won, his boss told him he could go home for breakfast before reporting in for duty, which he did an hour later!

Holden ran only one more marathon before retiring because the former AAA six miles and 10 miles champion, Jim Peters, who had been 8th in the Wembley Olympic 10,000 metres, was now being trained with new ideas of fast running by the 1924 and 1928 Olympic middle-distance and distance runner, "Johnny" Johnston. Even so, the old fox saw off the young cub in the Finchley 20 miles road race because it had been instilled in Peters that Holden was only good up the hills and could be beaten on the flat. The champion showed him that was not so by racing away to smash his own record by nearly three minutes and win by 96 seconds. Peters threw his shoes on the floor in exasperation, demanding, "How am I going to beat him?" His coach said he would have to do more training.

Two months later Holden and Peters met again in the Polytechnic marathon from Windsor Castle to Chiswick, but this time Holden was suffering mentally. He explains: "I had been offered a new job as groundsman at the Cannock Stadium which I had officially opened with Lord Burghley, and I could not rest for thinking about it. I worried myself pink-eyed as to whether I was doing the right thing in taking it. My employer, Mr Palethorpe, was very cross and gave me 30 shillings a week more than I would get at the new job, and that was a lot of money in those days. So when I went to the race I was not fit because the worry had got to me. I knew soon after the start that I was not right because I was just worrying while I was running. When he started to run well, I just packed it in".

Jim Peters ran under 2:30 to win easily. Holden stayed in his old job and told Jack Crump that now he had a successor he was retiring. "I said that I had done what I said I would do, holding the reins until someone else came along. Jim used to write to me for advice, and I told him he was silly to run for pretty platters as he was running in everything. I told him he should do what I had wanted to do, and that was win the Olympic marathon". As we now know, Peters did not, dropping out of the 1952 Games race after Emil Zátopek had politely inquired of him if the pace was right.

The start of Jack Holden's running career in the 1920s

John Thomas Holden was born in Bilston, in Staffordshire, on 13 March 1907. He was 5ft 5in (1.65m) in height and just under 10st (63kg) in weight when, as a lifelong member of the Midlands club, Tipton Harriers, he won the AAA six miles in 1933-34-35, the AAA 10 miles in 1934, the AAA marathon every year from 1947 to 1950, the National cross-country in 1938-39 and again in 1946, the International cross-country in 1939, and the British Empire Games and European Championships marathons in 1950.

His initial interest in sport was at a boxing gym where he kept in shape and had a few fights. He was a strong young man working in a foundry, and when a local publican staged a three-mile race, Holden was an onlooker and not only thought he could do better but told the winner so afterwards. When challenged, Holden claimed untruthfully he had run in and won a lot of races, but the next time the three-mile race was held he took part in it and won easily. His prize was a pig, and this was to cause him some bother later in his running career when he declared his winnings. He had to be re-qualified as an amateur and years afterwards was accused by a jealous rival club president of having been reinstated (which was a quite different matter) and therefore been disqualified from international competition. Holden, never one to mince words or to hold back, wrote to the local newspaper and the allegation was withdrawn.

It was because claims were made to the AAA that he had broken the regulations by working in a job connected with athletics when he took up work as a groundsman with Palethorpe's that he was described as a general labourer by his employers when a AAA official called to investigate the matter. In fact, there was much skulduggery in Midlands athletics in those days, which all seems to have stemmed from the involvement of bookmakers, with odds being fixed and deals done. Holden remembers winning one race for the third successive year by out-sprinting his old, rival, Jack Webster, of Birchfield Harriers, to make the trophy his own, and then being disqualified for not running the full two miles. Holden recalls laconically, "I dragged one foot over the chalk line when I made my effort. I then won the race three years in succession after that and kept the cup!"

Holden's attitude did not always please officialdom. He went his own way and would not toe the line if he felt he was in the right, and that might have cost him a place in the 1946 European Championships marathon in Oslo. After five years' war service in the RAF as a physical training instructor, he had one run in the Midlands marathon without racing flat-out and asked the selectors to consider him. They would not, and Holden believes that it was "out of spite because my face didn't fit for years. I was never a mama's pet and I wouldn't let them mess me about".

To show the selectors what they were missing, Holden asked his old friend, Joe Binks, who was the former world mile record-holder with 4:16.8 in 1902 and was now athletics correspondent for the "News of the World" Sunday newspaper, to organise a 30 miles track race at the White City. Holden won in 3:00:16.8 for a world's best time, passing the marathon marker in 2:36:39.4, despite having to run an extra four yards every lap in the second lane. This was a faster time than Mikko Hietanen, of Finland, had done to win the European title in Oslo on a short 40.2 kilometres course. To underline his point, Holden ran 3:02:09 for 30 miles on the road at Old Coulsdon, in Surrey, a month later and the next year became the first man to go under three hours with 2:59:47 on the same course.

The magazine, "Athletics", which was the forerunner of "Athletics Weekly", published an article in the autumn of 1946 in reply to the dozens of letters received from readers on the subject of Holden's non-selection for the European Championships which had taken place that year in Oslo. In the article it was said that Holden had not been omitted through spite but because of a train of events which had left the selectors with a problem. Holden had won the Midlands marathon but mistakenly did not enter the Poly race and then had to miss the AAA Championships event because he had booked his family holiday after not having had one for seven years while on military service.

To try and impress the selectors afterwards, he ran three time-trials over a carefully-measured three-lap marathon course and recorded times between 2:33 and 2:40, but it was not enough. Squire Yarrow, who had won the AAA race in 2:43:14, and Harry Oliver were chosen instead, and Holden characteristically sent them his best wishes for their success. Yarrow placed 7th in the European Championships, while Oliver did not finish.

During the 1930s Holden had proved he could hold his own on the track with any of the good home talent that was around. As well as his AAA titles and innumerable wins in Midlands races, he was 4th in the 1934 Empire Games six miles and 4th again in his last major track race in the AAA six miles in 1937. His best times were around 4:18 for the mile and 9:25 for two miles, plus 14:33.8 for three miles and 30:26.8 for six miles. He won his AAA six miles titles in 1933-34-35 in successive times of 30:32.2, 30:43.8 and 30:50.6, and ran his best time in finishing 2nd to Jack Potts in 1932 and then did 30:48.0 behind the winning 30:07.8 by the Hungarian, János Kelen, in 1937. Before becoming AAA champion at 10 miles in 1934 in a time of 52:21.4, he had been 4th in the same event to Ernie Harper in 1929. His main rivals included Alec Burns,

Encouragement for Jack Holden in the 1948 Olympic marathon, but blisters ruined his gold-medal hopes. Two years later he won both the Empire and European titles.

Arthur Penny, Robbie Sutherland and Jack Webster in the Midlands, and the Salford trio of Bill Eaton, George Bailey and Tom Evenson. Burns placed 7th in the 1932 Olympic 5000 metres and 5th at 10,00 metres in 1936, and Penny won the Empire six miles in 1934 when Holden had been the favourite but had lost form.

Altogether, Holden won 11 Staffordshire county track titles at the mile, three miles and four miles, and he was on seven occasions Midlands six miles champion and on four occasions the 10 miles winner. "I enjoyed the two-mile team races around the Midlands", he recalls, "but we never saw a cinder track until we went to London for the AAA Championships. After 1937 I lost interest really in track racing. I never ran for times except that occasion in the 30 miles on the track in 1946. As long as I won, that was all that mattered. There came a point in a race when I knew I had won, and once I knew that I'd won my only thought was to finish. I wasn't seriously trying once the race was mine. I was never one who could play second fiddle. I always wanted to be better.

"I never really concentrated on anything until I took up marathon running, and that became a way of life – almost my whole life – and training became second nature. It was a sport and I did it for fun to keep as fit as anybody else. If I had my time again, I would do the same".

When he gave up boxing to concentrate on running he gained selection in his first season of 1926 for the Tipton Harriers team at the National cross-country championships in their distinctive green-and-white hooped shirts which are still so prominent in competition more than 70 years later. His twice-a-week training runs were on the road or round a makeshift track laid out with markers and jackets on the Dudley cricket ground, and from the start he showed his toughness by walking five miles to one meeting, starting half-a-lap behind the others in a five-lap race, and turning the laughter of the crowd to cheers as he caught all the other runners and won the race. At another meeting he won the mile race and the two miles by a lap and then finished 4th in the 440 yards.

When he was 2nd to the future Olympic marathon silver-medallist, Ernie Harper, in the 1929 AAA 10 miles, Holden took his shoes off while leading at nine miles because he had got blisters, and still finished a lap ahead of the next man. That year he won his place in the England team for the International Cross-Country Championships and was never out of it until the selectors ignored him in 1947. His light and easy running style ideally suited cross-country and his consistency in the International was outstanding: 18th in 1929, then 7th in 1930 and 1931, 2nd (to Tom Evenson) in 1932, 1st in 1933-34-35, 2nd (to Bill Eaton) in 1936, a non-finisher in 1937 when he was ill, 6th in 1938, the winner again in 1939, and 6th and still first English scorer in 1946. He was in the winning England team every year from 1930 to 1936 and again in 1938.

Three times International champion before his National win

Yet, despite having won the International on three occasions by 1935, he just could not win the National title, and he explains why: "It was because I was so determined to win it that I trained too hard. Then after a week with no training in disgust at losing the National I got back to running stone cold and won the International. Eventually it dawned on me that I was a fool, and so I changed my training tactics and eased off, and I became the first man to win the National and International in the same year".

Having placed in the National in successive years from 1929 onwards 9th, 4th, 8th, 3rd, 8th, 3rd (to Alec Burns and George Bailey in 1932), 8th, 3rd again (to Sammy Dodd and Burns in 1934), 9th, 8th and 8th, he at last won in 1938 and then in 1939 (the year of his "double") and again after the war in 1946. He also won the Inter-Counties title four times and the Midlands title on seven occasions, including 1946. It was during his cross-country career that he changed jobs, having been laid off because of shortage of work at the foundry. He was due to be out of the country on the day that he was to sign on the dole as he was representing England in the International, and it was then that the philanthropic Mr Palethorpe stepped in and gave Holden the job which he kept until his retirement.

During our interview Jack Holden wrote out for me in a steady hand a list of his triumphs, including reference to many of the Royal Family to whom he had been presented. In one race with his old friend and marathon rival, Charles Cérou, in France they competed against horse-riders and cyclists and the winning horse dropped dead on the line. The prizes for the runners were set out on trestle tables, and it was inevitably Holden, who never took a single penny piece as a prize during his athletics career, who had his pick!

Voted "Sportsman Of The Year" in 1950, Holden completed his career in fine style by winning a 15 miles road race in Dublin after conceding up to 15 minutes in handicap start to his competitors. The time was very fast but could not be confirmed because the Irish officials would not agree to re-measure the course. At the height of Jack Holden's fame a public garden was named after him in Dudley. "Now", he says, "there's talk of a statue, but when they came to see me about it I told them that a statue was for dead men, so they would have to wait a bit".

Note: this article was first published in "Track Stats", Volume 38, No.4, November 2000. Jack Holden died on 7 March 2004, aged 96.

Sydney Wooderson, European champion 1500 metres 1938 & 5000 metres 1946, world record-holder 800 metres, 880 yards and One mile

"My six best races ... well, actually, seven"

Sydney Charles Wooderson was born on 30 August 1914. He was world record-holder for the mile (4:06.4, 1937), 800 metres (1:48.4, 1938) and 880 yards (1:49.2, 1938). He was European 1500 metres champion in 1938 and 5000 metres champion in 1946. He was the National cross-country champion in 1948. He was AAA champion at the mile every year from 1935 to 1939 and at three miles in 1946. He was undefeated in seven Great Britain international matches. So on the eve of his 85th birthday we went to visit him at his Dorset home to ask him to name his six best races.

Four of us had gone to see Sydney. Also there were NUTS member and celebrated historian and novelist Peter Lovesey and Tony Weeks-Pearson, a lifelong friend of Sydney's, together with an old rival of Tony's from Oxford and Cambridge days, John Knopf. Tony had himself been a fine distance-runner for the same club as Sydney's, Blackheath Harriers, with a fastest six miles of 29:17.2 for 6th place in the 1954 AAA Championships, and John had won the Inter-Varsity three miles for Cambridge the same year in a record 14:12.2. With Sydney was his brother, Stanley, a good runner in his day and a competitor in both the mile and half-mile world record races at Motspur Park in 1937 and 1938, The two octogenarians had just been for their daily walk, and while Sydney is a little heavier now and his eyesight not as good as it was, he still manages a mile or more each day.

Sydney actually recalled seven races because he could not decide whether beating Jack Lovelock for the AAA title for the first time in 1935 or the unexpected mile record in 1937 was No.3 on the list, so he settled on a tie. These are the seven in chronological order:

1. 1933: the Public Schools mile

"I had been 6th and then 2nd, and in my last year as a schoolboy at Sutton Valence I was determined to win, particularly as it was on the new track at the White City Stadium."

He raced home in 4:29.8, and it was the first time that an 18-year-old had been under 4:30. Behind him were two future internationals, Jack Emery and Dennis Pell.

2. 1934: the Southern Counties mile

Fresh from his Kent mile win, and trained and nurtured by the 1920 Olympic 800 metres and 1500 metres champion, Albert Hill, Sydney burst on the scene, knocking more than 19 seconds off his best time.

"It was my first major race, and I was determined to do well. I did, beating Lovelock and almost Aubrey Reeve, who was inches in front of me."

It was a crowded field of 28, starting in two ranks on a bumpy grass track, and among them were Jack Lovelock, the New Zealand holder of the British record in 4:12,0, and Jerry Cornes, silver-medallist in the 1932 Olympic 1500 metres.

The race was a pushing-and-shoving affair, and towards the end it looked as though Lovelock would take it, but two young men thought differently, Aubrey Reeve, of Polytechnic Harriers, ran the race of his life to win, and Sydney seemingly came from nowhere to take 2nd in the last few strides.

3=. 1935: the AAA mile, 1937: the world mile record

"Lovelock had just won the "Mile Of The Century" in America, and to beat him in the AAA mile was the best victory I had had up to then. But at the same time I cannot separate that from my mile record which I did not expect to do. I wanted to do something spectacular at the club's meeting, and thought it would be around 4:08, but instead it was 4:06."

Lovelock came back from the USA to find an extremely determined opponent who turned on a 61.4 last lap to win the 1935 AAA mile, 4:17.2 to 4:18.4. The 1937 mile record was achieved two days before Sydney's 23rd birthday, and by then Lovelock had retired without having had the chance to take on the little Blackheath Harrier when both were fully fit and finely tuned. A specially framed handicap mile was put on at Motspur Park with coach Albert Hill and former world record-holder Walter George among those watching. A previous British mile record-holder and AAA champion, Reg Thomas, was given a start of 10 yards as main pacemaker and Sydney was taken through laps of 58.6, 2:02.6 and 3:07.2 to come home in 4:06.4, bringing the record back to Britain for the first time in 42 years (Fred Bacon 4:17.0 in 1895).

5. 1945: the White City mile against Arne Andersson

This was the race that inspired Roger Bannister, who managed to get into the packed stadium with his father, to become the first sub-four-minute miler, and both Peter Lovesey, who was one of the many locked out of the stadium, and I, who heard the race on the radio, to become lifelong fans of the sport.

"I include this race because I had not done any serious training or racing until after the War. I had been very ill and Peter Wilson [a vociferous sports journalist who was known as "The Man They Could Not Gag"!] said I had had it. I was determined to prove him wrong and give a good account of myself."

On paper it seemed an ill-made match. The barrel-chested Swede, six inches taller and three years younger, had suffered no deprivation during the war years in his neutral homeland as a series of races with his arch-rival, Gunder Hägg, had brought the 1500 metres and mile records down to 3:43.0 and 4:01.6. Against him the Briton, who had only recently recovered from rheumatic fever, was short of food, like all his fellow-countrymen, and was lacking international racing. It was real David-and-Goliath stuff.

Watched by a packed crowd of 54,000, Andersson set the pace with laps of 60.8, 62.3 and 65.0 to reach the bell in 3:08, whereupon the little man went by the Swede, and they stayed that way until the home straight, when the stronger, fitter and healthier Andersson went by to win, 4:08.0 to 4:09.2. It was Sydney's fastest mile since winning the 1939 Inter-Counties race in 4:07.4 – and that was not the end of the matter.

A month later the 31-year-old Englishman went to Gothenburg to take on the Swede again. After a pace of 58.6, 2:00.1 and 3:02.0, Andersson went into the lead, but 200 metres from home Sydney went by him, passing 1500 metres in the best ever British time of 3:48.4. He was still ahead with 50 metres to go until the Swede's strength gave him victory by no more than three metres in 4:03.8. Sydney ran the fastest mile of his career, 4:04.2.

6. 1946: the European Championships 5000 metres

"I had not really trained or raced over three miles or 5000 metres. It was a complete change of distance, I was delighted with what happened. The experts said I had a better judge of pace over that distance!"

Sydney Wooderson leads Willy Slijkhuis in the 1946 AAA three miles and went on to win in a British record time. A month later Wooderson became European 5000 metres champion.

At the White City the previous month he had won an epic battle against Willy Slijkhuis, of Holland, in the AAA Championships three miles. It was Sydney's sixth and last AAA title, with a winning time of 13:53.2 and a last mile of 4:29.8 which exactly equalled his performance in his first appearance on the same track 13 years previously in the Public Schools mile. A few days later Sydney ran 13:57.0 to win the three miles in the match against France, defeating the French champion, Raphaël Pujazon.

In the European Championships 5000 metres in Oslo on 23 August Sydney lined up against all the world's stars at the distance except Gunder Hägg, the only man to have run under 14 minutes, who had been suspended by the Swedish authorities for breaking the stringent amateurism rules, as had Andersson. Even so, lining up in Oslo were Viljo Heino, Finland's world record-holder for 10,000 metres, together with Slijkhuis , France's Raphaël Pujazon and Belgium's Gaston Reiff (due to be 1948 Olympic champion), as well as a little-known Czech called Zátopek who did quite well later on!

Sydney stayed off the pace for the first mile, lying 10th in the Indian file, 20 yards back from the leader, and then moving up as others dropped back until 700 metres from home when the Dutchmen went with the Briton on his shoulder. The positions remained the same until 250 metres to go, where Sydney put in one of those bursts that made him such a wonderful champion.

He finished in 14:08.6 – the second fastest time ever run. He was five seconds in front of

Slijkhuis, 14 ahead of Sweden's Evert Nyberg, 15 ahead of Heino, 17 ahead of Zátopek, and 37 ahead of Reiff. The last lap was 61. His time was 23 seconds faster than Peter Ward's British best, and he passed three miles in an unofficial 13:42.0. Typically, he did not tell anyone about a nagging pain in his Achilles tendon in the days leading up to the event.

It was Sydney's last track race, but there was a special reason for him to go on running. He wanted to represent his club, Blackheath, in team competition.

7. 1948: The National Cross-Country Championships

"It was a new race, a new distance, and I got it right. It was the most exhausting race I ever ran and I never did serious cross-country after that."

Sydney had run cross-country before but not at the championship distance of 10 miles against the very best of English runners who in those days were regular winners of the International Championship.

From the start there were only four in contention over the tough, hilly Sheffield course: Wooderson; Jack Charlesworth, from the Aylesford Paper Mills club in Kent; Vic Blowfield, of Belgrave Harriers; and Albert Shorrocks, from Halesowen in the Midlands. They ran together in different permutations until the last half-mile, which was downhill, then on to the flat before turning uphill to the finish. When the spectators last saw them going out of sight Blowfield was passing Sydney, who looked as though he had had enough. Appearances were deceiving, as anyone who knew Sydney could have guessed, and using all his experience, determination, and never-quenched will-to-win he forced himself ahead and kept on going until the top of the hill and victory.

Sydney competed for England in the International Championships a fortnight later, finishing 14th and continued running cross-country for a couple more years as part of the Blackheath team.

Note: this article was first published in "Track Stats", Volume 36, No.4, December 1998. David Thurlow wrote a profusely-illustrated 56-page booklet to celebrate Sydney Wooderson's 75th birthday in 1989. The May 1997 issue of "Track Stats" (Volume 35, No.2) contains a vivid article by David tracing the 1930s rivalry between Wooderson and fellow-Briton Dennis Pell. In the February 2006 issue of "Track Stats", Volume 44, No.1, David examined in detail the controversy regarding the choice of the final torch-bearer at the 1948 Olympic Games, for which Wooderson had been thought to be an obvious favourite. Sydney Wooderson died on 21 December 2006, aged 92.

Doug Wilson, Olympic Games 1500 metres competitor 1948

Only in the sense that perfect motion is mechanical: the "other" race celebrating peace

On 6 August 1945 more than 50,000 people packed into the White City Stadium, in London, with many more left outside, to celebrate the end of World War II by watching two of the great Swedes who had been smashing records from 1500 metres to 5000 metres, Arne Andersson and Gunder Hägg. At that time Andersson held the mile record at 4:01.6 and Hägg the 1500 metres at 3:43.0, the 3000 metres at 8:01.2, the two miles at 8:42.8, the three miles at 13:32.4, and the 5000 metres at 13:58.2. All of these times revolutionised the standards at those distances.

The mile race in which the tall, barrel-chested Andersson, who had lived well and without worry for the past six years in neutral Sweden, beat the slightly-built Wooderson, just recovered from rheumatic fever in war-torn Britain, in 4:08.8 to 4:09.2, has been the subject of countless descriptions. What is forgotten is the "other" race at two miles between Hägg, the flaxen-haired fireman, and Britain's up-and-coming miler, Doug Wilson, who had high hopes of breaking Jack Emery's British record of 9:03.8, and if not of beating the Swede, at least of giving him a good race.

The two of them had met once before, socially, when Hägg was on his way via Britain to run in the USA in 1943. Because of Sweden's neutrality he was able to make a stop-over, and Doug Wilson was asked if he would train with him. So very early one morning the pair went out for a run in London's Hyde Park after meeting in the foyer of a South Kensington hotel. For 20 minutes they ran side-by-side in a fartlek (speedplay) session, not speaking much because Hägg had very little English. Doug, now aged 80 and living in Winchester, remembers talking more with Hägg's team-mate, Håkan Lidman, who was to win the European 110 metres hurdles title in 1946. "After that Hägg went off and did his stuff in the US and I did not see him again until the White City in 1945", Doug recalls, and he then describes the race graphically:

"Before the White City meeting I was criticised for running at the Rangers' meeting in Glasgow. I went on the train, and as there were no sleeping-compartments I had to sleep in the corridor, standing up in the gap between the carriages. It was not the best preparation for a race and I finished nowhere. I had a sleeper on the way back on the Saturday night – a round trip of some 36 hours, and most of it travelling – and then went training hard. I had high hopes on the Monday and went out training in the morning because I was so keen. Instead of building up my energy, I had trained with a fast three-quarter-mile, but I was exhausted after the terrible journey and needed to rest more than anything else.

"When I came to the race there was nothing there. I had over-trained again. I tended to do that. I tried to keep with Hägg, but I couldn't. My legs were heavy. I hoped to be near the British record and I was with him for the first mile. He must have gone away about the sixth lap and I couldn't go with him. I was terribly disappointed as he just went further and further away. It was a ghastly race".

Wilson actually led through the first half-mile in 2:12. Hägg was in front at halfway in 4:28.4, but to the delight of the crowd Wilson moved ahead again. It did not last long and with two laps to go the Swede strode majestically away to win by 120 yards in 9:00.6 for a British all-comers' record, with Wilson trailing in 9:19.0, compared with 9:13.8 which he had done three months earlier. "The Times" reported of Hägg:

"His victory was effortless once he had shaken off his only serious opponent, Wilson, early in the second mile. So far Wilson had made him go but no more than that. In the last half Hägg seemed tempted to relax, but he answered to the enthusiasm of the crowd who were more and more fascinated by the smooth beauty of his stride, which was mechanical only in the sense that perfect motion is mechanical".

Wilson was so fed up that he did not train for four days and by the following Saturday he was full of energy, running the race he should have done at the White City and setting a lifetime best of 4:11.4 for the mile, leading all the way on a grass track at the Morris Motors' Sports in Oxford. The 5ft 10in (1.78m) and 10st 12lb (69kg) Polytechnic Harrier never got within two seconds of that time again, although he did run a 3:51.6 for 1500 metres on a cold September evening in Sweden five years later, which was his most satisfactory race because it showed that at the age of 31, and after 14 years of active competition, he was still improving.

He now believes that he never reached his full potential because of his tendency to over-train, in contrast to Sydney Wooderson. "He always beat me, apart from one very slow race during the war when we were both unfit and Frank Close beat both of us," Doug says. "We trained together and got on very well. Sydney was a very nice chap, very quiet, but very determined, and I was never in his class". Doug thinks he would have run under 4:10 if he had trained less hard but would never have beaten Wooderson.

Yet he did become the leading British miler by beating the Dutchman, Frits de Ruyter, for the AAA title in 1946 and he held that position until Bill Nankeville, who was 6th in the 1948 Olympic 1500 and 3rd in the 1950 European 1500, came along. Doug remained among the leaders and was rarely beaten at two miles, which often seemed his best distance. This was an event in which he always had a tremendous finish, and I know this from personal experience because I was almost lapped by him and the future world record-holder at three miles, Freddie Green, in a desperate run to the line at the Waddilove Trophy in 1952 with the Birchfield Harrier winning by an inch in 9:15.6.

With modern training under 4:10 would have been achievable

First coached by Albert Hill, the double Olympic champion of 1920 who had taken Wooderson to glory, and then later by Bill Thomas, who was mentor to Jack Lovelock, Doug says, "I think I would have been a lot faster if I had done all the modem training and would have broken 4:10, but not by much. I enjoyed it, anyway. We had marvellous times and I had a lot of fun, not just on the track but also in the now defunct London-to-Brighton road relay".

Born in Holloway, North London, on 29 January 1920, he began running at 17 with Polytechnic Harriers and within a year he won the club mile championship in a gale ahead of the Olympian, Aubrey Reeve, and reached the AAA final. During World War II he ran regularly for the Civil Defence, to which he belonged, and for the AAA in charity meetings, often arranged by the British team-manager, Jack Crump, at Epsom. In 1943 he ran 4:14.0 behind Wooderson, and a year later he did 4:13.4 in a handicap race in Glasgow and his best ever two miles of 9:09.2 in Birmingham. He also set an English native record of 6:47.2 for 1½ miles at Tooting Bec in 1944 and ran his fastest half-mile of 1:55.0 on grass at Bedford.

In 1945, in addition to his two-mile race with Hägg and his mile best at Oxford, he ran 3:52.4 for 1500 metres behind Wooderson and Marcel Hansenne in the international match against France, set an Irish mile record of 4:15.6 in Dublin, and won the British Games two miles in 9:13.8 from future marathoner Stan Cox. In 1946 he celebrated his AAA mile win by beating Hansenne in 4:17.4 in the GB-v-France match, but he was a disappointed 6th in the European Championships 1500 in 3:53.2. Injury kept him out of athletics for most of 1947 before he came back strongly the following year, hoping to do well in the Wembley Olympics.

He ran a mile in 4:14.8 at Chiswick and 4:17.8 behind Alec Olney and Dick Morris in the Kinnaird Trophy meeting. Injured for the AAA, he clinched his Olympic place alongside Morris and Bill Nankeville with 3:57.8 for 1500 metres behind the Irishman, John Joe Barry, in the triangular international, and then shortly before the Games his coach, Bill Thomas, had him racing against Nankeville over three-quarters-of-a-mile, and Wilson did what he considers to be one of his finest runs, winning by two or three yards in 3:00.4 when very few had ever beaten the magic three minutes. At the Olympics, though, only Nankeville made the final, while Wilson struggled in 5th in his heat in 3:54.8, suffering from a heavy cold. He made slight amends with a 9:12.6 two miles at Motspur Park a fortnight later.

He went on for four more years and combined this with his appointment in succession to the former world mile record-holder, Joe Binks, as athletics correspondent for the Sunday newspaper, the "News of the World", which used to organise the major Bank Holiday meetings and the London-to-Brighton relay. In 1949 he ran 4:13.4 for 4th place in the AAA mile behind Nankeville, Morris and Len Eyre, plus a 4:11.0 behind Eyre on a track which was 11 yards short at Huddersfield, and he won the Southern three miles in 14:34.6 but struggled in last at 5000 metres in the match against France in Paris.

In 1950 he was 5th in the AAA in 4:15.4 behind Nankeville, won in 4:15.0 in a race in Liverpool, was very close to his best two miles with a 9:09.8, and ran 8:26.0 for 3000 metres in Gothenburg as well as the 3:51.4 1500 metres in Norrköping previously mentioned while on tour with his club. He competed rarely in 1951 and lost in the Middlesex mile to Derrick Burfitt, a former junior champion who never lived up to high expectations, but was again an AAA finalist and won the Liverpool Festival of Britain two miles in 9:24.0. In 1952 he ran a blinder on stage two of the London-to-Brighton relay and made his final appearance in the AAA mile in 7th place behind Nankeville.

Note: this article was first published in "Track Stats", Volume 37, No.3, September 1999. Doug Wilson died on 18 October 2010, aged 90.

Photo: Doug Wilson wins at the White City. This occasion was an international two miles race at the British Games on 6 June 1949, and Wilson's time was 9:15.6, ahead of Curtis Stone, of the USA, and Jean Vernier, of France. Wilson was AAA mile champion and also ran 5000 metres for Great Britain, but for him the two-mile distance was probably the one at which he was best. The meeting was sponsored by the "News of the World", for which newspaper Wilson became athletics correspondent.

Uncle Reg is injured, but here's his nephew to take his place instead for England

Eric Downer is now an 86-year-old retired land surveyor living in Harrogate, in Yorkshire, from where he told me that his uncle, Reg Gosney, was his mentor who had so impressed him with his running success that he took it up, too. Though there was 17 years difference in their ages, between them uncle and nephew established a remarkable record as contemporaries in the International Cross-Country Championships as Gosney was 7th in 1946, 15th in 1947, 10th in 1949 and 18th in 1950, and in the one year that he missed out in this sequence, 1948, Downer was 8th.

Downer explains, "He was very much the reason that I ran. I first visited him when I was five and remember being impressed by his Indian clubs and punch-bag. I wanted to be like him. He used to organise races on the beach during seaside holidays. We improved our ability by running against each other. We used to train together twice a week. If we trained more than that in those days people would think you mad. It was so different. I was given a cigarette-case for winning one race and a beer-mug for another, and I did not drink or smoke". He added further concerning his uncle: "One of the highlights of my career was when I beat him. He was a committed competitive athlete and he could not stand professionalism".

Eric Downer, who was born on 3 April 1927, was a natural athlete. He started racing in 1945 and by 1948, as a member of Eastleigh AC, he was in the Hampshire team for the Inter-Counties race. He finished 18th, nine places behind his uncle, who led early on but did not like the heavy and slippery course at Horsham, in Sussex. Then came his uncle's best race when he almost beat Sydney Wooderson, now retired from track running, having set world records at 800 metres, 880 yards, ¾-of-a-mile and the mile, plus winning European titles at 1500 and 5000 metres. It was only in the last mile of the Southern cross-country that the diminutive Blackheath Harrier broke away to win by 10 seconds. The junior race was won by Downer by six seconds to double the family success.

The tendon damage which Gosney suffered was to ruin his chances at the 1948 National on the hilly Sheffield course against Wooderson, who prevailed in what he described as the hardest race of his career. It was not Gosney who challenged him as his tendon trouble forced him to retire but Vic Blowfield, of Belgrave Harriers, 3rd in the Southern, who was leading until a short distance from the finish when Wooderson's will and experience brought him the title.

Incredibly, the Gosney family honour was upheld by young Downer, who finished 6th and won his first and only international cap. In that race the bespectacled Southampton University student was the first Englishman to finish, with England yet again 3rd but Jacques Doms, of Belgium, surprisingly winning the individual title, and not the favoured Frenchman, Raphaël Pujazon. That was the end of Downer's international running career because National Service followed and then working abroad as a land surveyor. He won several races in the Army and later back at University won the UAU championships. He also won the Hampshire cross-country title for the only time in 1951 when he finished nine seconds ahead of his uncle, then looking towards retirement at 41. In the Inter-Counties race Downer was 35th as Gordon Pirie made his breakthrough in 2nd place, giving the reigning National champion, Frank Aaron, a scare.

Uncle Reg's tendons were recovered by the cross-country season of 1948-49. He started with his usual win in the Hampshire championship – he was to win a total of 24 county titles on the track, road and country, with ten 2nd places and two at 3rd – and then was 4th in the Inter-Counties in a very tight finish. He did not compete in the Southern, but his nephew did, running for the Royal Army Service Corps, and came 12th. But Gosney was there in the large field for the National in Birmingham and was 4th, 38 seconds behind the winner, Frank Aaron, retaining his crown after a hard race with Alec Olney and Len Eyre, who would be the 1950 British Empire Games three miles champion.

Gosney was 3rd scorer this time in a fast International on Baldoyle race-course, Dublin, with Geoff Saunders, the English junior champion, and Aaron ahead of him as he came in 10th, 58 seconds behind the French winner, who was not Pujazon but the wonderful Alain Mimoun (three Olympic silver medals, plus marathon gold in 1956). England were 2nd team.

1950 was Gosney's last year as an international, the oldest ever at 40. He also became the captain of the English team. It was the usual progression beforehand: 1st in the Hampshire, 7th in the Inter-Counties at Leicester won by Aaron, 9th in the Southern, and then a good 3rd in the National at Aylesbury behind a runaway Aaron but only two seconds down on Olney. In the International in Brussels the captain was fifth scorer in 18th with his team again coming 3rd, but the winner this time was not a Frenchman – Mimoun was 2nd – but Lucien Theys, the local champion.

Retirement from competition but a full life of administration

1951 was Downer's year in the county (see above), but in 1952 Uncle was still there at 42, coming 2nd, and was still good enough for 42nd in the Inter-Counties at York. A year later Gosney was 7th in the county race and in 1954 he was 12th. He finished his active career, aged 47, because of sciatica, but he continued to run almost daily until his 90s. After World War II he had also turned to administration, time-keeping and coaching. He was secretary of Southampton AC for many years as it changed its name from time to time, and he scaled the county AAA ladder until eventually becoming president, team-manager, time-keeper internationally and locally until almost his death, and an AAA senior coach for the sprints, distances and field-events. Among his successes was June Bridgland, who he changed from a schoolgirl sprinter and high jumper into National cross-country champion and who won many other titles before tragically falling out of a train to her death in 1958.

Reg Gosney's whole time away from work was spent in athletics, combining racing with administration from being a novice, right through his international career and then 50 years' service afterwards. A truly wonderful effort and a shining example to others, and it is for this reason that much of this article is concerned with his contribution to athletics alongside nephew Eric Downer.

Gosney was the only distance-runner I ever saw using cork hand-grips. A few sprinters did when I ran handicap races in the late 1940s and early 1950s, but Gosney was the odd man out. I don't remember where it was I saw him, or even if it was in a photograph, but I do recall wondering why. Corks in the hand were all the rage in the late 19th and early 20th centuries, although whether the effect was psychological or physical was never proved. Top sprinters, like the 1924 Olympic Games 100 metres champion, Harold Abrahams, and coaches like Sam Mussabini ,recommended using corks, but there is no evidence that Abrahams ever did so.

Gosney was born in Southampton on 24 February 1910 and started running in 1930 as a young civil servant – he was to win their cross-country title and also the award for the most outstanding sports person nationally in the service in 1947 – when he started work at the Ordnance Survey centre in Southampton. He had already made a name for himself locally as a boxer and hockey player and had taken part in all the games he could at King Edward VI Grammar School in his home town.

For the first few years he ran competitively at everything from 880 yards to 10 miles on the road, but it was over the country that he showed most promise. His career did not really take off until 1937 when he finished 3rd in the South of the Thames junior cross-country championship (junior meaning not being placed in a race before, not his age, which was 27), with his club, Eastleigh, also 3rd. Like so many in those days, his entrance into major championship races was restricted because of having to work on Saturday mornings. He ran a lot of local races and did better over the country than on the track, as he was to do throughout his career. At 5ft 9in (1.75m) tall and 10st 3lb (65kg) in weight, he had an easy style, combined with a lot of natural ability, but with no athletics history in a family of long-lived people.

Then came World War II and like so many others his chances were spoilt. However, he improved greatly as an athlete because he was in a reserved occupation as a lithographic artist who finished off the vital maps that were made at the Ordnance Survey, where he worked all his long life (he died aged 93 on 10 January 2004 and was out running with his dogs until he was 90). During the war he won several races, but when the hostilities were finally over he made his mark at the top level of Britain's cross-country runners.

A fine winter season capped by 3rd place in the National

In a Southern Counties special race just before Christmas in 1945 he ran away from a high-class field by 22 seconds and was then 2nd in an inter-area contest. Into the New Year he won the Hampshire title by almost two minutes. In those days the county championships were held on the first Saturday in January, then the Inter-Counties, then the district and the regional, and finally the National at the start of March, with the International in the middle of that month. He won the South of the Thames by 15 seconds, with a future Olympic marathon runner, Geoff Iden, 3rd. Gosney missed the Southern because of work but finished a fine 3rd against two very experienced runners – the European and Empire 1950 marathon champion and four times International cross-country winner, Jack Holden, and Birchfield's multiple Scots international, Bobby Reid – in the National.

That was the first time I saw a photo of him, on the cover of the new magazine, "Athletics", which I spotted at a railway-station newsagent. I bought it, devoured it, and sent off for the previous four editions. The photo showed Gosney gripping corks and leading at the start of the last lap. Holden broke away towards the finish and won in style, 17 seconds ahead of the Hampshire man. In his first International, held over the race-course at Ayr, in Scotland, Gosney finished as 2nd scorer for England (3rd team behind France and Raphaël Pujazon) in 7th place, 14 seconds behind Holden, who was 6th. When he answered the "Athletics Weekly" questionnaire at his retirement from international racing in 1950 Gosney said this was his best race. He explained: "I judged my event so that when I had finished I felt that it would be impossible to have run further and yet I had retained form up to the finish". He added some notes on cross-country running and ended, "'One final word of advice – when training for cross-country try and avoid running on the road".

In 1947 he threw away his corks and immediately won the Inter-Counties championship in a very tight finish. He was chosen as No. 10 in a "portrait gallery" series in "Athletics" magazine, and the two-page article ended: "One unusual idiosyncrasy which has frequently been commented on is Gosney's use of running corks. An almost unheard of practice for distance-runners and seldom advocated these days even for sprinting, his use – or wearing – is merely a psychological relic of his early days. Once he had used them he did not feel at home without them and has maintained them ever since without making any use of them when running until this year when he decided to discard his corks for good. Within a few days of this appearing he may well be considering this a good omen, for success in the National is overdue and more than a possibility."

Sadly it was not to happen in 1947 as this was the year of the snow (and bitter cold), and when the heavily depleted field lined up at Apsley, in Hertfordshire, it was Bertie Robertson, of Reading, who had a day-of-days and finished 67 seconds ahead of the rest (which did not include the defending champion, Holden, who was stuck in the stuff), and Gosney was back in 10th, though it was still good enough to win an England vest. In the International on St Cloud race-course outside Paris he was 3rd England scorer (again 3rd to France and Pujazon) in 15th, with Alec Olney and Tony Chivers ahead of him.

On 20 May Gosney produced his best track performance in an invitation six miles at the White City against Viljo Heino, of Finland, then the best distance-runner in the world but soon to be overtaken by Zátopek. Gosney finished a distant 2nd to the Finn's British all-comers' record 29:22.4 but set a personal best of 31:55. His track personal bests were not generally very good compared with his speed over the country and included 4:39.8 for the mile (1942), 14:46 for three miles (1948), which is still the Hampshire veterans' record, and 31:15 for six miles (AAA championships, 1948). He was at the peak of his form in 1948, winning the Hampshire cross-country title by nearly two minutes from his nephew, Eric Downer.

Note: thanks to Peter Lovesey for assistance. This article was first published in "Track Stats", Volume 52, No.2, April 2014. Reginald George Gosney died in January 2004, aged 93.

Reg Gosney (left) and Eric Downer – uncle and nephew and both England cross-country representatives in the years immediately after World War II.

Dorothy Tyler, Olympic Games High jump silver-medallist 1936 & 1948

A "babe" in Berlin, a matron in Melbourne, a transformation in experience and style

Old athletes are not like old soldiers. They do not fade away. They simply change sports.

Dorothy Tyler did just that after a high-jumping career which continued over 28 years through four decades and included two Olympic silver medals, two other Olympic appearances, two Empire/Commonwealth gold medals, a European silver, 14 national titles, a world record, and three top-of-the-world rankings. Then she went into coaching before taking up golf at the age of 48 and winning many, many trophies and cups in that sport. She reduced her handicap to 10 at her best and still played – and won – three times a week into the 21st century.

Her last year of competition for her beloved Mitcham Athletic Club, from which she had received free membership when she had started out as a promising 11-year-old, was in 1963, but being the loyal club member that she was, she stayed on coaching girls to Olympic level both there and at the school where she taught for years until she was 60. She wrote an instructional book and continued producing articles, broadcasting on radio and television, lecturing, and advising on educational matters, having served on the leading administrative bodies in athletics and been a founder-member of the Olympians (British Olympic team members).

When I met her at her Surrey home she had just celebrated her 60th wedding anniversary at the age of 80 with her husband, Richard, a former 440 yards runner and rugby player, and she looks years younger. Their two sons and five grandchildren are sports-minded, too, and one son is still playing football at the age of 53. Silvery-haired, as upright as ever at 5ft 6in (1.68m) and weighing 8st 4lb (52kg) at her peak, Dorothy swam on the days that she was not playing golf, and she talked as enthusiastically as a youngster about her long, long athletics career.

She was born on 14 March 1920 at Stockwell, in South London. Her family, in which there was no history of athletics involvement, moved to Mitcham when she was aged four, and at the junior school which she attended there was no playground or sports field. Athletics was carried out in the gymnasium, and each girl was allowed to select only one event, with the youthful Dorothy Odam finding that she had a wonderful ability for high-jumping scissors-style off her right leg. By the time she was 13 she was good enough to place 2nd in the All-England Schools high jump with a spiked left leg (she still carried the scar), and she came under the wing of Muriel Gunn-Cornell, the British long-jump champion.

Dorothy always walked the two miles each way to and from school because she did not have the bus fare, and for fun she often hopped the full distance to strengthen her legs. Her two brothers were much older and she found the fun and friendship which she sought with the Mitcham club. She began a routine which she was to follow most of her competitive life: training was on Sunday mornings and Tuesday and Thursday evenings, with occasional Monday evenings in the gym, and netball and exercises during the winter.

She cleared 5ft (1.52) for the first time in 1935 and was 2nd in the Women's AAA Championships, but at the age of 15 she was considered too young to compete in the Women's World Games, in which her mentor from the Mitcham club, Mary Milne, did well. With her scissors style Dorothy ended the season with a best of 5ft 3in (1.60), which ranked as equal 4th best in the world. Early in 1936 she was selected for her first international match, winning at Blackpool and beating the up-and-coming 18-year-old Dutch girl, Francina Koen (later to become world-renowned as Fanny Blankers-Koen), with a British record of 5ft 4in (1.625).

After winning two Olympic silver medals Dorothy Tyler changed her jumping style from the scissors to the more efficient western roll, demonstrated here at the White City in 1951.

The long-legged 16-year-old innocent went abroad for the first time to the Berlin Olympics, mixing with the world's best athletes, with the VIPs, and with the Nazi hierarchy at an island party one night for which Goebbels had sent out the invitations. Dorothy recalls: "I'd never been further than Bognor, and there are pictures of me on the train to Berlin wide-eyed in wonder at what I was seeing. In fact, there had been talk that I was too young to go, but I did go and it was a terrific adventure.

"I had no nerves at all. I just wanted to get out there and jump. I don't think I trained much. I just jumped a bit and then talked to the men. We had three chaperones and were housed in a physical training college, unlike the men who were in the athletes' village. I was asked out by one of the Danish high jumpers, but the chaperones said that I could only go if I took the rest of the team – 11 other ladies – with me!

"Everything was highly organised. In fact, over-organised. My event went on for hours, and I lost in the jump-off as the bar went up and down. Under the rules now I would have won, but I didn't mind. I didn't feel fed up at losing. I was cheered on a by a group of British Boy Scouts, and I remember that no one was allowed a drink throughout the competition except the German girl, and she was brought one after three hours.

"The newspapers were not interested in the women then. There were no accolades. To me it was just a lot of fun, like the All-England Schools. I was a bit disappointed because I was used to winning, but it wasn't very important. We didn't think we were anyone special. We were just a bunch of friends enjoying ourselves. We certainly weren't prima donnas like some are today. I was young at 16 and even frightened to ask Jesse Owens for his autograph. When I finally plucked up the courage, he said, 'Gee, let me get my shoes off first'".

The winner of that Berlin Olympic high jump was Ibolya Csák, of Hungary, with Dorothy 2nd at the same height. The 1999 book by Ekkehard zur Megede, "The Modern Olympic Century 1896-1996", gives the full statistical story of the competition as follows:

1 Ibolya Csák (Hungary) 1.60, 2 Dorothy Odam (GB) 1.60, 3 Elfriede Kaun (Germany) 1.60. 4 Marguèrite Nicolas (France) 1.58; 5= Doris Carter (Australia), Annette Rogers (USA), Francina Koen (Holland) 1.55; 8= Helen Carrington (GB), Margaret Mary Bell (Canada), Alice Arden (USA), Kathlyn Kelly (USA), Wanda Nowak (Austria) 1.50; 13= Catherine Stevens (Belgium), Jantina Koopmans (Holland), Juno Nishida (Japan) 1.40; 16 Irja Lipasti (Finland) 1.30.

	1.50	1.55	1.58	1.60	1.62	Jump-Off 1.62	1.60
Csák	o	o	o	xo	xxx	o	
Odam	o	o	o	o	xxx	x	o
Kaun	o	o	xxo	xxo	xxx	x	x

Dora Ratjen, of Germany, was officially placed equal 4th but was later disqualified. After winning the 1938 European title she was recognised as a man and changed her/his name to Hermann.

On the podium the three medal-winning girls were crowned with laurel leaves, and Dorothy then had a great time socially before she went back home to Surrey and to Pitman's College, where she was learning to become a shorthand typist. Her Berlin success was the start of an international career that was to go on until 1956 when she won her 14th and last national title at the age of 36 and made her fourth Olympic appearance, at Melbourne, representing Great Britain for the 21st time.

In 1937 she was on top of the world – the undoubted queen of her event – and the only person to beat her was Ratjen, 1.65 to 1.61 in Krefeld. Dorothy remembers, "You could not miss the fact that she was a man. I knew it from the start. During the war they tried to take my world record away and give it to him, but after the war I was reinstated. There were three in the women's 100 metres in Berlin who were definitely men. You couldn't see that they were because they changed away from us, but when they spoke you turned round at once wondering how a man had been allowed into the women's quarters where men were definitely not allowed to go. One member of the British women's team was a man when I first started competing, but I was too young to say anything about anyone.

"They stopped men competing as women when they brought in sex tests, but drugs were a different matter. The first time I came across such a thing was at the 1950 Empire Games in Auckland when two, if not three, of the competitors were on drugs, though not the sort that are around today and help much more. A doctor gave one of the women competitors drugs and they definitely helped because she won her event. I remember three girls who took drugs in 1950 and two others at Melbourne in 1956. I was very much against it then, just as I am against it now".

Off around the world to win an Empire title

At the age of 17 she set off on a four-month adventure by sea to the 1938 British Empire Games in Sydney, having taken time off from her secretarial work with the National Fitness Council. On the long voyage everyone trained together and she met competitors from all sports, but she had to stay on board the ship when it docked en route in Perth because there was a poliomyelitis epidemic and no one under the age of 18 was allowed ashore.

She won the Empire Games high jump with a new record at 5ft 3in (1.60) and has great memories of the trip despite some setbacks. "The men had their village, but the women were put up in a third-rate hotel where the swimmers had their costumes stolen and Mary Holloway and I, who shared a room, had money taken from our cases. It was only a little money, and one of the team officials gave Mary and I £1 each to get us home! We didn't have much money in those days, though I didn't need it really as I was living at home, but we couldn't afford to buy any clothes and Mrs Cornell had lent me an evening dress for the trip. We had a tremendous time with parties and official and unofficial social events and by the time we got back we were hardly fit for sport!"

It made no difference to Dorothy's athletics career because she won the national title both indoors and out and her performances were very high in the world rankings. This was also the year that she met her husband-to-be, Richard, at a training evening after he had transferred from Polytechnic Harriers.

In 1939 she broke the world record with 5ft 5⅜in (1.66m) at Brentwood, in Essex, and Dorothy recalls: "It was really 5 feet 6 inches and I soared over that easily with my scissors. I was miles higher and had to land in the sand which they had dumped in the middle of the field. Our team had gone over in a coach, as we always did, and it was a day out for fun. I won a beautiful cut-glass bowl which was so heavy I could barely carry it. Someone dropped it a few years ago!"

Reinforcing her position as the best in the world she cleared 5ft 5in (1.65) to win the national title and then 1.65 in Berlin a week later on 29 July to beat an international field. Together with her world record, these were the best three performances in the list, but that was to be her last serious competition for nine years. She married Richard in 1940 and a year later joined the Women's Auxiliary Air Force, where she served as a driver (including a posting to the "Dambusters" 617 Bomber Squadron at Scampton, in Lincolnshire) and then as a PT instructor. She also played netball for the national WAAF team and hockey, cricket and netball for her air-force station near Hull, but took part in no athletics after initial training. Her husband was an army "Desert Rat" in North Africa before fighting through Europe.

She was demobbed in 1945, and her two sons, David and Barry, were born in 1946 and 1947. So, apart from brief appearances winning the Southern title, placing 2nd in the Women's AAA Championships, and clearing 5ft 1½in (1.562) at the famously inspirational post-war White City meeting on August Bank Holiday to rank 3rd in the world for the year, she was out of athletics altogether. She recalls, "I missed both the 1940 and 1944 Olympics planned for Tokyo and Helsinki, and there was no reason why I should not have won both. I certainly would have jumped higher. The war took six years out of my life, and everyone else's, too, of course, but it was also six lost years technically. The straddle and the western roll would have come in much earlier in the UK and I would have learned the roll earlier and would have gone much higher, but I did not change until 1951 when I came under Arthur Gold's coaching".

In 1948 Dorothy returned to athletics, determined to see what she could do, but because she had been out of competition she was not on the "Probables" list for selection and so did not qualify for the food parcels given to prospective Olympic athletes because of the country's shortages. Instead, she won her place in the team with victories in the Surrey, Southern and WAAA Championships and finished 2nd again in the Olympic final at Wembley. She and the American, Alice Coachman, both cleared 5ft 6⅛in (1.68m) for a lifetime best, but Dorothy lost on the "fewer failures" rule as the American cleared first time and she did so at her second attempt. The details were as follows:

1 Alice Coachman (USA) 1.68, 2 Dorothy Tyler (GB) 1.68, 3 Micheline Ostermeyer (France) 1.61, 4= Vinton Beckett (Jamaica), Doreen Dredge (Canada) 1.58; 6 Bertha Crowther (GB)

1.58; 7 Ilse Steinegger (Austria) 1.55; 8 Dora Gardner (GB) 1.55; 9= Simone Ruas (France), Annemarie Iversen (Denmark) 1.50; 11= Carmen Phipps (Jamaica), Shirley Gordon (Canada), Claudealia Robinson (USA) 1.50; 14= Catherine Bourkel (Luxemburg), Anne-Marie Colchen (France), Emma Reed (USA) 1.40; 17= Olga Gyarmati (Hungary), Elizabeth Clara Muller (Brazil) 1.40; 19 Elaine Silburn (Canada) 1.40.

"Coming 2nd was not as important as it is today", Dorothy says. "You were so thrilled to have done what you did. You didn't get the coverage that you get today, where it's only to do with money. We weren't celebrities because there was no TV where you were on every week. I think it was more fun then. We were all friends, and I don't think they are now. I don't think I would like to be taking part now". It was at Wembley that Dorothy became friendly with the Dutch multi-gold-medallist, Fanny Blankers-Koen, against whom she had competed as teenagers a decade earlier.

A fortnight after the Games Dorothy was appearing for her club at the Motspur Park track, in Surrey, and took part in the long jump. At the age of 28 it was her first season at the event but she cleared 18ft 9½in (5.725), which was three centimetres further than the distance of 5.695 (18ft 8¾in) with which Olga Gyarmati, of Hungary, had won the Olympic title.

Realising how lucky she was to have a supportive mother and husband, Dorothy was able to go off on another long trip in 1950 to the Auckland Empire Games, where she retained the title she had won 12 years before, adding two inches to the Games record. She was also 4th in the javelin and 6th in the long jump, but failed to qualify in an 80 metres hurdles heat in which the first three broke the record. "I was captain of the English team", she recalls, "and on the voyage to New Zealand one of the boxers took us for PE and we ran round the deck to stay fit. At the Games we jumped into pits which were filled with pieces of wood which were scratchy, and it wasn't at all pleasant.

"I didn't jump well because the event was held in a corner of the stadium, making it the wrong angle for my approach. I had to turn my body round to approach the bar and make sure that I landed in the pit. Then, in addition to all that, the event started an hour late, and we had to stop at a crucial point because of some dispute in the men's discus which meant that one of the competitors had three extra throws which went straight over the pit! But it was a good social occasion, and we had a great deal of fun. We toured the other islands and I won all my events. Luckily, the children recognised me when I got back! It was my last long trip away".

1950 was also the year in which Dorothy suffered pneumonia but came back to win the Surrey high jump, javelin and 80 metres hurdles in an afternoon and then finish 2nd at 5ft 5in (1.65m) in the Southern Championships to 21- year-old Sheila Alexander, who was to be the first woman to break the world record using the straddle technique. At the European Championships in Brussels Dorothy again finished 2nd to her team-mate, Alexander, as both cleared 1.63.

Sheila Alexander (now Mrs Lerwill) and later Thelma Hopkins, from Northern Ireland, were two young eagles who soared higher and higher to world records, beating their older mentor, and how many other countries could ever claim to have had three world record-holders in one team? "It poured with rain in Brussels", Dorothy says, "and they put oil on the take-off area and burnt it to dry it out. I was the first to jump and the surface gave way under me and I fell into the pit without jumping, but they still insisted that it counted as a jump and thus a failure against me."

In 1951, at the age of 31, she changed from the untutored scissors style which she had been using to the western roll, and for the first time she had a coach in the person of the former international, Arthur (now Sir Arthur) Gold. She explains: "Everyone was jumping higher and I needed to change, too. They all said I was too old to change, but they were wrong, and Arthur was the only one who wanted to coach me. I wish now that I had had a go at the straddle, but at the time I thought it was a bit dangerous. Sheila was the first to go for the straddle, and when she beat me in the national championships I was so angry that I went over and won the long jump!

"I don't know what I would have done with the straddle, but the western roll took me almost as high at the end of my international career as I had done at the very peak of my career in 1948, when I was jumping better and more satisfyingly than at any other time. High jumping now is not what I call jumping. It's rather like throwing a weight at the end of a piece of string, with the head heavier than the rest of the body. You throw the head over, and the weight is like the stone on the end of the string which takes the rest of you over on your back."

Trying the pentathlon (shot, high jump, 200 metres, 80 metres hurdles, long jump) for the first time, she made the most of her natural talent and won the national title by a margin of 276 points with a record score of 3,224 (1950 tables, 3,953 on the 1954 tables).

In 1952 she won another national high-jump title and went to the Olympics again but suffered a groin injury during a club match beforehand which spoilt her chances in Helsinki. Her coach would not let her train until the injury healed and she could only finish 7th, with Sheila Lerwill 2nd and 16-year-old Thelma Hopkins 4th. In 1954 dysentery and ensuing exhaustion put Dorothy in hospital and she almost went from her sick-bed to the Empire Games stadium in Vancouver where she finished 2nd to Hopkins (5ft 6in) in her third appearance at the Games and ahead of Lerwill and was also 5th in the javelin.

The next year she jumped 5ft 5in and narrowly missed the world record. She also had a victory over Aleksandra Chudina, the Russian world record-holder and prolific all-rounder, but even so she recalls that people were saying by this time, 'Why don't you give up and let someone else have a chance?' Dorothy told them: "By jumping over a bar I go round the world. I'm not getting paid for it. It's only for the glory. So I'm going on!"

After yet another national title in 1956 she went to the Olympics for the last time, finishing 12th, and then retired from international competition. She readily admits: "I was lucky to go to Melbourne. I only just made the qualifying height because Arthur kept entering me in all sorts of things. There were some very, very good jumpers at the Games, and even though I was 12th, I still beat one of the British girls".

Though retired from the global scene, Dorothy remained a tower of strength for her club, always ready to take part in several different events. She placed 2nd to a promising 18-year-old, Mary Bignal, in the 1958 Southern pentathlon and regularly cleared 5ft 2in or 5ft 3in every year until her last in 1963, when at 43 she still got over 5ft 1in. Then she went on to become, amongst other things, the first woman to qualify as a coach for male athletes, an international judge and referee for field events, a Great Britain team manager, and a member of many committees, including those involved with Olympic selection, with WAAA rules, and co-ordinating with the Royal Ballet on an unusual high-jump training programme.

Dorothy Tyler does have some regrets. She never won the trophy as the outstanding athlete at the WAAA Championships, despite competing for 20-odd years. On two occasions her name has been put forward for the Honours Lists but without recognition. Her old club, Mitcham, no longer exists after amalgamation. Athletes today, she feels, over-train because they never take a rest.

"I had my natural talent and I was very fit," she concludes. "I still am very fit".

Note: this article was first published in "Track Stats", Volume 38, No.2, July 2000. In 2001 Dorothy Tyler was appointed an MBE. She died on 26 September 2014, aged 94.

Out of the blue, the reluctant Scotsman who surprised the US sprinters but preferred cricket

Olympic sprinters have come in all shapes and sizes – from the Frenchman who insisted on wearing white gloves because he was running in front of the King of Greece in 1896 through Abrahams, Owens, Morrow and Carl Lewis to 2008. None has ever appeared out of the blue with such natural power and brilliance to become the fastest white man in the world, and then gone with the same speed to return to the game he really loved, cricket, than the 6ft (1.83m) tall 14st 4lb (91kg) power-pack of Scottish smoking excellence, Alastair McCorquodale.

It started on an Army training exercise in the early summer of 1947 with the carrot of a weekend pass – "always the point of the exercise", he recalled at his home in Grantham, in Lincolnshire – and graduated the next year to picking up almost all the staggered start on the first leg of the British Empire-v-USA match 4 x 110 yards relay against Barney Ewell, the Olympic 100 and 200 metres silver-medallist of a few days before. McCorquodale already had an Olympic relay silver medal and 4th place in a blanket finish to that 100 metres to his credit. He walked off the White City track on to a cricket field and never ran competitively again.

At Harrow School McCorquodale had been an outstanding cricketer; a first-class bowler and batsman who performed so well in the traditional match against Eton in 1943 and 1944 that he was selected to play for the Public Schools. He was an excellent all-round sportsman (great rugby player, too) and won the sprint events in the annual school sports in the summer in fast times and the Victor Ludorum prize as overall champion in 1944 and 1945. Unlike most public schools and Oxford and Cambridge Universities in those days, Harrow's sports actually were in the summer, not in the cold of March. He went into the Coldstream Guards towards the very end of World War II and served in Germany as a Lieutenant.

It was in the early summer of 1947 that his sensational athletics career began. He recalled: "I was instructing at the School of Infantry at Warminster on Salisbury Plain, and the Company Sergeant Major came up while we were on exercise and said he was a hell of a good hurdler and was running in the Salisbury and District area sports on the Saturday. That's the lowest point in the Army championships. You proceed from there to through Command and then to the finals.

"For a joke I challenged him, and drew a pair of spikes from the stores, and he fell over at the first hurdle. I won that and both sprints and the shot put and long jump. I then went on to Command, and having won there to the Army championships, and I won the hundred in 9.9 at Aldershot. I was always very fast at school but was not interested in running, just cricket. I got a weekend's leave pass every time I competed, which was the object of the exercise. Because I had won the Army 100, I was entered for the AAA championships and came 5th."

A photo in "Athletics" monthly magazine, the forerunner of "Athletics Weekly", shows him very close up to the winner, Emmanuel McDonald Bailey (supreme in British sprinting except when injured until 1952), with John Wilkinson and Jack Gregory even closer. Time: 10sec. "They issued a list at the end of 1947 of people who might be eligible for the Olympic Games the next year and I was on it". He was also ranked 7th on merit in the 100 yards by team manager Jack Crump in his annual survey in the magazine.

McCorquodale continues: "I came out of the Army at the beginning of 1948 and went round to see Jack Crump at the AAA offices, and it so happened that Harold Abrahams was there. I asked, 'What should I do?' They said I should get hold of Guy Butler because he was the best coach and also join the club where he was coach, which was the London Athletic Club. Because of the war I had missed my chance to go to university and join Achilles with the university chaps. I was born at the wrong time because I had to go to war and not to Oxford or Cambridge. I met Guy Butler, and he was very good, but there was not much he could do for me in the time. The first thing was to get me a pair of running-shoes made, size 11, and I went to George Law, the only shoemaker around at the time. Guy Butler worked out a programme for me and I just went from there to the finals at the Games".

Butler was another Harrovian and a former Olympic gold medallist for the 4 x 400 metres relay in 1920, and the first thing he did was to get McCorquodale fit. He said: "I was not really fit. When I was at school, playing games all the time and not smoking and drinking, I was fit, but not when I came out of the Army. I was smoking and drinking and not fit at all. He gave me a programme, and I started going for runs, doing three to five miles in the dark around Bray where we lived. It was hard work, and my first race was a 440 yards at Wellington College in a match against the boys in the spring after which I was sick". But he was stronger and fitter, and twice a week he would go for training at the White City, learning how to start and run fast. McCorquodale said: "I did not do anything else except go there and do what he told me to do".

He was also busy at work with the family printing and publishing company which produced the Olympic Games programmes, and he was living outside London in Windsor. So putting cricket aside for a couple of months, he joined the Olympic trail. He said: "I suppose I got satisfaction from it but not much pleasure. You are in a team, but you do your best to beat the other fellow. I did not have many friends in the sport because there was not time. I was keen on all sports. Like all sports, once you have got a taste for it and start winning you go on to see how far you can go. You get self-satisfaction from it. If you have success you go on until such time as you have reached a peak. The peak of sprinting is the final of the Olympic Games. After that there is not very much more to go for and nowhere else to go".

His first major wins and a return to his home town

His first outing in his bid to reach that Olympic final was in the Southern championships 100 yards at Uxbridge on 12 June when he ran the Welsh rugby international, Ken Jones, to a foot in 9.9, with McDonald Bailey 3rd. This was the first sign showing of the muscle injury that was to wreck Bailey's Olympic chances. The following Saturday at Chiswick, McCorquodale – the reluctant 6ft sprinter in the black baggy shorts – came out and convincingly won both sprints in the annual Kinnaird Trophy (for the top clubs): the 100 by half-a-yard from Bailey and John Fairgrieve; the furlong by a yard from Nick Stacey, with Fairgrieve a stride back 3rd. Fairgrieve would later in life become a consultant surgeon and Stacey a bishop.

A few days later McCorquodale, who had been born in Hillhead, Glasgow, on 5 December 1925, ran 11.6 for the 120 yards at half-time during a football match at Hampden Park in the city of his birth, and that is a time which still stands as a Scottish record. He said: "The whole thing was muddled up with football and they booed one of the teams when they came out on the field". The next weekend it was the AAA championships, and in a tight 100 he nipped between the Australian, John Treloar, and Bailey, 9.9 to 9.8, for 2nd, and because both of the others were injured McCorquodale took the 220 in 22.2 by two yards from Fairgrieve – thus a novice in every sense winning such a title.

A few days later in his club championships, which also formed an invitational meeting at Motspur Park, McCorquodale did another double, 9.9 and 22.1. Squeezed into the time between then and the Games was a triangular international (Scotland, England and Wales) in Manchester, and wearing his native colours he took the 100 metres in 10.8, an inch or two in front of Ken Jones and the still struggling Bailey.

In his editorial in "Athletics" to welcome the Olympics, editor Jimmy Green wrote: "We do not expect too much this time but tend rather to look forward to 1952, for our youngsters are undoubtedly the best ever. But some of our athletes will rise to the occasion and we may find some heartening performances, particularly from the women". He was right about that, and GB would have had a mighty haul of gold but for a certain Dutch woman, but the three men he singled out – Jack Holden (marathon), John Parlett (800 metres) and Harry Churcher (10 kilometres walk) – did not perform to expectation. McCorquodale, with his fabulous talent, did.

On the opening day at Wembley, Friday 30 July, he lost his first-round 100 metres heat by inches to one of the favourites, Barney Ewell, of the USA, with both timed at 10.5. Soon after, he lost the second-round heat to the American favourite, Mel Patton, the fastest white man in the world, 10.5 to 10.4. The next day, 31 July, he stormed through in 3rd place in his semi-final in 10.7 to qualify for the final just behind the two Americans, Harrison Dillard and Ewell.

Dillard was a wonderful example of athletic guts and determination. He was the world's best high hurdler for two seasons, with a winning streak of 82 races, but messed it up in the US trials and did not qualify. He used the second string to his bow to gain selection for the Olympic 100 metres, won that (and another gold in the sprint relay), and then came back four years later to win the gold in his own 110 metres hurdles event.

No doubts about Dillard but 2nd place is desperately close

The Wembley 100 metres final was never in doubt once Dillard (10.3) inched ahead, although Ewell at the end thought he had won. In a desperate finish for 2nd the strong Scot in lane three was just beaten by Ewell and by Lloyd LaBeach, of Panama, in 10.4. The place times given after the race were adjusted later as they were so obviously inaccurate at 10.4, 10.6, 10.6. Behind McCorquodale were Patton and Bailey (Trinidad-born but running for his adopted Britain and still suffering from his injury), and so the Scot became the fastest white man. It was unexpected by all the pundits and surprised him, too. He said: "You do your best in the Olympic Games. It was not quite good enough, but it was my best. You could not run in a bigger race than the Olympic Games and I thought I would leave it at that".

But there was still the 200 metres and the relay to run before he could get back to cricket.

On Monday 3 August he won his first-round 200 metres heat in 22.3, and in the second round he came up against Patton again. The American was itching for revenge and got it in 21.4 to the Scot's lifetime best of 21.6 (Patton went on to win the final in 21.1). The semi-final was a race too far and McCorquodale finished 5th in 21.7 (and this was a man who had never run a 200 metres or 220 yards on a proper track before June) behind the winning 21.5 for Cliff Bourland of the USA.

Still to come was the relay, and at that discipline he was a real novice. So they stuck him on the first leg. He said: "I had no idea. It was the sort of thing you learnt to do at university which I had missed. It was all pretty amateur in those days and is an entirely different ball-game now. We were never together, but I think the others were training more than me, and they trained quite intensively during the Games, but I was racing every day. That's why I ran the first leg so that the only thing I had to do was to hand the baton to the first of the others".

It worked. In the qualifying heat he powered round the first bend and put the baton into Jack Gregory's hand, and with Ken Jones and Jack Archer to follow (Bailey still injured and out) they ran only 0.3 slower than the USA's 41.1. It was clear that failing a miracle (and they do happen, as it did when the perfect German girls dropped the baton in Berlin in 1936) Britain was at least going to get a silver and the first men's medal at those Games.

The finish of the 1948 Olympic 100 metres. Left to right: Harrison Dillard (USA) 1st, Alastair McCorquodale (GB) 4th, McDonald Bailey (GB) 6th, Lloyd LaBeach (Panama) 3rd, Barney Ewell (USA) 2nd, Mel Patton (USA) 5th.

The British Olympic 4 x 100 metres relay squad, left to right: Jack Archer, Ken Jones, Jack Gregory and Alastair McCorquodale. For a day they were Olympic champions until the USA team was reinstated.

But for several hours the miracle happened again, and it was not the fault of a dropped baton but because of the indecision of a rather inexperienced official who thought that the Americans, Ewell and Lorenzo Wright, might, and only might, have passed the baton outside the zone. So the bewildered Americans were disqualified; the delighted crowd roared the Britons onto the victory stand; and ... next day it was all change again, and the Americans were given their rightful medals when the jury quickly realised that there had been no infringement.

The British team really impressed everyone by their technique. "Athletics" described it: "Never have I seen such brilliant baton-changing by one of our relay teams – a brilliance repeated by the British Empire team later against the USA". And in the report of the Games it said that it was a pity that the disqualification "tended to push into the background that the performance of the British team did more to rouse British enthusiasm than any other in the Games. Our baton-changing was perfect".

McCorquodale's performances were outstanding and showed tremendous promise for the future. That a man with so little training, even though his natural talent was extraordinary, could run so fast was astonishing. But it did not affect him. Not even after he had the best run of his oh-so-short career on the first leg for the British Empire against the USA at the White City. He was pleased at his success, but athletics did not attract him. He ran because he was asked to do so for his country.

He went off so fast in the inside leg that he all but caught Barney Ewell by the hand-over to John Bartram, of Australia, which set the others – John Treloar and Jack Archer, the architect of the team's slick baton-changing – for a win by four yards in a British record of 41.8. McCorquodale remembered: "It was the fastest I ran, but I did not want to do any more. I wanted to go back to cricket, and I never stepped on a track nor ran again. If I had gone on, it would have been very unsatisfactory being over the top and not winning. You have to get out at the top. I had gone as far as I could".

His cricket career as a left-handed batsman and right-arm fast bowler lasted over many years, playing for Middlesex in three first-class matches in 1951 and for their second XI many times, also going on an MCC tour of Canada in 1951. Even so, he recalls sadly: "I was not good enough and I did not get the time because of business". But he enjoyed it more than his running. "I found it more social and friendly", he said.

His only contact with his team-mates from 1948 was at their 50th reunion where he met McDonald Bailey again (he is still alive but blind) and Fairgrieve. McCorquodale said: "It was all so different then, nearly all amateur. Now they are all professionals. A different ball-game. But they were beginning to be even then. Roy Cochran, who won the 400 metres hurdles, was advertising running-shoes before the Games were over".

Alastair McCorquodale had one other link with his Olympic past when he was on business in Perth, Australia, and tripped over one of the plaques they have in the main street honouring their heroes. He said: "I looked down, and the one I had tripped over was that of John Winter, the high-jump winner on the first day of the Olympics when I was running the 100 metres".

Note: this article was first published in "Track Stats", Volume 45, No.4, November 2007. Alastair McCorquodale died on 28 September 2009, aged 83.

Lorna Lee, Olympic Games long jump competitor 1948

An unexplained mystery in Wembley's graveyard of many a hopeful medallist

On 26 June 1948, during the Women's AAA Championships at Chiswick, near London, something very strange happened. Three women, all unheard of, long jumped 18ft (5.48m) and over and put themselves in line for a medal and certainly a top-six performance at the Wembley Olympic Games on 4 August. Why it did not happen and why they lost their form – something around half-a-metre each – in the days between the two events is a mystery that at last looks as though it might be solved.

This is because John Lee, editor of a publication called "Dawn", the house magazine of a large group that owns old people's residential homes, was visiting one of them in Essex and saw the black-painted silhouette image of a long jumper in full flight on the door of one of the residents. He was told that it was the room of Joan Shepherd, one of the three British competitors in the first Olympic women's long jump at Wembley in 1948. He asked if he could interview her, and did so, but at the time she was suffering from locked-in syndrome, and although still sharp she could not talk and could only communicate by blinking her eyes. She has sadly died since, aged 88. Lee then researched her busy life (including winning the famous Dunmow Flitch for happily married couples in 2000) on the internet. In the course of that he discovered that she blamed her failure at Wembley on a last-minute change of the rules which made it illegal for the competitors to mark their run-ups.

He contacted Essex Ladies AC, Joan's club, and talked to Jean Desforges, who broke Joan's Women's AAA record and was European champion in 1954, but she was much younger and referred him to another club member, Dorothy Manley, the silver-medallist at 100 metres in 1948 who is now the wife of John Parlett, a 1948 800 metres finalist and 1950 European 800 metres and Empire 880 yards champion. Dorothy was a friend of Joan's, and she and her then husband used to go out regularly with Joan and her husband, Jack, but Dorothy says that Joan never mentioned the matter of the Olympic rule change to her. And what makes it so intriguing is that there is no mention of such a ruling anywhere else; neither in the official Games report, nor in any coverage of the Games in newspapers, books or magazines. Margaret Erskine, who was 2nd in the WAAA long jump of 1948, has also died, and for a long time I could not find Lorna Lee, who was 3rd.

Is it true that the rules were changed? Under the WAAA rules published in 1949 (kindly provided for me by the Parletts) there is no mention of marks for the long jump, but there is for the high jump, and this states that "a competitor may place marks to assist her in her run-up and take-off and a handkerchief on the cross bar for sighting purposes".

What is certain is that all three of the British competitors in the 1948 Olympic women's long jump lost their form completely. Others in the British team did so at the Games, as in the 5000 metres, but having a bad run is quite different to losing all form in a jumping event in which a contestant has at least three attempts.

Consider the facts. Post-World War II, British women's long jumping was not up to much. The golden day had been in 1930 when the fabulous Muriel Gunn (later Mrs Cornell) leapt 19ft 2½in (5.85m) for her eighth consecutive British record which would last until 1952, when Shirley Cawley did 5.92 for the bronze medal at the Olympics, and this was improved to 6.10 by Jean Desforges a year later. Until the WAAA meeting of 1948 no British woman had jumped over 18ft since World War II, apart from a youngster named Mona Lee, who won the under-16 group of the All-England schools' event in Hull with 18-2¾ (5.55) in 1947 to head the British rankings and never did anything again – or so we all thought, but I will come to that later.

Then it all came right. Joan Shepherd, who was tiny at 5ft 1¾in (1.57m) and 7st 6lb (47kg), won with a great leap of 18-8½ (5.70). Her previous best was 18-1⅛ (5.52) in winning the Southern, which had improved 40 centimetres on her personal best from the previous year. The WAAA winning leap put her almost at the top of the world rankings in 4th place before the Games and was to still remain 8th at the end of the year. Nearly as good in 2nd place was Margaret Erskine, of the Birmingham Atalanta club, with 18-2¾ (5.55) for a life-time best (she, like Joan, was aged 24), and 3rd was 16-year-old Lorna Lee, of Tonbridge, with 18-0 (5.48), another personal best, who turned 17 a fortnight before the Games.

The previous year Shepherd, an industrial chemist, had a best of 16-9¾ (5.12) in coming 2nd to Kathleen Duffy in the WAAA after winning the Essex and Southern titles. She had transferred to the long jump from the 220 and 440 yards which she had been running for the previous two years. For Erskine 1948 was the first year that she had tried the long jump, but she went on to win the WAAA title in 1949 and 1950 and was 3rd in 1951 – although with nothing like the distance she jumped in 1948 – and also won the Midlands 100 yards title. It was again a first year for Lorna Lee, who then won the Southern in 1949, with a personal best of 18-2½ (5.55), and was 3rd in the WAAA but after finishing 6th the next year was not heard of again for a very long time.

Particularly good chances of a British medal at the Olympics

When it came to the team selection Lee was preferred over the 1947 WAAA champion, Duffy, who had jumped 18-1 (5.51) behind Shepherd in the Southern but did not compete in the WAAA championships. And there was a fifth 18ft-plus long jumper in 1948 – Dorothy Tyler, still eight years from the end of her unequalled Olympic high-jumping career but already an evergreen.

There was no national press coverage of this wonderful improvement by the WAAA trio, even greater than normal in the British long jump pits, the graveyard of many a hopeful, and it made the chances of a British medal at the Olympics look particularly good. The world record-holder, Fanny Blankers-Koen (6.25 set in 1943), was not competing as she was already booked for four events – in every one of which she would win a gold medal. But on 4 August, when the women's long jump was held for the first time in the Olympics, there was that bitter disappointment for the British.

Instead of being among the leaders in the qualifying round, the British girls were at the tail end of the field. Erskine was 19th with 5.14, 41 centimetres less than at the WAAA. Lee was 20th with 5.12, 36 centimetres less. Shepherd, who might also have been injured, although there is no evidence of that, was a colossal 69 centimetres less, with 5.005. The winner with 5.695, half-a-centimetre less than Shepherd did in the WAAA, was Olga Gyarmati, of Hungary, who was to go on to reach the final again in the next two Olympics (10th in Helsinki, 11th in Melbourne). Gyarmati became a British citizen later after escaping the uprising in her native country and then went to live in the USA, but I was unable to get a reply to the letter I wrote to her, and I learned later that she died in October 2013. Had the British girls reproduced their Chiswick performances, they would have won Olympic gold and been 5th and 6th.

I was in the stands on that day at Wembley and cannot remember any problems. There were certainly no complaints about the men's long jump. But women's long jumping did not attract any attention then and is not the most popular event now. Mary Rand and Sheila Sherwood put it temporarily in the public domain, but few others in Britain have done so.

Among the salient features of the organisation at Wembley were the delays, including on the opening day the men's 400 metres hurdles heats, where the barriers had been set out wrongly, and later on during the decathlon, which continued until late into the night, hours behind schedule. So it is understandable that the officials for the women's long jump, held on the sixth day of competition, should have been under pressure to hurry things along. They had 26 competitors to cope with, each of them allowed three jumps, and even with no more than two minutes allowed per effort the qualifying round could have lasted as much as some 2 hours 40 minutes.

Only 10 of the competitors reached the qualifying distance of 5.30m, and whether they did so at their first or second attempts we know that at least 59 jumps must certainly have been taken. Preventing the competitors from marking their run-ups would surely have saved only 10-to-15 minutes. There had been 21 entries for the men's long jump five days before and the qualifications and final had been properly organised to take place on the same day. So why hadn't provision been made by the organising committee for the women's long jump to be arranged in advance along the same lines?

Among the officials a highly experienced referee and British long-jump internationals

There was no questioning the extent of the experience of the referee for the jumping events. He was Dr Sydney Best, who was headmaster of Doncaster Grammar School (now known as Hall Cross Academy) and had been elected vice-president of Yorkshire County AAA in 1926 and had served as committee chairman in the late 1930s and would do so again in 1949. He was appointed honorary coaching organiser for the North of England by the AAA in that latter year, and he was to be president of the Northern Counties AA in 1956. Among the 12 other male officials named for the Wembley Olympic jumps (including three more future NCAA presidents) was Sandy Duncan, a British international long jumper of the 1930s. One of the five women acting as field-event judges specifically for the women's events was the still reigning British long-jump record-holder after 22 years, Muriel Cornell. It seems most probable that Mrs Cornell, who died in 1996, was on duty for the long jump that day, and I wonder what she thought of the proceedings?

If the judges had ruled at the last minute that the jumpers could not mark the run-up it would have been catastrophic. It would be like going into a vast shopping-mall without a map and trying to find the store you wanted. Just standing on the runway without a marker to show you what you were doing, where you should be, where you should start from, would have made the competition hopeless. Some of the other 26 competitors are in all probability still alive – they would now be aged in their 80s or more – and maybe they know the answer. The officiating that day was certainly not up to the mark because Judy Canty, of Australia, was inadvertently allowed an extra jump after finishing out of a qualifying place before the judges discovered their mistake. Nevertheless, though she was a centimetre short of the qualifying distance, as was an American, Emma Reed, both were allowed through to the final to make up a round dozen.

And then I found Lorna Lee – now Mrs Lee-Price, living in Cardiff, aged 81, and no relation to the researcher, John Lee – and in her letter to me she wrote, "At long last I am relieved to have it confirmed by Joan (sorry to hear that she has passed away) that we were not allowed to mark our run-ups. I have maintained this for years but don't believe anyone accepted what I said was true because it sounded so unbelievable. The only explanation I can think of was the fact that originally we were told there would not be a preliminary jump-off. We were given very little time to get from the School of Domestic Science, where we were staying, to Wembley Stadium because the final was now taking place the same afternoon.

"At 11a.m. we were told to rush to the stadium, and when we got there we were told that we

Lorna Lee competing in the 1948 Olympic long-jump qualifying round.

could not mark our run-ups. Some were lucky and hit the board. I took off 18 inches from the board, and then off the wrong foot. No one can jump properly without a proper run-up, and all of us would have got into the final if we had been allowed to jump fairly. We only had to make 17ft 4in to qualify, but none of us were able to achieve that. We were all very disappointed, and I got very upset about it. For a long time no one would believe me when I told them". A fortnight later Lorna Lee jumped 18-5 (5.61) in an inter-club match.

Born on 16 July 1931, she had started long jumping in 1946, clearing the pit completely when a teacher at Wycombe High School, in Buckinghamshire, first suggested she tried the event. The next year she won the All-England Schools under-16 title at Hull, but she was mistakenly named as "Mona Lee", and that is why she has appeared in ranking-lists as an apparent "one-year wonder". When she was selected for the Olympics, her father bought her a £10 pair of spiked shoes – a lot of money in those days – and she was declared a "brazen hussy" by an official for slightly altering the cut of her shorts for easier leg movement.

Isn't this account of the 1948 Olympic women's long jump intriguing?

Author's note: many thanks to John and Dorothy Parlett for telling me about this Olympic controversy, and to Michael Sheridan for his immaculate research into the period from which the background facts are taken.

Note: the article was first published in "Track Stats", Volume 51, No.4, October 2013.

Glad that the Games would be in London, happy with the food parcels, honoured to be selected

In the days leading up to the opening of the 1948 Olympic Games two handsome young men were often seen at Wembley Stadium, running round the track while holding a heavy unlit torch. One was the Greek God look-alike and international 400 metres runner, John Mark, medical student and former president of Cambridge University Athletics Club. He was 6ft 2in (1.88m) and blond and had been chosen to carry and light the torch in the packed stadium on the day the Games opened. The other was John Fairgrieve, another medical student, an international sprinter and Cambridge wing-threequarter rugby Blue, who was three inches shorter and dark-haired.

Fairgrieve was his friend Mark's deputy and the man who would stand in for the torch ceremony if anything went wrong. As we all know, it did not, and on that boiling hot day at the end of July John Mark caused a gasp of astonishment at his genuine beauty as he entered the stadium, the torch held high, and ran round the track and up the stairs to light the flame that had been brought from Greece; a total of 1,415 runners having travelled 1,964 miles carrying the 960-gramme 47-centimetre long stainless steel torches designed by Ralph Lavers. Fairgrieve and Mark had met as schoolboy rugby players: Mark had trials for the Cambridge side but never played in the Inter-Varsity match – and there was one more difference. Fairgrieve made the Great Britain team for the Games at 200 metres, but Mark was not good enough for the 400 metres.

John Fairgrieve, now 85 and a retired consultant surgeon specialising in vascular surgery at Cheltenham General Hospital for 30 years, talked to me about those "Austerity Games" – although he and his team-mates never thought of them in those terms. They were just proud to be part of the Games, glad that they were being held in London, and happy with the benefits that came the way of those chosen, particularly the food parcels. Fairgrieve received his from a family in New Zealand but did not make a hog of himself on the contents. Rationing had made people accustomed to shortages, and as a medical student he knew the dangers of suddenly eating too much of the meat and eggs and other goodies that arrived.

He said, "In the food parcels I got there would be two pounds of choice meat and eggs, but no one with our rationing could have sat down and eaten that. We were just not used to it. We were very lucky to have the chance. When we were in the Olympic team camp at Uxbridge where the men were housed I would go down to the dining-hall where you could help yourself to anything you wanted. Three eggs or loads of bacon. It was marvellous to go and look at it, but you knew it was not good for you after what we were used to and I ate what we ate normally".

He continued, "John Mark and I were very good friends. He was chosen for the torch ceremony because of his looks. He was a good quarter-miler with a long stride and very fit. He looked like a Greek God and that's why they chose him. I was his deputy in case anything went wrong. I think Sir Arthur Porritt was the master-mind behind it all. He probably thought 'Look, I'll find a student runner. Have we got any among the medical students?' " Sir Arthur, a New Zealander, was a senior surgeon at St Mary's, where Mark was a student, and also on the organising committee for the Games. He had won a bronze medal behind Harold Abrahams in the 1924 Olympic 100 metres final and was one of King George VI's royal surgeons.

Fairgrieve recalls, "Sir Arthur was instrumental when it came to choosing. They were looking for a good-looking sort of chap as a fine example of British youth. He had to have a deputy in case of illness. I used to go down to Wembley with him two or three times and run round the track carrying one of the torches. We did a couple of laps just to get the feel of it. The torches we used were solid silver, unlike the ones they carried on the relay which were quite light. Our one was much heavier. It weighed a hell of a lot. You started the lap with it over your head and by the time you reached the bowl it was down to your knees. I could not keep it up, but John could. I was delighted for him to carry it because I'm sure I would have dropped it. It was a great responsibility if one had dropped it, particularly on the steps, and it would have been totally disastrous. He did it very well. Afterwards one of the torches was given to the King and Queen and another to John who kept it in a glass case at his home".

John Mark became a general practitioner in Liss, in Hampshire, and died from a stroke when only 66 in 1991. Fairgrieve says, "He and I had been friends since playing rugby against each other as schoolboys. He was a wing-forward and went on to play representative games". Fairgrieve, 5ft 11in (1.80m) tall and weighing 12 stone (76kg), on the track, did just as well. He was a part-time amateur who fitted in some athletics with his medical studies. He had run 2nd to Alastair McCorquodale in the 220 yards at the AAA Championships in 1948 and at the Games finished 2nd in the seventh heat of 12 in the first round of the 200 metres in 22.2, which was the same time as the winner, Gerardo Bonnhoff, of Argentina. In the second round, running in the outside lane six, Fairgrieve was just pipped for 3rd and qualifying by a South African, Abram van Heerden, in 21.9, with the eventual bronze-medallist, Lloyd LaBeach, of Panama, winning in 21.7 and Les Laing, of Jamaica, 2nd in 21.8.

Fairgrieve remembered, "I was very close to getting 3rd, but I was in the outside lane. So you had no one inside you to set your sights on. If I had been in an inside lane I might have run a wee bit better, but it was just the luck of the draw". He was not picked for the 4 x 100 metres relay in which the UK team finished 2nd and were promoted to 1st for a while after the USA team was disqualified on a possible change-over fault. Then the Americans were reinstated and so the hope of British gold went.

He was proud and honoured to be selected for the Games, but he thought the training beforehand was ridiculous. He said, "I was a part-time athlete. My medical studies came first. Before the Games Sandy Duncan was appointed my coach along with a group of others. He would get the three or four of us down to Victoria Park track – near where the new Olympic stadium is – to practise starts and other things. I would get up early at my home in Blackheath in south London and get the train to Charing Cross, do a full day at the hospital, and then finish around 5, 5.30. Then I would catch a train or bus to the track, and we would finish there around 7, and I would get back across London to Blackheath via the Blackwall Tunnel. Mother would have a meal waiting for me at 9 and then to bed.

"The next day was exactly the same. I was going to Victoria Park two or three times a week. It was not the way to train. It was absolutely ridiculous in those days. Nowadays that's what you have to do. As a medical student then the most important thing to do was pass your exams and put your training to one side".

"I was at the Uxbridge camp throughout the Games. They had a special stand at the stadium for the competitors to watch all the events and we would travel there on a coach. Six or seven of us in the relay squad shared a room and we had a gamble on placing the first three in the men's 100 metres. No one got it right, even though we knew all the runners and what they had done. The only person who made any money was the chap who organised it. He was quids in".

Fairgrieve was born in Greenwich, in south London, on 18 April 1926, and he had a successful athletics and rugby career at Imperial Service College, and after the college closed during World War II because pupils could no longer come from abroad, he went on to Haileybury, another

John Fairgrieve (far left) in action in his 1948 Olympic 200 metres heat. The winner (right) was Gerardo Bonnhoff, of Argentina.

public school. He went up to Caius College at Cambridge to study medicine in the autumn of 1945 where he gained his blue for both athletics and rugby, winning the 100 yards in the Inter-Varsity match in 10.4. His rugby career suffered badly due to injury, and during his time at Cambridge he had to have three of his four cartilages removed. It hit his rugby but not his athletics.

In 1946 he beat John Mark in the Cambridge sports 440 yards, but his friend turned the tables in the match against Oxford (though losing the 880 by inches) and Fairgrieve won the 100 yards in 10.5. He repeated this the next year when he won the inaugural 220 yards in the match in 23.2. Then 1947 was his most successful year. The main man in sprinting was Emmanuel McDonald Bailey, who came from Trinidad but ran for Britain in two Olympics, gaining bronze in the 100 metres in 1952 but coming 6th in 1948 through injury. Fairgrieve only beat him once, in a 120 yards handicap sprint at the Rangers sports in Glasgow off four yards where he hung on to win by four inches!

The outstanding native-born sprinter that year was John Wilkinson. He was a great talent at 19 who ran the fastest 200 metres by a European in 1947, 21.3, and won the World Student Games 100/200 metres double in Paris in 10.6/22.3 into a strong wind, with Fairgrieve achieving a lifetime best 10.7 and 21.6 in the heats, finishing 2nd in the 100 metres final in 10.8 and 4th in the 200 metres. He also finished 2nd to Bailey in the AAA 220 yards in 22.2 and was 3rd in his debut international against France at Stade Colombes in a metric 22.1 behind Wilkinson.

Fairgrieve recalls of Wilkinson, "John was a bit of a chump. He came to the hospital and started to smoke and put on a bit of weight and let himself go to the dogs, and when the time came he could not produce his results again". He also says of the France-GB match, "I still have a bit of that track left in my knee. I was in the medley relay and ran the second leg, 200 metres, and the third man, Paul Vallé, started too fast and I had to lean forward to give him the baton and fell. There is still part of the black dirt from the track in my knee. They could not get it out".

Fairgrieve had just three years at the top in athletics, and he never allowed it to get in the way of

113

his studies, but he enjoyed his running very much and had no regrets. He raced regularly between May and August for Cambridge University and later for United Hospitals when he was studying in London. He ran in their matches, in the Kinnaird Trophy, the Southern Championships, and the AAA Championships, in which he was 2nd in the furlong twice and was in the 1948 AAA title-winning Achilles 4 x 110 yards relay team after being 2nd the year before, and then in representative matches. He often won and was nearly always in the first three, with best times of 10.0 for 100 yards and 22.2 for 220 yards.

He fitted his training around his heavy medical studies and would either be at the track or would go for a run in the evening from home, three or four times a week. He said, "I preferred the 220. I was rather a slow starter and it gave me a little bit more time to get going", and he twice won that event at the triangular England & Wales-v-Scotland-v-Ireland matches which were held just after World War II. "The first year I was running for England and I won", he recalled. "By the next year the Scots had realised I was one of them as my parents were Scots and so they picked me and I won again this time for them".

His performances were good for those days but not world-class. He was never the best in the country, but he was always thereabouts. In his first year there was McDonald Bailey who would reign supreme in Britain until the early 1950s. In 1948 McCorquodale came out of the blue and finished in 4th place in the Olympic 100 metres final and then went back to cricket, to be replaced in 1949 by Nick Stacey (later a bishop) and Ken Jones, a rugby international whose biography was published in 2011.

Fairgrieve was 5th in the 1949 AAA 220 yards, 2nd to Wilkinson in the Inter-Counties for Kent, and in the winning Achilles 4x110 yards team at the London AC relay meeting. Then he finished with sprinting. He said, "In 1949 I stopped because I was coming up to my final exams and partly because I could not really be bothered to train very seriously. I knew that when I qualified and went into the Army to do my National Service I would have the chance to train, but I could not reproduce the form. So I played rugby for the depot – we usually reached the finals – and then I was the medical officer on a troop-ship to the Far East for the second year.

"I had my fill in Olympic year. I was running pretty well. In those days it was not like it is today. It was very much an amateur sport in which you gave as much time as you could. These professionals work at it all the time. The game is totally different to anything we experienced. I could not have spared the time in my day. The performances now are quite a lot better than ours. It was the same on the rugby field. The standard now is much better than the amateurs."

There were no drugs in his day. Fairgrieve, son of a mechanical engineer who won the Military Cross at the Somme in World War I, said, "As far as I was aware there were none. I knew of no one who took drugs. The only thing that anyone could have taken was amphetamines, which were available for patients. I suppose that might have enabled one in a quicker start, but it was just not mentioned".

He has four daughters and 10 grand-children and lives with his wife in a village just outside Gloucester. As a surgeon he has had his own fair share of surgery, too. Apart from losing three of his four cartilages, and never having had any trouble with them, so skilful were the surgeons, his hips went in later life, but the operations on them were not such a success and now he has motor neurone disease. He concluded our interview by saying, "I hope I will be fit enough to be at the Games in London".

Note: this article was first published in "Track Stats", Volume 49, No.4, December 2011. John Fairgrieve died on 20 July 2014, aged 88. He had been a spectator at the 2012 London Olympics and saw Usain Bolt win the 200 metres.

Dorothy Manley, Olympic Games 100 metres silver-medallist 1948

Three months under Sandy's keen eye, and the high jumper gets 100 metres silver instead

In the early spring of 1948 the international long jumper and AAA coach, K.S. ("Sandy") Duncan, took over a group of Olympic "possibles" at Victoria Park track in East London. Among the girls was dark-haired and attractive Dorothy Manley, who was on the list as a high jumper, but it was her running as she warmed up that caught Sandy Duncan's eye. He did not think she could make the grade as a high jumper – the first choice, Dorothy Tyler, was so much better and was to win the silver medal for a second time – but there was something about the newcomer's stride and action that he liked and thought he could improve upon.

Dorothy Manley, 1.65m (5ft 5in) tall and 7st 12lb (50kg) in weight, worked as a shorthand typist in the city, commuting each day from Manor Park, in Essex, and in three months she was transformed by Sandy Duncan from a county sprinter into an Olympic silver-medallist at Wembley behind the magnificent and unbeatable Fanny Blankers-Koen, of Holland. In fact, without the overwhelming presence of the Dutchwoman, Britain would have had three gold medals in the 100 metres, 200 metres and 80 metres hurdles, as Audrey Williamson and Maureen Gardner joined Dorothy Manley as silver-medallists.

Behind Dorothy's success there was also a story of determination and triumph over heartbreak because during the three months of training four nights a week and on Sunday mornings, racing most Saturdays, and her daily job, she was also travelling 16 miles twice a week to see her fiancé, Peter Hall, who was a production engineer but was seriously ill in hospital. Each night she was crying herself to sleep in despair as to their future. They were to marry and have three children (and four grandchildren and five great-grandchildren). After his death in 1973 she married an old friend, John Parlett, the 1950 Empire Games 880 yards and European Championships 800 metres champion, six years later. For this article in "Track Stats" I met and talked to them.

Dorothy was born in Manor Park on 27 April 1927 and her athletics career was short, starting with schoolgirl victories and then county titles at sprints and high jump for her club, Essex Ladies. Once Sandy Duncan, who was general secretary of the British Olympic Association for many post-war years, had taken over her training she shot up the ladder and continued at the top with European Championships medals, including the third leg in a wonderful victory over the Russians and the Dutch in the 4 x 100 metres relay in 1950, until suddenly in 1952 when building up to the Olympics that year she found she could no longer run. She was able to walk and jog but could not sprint at all any more.

She recalls: "It was weird. My legs just packed up on me, and I had lost my ability to move them to sprint. I could not even get through the heats of the Women's AAA in 1952. So I gave up. I had no idea what was wrong or why it happened". A year later she was diagnosed as suffering from a poisoned thyroid gland, but she never ran again. Once the problem was cleared up she was able to have children, and they became her life.

This experience on the track was all so different and sad compared with the start in the 1948 season, when with Sandy Duncan's guidance she moved into the front rank, winning big races against the best and taking her fastest time down by almost a second, making more use of arms, body, leg lift, stride and action.

She should have won the Women's AAA 100 metres, but Maureen Gardner, next to her, made a move before the start and they both expected the race to begin again, but the gun went off and they were left. "I finished 5th", Dorothy says. "They offered me a re-run, but I said all I wanted to know was whether it would affect my chances of getting in the team, and they said 'no' because I had already proved from other races that I should be included. So I let it go". With Winnie Jordan and Doris Batter 1st and 2nd in the Championships, Dorothy was in the Olympic 100 metres. It was her first international race.

She missed the opening parade because Sandy Duncan said she should not go out in the 80-degree heat with her race so close, and so she watched from the grandstand, instead. On the second day of the Games, 31 July, at 2.45pm she lined up for her 100 metres heat, wearing her home-made vest (all the girls had to make their own from materials provided) and with a ribbon in her hair. She said a prayer because she believed she had a God-given talent, and she was, and still is, a committed Christian, She won in 12.1, one-tenth slower than her lifetime best, with only the Dutch mother of two faster.

The next afternoon she won her semi-final in 12.4, and at 4:45pm in the pouring rain she lined up on the outside lane for the final. She says: "I was notoriously bad at starting, but on this occasion I think I got the best start of my life. In fact, I was away so well, and was in front of Fanny, that it went through my mind that I had made a false start, and I expected that we would be recalled. Now, I should not have been thinking that, and I obviously lost a little bit, but it would not have made any difference because Fanny would still have beaten me. She was fantastic and much faster and stronger than any of us".

The silver medal – excited, emotional and a single regret

Fanny won in 11.9, with Dorothy a stride behind in 12.2 (which would also have got her into the 1952 Olympic final), just ahead of Shirley Strickland, of Australia. "I was 2nd and I was so excited, overjoyed, and then there I was on the podium getting the silver medal. I was still a bit dazed and I was so emotional that I did not notice the Union Jack being hoisted. It's something I have always regretted."

The 1948 Olympic Games women's 100 metres final: 1 Fanny Blankers-Koen (Holland) 11.9, 2 Dorothy Manley (GB) 12.2, 3 Shirley Strickland (Australia) 12.2, 4 Viola Myers (Canada) 12.3, 5 Patricia Jones (Canada) 12.4, 6 Cynthia Thompson (Jamaica) 12.6.

It is interesting to compare Dorothy's attitude and her experiences before the Games with the hysterical razzamatazz that comes before and after every major championship now. She says: "I did not think of myself as a champion. I just thought, 'That's not me'. There was no great build-up at the time. I did not expect to get gold and I was just happy to be taking part. Someone said I did not put everything into it, that I did not have the 'win at all costs' attitude, and I said I did because l enjoyed it so much".

There was no fast car to take her down the competitors' special motorway lane to the stadium, as there was at the 2012 Games in London. She went by ordinary-service bus with the other girls and everyday passengers or by underground rail from the team house at a teachers' training college in Ecclestone Square, in Victoria. She recalls: "One of the girls said it was a red-light district, and I was so naive in those days that I did not know what she was talking about. I was not a girl of the world".

On the last day of the Games Dorothy ran the first leg in the 4 x 100 metres, in which Britain had won its heat in 48.4, but the team finished 4th in the final to Holland, Australia and Canada in 48.0, half-a-second behind the winners. Holland won only because Fanny Blankers-Koen, who had gone into London to buy a coat, managed to make it back with 20 minutes to spare after a delay on the journey. Her coach and husband, Jan, was tearing his hair out at Wembley, but Fanny picked up seven metres on the last leg to win her fourth gold medal.

The 1948 Olympic Games women's 4 x 100 metres relay final: 1 Holland (Xenia Stad de Jong, Jeannette Witziers-Timmer, Gerda van der Kade-Koudijs, Fanny Blankers-Koen) 47.5, 2 Australia (Shirley Strickland, Joyce King, June Maston, Elizabeth McKinnon) 47.6, 3 Canada (Diane Foster, Nancy McKay, Patricia Jones, Viola Myers) 47.8, 4 Great Britain (Dorothy Manley, Muriel Pletts, Margaret Walker, Maureen Gardner) 48.0, 5 Denmark (Grete Nielsen, Bente Bergendorff, Birthe Nielsen, Hildegard Nissen) 48.2, 6 Austria (Grete Jenny, Marie Oberbreyer, Grete Pavlousek, Elfriede Steurer) 49.2.

After the Games Dorothy's father took her to one side and told her not to let her success go to her head. It never did, and he was later to buy her the ironing-board she needed for her new home when she beat for the first time her great rival, Sylvia Cheeseman (later Mrs John Disley), at 200 metres. Dorothy finished an excellent season with the anchor leg for the British Empire against the USA at the White City. Then it was back to the normal routine, if you allow for the fact that her fiance was still seriously ill and the planned November wedding had to be cancelled. The marriage eventually took place the following April and she continued with her running career.

A switch to 200 metres and selection for the Empire Games in New Zealand

It was in 1949 that she changed from 100 to 200 metres while still taking part in the high jump for her club and winning the Essex titles. She was 2nd in the Women's AAA 100 metres in 12.2, 3rd for England against France and Holland (guess who won?), and she also ran 24.9 for 220 yards at the Highland Games behind the same lady and Cheeseman. Her performances earned her a place in the English team for the Empire Games in Auckland early in 1950, and this involved a four-month stay away from home on unpaid leave for a girl who was always homesick.

Dorothy says: "I changed to the 200 because I preferred running the distance. Originally I could not do it through lack of stamina training, but once I achieved that I really enjoyed it. Running round the bend gave me a feeling that you seemed to be going faster than on the straight. I did not know it at the time, but my left leg was half-an-inch shorter than my right".

John Parlett had also run in the 1948 Olympics and had finished a bitterly disappointed last in the 800 metres final after a lifetime best of 1:50.9 in the semis. He, too, qualified for the Empire Games team and met Dorothy in London before they sailed for New Zealand. They had also met briefly at the 1948 pre-Games training at Butlin's holiday camp when John sat opposite this girl with a winning smile. So he recognised her smile when they assembled for the long sea journey.

Dorothy says: "We sailed out on the 'S.S. Tamaroa' which was mainly a refrigeration ship which went round both New Zealand islands to pick up lamb at every port before bringing the sheep and the athletes home. It was a very happy trip, very much a social occasion, with everyone mixing – athletes, swimmers, boxers, rowers, wrestlers and cyclists representing England, Scotland and Wales, and three Nigerians. The trouble was that we did not do very well until after the Games on a tour of New Zealand, when I started winning races, even on the day we sailed for home. By then we were fit again, having eaten so well after all the rationing at home and put on weight".

She failed to reach the Games finals in the sprints but won a silver in the 660 yards relay (2 x 220 yards, 2 x 110 yards) and was 4th in the high jump, an event in which she had been entered but no one had told her so until she reached the stadium. Parlett, who won the 880 yards, experienced a similar surprise, not being aware that he had been entered for the mile. He saw his name on the programme when he reached the stadium to watch but did not have his kit with him and so could not run.

Dorothy arrived back in England in March, when there was a major row concerning the alleged boisterous behaviour and other minor indiscretions of certain girls in the team. All of this became a storm in a teacup and the "heavyweight" officials of those days, including Harold Abrahams and Jack Crump, sorted it out with a severe telling-off for the women's rulers for their lack of natural justice.

In June Dorothy was involved in a strange race in Amsterdam against the controversial Dutch sprinter, Foekje Dillema, who two years later became a man. She was so suspect that Fanny Blankers-Koen would not run against her. Dorothy did, and was 2nd as Dillema ran 24.1 for 200 metres.

The change of event provided Dorothy with her only WAAA title, when she beat Sylvia Cheeseman at 220 yards by a foot in 25.2. She also won against France in 25.2 for 200 metres and was 3rd in the European Championships, in Brussels, a second behind Fanny. She did not qualify in her heat of the 100 metres because of an incident in the changing-marquee half-an-hour before the start. She explains: "We used to take a concoction of glucose and lemon-juice, and I took a swig and it caught my breath. I found some foreigners, but they laughed when I asked for water, not understanding. I was choking because I could not breathe, and then I found the Ovaltine man – we got that free – and he gave me a drink. It was bizarre, but it meant that when I went to the start I was still shocked".

Not even Fanny can match the British women in the relay

Far better was the 4 x 100 relay, which she considers her best race. She ran the third leg to hand over the lead to June Foulds, and not even Fanny at her majestic best could prevent the British winning gold in 47.4. In the match against France in Paris in September, Dorothy again did 25.2 to win the 200 metres and was in the winning relay team.

The 1950 European Championships women's 200 metres final: 1 Fanny Blankers-Koen (Holland) 24.0, 2 Yevgeniya Sechenova (USSR) 24.8, 3 Dorothy Hall (Great Britain) 25.0, 4 Sofia Malshina (USSR) 25.0, 5 Bertha Brouwer (Holland) 25.0, 6 Zoya Dukhovich (USSR) 25.5.

The 1950 European Championships women's 4 x 100 metres relay final: 1 Great Britain (Elspeth Hay, Jean Desforges, Dorothy Hall, June Foulds) 47.4, 2 Holland (Xenia Stad de Jong, Bertha Brouwer, Grietje de Jongh, Fanny Blankers-Koen) 47.4, 3 USSR (Yelena Gokieli, Sofia Malshina, Zoya Dukhovich, Yevgeniya Sechenova) 47.5, 4 France (Rosine Faugouin, Micheline Ostermeyer, Colette Aitelli, Yvette Monginou) 48.5, 5 Italy (Maria Musso, Laura Sivi, Micaela Bora, Vittoria Cesarini) 48.7, 6 Yugoslavia (Spomenka Koledin, Milica Sumak, Mira Tuce, Alma Butca) 49.8.

1951 was a year when she should have improved but did not really do so. She lost her title to Cheeseman and again ran 2nd to her in the match against France in slightly slower times than the year before. She did clear a lifetime best of 5ft 1in (1.55m) in the high jump in one of the club matches in which she also loved to run the relays. The highlight of the season was the 4 x 220 yards world record at a floodlit meeting at the White City on 26 September: she, Cheeseman, Barbara Foster and Margaret Brian ran 1:41.4. The same night John Parlett (with Bill Nankeville, Frank Evans and Albert Webster) was in the world-record British 4 x 880 yards team.

Baton-changing from Dorothy Manley to Jean Desforges, the 1954 European long-jump champion, on their way to winning the 1950 Women's AAA 660 yards relay title for the Essex Ladies' club. This event (2 x 220, 2 x 110) was held from 1923 to 1960.

As usual, Dorothy did not train during the winter, and it was not until the next summer that she found that she had lost her sprinting talent. She says: "I had been to the training-camp preparing for Helsinki and I was getting a terrible burning sensation in my throat and neck. I had not improved in 1951 as well as I had done before and did not know why. And now my legs did not go and it was a very queer sensation. I found out why at the clinic in 1953. The doctor asked me how long I had had the swelling on my neck. I had been trying to dismiss it. She told me to go straight home and see my doctor, and within a week I was in hospital and it took five weeks to get me into condition for the operation. I had thyroid toxicosis, a poisoned thyroid gland. That was why I had not been able to conceive. After I had my daughter, I did a bit of running near home, but then the boys came one after the other and I was looking after them, which mattered much more to me than medals".

That was the end of her running career. "I enjoyed it very much" she recalls, "and it fitted into my life, but I would not like to be running now. You cannot compare it. I would not like to be running, with a manager telling me what to do. I was a free spirit, but I never let the side down".

She and John met again by chance in 1979. She was a young widow, he a divorcee, and they were married and still are.

Note: this article was first published in "Track Stats", Volume 44, No.1, February 2006.

Jack Braughton, Olympic Games competitor 5000 metres 1948

Racing until the age of 80. Still sprinting between lamp-posts at 90. The amateur realist never rests

On Saturday 31 July 1948 Jack Braughton took the morning off work and caught the No. 12 London Transport red bus from Peckham Rye to Wembley Stadium. The fare was 2½ old pence and he lost half-a-day's pay. He was off to the Olympic Games to run for Great Britain in heat one of the 5000 metres. Just over 15 minutes after the start of the heat he finished in 10th place and failed to qualify. He changed clothing and then caught the bus home for tea, a journey of over an hour. His participation in the Games was over.

How different it all is now, but for Jack that one race was a wonderful moment in a very long career. For he had been chosen to run in the greatest sports event in the world, the first Olympic games after World War II. Now aged 90, still running and ballroom dancing four times a week, he looks back on it with pride. He started running as a boy at school, choosing running against a possible career with Grimsby Town football club, and thus following his father's example,. He joined Cleethorpes Harriers, on the Lincolnshire coast, and then, when the club closed, he went to neighbours Grimsby Harriers, for whom he won the junior Eastern Counties cross-country championship in February 1939.

During his Army service he ran a bit, winning his battalion championships, and later, having married on D-Day, 6 June 1944, was posted out to India. There, as a building engineer with the Indian Army his group was sent to work on aircraft runways, and he won the state 1500 metres and came 2nd in the Indian championships at Mysore. He remembered, "I was a Warrant Officer and had a bearer called Jacob who looked after me. I hadn't done any running for a while and one night I saw him coming back from a run and I suggested that I went with him. He agreed and said if I went with him I would be safe". That's how Jack started on the trail that was to lead to Wembley.

He said, "When I got back to the UK I started running again. That would be 1946-47, and I went down to the Tooting Bec track in south London to join Belgrave Harriers. I had run with some of them, people like Charlie Smart, who was a good distance runner. I thought they trained there, but it was like being in a foreign country. I met the very young Gordon Pirie and Blackheath Harriers members. The Blackheath captain was an ex-Olympic sprinter, Charles Wiard, and after they had asked me what I did, I joined them. That was Sydney Wooderson's club and I ran against him. We had just moved into a flat at Peckham. So I went training at Hayes, where the club's headquarters is, and at the Ladywell track at Catford in south London. In 1948 I had my best year".

He had raced well in 1947 and Jack Crump, the British team manager, had ranked him 5th best three-miler on merit in Britain for the year. He finished 14th behind Wooderson in the 1948 Southern cross-country and 28th in the National in Sheffield, again behind Wooderson, who won a thrilling race with Vic Blowfield, of Belgrave, for his last major title before retirement. Blackheath finished 3rd in the team scoring.

Jack was working as a building-site manager, first in the private sector and then for many years with the Greater London Council. He only trained twice a week, but it was bringing results because in the London-to-Brighton road relay he ran a brilliant last leg to bring his club in 3rd, 16 seconds faster than his closest opponent. He went on to win the Surrey three miles, which would be a title he held until Pirie took over in 1952, in a personal best of 14:49.4 but did not run in the Inter-Counties Championships for his county. Peckham, where he lived, was in Surrey in those days. He remembered, "I was never picked for Surrey. I asked their team manager, George Pallett, why not and he said they never knew whether I was fit! I told him he should read the results in 'Athletics' magazine".

He dropped out of the Southern because of illness, then did 8:49.0 for 3000 metres, and in the AAA Championships three miles he ran 14:24.4 for a new lifetime best by 20 seconds, to finish 4th behind Willy Slijkhuis, of Holland, who would be the bronze-medallist in the Olympic 5000 metres. In 2nd and 3rd places in the AAA event were Alec Olney, of Thames Valley Harriers, and Bill Lucas, of Belgrave. Jack said, "It was one of the few times that Bill Lucas ever beat me. I knew I had to finish in the first three home runners to get in the team because they had announced that. So I was very happy to come 4th and get the third place on the team".

So it's the Olympics? Well, he can run in his own time, not mine

He had no coach, no mentor, just his own twice-a-week training, mixing speed-play with fast and slow bursts over the recreation ground and fields locally. His neighbours did not even know he was a runner, let alone an Olympian, until they saw him on television winning at the Surrey championships. He said, "My boss where I was working as a building site manager in the private sector would not give me time off for the Games. The team manager got in touch with him and was told that 'If he wants to run he runs in his own time, not mine'. I asked him, and he said the same. So I stayed at home for most of the Games doing a normal day's work. I took two days off unpaid.

"That was the way it was then. I did not get any help with my training, I did not get any food parcels, nothing, but I was very proud to be selected. We were living in a flat and saving for a house. My son, Graham, had not been born then and we could not afford to lose my pay".

He was not the only one in this predicament. Years later he met race-walker Harold Martineau, who was 5th in the Olympic 50 kilometres event and Martineau told him he had the same problem. Jack only went twice to the Games; the first time to the Opening Ceremony to march with the team and lose a day's pay. He went by public transport to the male athletes' village at Uxbridge to pick up his track-suit and blazer. He said, "My track suit was laid out on my bed – which I never used – ready for me, but someone had changed it and it would not fit me. I had given my dimensions for trousers, blazer and track-suit. Somebody had got a track-suit which was too tight for them. So I had to have the one on the bed. I went there again to warm up for my heat and met Zátopek. Somebody nicked my watch. I never got that back and I suspected a very well-built shot-putter who had just come out of prison".

Author's note: then came Jack's heat in front of a packed Wembley Stadium, including me. I remember the disappointment when all three of our men failed to qualify. I don't know whether it was the occasion or nerves or the sultry strength-tapping weather, but whatever it was all three were not the men of the AAA Championships of almost a month before and they ran without any show of aggression.

Jack said, "I did not get much out of it. There was not much to cheer about. I was just not fit enough. End of story. I ran much slower than I did normally. Just one of those things. I had no coach, no one to fall back on. In those days it often went that way. The people in charge were always looking for university students and people with plenty of time to train. Some time later I had a letter from the AAA asking if I could take six months off and go to New Zealand to race. Of course I could not afford to take six months off. You had to be able to afford it. It has all changed now. It has gone right the other way".

His Olympic heat was won by Evert Nyberg, of Sweden, in 14:56.2 from Vaino Koskela, of

Finland, a tenth behind, with Curtis Stone, of the USA, 3rd another three-tenths behind and Marcel van de Wattyne, of Belgium, 4th in 15:14.0. Jack trailed in untimed, bitterly disappointed. The next heat saw Erik Ahldén, of Sweden, have a great battle with Zátopek, winning by inches on the line in 14:34.2, and the last heat saw Slijkhuis jog in two-tenths of a second ahead of the man who would win the gold medal, Gaston Reiff, of Belgium (Zátopek's mad dash over the last 300 metres in the driving rain just failed). After his heat Jack caught the bus home and had tea with his wife who had not gone to watch but asked if he had enjoyed the run. His mother had refused an offer from her local newspaper in Grimsby to bring her down to London.

Braughton said, "I never went back to the Games, just went to work as usual. No one else wanted to know if you were there at the Games. No one queried why you were not there. I could have been dead and buried as far as they were concerned. I just turned up and did what I had to do. It was just like any athletics meeting. No one asked. It was not much of a thing in those days. There was no money in it. It was just a sport that people enjoyed. I did not allow athletics to interfere with my home life. That had priority. Until I was 80 I was racing and enjoyed it. I never ran for Britain again. I did not have the time. I did not look to do it. I was just happy to get out and run, and that is what I did, and I was always available to run for the club. Eventually, like everyone else, I had plenty of time to get out and run. Later I was able to make time but sadly not in 1948. But I enjoyed my life".

A marathon debut and a personal best at three miles a week later

The Olympics were not the end of his career, far from it. He ran 14:32.8 for three miles in 1949 and continued to win county titles. Probably his best achievement came in 1955 when, trained by Franz Stampfl, he caught the coach's anger when he ran in the Poly marathon a week before the Southern three miles. In each he did a lifetime best. He only ran the marathon to make up the numbers in the team event when one of the Blackheath men dropped out. He finished 6th in his first race over the distance in 2:36:44, 10 minutes behind the winner, Bill McMinnis. When Stampfl heard about this he was furious. But his anger subsided when Jack finished 7th in the Southern in 13:51.0 – the first three miles in Britain where eight runners broke 14 minutes. The winner in an inches finish was Frank Sando from Ken Norris in 13:29.8.

"At 80 I ran out of opponents", Jack said. He won veterans' titles and broke age records until then. He was a familiar figure all over the country, always wearing his woollen bobble hat.

In their book, "The Centenary History of the Blackheath Harriers", Tony Weeks-Pearson and D.K. Saunders described him thus: "This man was one of the most relaxed and graceful movers the club has ever had and a great asset on track, road and country. The outstanding distance runner of the club track team in this period (1948-1950s), he possessed the smooth inexorability of leg action that one associated with the superlative Finnish distance runners and performed with distinction over a variety of distances from the half mile to the marathon. Apart from some fine runs in the London-to-Brighton relay, he was one of the only ones to attempt to challenge the overwhelming supremacy of Jim Peters and Stan Cox at the marathon. He was also one of the few runners directly following the war to see the necessity for British distance men to increase their training in order to match the performances of continental athletes like Zátopek. But there was always a hard-headed common-sense and realism about this northerner which recognised a limit to what amateurs like himself could achieve in this coming age of full-time athletics".

Jack said, "I'm still pretty fit. I slip out and jog round the park at the rear of my house. One neighbour who had watched me said to another 'He doesn't seem to get any faster, does he?'. I enjoy running two or three miles. I race between lamp posts, jog between two, race between three. It keeps me fit". And so does his ballroom dancing four times a week. He is also a director of the companies that look after the Blackheath Harriers club headquarters and the track at Bromley, and he helps with judging and anything else "whenever I am needed".

The happy 90-year-old widower concluded, "If I die tomorrow I have had a good time. That's what life is all about. Not to have won but taken part."

Jack Braughton was born in Grimsby, Lincolnshire, on 22 February 1921. Height: 5ft 8½in (1.74m). Weight: 10st 2lb (64kg). Best performances: 1 mile 4:12.0, 2 miles 9:23.0, 3 miles 13:51.0, 6 miles 30:01.0, Marathon 2:36:44.

Note: this article was first published in "Track Stats", Volume 49, No.2, June 2011. Jack Braughton died on 30 October 2016, aged 95.

Wearing his habitual woollen hat and his 1948 Olympic uniform, Jack Braughton takes part in a typical grass-track meeting of his post-war competitive era.

Sylvia Cheeseman, Olympic Games bronze-medallist 4 x 100 metres relay 1952

Wonderful times, travel, fun, friends. Never a false start. Always the chance to catch up

The article that the 17-year-old Sixth Form grammar school-girl read in the newspaper stated that the first post-war women's athletics championships were going to take place the next weekend. She was an outstanding sprint talent but had only run in a school relay team, though it was a mighty successful one that had beaten every other school in the London area. Not surprising really because two of the team were to become Olympians.

The school-girl rang a sports news agency that she found listed under "Athletics" in the phone-book and they gave her the number of the Women's AAA. The lady she spoke to was helpful. After telling her caller that the entries were closed for the 1945 championships she suggested getting in touch with the nearest club to her home in Richmond, which was Spartan Ladies. Within a year the girl was a winner at the Women's AAA Championships and was on board the ship to Oslo to run for Great Britain in the first post-war European Championships. There, in the first heat of the first event on the first day, she was drawn against the great Fanny Blankers-Koen (of whom she had never heard), who brought out her starting-blocks. The novice watched in awe and amazement as she dug her own starting-holes. She lost, coming 2nd in 12.8 to Fanny's 12.4.

Sylvia Disley (née Cheeseman), dark-haired, attractive, vibrant, loquacious and not looking her age, sat on the sofa in the upstairs lounge in the very pleasant home where she and her husband to whom she has been married for 51 years, John Disley, live near Hampton Court, in London, and talked. "I was very disappointed", she remembers. "I didn't know who Fanny Blankers-Koen was. Later we became very great friends. She was a great one for one-upmanship. She would say she had hardly run, say, the 200 metres and her times were terrible, and then after telling this great big lie she would run a fantastic race".

Sylvia was 5th in her 100 metres semi-final in Oslo (Blankers-Koen fell in the other semi-final) and then came 5th in the final of the 200 metres in 25.8sec. The British 4 x 100 metres relay team was 4th. For a school-girl who had still to take the equivalent of GCE "A" levels, it was not a bad performance. It was her first trip abroad, and on the way out on the ship she had talked on the deck one evening to the legendary Sydney Wooderson, who would take the 5000 metres title in Oslo in the 2nd fastest time ever run. "I remember he said about the Olympic Games, 'I don't think they are all that they are cracked up to be', and I have always remembered that. I always think how right he was. Steve Ovett much later said the same, although he won a gold. You have to be lucky on the day. For every gold-medal winner there are scores of people who do not win. You have to be philosophical about it".

Yet she is not. The one subject that she is reluctant to talk about is her participation in the Olympic Games of 1948 and 1952. She did not perform at her best, and that left her with the feeling that her athletics career was not properly fulfilled. It's a shame because her record is an excellent one, including a bronze medal in the sprint relay in Helsinki in 1952 as the superb all-star Australian team led by Marjorie Jackson dropped the baton when 100 per cent certainties for the gold, just as the German girls had done in 1936. "But the thing of which I am most proud", Sylvia says, "is winning seven Women's AAA sprint titles, and no one has done that ever since."

Born on 19 May 1929, athletics started for her as a little girl – mother a concert pianist, father a bass player so good that Sir Thomas Beecham made him a founder-member of the Royal

Philharmonic Orchestra, and a sister who was an international model – when she discovered she could beat all the other boys and girls when it came to running. When she won a scholarship to grammar school in Isleworth she decided that she could win the school athletics championship but was told at the age of 13 that she would not do so because the favourite was Doris Batter (who was also to run in the 1948 Olympics). Sylvia arrived late, knew nothing about racing, and just ran when the whistle was blown (yes, they used whistles in those days). Doris Batter went like the wind, but Sylvia caught her at 80 yards and won in the manner that she was always to do.

"It was the pattern for the rest of my career", Sylvia says. "I always had the stamina to get ahead at the end. I just could not start until I was taught to do so. I was quite capable of falling over or getting my legs crossed. It happened once in the semi-final of the Women's AAA championships 100 when a man from our club kept shouting for me to bend my arms, which I did and fell flat on my face when the gun went! That's why I chose the 220 yards as my main event because it gave me the chance to catch up".

When she joined Spartan Ladies she was picked for the "B" race in an early-season meeting in 1946 on a wet thick grass track at Epsom. She turned up and ran in sixpenny plimsolls and a divided skirt and won in a faster time than the internationals who had competed in the senior 100 yards. Later, as a competitor at the European Championships, she learnt two lessons: not to look round as she had done at least twice, according to Harold Abrahams, and also that some of the female competitors had stubble on their chins and spoke in deep baritone voices. Two of those who beat her were later thrown out when the authorities brought in scientific sex testing.

The first starting-blocks and a pair of spiked shoes

In 1947 Sylvia passed her school examinations, although university was not an option for her because of the government policy of giving priority to men and women returning from the services. She remembers, "In my last year at school, when I was head girl, we had a new games master – the school was co-educational – who had been in Africa during the war with Geoff Dyson, and he put me in touch with Geoff, who had just been appointed chief national coach. I went with him to Parliament Hill Fields track to do an exhausting afternoon of circuit training, and he told me I did not know how to start. He was already coaching Maureen Gardner, whom he was later to marry, and he suggested that we apply for the games course at the Loughborough College summer school. In the afternoons, when the men had finished with the track, we had top-class coaching and Sandy Duncan taught me how to start. Since then I never had a false start in my career. I still cannot understand how people do it. There is no excuse for it. I was the first woman in the country to get starting-blocks, and I never had any trouble after that. I was also given spikes to replace my plimsolls".

Having won the WAAA 220 yards in 25.7sec in her first year of competition in 1946, she retained her title the next year in 25.0 and was 2nd to a stubbly Frenchwoman in the GB match against France. Being coached by Duncan, a pre-war GB long-jump international and one of the country's best Olympic managers of the future, meant her travelling across London and finding part-time jobs that fitted in. She tore a hamstring, which took a long time to heal, but she prepared for the Games and won the WAAA 200 metres (not 220 yards) in 25.7 from Margaret Walker and Audrey Williamson. Yet at Wembley it was all different with Williamson getting the silver medal behind Blankers-Koen and Sylvia going out in the semi-finals. "I don't like to think about it", Sylvia says. "I just did not do my best. Geoff Dyson used to say that it was 90 per cent perspiration in training but 90 per cent psychology and only 10 per cent perspiration on the day. The Olympics have that extra stress. I was also a stone overweight, partly due to the hamstring problem".

She considers 1949 to have been her best year. She had her tonsils removed and was working on the fringes of the newspaper industry in which she was keen to become a reporter. She was recovered from her injuries and won her fourth successive WAAA title in the longer sprint (25.4 for 200 metres) and also won the 100 metres to complete the double. She ran 2nd for England at both 100 and 200 metres in a match against Holland and France at the White City, beaten in both races by a Dutchwoman, Foekje Dillema, who was later identified as a man. Sylvia's 200 metres time of 24.8 equalled the British record set by Dorothy Saunders in 1937 and she may well have done another 24.8 for 220 yards a few days later when only Fanny Blankers-Koen's final stride managed to defeat her by inches at the Highland Games in Edinburgh. Fanny's time was 24.8, but Sylvia's was not reported, even though 2nd place to Fanny at 80 metres hurdles was timed in a Scottish record. In any case, Sylvia then improved to 24.5 in a club match a week after that and was in a record-equalling 660 yards relay team (2 x 220, 2 x 110) and ended the year joint 2nd fastest in the world at 200 metres with the South African, Daphne Robb, to Fanny's best of 24.3.

Then came the incident which almost 60 years later still rankles

Sylvia was selected for the England team for the Empire Games in Auckland in February 1950, and this meant a four-month trip sailing there and back on the "S.S. Tamaroa", from which she sent progress reports to "Athletics Weekly". The women's team manager was Mrs Ruth Taylor, a middle-aged lady and wife of a rich Northern industrialist, and she took an instant dislike to Sylvia, who she called "Cheeseman", though referring to all the others in the team by their Christian names. The result of her antipathy was a report to the WAAA accusing Sylvia and her friend, Doris Batter, of not being amenable to discipline, and the WAAA promptly suspended the pair for a year without a trial or the girls even knowing what charges had been brought.

It led to an immediate appeal by the girls, and the two leading athletics officials of the time, Harold Abrahams (a barrister as well as an administrator) and team manager Jack Crump, set up a tribunal to hear all the charges and the evidence, with a chance to cross-examine. The tribunal found that the charges were "of very small significance" and that though there were faults on both sides Mrs Taylor took her responsibilities too seriously and "her ideas of what discipline should be were exaggerated".

In the report which dismissed the charges, Abrahams and Crump stated quite clearly what they felt: "It is almost inconceivable that the General Committee of the Women's AAA should have entirely ignored some of the elementary principles of justice. They found that these two athletes were not amenable to discipline on the uncorroborated and unchallenged word of the Team Manager. No opportunity was afforded the two athletes of cross-examining or repudiating the statements of Mrs Taylor, and indeed they had no knowledge (until after they had been condemned and their punishment decided upon) of what the charges were".

The matter caused an outrage at the time, and would still do so today. Sylvia remains very angry about what happened, and particularly because the WAAA would not tell her what the charges were, nor what the evidence was. Of her accuser she says, "She was an old battle-axe who took against me for some reason. She was a Northerner who hated all Southerners. I was always polite and obedient and stuck to her rules. I wanted to sue and to take legal action, but in those days we could not afford it. There was no money in the sport. We competed for fun". It was not until August, five months after the team had returned from New Zealand and two months after the two athletes had been suspended, that the tribunal gave its verdict. You can read all of it in the issue of "Athletics Weekly" for 5 August 1950.

Sylvia gives examples of what the charges were: "She accused me of being on the deck in my dressing-gown and pyjamas with my swimmer boy-friend, which was totally untrue. On another occasion we relay runners went on strike because she said that I was not to run the first leg but

Sylvia Cheeseman wins a 100 yards race from Doris Hatton (née Batter) at the Parliament Hill Fields track in North London in 1952. They both went to the same school and both were selected for the 1948 Olympic Games.

could not say which leg it should be. We stayed sitting down and no one talking for over an hour until Sandy Duncan came and had a word with her and the original order of running stayed. My case was helped, I think, because the press was on my side. They ran articles about me living at home with my mother, and my working for the 'Sporting Record' and later 'World Sports' before joining 'The Star' evening newspaper as a reporter, and being a clean-living, hard training twice a week, home-loving girl. And it was true". She had her photograph on the front page of the "Daily Express" with the headline, "Who is Sylvia? What is she?"

She does, however, think there was a touch of revenge that left her out of the European Championships, even though she only lost her 200 metres title at the WAAA Championships by inches to Dorothy Manley (later Mrs John Parlett). "I had a throat infection and had a penicillin injection that morning from a doctor who told me not to run, but I did and only just lost", Sylvia says. "They did not pick me. They were getting back at me". In September she ran 2nd against France at 200 metres and won the Waddilove Trophy 100 yards just to show she was not finished.

In 1951 she had a good year, retaining her WAAA title, winning against France, and being in the 4 x 220 yards/4 x 200 metres teams that broke the world record. One of these records was at Motspur Park in September running for her club, and then came another at the White City a week later. "It was under floodlights, and I just loved running under the lights as it gave me a lift", she enthuses. It was a good note on which to end a pre-Olympic season.

But things again went wrong in 1952, and after winning the WAAA title in 25.9 for 220 yards with a swollen knee her form had gone by the time she got to Helsinki for the Olympics. She went out in the 200 metres semi-finals in 24.7, though getting a bronze medal in the 4 x 100 metres relay, and then came wins against France and Italy in 24.7 and 25.0 and a share in another 4 x 200 metres world record as part of a Southern Counties team late season under the White City floodlights. "I needed a sports psychologist that year", she says. "I did think of becoming one later on because I think you need to have been in the sport in that position to do it really well. One of my daughters who took part in athletics, and might have done well if she had persevered, is training to do it now".

That was really the end of Sylvia's career. She ran occasionally in the years that followed, but injuries to an Achilles tendon and a hamstring put paid to any chances of getting back to international level. In 1957 she married John Disley, and they have two daughters, each with two children. Sylvia's journalistic career took her as a freelance to China, to Paris for fashion shows, and all over Europe until she wrote a book about a dancer and retired. "I had some wonderful times, travel, fun and friends. It was good", she concludes.

Note: this article was first published in "Track Stats", Volume 47, No.3, September 2009.

Bill Nankeville, European Championships bronze-medallist 1500 metres 1950

Not afraid to hold his own: Britain's master of the miling art of "argy bargy"

George William Nankeville (always known as Bill) was the "step" from Sydney Wooderson's successor, Doug Wilson, to Roger Bannister, who set up the base-camp from which Seb Coe, Steve Cram and Steve Ovett eventually reached the summit of British and world miling. Nankeville was a fine miler with his tall, upright, barrel-chested style and his brightly-coloured shorts, and he was a doughty competitor who was not afraid to hold his own in any argy-bargy that he might find – particularly when racing against fellow-Europeans in the late 1940s and early 1950s who were then the world's elite.

He survived two major incidents in his life to become Britain's leading miler. At the age of 15 he was playing cards in the tool-room of the aircraft factory where he worked, helping to make Wellington bombers, when 135 people were killed in a German air-raid and yet he escaped injury. He was not so lucky when he was given a car-ride while serving in Germany at the end of World War II. The vehicle crashed and he did not regain consciousness until he was back in England to find that all his ribs were broken and that he had contusion of the lungs.

He overcame this setback, and his running career, which had already started in the services, really took off when he became an Olympic "possible" in 1947 after finishing 3rd in his first AAA mile final to the Hungarian, Sándor Garay, and to the Dutchman who was to become a regular rival, Willy Slijkhuis. The following winter the AAA provided Nankeville with coaching from the legendary Bill Thomas, who had advised Jack Lovelock, Empire mile champion Reg Thomas, Olympic silver-medallist Jerry Cornes, and many Oxford University athletes. Under Thomas's tutelage Nankeville was Britain's No.1 until 1951, when the up-and-coming Bannister was just that bit faster. Nankeville's career included 6th in the 1948 Olympic 1500 metres (3:52.6) and 3rd in the 1950 European Championships 1500 metres (3:48.0) to Slijkhuis.

Nankeville was then in the form of his life and one of the favourites for the 1952 Olympic 1500 metres title ahead of the eventual surprise winner, Josy Barthel, of Luxemburg, whom he had always beaten when they raced, but all his plans went wrong on the turbulent flight out to Helsinki. In a rickety and drafty plane he became so ill that he went down with flu and was eliminated in the 1500 semi-finals. The marathon runners, Jim Peters and Stan Cox, suffered a similar experience on the same aircraft, and that was thought to be the reason for their failure in the Games.

Nankeville was the holder of three world relay records, at 4 x 880 yards, 4 x 1500 metres and 4 x 1 mile, along with Bannister, Chris Chataway, and the 6ft 4in (1.93m) tall Cambridgeshire miler, Don Seaman, whose promising career was cut short at the age of 22 with Achilles tendon troubles. At 5ft 10½in (1.79m) and 10st (63kg) in his racing days, and born on 24 March 1925, Nankeville went to the same school as the great cricketing twins, Sir Alec and Eric Bedser (who still play 36 holes of golf most days at the age of 81), and became a member of Walton Athletic Club, in Surrey. He won the AAA mile title on four occasions, in 1948-49-50 and again in 1952, when he beat a future world record-holder, John Landy, and lost to Bannister in a fast race in 1951, 4:07.6 to 4:08.6.

Nankeville enjoyed his finest season in 1953, but Bill Thomas's death that year was the main reason for his retiring from athletics at the age of 30. Recollecting the facts 45 years later, he recalled: "I was upset when he died, and things went sour. It was never the same again without

129

Bill. The main difference between doing it yourself rather haphazardly and having a coach was that you had someone to lean on and had a programme to work to. Bill was wonderful. He made everything. He inspired confidence and he worked me tremendously hard. He was one of the old school of coaches like the professional boxing trainers. He did not do it very scientifically. He did it naturally. When I first asked him to train me his reply was – and I can still remember the exact words – 'Yes, lad, but you'll have to learn to run first!'."

Training became gentle jogging on Sundays, a two-mile warmup and then some 300-yard or 600-yard efforts or an occasional ¾-mile time-trial during a 75-minute session on other days, followed by a race on the Saturday. But it did not always go smoothly, and Nankeville remembers that "to begin with in 1949 I went through such an awful time that I was going to pack it in, and my wife didn't come to watch me when I ran in the AAA that year because things were so low, but in the rain and storm that afternoon things suddenly came right, thanks to Bill, and I ran my best performance, 4:08.8, for a Championship record. No one could have beaten me that day, and I was three seconds clear of the field".

A good lunch. A glass of wine. Then an introduction to international athletics

His running career had started at school. He tried the sprints but without success, and so his teacher suggested the half-mile. Nankeville clicked. He was a natural, and he was 3rd in the All-England Schools final at the age of 14 and won the Southern junior title when he was 17 and working in the aircraft factory. When he joined the army his Belgian foreman at the factory gave him the address of relatives in Brussels, and when he went there to enjoy a good lunch and a glass of wine, he inquired about athletics. He was taken straight down to the Union St Gilloise club to which the great Gaston Reiff (Olympic 5000 metres gold-medallist in 1948) belonged, and the young English soldier promptly won an 800 metres race wearing baggy NAAFI shorts and battered spikes.

"That's how it all started," he says, "and I was in the winning round-Paris relay team, but after another relay win in Hanover I was involved in the car crash". A few months later, and fully recovered, Nankeville was back in Berlin and won the British Army of the Rhine 800 and 1500 metres titles. He became friends with Gerhard Stöck, the 1936 Olympic javelin champion, and joined his club in Hamburg where Stöck and another German named Stackmatt coached him to victory in the European inter-army championships 1500 metres in 4:01.6.

Back in England for an Army physical training course in 1947, Nankeville finished 3rd in the AAA mile in a time of 4:18.8, a long way behind Garay's 4:10.6. Virtually self-taught, he made his international debut with a time of 4:00.2 for 3rd place at 1500 metres in the match against France in Paris, broke four minutes for the metric mile for the first time with 3:59.0 when representing the Combined Services, and ran an estimated 1:52.4 from a 10-yard start in a handicap half-mile in Glasgow. The difference that Bill Thomas's coaching made to him in terms of mixing stamina and speed in training most days was obvious in Olympic year when he won the AAA mile in 4:14.2 despite a stomach upset and then ran a great race in the mud and the rain at the Wembley Olympics to finish sixth, 2.8sec behind the Swedish winner, Henry Eriksson, 3:49.8 to 3:52.6.

The next year was even better. After a rough race in the Southern mile in which Dick Morris, who had also run in the Olympic 1500 metres, beat him but was disqualified, Nankeville came good in the AAA, defeating Morris among others. Earlier in the year he had gone on an hilarious trip to Lahore with Jack Crump as team manager during which the English team of five took the salute at a military parade, and then won all their events, but had no money because the British authorities had not provided expenses. So Nankeville and his team-mates had to rely on the hospitality of a travelling British salesman!

Another win at the White City for Bill Nankeville, wearing his famous purple shorts. This was at 1500 metres at the British Games on 31 May 1952 in 3:49.0, beating Peter Robinson (Cambridge University), Don Gehrmann (USA) and Don Seaman.

Nankeville had become a sales representative himself after leaving the army, working for a leading sportswear company before eventually setting up on his own, selling many and varied goods – and still doing so now from time to time. As he says, "We were relatively poor, and that gave me a driving ambition to do better than that in running and in business".

He ran 4:10.4 for the mile when losing to Jean Vernier (one of French middle-distance twins) in the GB-v-France match at the White City on 1 August and then beat his friend, Gaston Reiff, at 1000 metres in Brussels, winning in 2:24.4 after going through 800 metres in a lifetime best 1:53.4. With laps of 63, 67, 63 and then 58.8, Nankeville retained his AAA mile title in 1950 in 4:12.2 ahead of the British Empire three miles champion, Len Eyre, and Alan Parker, who was to be a 1952 Olympic 5000 metres finalist. Nankeville ran several other fast races at 1500 and the mile, but saved his best for the European Championships 1500 final in Brussels, where he was leading almost to the tape before losing out to Slijkhuis (3:47.2) and the Frenchman, Patrick El Mabrouk (3:47.8), to clock the fastest ever by a Briton of 3:48.0.

Bannister took the bronze medal at 800 metres in those same championships but returned to the mile in 1951 and, as previously mentioned, beat Nankeville for the AAA title, with the 1950 Empire/European champion at two laps, John Parlett, in 3rd place. Against France at the White City, Nankeville won from Parlett and El Mabrouk in 4:11.0, and he then ran the first leg of the world-record-breaking 4 x 800 metres in 1:53.4, followed by Albert Webster (5th in the 1952 Olympic 800 metres), Frank Evans and Parlett for an aggregate time of 7:30.6. Nankeville's build-up to the Olympics under Bill Thomas's watchful eye was impressive and formed the basis for his great hopes for gold.

Another AAA mile title, but Olympic hopes are dashed on the flight to Helsinki

He ran 2:58 for ¾-mile in training, recorded times of 3:54.6 and 3:49.0 for 1500 metres, and set an English native record for 1000 yards in finishing a stride behind the American indoor specialist, Don Gehrmann, at the White City. He retained his AAA mile title in 4:09.8 ahead of Landy and David Law, who was also to figure in the 1954 British Empire Games final. Then, with his legs drained from the flu bug, he was 9th in his 1500 semi-final at the Helsinki Olympics and had to watch as Barthel ran the race of his life to take the gold and Bannister finished 4th.

During the 1953 season Nankeville was involved in two more successful relay record-attempts. The first of them was the 4 x 1 mile in 16:41.0, 17 seconds ahead of the Great Britain "B" team, with Chataway running 4:11.8, followed by Nankeville's best ever of 4:06.6, Seaman's 4:15.0 after setting off too fast, and Bannister's 4:09.4. Then came the 4 x 1500 metres with Ralph Dunkley, David Law, Gordon Pirie (in his year of years) and Nankeville (running the last and slowest leg of 3:53.6) achieving 15:27.2, nearly two seconds ahead of the Swedish national team. Running superbly, Nankeville set a personal best 800 of 1:52.4 behind future world record-holder Roger Moens, of Belgium, at the British Games, was 3rd in 4:10.4 behind Bannister (4:05.2) and Seaman in the AAA mile, and then had times of 3:52.0 for 1500 metres against Germany and a personal best 3:46.6 against Sweden while on tour with the GB team. He ended the season at home with his fastest winning mile time of 4:07.4.

The 1954 season, though, was a disappointment and he gave up athletics at the end of it to concentrate on business. He did not run fast enough in the early-season races to challenge for an Empire Games place and was out of the first six in the AAA mile and not good enough for the European Championships team. He finished his career with a meeting record 1:58.4 for 880 yards, representing his Walton club.

How good was he? Well, he reckons he could have run 4:02, given regular competition on the Continent where the racing was fast and furious. "We didn't get the chance of races there and we didn't have the pacemakers like Bannister did," he points out. But he knows that he was not a four-minute miler and believes that Sydney Wooderson would have beaten four minutes long before Bannister did if there had not been a war. He remembers how the university runners like Bannister and Chataway had the advantage over those who worked for a living.

"They had much more free time and could train every day. They had long holidays and there were no problems for them in getting away for internationals and long trips. It was a bit of 'them and us', and they kept mainly to themselves. They were very nice but a different breed. You tend to be different if you go to Oxford. You get an air of superiority and of supremacy. Bannister was up in the sky but a nice enough guy."

Nankeville also believes that the difference between the tracks on which he ran and the all-weather surfaces of today is worth about two seconds per lap in the mile. "The tracks we raced on were cinders, which were sometimes inches deep and not rolled, or they were grass. The food after the war was awful. It was stodgy, but there were still some great eaters like Derek Pugh (1950 European 400 metres champion) who would get through three lunches!

"Glucose gave us a boost, but drugs were unheard of. We trained and raced together, and at one time I was the only one who owned a vehicle – an old van with no heater. Athletics was not so serious then. A lot of fun. Happier times, I think. There was no money like now, and often very little in the way of expenses. One other thing I have noticed is that there are far more injuries now. No one pulled muscles in our day".

Now, at the age of 75, Bill Nankeville's main interests are as an assistant to his nationally-known comedian son, Bobby Davro, and in working for golfing and boxing charity events.

Note: this article was first published in "Track Stats", Volume 38, No.3, September 2000.

Sheila Lerwill, world record-holder High jump 1951-54, European Championships gold-medallist 1950, Olympic Games silver-medallist 1952

There are more things to life than merely winning an Olympic silver medal – like netball!

The tall erect but silver-haired lady who walks like someone 20 years younger as she strides across the South Downs above her home by the sea in Sussex with her lurcher dog, Jet, is there every day at 07:30. She walks hard for 90 minutes and more and only uses her stick for down hill. Uphill invigorates her. At the age of 81 she is extremely fit and active despite two hip replacements.

Her name is Sheila Lerwill (née Alexander), the first British woman high jumper to hold the world record after World War II. Before her was her great rival, Dorothy Tyler (née Odam), who set the record in 1939 and celebrated her 90th birthday in May of 2010. Sheila remembers her many battles with Dorothy and the difference between them – she a team player, Dorothy not – and talked about that and her career and her great love, netball. That sport always came before athletics, and playing for England meant more than winning an Olympic silver medal at Helsinki in 1952, feeling she had let everyone down by not winning the gold.

It is a different story to many of that era in that she was not totally obsessed with high jumping, and marriage and the social life that she and her husband, Michael, who sadly died in 2008, found in Iraq when he went there to work changed her outlook. In 1956 she came back to Britain to train and try for the Olympic gold that she felt should have been hers four years before, but could not go because her mother dashed all her hopes when she said she would not look after her baby daughter while Sheila went round the world to Melbourne for the Games. She finished her athletics career with no regrets, once she had recovered from the shock and anger.

Born in Surrey on 16 August 1928, high jumping began for her at the age of 10 at school in south London when the annual sports day was held and she was asked what event she would like to do. She had shown great promise as a shooter in netball and knew she could jump. So she said she would try the high jump, and she won. She was selected for an inter-schools competition, and although she did not win against much bigger and taller girls she cleared 3ft 9in (1.14m), which was excellent in those days for a girl her age. She was 5ft 7in (1.71m) tall and weighed 9st 7lb (60kg) in her competitive prime.

After retiring from athletics she concentrated on netball, and her ambition was to be a physical education teacher, but this came to an end when her teacher told her that there were only three scholarship places (the only way she could afford to go to college) in the country and she was unlikely to get one. One day soon after, when she was 18, her then boyfriend told her he used to train down at Tooting Bec track, and she said she would go with him. The coach in charge asked her what event she wanted to try and she said she preferred the high jump. By the end of the year she was ranked 6th in Great Britain and 74th in the world with a scissors jump of 4ft 10in (1.47m).

She had joined the Surrey-based club, Selsonia Ladies AC, and was in the list of "Olympic Possibles" issued at the end of the 1947 season. She was 3rd in the Women's AAA Championships behind Tyler, improving slightly to 4ft 11in (1.50m), and so the WAAA had appointed George Pallett as her coach. He was a former international and already coach of internationals at another club, Spartan Ladies, where he was a vice-president, but the relationship did not have a good beginning.

She remembered, "He was rude to me. He said, 'If you think I like training women, think again.

I don't really think of women in this sport. You must abide by what I say'. Good God! He had said it to the wrong person and I told him so. It was the attitude of the time, though. A few years later a promising male sprinter came to join the group, took one look at me and said, 'I'm not going to train with women. What is she doing here?' " By that time Sheila had an excellent relationship with Pallett, and he told her that for once she should show what it was like to train with women. She led the running pack at a very fast pace – she had won a team medal for cross-country as a senior – and the sprinter said nothing more about women after that.

Sheila said, "I remember George saying to me at the start that I would get nowhere with the scissors, but the straddle would get me much higher, but that it would take time". He was right. It did – three years later – and it was very hard work mastering the style of crossing the bar face down as she hurt her shins a lot in the early days. By the time that she was the best in the world the coach was a very good friend; so much so that she visited the Palletts out in Australia when they emigrated there after both she and her coach had retired from the sport.

She cleared 5ft 2in (1.57m) in 1948, but missed Olympic selection, and 5-3 (1.60) in 1949, and by 1950 George Pallett had been proved absolutely right about the straddle. It was the technique by which she would become a top competitor, the first woman athlete to use it. She regularly beat Dorothy Tyler and at the beginning of August set a British record of 5-6⅛ (1.68) at Aylesford, in Kent, with Tyler 2nd. The rivalry between the two over the years was intense, with Sheila winning many more than her opponent, but they were never friends. Sheila said, "Let me put it this way. She was an icon. I was a team player, always had been, always will be, but she was not. She used to isolate herself. I would always help someone in the team, she would not".

The rivalry with Dorothy Tyler – "never quaking at the knees!"

"When I was picked for my first international, which was the European Championships in 1950, we were the two in the high jump, but she did not give me an ounce of help about the format. That was how it was. We met in competition regularly in inter-club matches and the three major competitions for women, and then what international events there were. It was the press who made up the stories about the rivalry. I was never quaking at the knees or anything like that because I always knew I could beat her. It never struck fear in me because I knew that. I was very good! And also my first love was netball and I would always play that if the two clashed". She went on, with a smile, "She was as consistent as could be. I always knew she could not get that much better because age was against her, but Thelma Hopkins, who won the silver in Melbourne in 1956, always had potential. She was a sweetie".

Sheila had not been considered for the 1950 Empire Games in New Zealand because she was not a multi-eventer, which was necessary to help cover the costs of travel in those days, and she says of the European Championships in Brussels, "I was very naive then. I had not been picked for the 1948 Olympic Games, and it never occurred to me that I would be. I did not even know what the Games were. I did go to watch, but I was bored by them as a spectacle. I was there on the day of the women's high jump, at that end of the stadium, and I have to admit that I left before the end with that great climax to beat the crowd. I missed the last 15 minutes when Dorothy Tyler won the silver medal for the second time".

She continued, "I was shocked when we were booking in at Brussels for the European Championships and the Belgian official told me I was favourite". He was right, and she won with Tyler 2nd. "After that it never occurred to me that she could beat me". And that was how it went on. Three weeks before the Brussels final she had set a British record of 5-6⅝ (1.692) in beating Dorothy Tyler yet again in the Southern Inter-Counties match at Aylesford, in Kent, on 5 August. The next year Sheila gained the world record from the great Fanny Blankers-Koen, who had held it since 1943 and who Sheila credits for starting the rise of interest in women's athletics, clearing 5-7⅝ (1.717) in the Women's AAA Championships before few spectators at the White City, London, on 7 July. It was ratified by the IAAF at the slightly higher 1.72m, but also listed by them as the slightly lower 5-7½! It stood for almost three years. "I was ever so pleased and very smug – ever so pleased it was over and done with. It had been an objective and I had done it. It was good. How could it not have been? I was not surprised because the whole motivation had been towards getting the record. All I knew was that as people measured it, it was above the height of a lady who had been the women's team manager and was standing nearby".

The only letter she received from anyone at her old school was from the teacher who had dashed her hopes of ever becoming a PE teacher – "obviously on her conscience". The record came just a few weeks after she had fulfilled her potential in her first love by playing shooter for England in the netball home internationals. She had cleared the bar at her first attempt but failed at 5-8 (1.73), and going on to another height in the competition was something that had never entered her head when she had set the British record the year before: "I just stopped there and then. I had nothing left. I was very naive. How could you set a record? I loved high jumping, but I was not used to the mechanics of world-record-breaking".

Going to the Olympics as the favourite, but nerves took their toll

So she went to the 1952 Helsinki Olympics expecting to win the final on 27 July, for which there were 17 qualifiers. She didn't, finishing 2nd to the South African, Esther Brand. Sheila explained: "I did not win because of nerves. Another member of the British team, sprinter Sylvia Cheeseman, had come into my room in the early hours, saying my cough was keeping her awake. And she had brought me a cold drink. But it was not a cough like that. It was a nervous cough, a nervous tic that had manifested itself the night before the event. What it made me do was to clear the heights at the third attempt. Normally I would clear first time. I often missed heights out knowing that I would clear the higher one at the first attempt, but this time it was third time and a high jumper knows you don't do that sort of thing.

The height-by-height progress of Brand and Lerwill in the competition was as follows:

Brand – 1.40 o, 1.45 o, 1.50 o, 1.55 o, 1.58 o, 1.61 o, 1.63 xo, 1.65 xo, 1.67 xxo, 1.69 xxx
Lerwill – 1.40 o, 1.45 -, 1.50 xo, 1.55 o, 1.58 o, 1.61 o, 1.63 xxo, 1.65 xxo, 1.67 xxx

"Nerves? How could you mess it up? Franz Stampfl, the coach to Thelma Hopkins, who placed 4th, was so concerned for me that he was telling people to be quiet when I jumped. The silver medal does not mean a dicky bird to me. I could have chucked it in the North Sea. Those are my feelings over the years and they have not changed. I felt I had let everyone down. Everything to do with my country and everything else – I felt I had let people down. I was the sort of person who believed that the world record-holder goes into the Olympic Games and comes back with the gold medal and a new world record on top. They are to me wonderful people. That is why my medal does not mean a dicky bird to me.

"Franz Stampfl said, 'It will go into the record books and in 50 years' time it will still be there', but he didn't know me, did he? It didn't affect me at the time, but my parents received letters saying what a bad sport their daughter was. It upset them and, of course, the police were involved but eventually it all died".

Sheila had met and married Michael Lerwill, an ex-Army officer who was interested in sport but was the Sunday-rugby type. He worked at the engineering firm where she was a personal secretary. When he and his team-mates once went to Tooting Bec track to train, they did a lap,

Time for a tea-break at the Tooting Bec track. George Pallett and his training-group, including a youthful Sheila Lerwill (far right). *Photograph supplied by Kevin Kelly.*

stopped for a cigarette, did another lap, and then changed quickly to get down to the pub. Sheila said, "I told him, 'Don't ever embarrass me by talking to me if I'm there when you are!' "

Being married changed her outlook. As well as her job as a secretary there was a husband to look after and a move to Basra, in Iraq, where he was a manager with a fruit-exporting firm. Before she went she set another world best, for the indoor high jump with 5-6 (1.68) at Wembley on 13 November 1953, although this seems to have been an exhibition jump as part of the "Festival of Sport". She came back to try for the Empire Games and European Championships teams the next year. She was selected for both, but the old spark had gone. She finished 4th, in Vancouver, with Hopkins 1st and Tyler 2nd, and then 4th again (Hopkins winning once more) in Berne, jumping much lower than she had done in Brussels and Helsinki.

She said, "In Vancouver I was awful, although I did have a good life socially. The truth is that I was homesick for Michael. I had specifically come back from Iraq. We were very impecunious and I used to do agency work because I stayed with my parents. It took its toll. I forgot to compete. I had learnt for two months in Basra that one could enjoy life. There were parties, cocktail parties and drinks. There was more to life than your nose to the grindstone, running and training in all weathers. It opened my eyes to the fact that there was another life out there. I was no good at Berne. Thelma came into her own, and the first person to congratulate her was me. I had switched off. I wanted to go back home, I wanted to go to Basra".

She did go back and did not compete in 1955 as Hopkins took her place as No.1 in British women's high jumping, but she returned in 1956 determined to win a place in the team for the Melbourne Olympics and the gold she had so hoped for in 1952. She explained, "My daughter, Tricia, was born in 1955. I came back to Britain for six months in 1956 to make the team. I started training with George, and I could not believe it but the spring and height was still there. It was timing that was haywire. I was back to live training and it all came together. I won the Surrey title and there was a headline in the local paper, 'Unknown housewife wins county title'. It was so typical of life – out of sight, out of mind".

She thought she had a chance of the gold: "I would not have been so nervous. I was full of confidence, but it all went pear-shaped. I had my small daughter, and my mother asked, 'Who is looking after her if you get into the team?' I said, 'What are you talking about? Of course I'll get in the team'. I was training well. The local school was providing the equipment and I was full of confidence. In July before the WAAA Championships my mother said, 'I suppose you know I won't be looking after your daughter. It is up to you'. And that was it. It was a family hiatus. There was nothing I could do. It was the end of my hopes. There was no one else to look after her. I never jumped again. Was I cross? I was incandescent. I was shattered. I determined that as my children grew up I will always be there for them – and I was.

"I made it up with my mother. I was the only child and you have to do it. When my parents were in their 80s I had them to live with me, and after my father had gone my mother used to say that she was so lucky to have me. But I never forgot. That was the end of the story as far as jumping was concerned. I put it all behind me because when you have offspring they are the priority. I walked away from it. There are more things out there in life". That was the end of her career, and Thelma Hopkins won silver in Melbourne while Sheila was back in Basra. "It was all so long ago", Sheila said.

After she retired and had gone back to Iraq she survived the revolution there in 1958, and she only regretted that because she was out of the country she could not help in the administration of British athletics. She has always loved that side. Instead, she raised her family, a girl and boy (he like his son reached the fringe of international hockey), and now has four grandchildren. She worked for 10 years with the Samaritans and six years with bereavement counselling – "more rewarding than anything else I could have done" – and was a very active member of her local tennis club, as she still is.

Looking back she said, "Women in athletics were only just coming into their own when I was competing. I think Fanny Blankers-Koen had a lot to do with the rise of women athletes. She was an icon. Her four gold medals at Wembley did a lot of good. But money has ruined athletics as it has many sports. I know it is wonderful we have people very impecunious who need money in order to train and get it. Then I hear from someone from my era that they hear subsequently that someone has trained so much they are injured because we don't have enough coaches to train them!"

Sheila was never one to blow her own trumpet or dance in the limelight. She said, "When my son, Clive, was aged nine a master at his school said, 'I hear your mother won a medal at the Olympics'. Clive replied, 'Did she?', and when we were recently putting all my cuttings into scrapbooks after they had been in a box for many many years my daughter said, 'You have never said a word about this. I had no idea you were so high profile'. But that was me. I was never bothered about a cabinet full of trophies, or showing off."

Note: this article was first published in "Track Stats", Volume 48, No.2, June 2010.

There was no gap between the club athletes and the celebrities then. How do we close it now?

Terence Langley Higgins was born 18 January 1928 in Dulwich, South London, and educated at Alleyne's School, Dulwich, and Cambridge University. He was a member of Herne Hill Harriers. He began employment in the shipping industry, and he was then a mature student at Cambridge University, a lecturer at Yale University, a Unilever economic adviser, and Conservative MP for Worthing from 1964 to 1997, appointed Privy Councillor and knighted as Lord Higgins in 1997. At 5ft 11in (1.80m) tall and 10st 10lb (68kg) in weight, he competed in the Empire Games of 1950 and the Olympic Games of 1952. His best performances were as follows:100 yards, 10.2; 220 yards, 22.0; 400 metres, 47.8; 440 yards 48.1.

Terry (now Lord) Higgins shares a couple of common bonds with Sir Arthur Marshall, Britain's longest-lived Olympic athlete who died aged 103. Both were selected for the 4 x 400 metres relay at the Olympic Games, in 1924 and 1948 respectively, but never got a run, though Higgins had his chance in 1952. Both were knighted; Sir Arthur for services to the aircraft industry and Terry for his political work as a Tory front-bench Treasury spokesman. Lord Higgins was latterly Shadow Minister for Work and Pensions in the House of Lords and is one of the longest-serving athletes-turned-politicians in British history.

Higgins was left out of the relay team in 1948, although he took part in the Opening Ceremony and all other activities. Sir Arthur did not make it, even though his great friend, Eric Liddell (with whom he went night-clubbing in Paris when that meant going out for afternoon tea), was not in the team because the race was on a Sunday and he was preaching and would never run on the Sabbath. There were others who were preferred for the bronze-medal quartet — Guy Butler, Edward Toms, George Renwick and Richard Ripley. Higgins was also left out, but the GB team (Les Lewis, Martin Pike, Derek Pugh and Bill Roberts) never made it past the first round.

Ahead of the Games, Higgins had run an impressive non-winning 48.8 for 440 yards but missed out after a poor performance at the AAA Championships. Later that year he made his first major breakthrough in the European Combined Services Championships 400 metres in Brussels in September, where he won in 48.6, a clear 10 metres in front of Dupoix, of France. Higgins had started his career as a natural talent who won schoolboy titles, crowned by the Public Schools 440 at the White City in 1946. He went to work for the New Zealand Shipping Company, which encouraged good athletes because it enabled them to win the shipping sports meeting titles. This was an important event of the era, as were the banking, civil service and insurance sports.

In his first year as a senior in 1947 he had managed 51.2 for the AAA v London University, was 3rd in the Surrey county "quarter", and 2nd to Les Lewis in the RAF Championships. Much better was to come in 1948 when he won the RAF title and competed well for Herne Hill Harriers, winning the club titles at 100, 220 and 440 yards and being club record-holder several times at the 440 (he is now a patron). He set his first club record when giving Les Lewis a hard race, 48.8 to 48.5, in the Southern Championships and was 3rd in the Kinnaird Trophy meeting. Yet it was not enough to gain him a run in the Olympic relay team (which was not announced until the night before the heats). Looking at the statistics, he was certainly worth his place.

Back into civilian life again in 1949 after his National Service, where he had been given an extra pint of milk a day and was allowed to jump the queue for additional rations because he was an Olympic "possible", he was 3rd at the AAA Championships 2nd in the Southern, 3rd incredibly for

Surrey in the Inter-Counties 440 hurdles in 57.4, and won for the AAA v the Combined Services. His 440 flat races were always in the 49sec range. He was also part of a London 4 x 220 yards relay team at Birmingham at one of the first floodlit meetings that were to become a regular fixture, setting a British record of 1:27.4 with John Wilkinson, Nick Stacey and the Jamaican, Les Laing. This time was not beaten until 10 years later when another London team of David Jones, Brian Smouha, Peter Radford and David Segal ran 1:26.0.

Talking over tea in the House of Lords, he said, "It was work, training, sleep, work, training, sleep, but it was fun". He trained for around 90 minutes six days a week in the summer, with long slow jogs of up to six miles during the winter under the eagle eyes of the club's coaches, George Pallett and the legendary Bill Thomas. His performances brought him 1950 Empire Games selection, and he went off to New Zealand with a double purpose – to run and to have a year's experience at the New Zealand Shipping Company's various offices.

The Games went fairly well for him, going out in the semi-finals of the 440 yards after running 49.0 in his heat and then missing out in the 440 hurdles heat ("When you went that far you did not just run your own event", he explains) but winning a silver medal in the 4 x 440 relay, where he ran his first leg well, handing over to the 880 yards champion, John Parlett, who kept the team in the hunt, and was followed by Derek Pugh, with Les Lewis (who had finished 2nd by a whisker in the individual race to the Australian, Edwin Carr) coming home a few yards behind the Australians.

Returning home to run in the gigantic shadow of Arthur Wint

After the Games many of the team toured both the South and North Islands and competed in a number of invitation meetings. Higgins was 2nd to the Games finalist, Jack Sutherland, in 49.4 at Christchurch, and he then ran a very fast grass-track 300 yards in 31.0 at Lower Hutt and an excellent 49.4 on a poor track at Wellington Basin Reserve in a bit of a gale, beating the NZ champion and Games bronze-medallist, Dave Batten. This was after finishing 2nd to another bronze-medallist, Don Jowett, in a 22.0 220 yards. Some of the team, such as Lewis and the high jumper, Peter Wells, settled permanently in New Zealand.

Among the leading lights at 440 yards during Higgins's racing career was Derek Pugh, who had placed 3rd in the European Championships 400 metres in 1946 and 2nd in the relay and then won gold in both events in 1950, with 47.3 in the individual event. Les Lewis was 5th in that 1950 European final and was also in the winning relay team. In addition, there was Derek Johnson, Alan Dick, Martin Pike, Peter Fryer, Peter Higgins (no relation) and others on their heels who raced against each other week-in week-out, but literally towering over them all was the 6ft 4in (1.93m) Jamaican, Arthur Wint, of the nine-foot stride, who not only won two Olympic gold medals (400 metres in 1948 and 4 x 400 in 1952, plus two silvers at 800 metres) but also dominated the British scene from 1946 until 1952 after coming over to join the RAF during World War II.

Wint was a much-loved athlete and Higgins had many battles with him, never finding that extra stride that would take him past. They also regularly ran relays in the same team and Higgins remembers passing the baton to Wint, later to become Jamaican High Commissioner: "I don't understand why our coaches now encourage the use of risky baton-changing techniques which include passing the baton downwards. It has always seemed to me there is only one safe way – the man who is going to take the baton starts with his arm stretched out behind him to get maximum free distance with his hand pointing down to take the baton, and you ran up and smack it into his hand where it is gripped. With Arthur it was so easy because there was this great big hand just aching to take the baton and be away."

Higgins worked with his company in New Zealand after the Empire Games and did not come back until March 1951, having missed the entire 1950 British season, but his return produced the best season he was to have. He was 2nd in a 400 metres at an international meeting in Amsterdam with 48.9. He then improved to 48.9 for 440 at the shipping sports, won at the British Games with 48.7 for yards, was beaten by a foot in a gale by Peter Higgins, for the first time, lost to the immortal Herb McKenley by a stride or two in 48.5y on the dead White City track, and was one-tenth slower at the AAA Championships when Derek Pugh set a new English native 440 yards record of 47.9. As always, Higgins suffered from hay fever every season until the Championships. He said, "The moment you stopped warming-up your pulse-rate dropped and you began to sneeze. The only anti-histamine available was Benzedrine, which is now used as a sleeping tablet".

His AAA run won him his first international vest for the winning 4 x 440 yards team (Higgins, Stacey, Pugh, Wint) against France in a record 3:13.6. Better was to come as his training paid off and he was selected for the exciting but illness-struck first tour of the Balkans, which was also the first major overseas excursion by the GB team since the war. It started against Yugoslavia, where he ran a lifetime best behind Wint, 47.8 to 47.2, at a meeting in which the highlight was Roger Bannister's first big defeat by Andrija Otenhajmer in front of his home crowd in a national 1500 metres record of 3:47.0, with Bannister setting a personal best 3:48.6, and both of them high in the world rankings.

Higgins anchored the 4 x 400 relay and went on to Greece where he was again in the winning relay team. By that stage of the tour many of the British athletes were suffering from stomach problems, but this did not stop Higgins, who won the 400 metres in 48.6 in the final match and was also in the winning 4 x 400 team. He recalls that the athletes were in trouble for accumulating an enormous hotel bill for real lemonade that cost about £1 a pint when beer was around a shilling (5 pence)!

"Hustling Herb" is hustled out of yet another win

He came home to finish the season in style with two floodlit wins – including 48.5y in Birmingham – and then to a meeting at Motspur Park in aid of the Jamaican Hurricane Relief Fund where he did what very few people ever did (and I can't remember any other Briton doing it) by beating the great Herb McKenley. Writing in "Athletics Weekly", James Audsley pooh-poohed the win, writing, "It should be added that McKenley has not been training and was quite unfit for such a race". That may be so, but "Hustling Herb" had a string of sub-47s up to the end of July and was always ready for a race. McKenley, as was his wont, went like a bat out of hell from the start, but Higgins judged his race well and used his training and his ideas on racing to the full, coming at the end to win by inches in 48.8y.

As Higgins now says, "Not many people ever beat him, and I was thrilled, really thrilled". James Audsley may have been off-colour because in the same report he has a dig at Norris McWhirter, saying that in the 4 x 110 yards relay "Wint played an unfamiliar role with success when he outpaced McWhirter on the last stage".

Higgins was 3rd in the year's British rankings to Wint and Pugh and was on the "possibles" list for the 1952 Olympics. Before the 1952 season began he gave some interesting answers in the popular "Athletics Weekly" questionnaire. To the question, "How long did it take you to reach Championship standard?", he said: "I have been fortunate in that when I took up athletics seriously in the first post-war season the standard was comparatively low. Since then I have managed to progress as the standard has become higher". He said that he trained as many days as possible and he offered various advice to a novice, particularly stressing that it is essential to run at least the first 60 yards of a quarter-mile flat out and "not to attempt to relax and stride until maximum speed has been attained".

He also said that he did not believe there was any advantage in running heats slowly with the idea of conserving energy: "Last season I ran only one heat or semi-final slower than 50sec and yet my standard of performance was better than in the previous seasons". He added that it is not enough to run just one fast time because championships require more and it was important to train to build the stamina as well as speed. "I do not understand", he wrote, "why athletes now look round if they are in the lead. It's dangerous if someone is close behind and merely prolongs the agony". Nowadays he compares making a speech with running a quarter-mile, saying with a smile, "It's very much the same. You start with a sprint, then float along, and finish sprinting again".

Sadly in 1952 the formula that had worked so well the previous year and had showed so much promise – perhaps to a place in the semi-finals of the Helsinki Olympics if he could improve that much – did not happen. He started the season well with a 48.9y heat in the Inter-Counties Championships and a tenth slower in the final which he won. At the AAA Championships he did 49.6y and 48.5y in his heat and semi-final and was then 3rd in the final in a disappointing 49.1y behind Wint and Lewis but was in the Olympic team for the individual race and the relay. Just before the Games he ran 48.1m to win at the Triangular International match, but after running 48.7 for 2nd in his heat in Helsinki he faded to 49.1 in his quarter-final. The British team was outclassed in the 4 x 400, finishing 5th in a respectable 3:10.0 to Jamaica's 3:03.9, with the USA one-tenth behind in 2nd place.

Stacey sprints past Whitfield – and gives his team-mates a worrying moment

Lord Higgins remembers how the team of himself, Les Lewis, Alan Dick and Nick Stacey (later a Bishop) qualified for the final: "We told Nick, who had reached the semi-finals of the 200 metres, which was his speciality, that when I handed the baton to him for the last leg he was to stick just one yard behind the American. I handed over to him just as we had planned, a yard behind, and to begin with Nick did just that, but on the far side of the track he went past and built up an eight-yard lead on the American and then faded. Luckily, we were far enough ahead to get through, but it was a worrying moment". The American who Stacey had passed was Marvellous Mal Whitfield, gold winner at 800 metres in 1948 and 1952!

Higgins was still 3rd in the British quarter-mile rankings at the season's end, behind Wint and Dick, but his business career was beginning to take off and his running suffered in his last few years on the track. In 1953 he raced sparsely as he was suffering from an Achilles tendon injury and was a poor 5th at the AAA Championships in 50.2, only once ducking under 50sec during the year. In fact, he only once went under 49sec in his remaining years, when finishing 5th again in the 1955 AAA final in 48.8. He said, "Sadly I never won the AAA. Arthur usually won it, and when he didn't there was Pugh, and when Pugh didn't an Irishman called Reardon came and beat me".

In 1954 Higgins was at Oxford on four-minute mile day and ran in the only race after Bannister had finished. He recalls, "It was something of an anti-climax and did not attract much attention". This was understandable but also rather a shame because Derek Johnson ran a 440 yards ground record 48.0, 1.6sec ahead of Higgins. Later in the season Higgins won the Southern title in a slow 49.4 and was 4th in the AAA final, again in 49.4, behind Peter Fryer, Johnson and his namesake, Peter Higgins. He was thus too slow to be considered for the Empire Games or European Championships, but he was in the winning England medley relay team against Belgium and ran the first leg in the British Games relay against the USA which the home team won by a gossamer thread – an "Athletics Weekly" cover photo showing how tight the finish was between Derek Johnson and Josh Culbreath.

The Herne Hill Harriers team which won the AAA 4 x 440 yards relay in 1954 – left to right, Dave Rawe, Clay Gibbs, Eddie Hartley and Terry Higgins. This event was contested from 1927 to 1969, and then at 4 x 400 metres to 1977, held separately from the AAA Championships meeting. *Photograph supplied by Kevin Kelly.*

Higgins's last year in the top rank was 1955, when he was consistently around 49sec and managed his season's best of 48.8 in the AAA final behind the English native record 47.7 set by the 6ft 4in (1.93m) Fryer. This brought Higgins international selection for GB v Hungary and he ran the second leg in the 4 x 440, dropping a few yards on the European 800 metres champion, Lajos Szentgáli, but keeping the team in the race until Fryer had an off day and lost a five-yard lead.

In the autumn Higgins went up to Gonville and Caius College at Cambridge as a mature student reading economics, and he continued with his athletics, winning the freshmen's 440 yards in 50.9 on a bitterly cold Fenners track in October. He won the "freshers" quarter against Oxford and was in the winning 4 x 220 team at the relays match but on the losing side at 4 x 440. Then his studies and his political activities took over and after finishing in last place behind Johnson in the full match against Oxford his running was mediocre. "It was very painful", he recalled, "being active in the Union, studying economics, and running 440 yards in the cold without training is something I would not recommend".

He ran in the 1956 Inter-Varsity relays but failed to make the team in 1957 and 1958. By then his life was in politics and he became President of the Union and a top man in the University Tory party, going off to Yale as a lecturer in the Department of Economics. He came back to the New Zealand Shipping Company and then was appointed economic adviser to Unilever. He won the Tory seat at Worthing in 1964 and he held it for 33 years until elevated to the Lords in 1997. During his time in Parliament he was Minister of State to the Treasury, Financial Secretary to the Treasury, Chairman of the Treasury Select Committee, and a member of other important

143

committees such as Public Accounts and the Executive of the 1922 Committee. Now, as a Privy Councillor and Shadow spokesman on Work and Pensions in the House of Lords, he works as hard as he has ever done – Lords are unpaid – and he commutes each weekend to The Hague, where his wife, Rosalyn, is a Judge of the International Court and where he plays golf.

Like any athlete of the 1950s looking back half-a-century, he sees that the differences are enormous. It is impossible to equate those days and the performances then with what goes on now. Or is it? As he rightly points out, "The performances at club level now are no higher than in my day 50 years and more ago. There was then no gap between the ordinary club athlete and the celebrities, as there is now. I don't know how to close it. One wonders if they did not go to Florida, or wherever, for their warm-weather training whether they would win or not. Training full-time makes them very vulnerable to what used to happen to the Americans and the Russians. They would perform wonderfully until it came to the main events, when they were stale and then they failed. It is worth thinking about".

He added; "We are not getting the people into athletics. And when they do, they often drop out before they reach their maturity. There are so many other things to do now compared with the post-World War II period. There used to be the routine of club events, county, area, AAA Championships, and then internationals if you were selected – but that has all gone. We were not paid. We did it for fun, with £15 limit on the prize value and not in cash. Once you brought money in, the temptation to use drugs was there, and that is what really changed it. It was anything to make you better to win – just like the East Germans and the Russians".

Note: this article was first published in "Track Stats", Volume 43, No.2, May 2005.

Diane Coates, British javelin record-holder from 1949 to 1952

A club match at Reading – "Come and have a go, Di. Just throw it as far as you can"

On 28 May 1949 Oxford Ladies Athletic Club was struggling for points in the field events at an important inter-club competition at Reading, in Berkshire. The club secretary had an inspiration. She asked 17-year-old Diane Coates, a promising high jumper and long jumper, tallish and perfectly proportioned, if she would help out. Diane, now 72 years of age but still of erect build, as befits an international athlete, county cricketer and hockey player, and a fine six-handicap golfer who won the Channel Islands championship, recalls:

"Susan Parrott came up and said, 'Di, we're doing well. We've been told you're good at throwing a ball. Come and have a go with the javelin', and I asked 'What's that?' I was good at throwing. When I was growing up, my brother, Tony, and I had to entertain ourselves, and one game we played for hours was throwing a ball over the roof of the house, with one of us on either side. I was also good at throwing in cricket and with snowballs! I agreed to throw the javelin, having already competed in the jumps and waiting to run the last leg in the 4 x 110 yards relay. I had never seen a javelin before. They showed me the binding, and where to hold it, and the arc of the throwing area".

Unlike the famous occasion when a Danish international javelin-thrower was demonstrating to fellow athletes and Cambridge University novices and showed them all the intricate steps of the Finnish masters but with disastrous results, Mrs Parrott then sensibly gave the order, "Just throw it as far as you can". Diane did just that – out to over 99 ft (30.18m), which was to take her right up into the top echelons of British throwers. By the end of the season she was the best in Britain, and within three years she was far and away the best ever. She now forms the bridge between total obscurity for Britain in the event internationally and the arrival of Tessa Sanderson and Fatima Whitbread in the 1980s as world leaders.

By the time of the Olympic Games in 1952 Diane was to hold her own against anyone except the Eastern Europeans, and she even won in three successive matches against France, which was unheard of in a stretch during which the standards in British men's and women's throwing events were awful. Unfortunately, her triumphs came at a time when there was practically no coaching at all for women in field events – particularly outside London – and very little interest in those who took part in them. Often there was no interest at all. Diane admits that she was naive when she literally threw herself into the big time. She was self-coached, following the advice given in the training bible of the American coaches, Bresnahan and Tuttle, and of the British international Tony Hignell, published in the book, "Athletics", written by members of the Achilles Club.

Added to that were pieces of paper that another international, Malcolm Dalrymple, gave her which showed the footwork of the Finnish "father" of the javelin, Matti Järvinen, and the leading British thrower, Mike Denley, and a flip-book depicting the action of a leading Finnish thrower. There was a also a lot of encouragement from her clubmates, of which the leading light was Maureen Gardner, who had finished 2nd to Fanny Blankers-Koen at 80 metres hurdles in the 1948 Olympics. That was her back-up plan.

Diane trained at Iffley Road (and, yes, she was there on that famous 6 May 1954), and during the winter she borrowed the javelin, and using a special carrier which her father had made for that and for her hockey stick she went out into the farm-fields near the city of Dreaming Spires to throw. She was to do the same when she was at teacher training college, going out on to the Downs above Eastbourne, and it was there that she threw her greatest distances of around 165ft (50.30m), which would have put her among the East Europeans. She recalls: "I always knew there was more to come, but in competition it never came"

The trouble was that athletics was far from being the main thing in her life. She enjoyed it and wanted to do well at it because her sporting parents had instilled a belief that whatever you did you must do it to the best of your ability, but she had to mix it with her career as a physical education teacher and with all the other sports which she played. "On one occasion", she remembers, "a cricket match clashed with the county athletics championships. My mother persuaded them to put the javelin on last. So after the match, where I took three wickets and made 39 to win the game, I got on my bike and rode to Iffley Road and won the javelin!"

But it was not just the other sports which interfered with her javelin-throwing. As a PE teacher she had to be present on Saturdays for the various matches in different sports which her pupils had to contest. After leaving training college she was stuck – like many other non-Oxbridge or non-services athletes in those days – in a job which did not give time off for sport, and there was, of course, no money to be made in athletics then. She gives an example:

"In 1952 I was in the college cricket team with regular Saturday matches. So to take part in any athletics I had to get permission. I had Jack Crump, the British team manager, down to give a talk, and I persuaded him to ask the college principal to come to watch the Women's AAA Championships. I got permission to compete. My last throw was a lifetime's best – 45.30 – and it proved to the principal, who was a dancer, that javelin-throwing was aesthetic and not just brute strength and ignorance, which I thought was what many people felt about the throwing events". Shortly afterwards Diane finished 15th in the Olympic javelin final: "I qualified with my first throw, but in the final, unfortunately, I was trying a little bit too hard and did not throw as far as I could. If I had thrown anything like my best, I would have come 6th".

Not even aware that there was a Women's AAA Championships

Born on 25 June 1932, Diane had joined the Oxford club on her mother's advice in 1948 to use up some of the tremendous energy she possessed, even after all the other sports in which she took part, and admits that after her first throw and win in that May-time inter-club competition the next year she still knew nothing about the sport – and was never to meet Ellen Allen, the unexpected WAAA champion later that summer. Diane did not compete in that WAAA event simply because she did not know there was such a competition, despite having won the Southern title. There was nobody around to tell her. She would have won the WAAA title easily, but because she did not take part she was not selected for the triangular match against France and Holland in which the better Briton was Bevis Reid with a pathetic 103-0½ (31.40) and the other British competitor (who shall remain nameless to spare her blushes) managed 77-9 (23.70).

Someone did tell Diane about a pentathlon at the White City later in the year, and she took part just to show how far she could throw the javelin, which she won with over 120ft (36.58). Although she was the best by far in Britain, and certainly one of the best in the Empire (as it was then called), she was not selected for the Empire Games in New Zealand early in 1950. Diane says, "There was not the money, and then there was the expense and the time it took to get there and back, and they only took people who could compete in several events". Instead, she won the Southern title again the following summer, giving a major fright to two male officials who stood at around the 120ft mark and patronisingly waved her on to throw in the belief that she would not reach them. She did – and the javelin went sailing over their heads. She recalled: "They soon got out of the way!"

Diane Coates throwing at the White City on 7 August 1950. The javelin was one of five women's events that day described as "European Games Trials" and held in conjunction with the annual men's match, England & Wales v Ireland v Scotland.

She won the first of her four WAAA titles and did well enough in the shot and discus (both self-taught) to almost reach British international level. She had her afternoon of afternoons in a meeting at Aylesford, in Kent, where she broke the British record three times – "the record was there to be broken, but it took years for it to be ratified because the right officials were not there" – which gave her great enjoyment and satisfaction, although she was not aware of just how good her record was. Every throw that day went smoothly, with the last of them the best.

She was selected for the European Championships in Brussels, and this was the first time that she had been abroad, which was very exciting for anyone in those days, and particularly so for a young girl from an Oxford council estate. It was also the first time that she had used a cinder run-up. She was not allowed to take part in the march-past because her event was one of the first on the programme and when it started none of the competitors were allowed to use the track as an additional part of their approach. "So I measured out eight paces, which was my run-up for bowling swingers left and right at cricket, and stuck to that afterwards", she remembers. "At the White City we had to compete on grass, and it was usually after the international horse show with the grass in a poor state. It would not be allowed nowadays".

She was not in awe of the mighty East European athletes – one of whom, she remembers, had a man's voice – because she knew nothing of them, and she did well to finish 10th with 37.50. "It

147

was all new to me", she explains. "I just enjoyed what I was doing". Immediately afterwards, she had another foreign trip to Paris, where she became the first British woman in modem times to win the javelin in a head-to-head international – and had the additional pleasure of sewing Roger Bannister's British badge on to his vest!

She was very good for the next two years despite no backing and a great deal of criticism from a leading coach, George Pallett, who she did not know but who made derogatory remarks in print about her throwing ability. She remains annoyed to this day. By the summer of 1953 she was having great difficulty combining competition with other sports and with her first job, which she had started just in time to clash with the matches in Germany and Sweden, for which she had to turn down selection.

She says: "After that my job came first. The less competition and training you do, the more rusty you become. I mixed my training with sport in which the children were taking part. My career meant a lot to me in those days, and there was no way round it. Nowadays, athletes are professionals, but I did so many other sports and I don't think I would be happy to have done this one specialisation. To me, to belong to a team in whatever sport was important. I started as a team person, and doing events which I knew nothing about but which were challenging. I trained when I had a moment and competed when I had a weekend off, which was very rare in term-time. When I did not make the Empire Games in 1958 because there were others who were better I took a party of children to watch, including the javelin".

From 1953 until 1958 Diane taught PE in Northamptonshire and Hertfordshire and still competed occasionally, though not matching the early highlights. "I had some wonderful trips to Moscow and Prague and enjoyed every minute of them – the people I went with and the people I met. I was not disappointed at the end. I suppose there were coaches about by that time, but they were in London, and I never came across them. Not living in London, you did not hear about things to take up the challenge to catch up".

When she retired from teaching she went to Jersey, in the Channel Islands, where she qualified as a WAAA senior coach – one of the films she had to criticise in her examination was of herself described as "too straight at point of release" – and she then became a six-handicap golfer but has now been forced to give up the game because of back problems also associated with her javelin throwing. She still takes an interest in athletics and believes that the enjoyment which she experienced sometimes seems to be lacking in competitors these days. She says, "I don't know whether Sanderson and Whitbread were coached from the start, but I would never have wanted to look as they did after all that weight-training. I don't know whether they enjoyed throwing, but they always looked stilted, over-coached. Now Jan Zelezny and Denise Lewis always look as though they enjoy every minute of it – like I did!"

Note: this article was first published in "Track Stats", Volume 43, No.1, February 2005.

"Bloody well get a move on!" shouted Dyson . . . and so the Welsh mountaineer got the bronze

The man with the microphone who was announcing at the Loughborough College freshmen's sports on 23 October 1946 watched the 18-year-old Welsh youth pounding round the track in the three miles – and told the small crowd that after the first four laps the freshmen's mile record had already been broken. "He doesn't know what he's doing", the announcer forecast. "He'll blow up".

The prediction was wrong. The 5 ft 11 in (1.80m) runner went on to set a three miles record in a promising time for those days of 15:34, and the announcer spoke to him afterwards. "Come and see me at the Olympic Games on the last day", he said. So the young runner who by then had improved enough to finish 3rd behind Roger Bannister in the UAU mile did just that two years later. He recalled: "In those days you could do that at a major meeting, find someone. He asked me if I had seen the steeplechase in which all three British competitors had finished last in their heats. I said that I had. He said, 'That's what you're going to be. Still think of yourself as a miler, but you're going to be a steeplechaser'. And that was that".

It was not until the end of the next year that the Welshman tried a steeplechase at a military meeting in Bordeaux in September while carrying out his National Service in the army. He had run earlier that afternoon and set his best time of 4:09 for 1500 metres, finishing as ever behind Captain Dick Morris, the Army champion for whom he was always the second string. For the steeplechase event there was no water jump but five hurdles to the lap and he finished 2nd to a Frenchman, Ben Said Abdallah, whose time of 9:29.7 was listed in the world's Top 40 for the 1949 season. The next year the young novice burst on to the British scene and was to rule the roost not just in the UK but at the very top globally until Thursday 29 November 1956 when – coming back from virus pneumonia which had taken a critical month out of his pre-Olympic training – he was beaten for only the second time in 27 meetings by Chris Brasher.

The Welshman was John Ivor Disley and the announcer was Geoff Dyson, the first AAA national coach, who saw the potential and put him into his squad of Cinderella-event "guinea-pigs": shot putter John Savidge, hurdler Maureen Gardner (who Dyson was to marry), pole vaulter Geoff Elliott, and long jumper Shirley Cawley, all of whom were to have brilliant careers. Disley was a natural athlete, a master mountaineer and a frustrated Everest climber, and he was the man who put the spark back into British steeplechasing. It was a spark that had been doused after the glory days of Tom Evenson and George Bailey, 2nd and 5th at Los Angeles in the 1932 Olympics, and had lain dormant for nearly 20 years.

It was Disley who led the way and was joined by Chris Brasher and Eric Shirley when they realised that because of the depth and strength of Britain's milers and three-milers in those days (and you don't need me to list them!) their best chance of international glory was in the steeplechase. Disley reckons that Shirley was a better runner than he and Brasher, but Shirley's greatest enemy was the nerves from which he suffered before a race. These three were followed by Maurice Herriott and Ernie Pomfret and then by men like Mark Rowland, Colin Reitz, Roger Hackney and Tom Hanlon until our present low level where Disley and Brasher would still almost make the British team!

Through 1950 and 1951, as he trained six days a week, mixing the Swedish system of varied-pace running ("fartlek", which translates as "speedplay") and middle-distances with hurdling technique, and supervised by Dyson on Saturdays at Motspur Park, Disley was by far and away the best in Britain, twice placing 2nd at the AAA Championships to the Yugoslav, Petar Segedin, who was one of the best in the world. Disley recalls: "That I never ran any decent mile times was because in every meeting I was running this steeplechase. I liked it, but you could not raise yourself in the early years because no one else did it. There was no home opposition". By the time he retired Disley was to run a mile in 4:05.4.

Dyson was his guiding light and it was with him that Disley stayed in London when he first started his teaching career. It was also Dyson who advised him to join London Athletic Club "because it was the oldest athletics club in the world and Geoff was a bit of a snob about things like that". Dyson was a superb coach whose own excellent athletics career before World War II, during which he had run 14.8 for the 120 yards hurdles, was cut short when the AAA declared that he was a professional because as an army officer he had coached athletes as part of his job. If it had been any other sport, it would not have mattered.

Disley mixed his running with mountaineering, and it was in a climber's hut that he first met Brasher, who was leading a Cambridge University Mountaineering Club group on a climb in Snowdonia in 1948. Brasher was the club president and Disley remembers: "My first recollection was his voice. It was a loud voice shouting at someone, 'You don't make porridge like that'. I knew then that he knew less about it than most people, but what he was doing was setting out his leadership for the climb so that people would accept what he said and do it. We climbed a lot together. He was very competent, and we were both on the list for the Everest team that was going to go out after the monsoon in the autumn of 1953. That was all spoilt when two very tough New Zealanders turned up". Disley and Brasher also had a licence to do the climb in the spring of 1953, as had the British team led by Sir John Hunt, who invited them to join him. As everyone knows, it was a New Zealander, Edmund Hillary, who reached the top of Everest with Sherpa Tensing.

How Disley nursed Brasher into the Olympic team ... and Brasher won gold

"Chris and I were great friends from then", Disley continues, "and we raced against each other and went on holidays. I could see from the start that his athletics career with the mile or three miles, at which he had been successful as an undergraduate, was not going anywhere when he got into the real world. He looked at my record, and I think that he was the first serious runner to see that there was an opportunity, and then later Eric Shirley did the same. Chris and I trained together in Snowdonia, and we were knitted together by the time our careers finished, and then ever afterwards".

They ran together for Britain eight times in head-to-head internationals and in two Olympic Games. The only occasions that Brasher beat him were at a London early-season meeting in 1952, when Disley had driven through the night after running and climbing for over seven hours to break a Welsh mountaineering record, and then in the Melbourne Olympic final in 1956. Disley had won the bronze in Helsinki four years before – of which more later – and was the favourite in Melbourne, and it was only because of him that Brasher was even in the team. Up to the AAA Championships on 14 July that year, Brasher had done nothing of note at all, with a best of 9:14.6, and even in the AAA race he improved no more than 12 seconds on that time, while Shirley and Disley finished 1-2 in 8:51.6 (a championship record) and 8:53.4.

Brasher was not in the original team list, but on 4 August, again at the White City, Disley paced his friend to 2nd place against Czechoslovakia, running a brilliant record-breaking 8:46.6 even after driving through the night from Wales and then bursting a shoe as he approached the last water-jump, with Brasher setting a lifetime best of 8:47.2. Disley recalled: "The air-fare to Australia was enormous then, well over a thousand pounds, and if he could qualify they would

Above: the 1952 Olympic steeplechase medallists – left to right, Kazantsev, Ashenfelter and Disley. Below: Disley and Brasher finish 1-2 against the USSR in Moscow in 1955.

have to pay. So we worked out what it was divided by the seven-and-a-half laps we were going to run, and as we went round we calculated on each lap how much he had saved towards his fare. It was about £200 a lap, and we shouted out the running total as we finished one-two".

Brasher kept on improving, but Disley went down with virus pneumonia in September. He was in bed for over a week and unable to train for four weeks. He said: "When the Games came I was a month short of training, I had to run in the final meeting for the athletes before we left, to show I was all right and I did a reasonable time for 1500 metres in a match between the Olympic team and Oxford and Cambridge in November because, luckily, the race was not fast".

As for the Games, Disley says, "I think I would have won if it had not been for the virus. Even so, I was winning at one stage on the last lap, but when I put my foot on the accelerator nothing happened and I finished 6th in 8:44.6, which was almost my lifetime best". After the race there was a protest that Brasher had obstructed the bronze-medallist, Ernst Larsen, of Norway, at a hurdle on the last lap. This was later overturned when Larsen and the other competitors said that Brasher had not infringed them. Disley said: "We did not think it was a dirty race. The Australian officials had not seen a race like this before. There was a lot of the pushing and shoving there always is, but the officials were not used to it and took action. Larsen was very honourable. He said that Chris had not hindered him in the slightest".

It was Stampfl's influence that had helped Brasher to gold

What was exceptional about the race was Brasher's running. He had gone out to Melbourne early and came under the influence of Franz Stampfl, the man who had guided Bannister to the first sub-four-minute mile two years earlier, and ran personal bests in two races before the Games. Brasher was taking medicine given to him by Stampfl to counter his asthma and one member of the British team thought this might have been of help to him. Disley's reaction almost 50 years later is philosophical. "But so what? It's not much consolation when you've lost".

Disley's major international baptism had been at the 1950 European Championships in Brussels where he finished a distant 13th in a race won by Emil Zátopek's fellow-Czech, Jindrich Roudny, from Disley's AAA rival, Segedin. At the 1952 Olympics Disley was an outside chance after a superb world best of 9:44.0 at the AAA Championships for which the two-mile steeplechase event was run instead of 3000 metres, and he recalled: "At Helsinki I was pretty fit, and I think I would have got a silver medal if I had not decided long before the race that the German, Helmut Gude, who headed the world rankings, was going to win. I did not know that he had 'flu three weeks before the race. I watched him, and then Geoff shouted from the edge of the track, 'Bloody well get a move on!' "

"If he had come shouting a lap earlier I might have got silver, but I would not have beaten Ashenfelter". The warning made Disley, who was at the back of the field with Brasher with five laps to go, wake up and run like the star he is. But it was too late. The US FBI agent, Horace Ashenfelter, won in a sensational 8:45.4 and Disley almost caught the Russian, Vladimir Kazantsev, on the line in 8:51.8, with Brasher 22 seconds adrift in 11th place.

Three years later, when Disley and Brasher ran in Moscow against the USSR pair of Vasiliy Vlasenko, an ex-world record-holder, and Mikhail Saltykov, who had done 8:52.8, Disley was introduced as world record-holder, which was technically correct because the time of 8:40.2 by the Pole, Jerzy Chromik, had not yet been ratified. The race in the first-ever international between the two nations in front of a crowd of 70,000 – Disley particularly remembers the noise – was as hard-fought as could be until the end when Disley swept away, with Brasher five seconds adrift but ahead of the two Soviet athletes who had set the earlier pace. Disley's time of

8:44.2 was his lifetime best and the ideal end to what had been his best season. The McWhirter twins (later of "Guinness Book of Records" fame), writing about Disley's achievement, worked out out that his steeplechase time was worth a 4:02 mile, which was a bit faster than his best for the distance that year of 4:07.0.

Disley mixed running and climbing but suffered severe Achilles tendon trouble. He was the first athlete to have this operated on by a surgeon, who told him that if the technique was successful he would use it on his race-horses. The problem would eventually put Disley out of running, and it ruined his chances in front of his home crowd at the Empire Games in Cardiff in 1958, where he was a non-finisher in the three miles. There was no steeplechase, and although he had won three AAA titles he could never be an Empire champion because there had also not been a steeplechase at the Games of 1950 or 1954. Nor, for that matter, would he ever win the Welsh title.

In 1960 he was only able to run one steeplechase because of injury, finishing 4th in the Inter-Counties event to the young tigers and then three days later running a 4:13.6 mile. Yet the selectors for the Rome Olympics still had great faith in him. And why not? Fit, he was still the best of the bunch. Disley said: "They arranged for me to run a six-lap trial at racing speed for an 8:40 at Motspur Park one Saturday morning and sent coach John Le Masurier to watch. John said, 'Yes, you're fine', but my leg was so sore, and I knew that there was no way I was going anywhere to run. So I said, 'Thank them, but tell them I think that I'll have to withdraw' ".

And that – on the track – was that. Born in Corris, Gwynedd, in Wales, on 20 November 1928, he is still extremely active with the organisation of the London Marathon, of which he was co-founder, and with climbing and as international measurement co-ordinator for the IAAF, among other things. Of his competitive career, he says: "I enjoyed it all, and there was a lot of good company. I don't know that you would find as many fraternal friends nowadays". Many of his friendships have lasted over the years because his group was so varied, including shot-putters, throwers, hurdlers and jumpers, not just middle-distance runners. "There was a good mix of clubs and of Oxford and Cambridge, and there were many cub meetings which you don't get now. And it was more fun because you also did a day job. Athletes get very introspective now because they earn their living and it's much more serious".

As for the future of steeplechasing in Britain, where the standard now is so poor, he says, "There are no milers. If there were some good milers, people would be pushed somewhere else. It's as simple as that".

Note: this article was first published in "Track Stats", Volume 43, No.1, February 2005. John Disley died 16 February 2016, aged 87.

"I felt peace at the top of that hill – and at that moment Pirie was beaten and there was only Zátopek between me and the gold medal"

The North/South divide in England has existed as long as there has been history. It covers all aspects of life. The grim-faced, mean Northerners and the soft Southerners who believe that civilisation ends at the Watford Gap have been locked in perpetual battle, whether it be politics, poverty, play-writing, culture or accent. But it really manifests itself in sport, with football taking pride of place. The South has Arsenal, Spurs and the Hammers; the North has Manchester United and City, Liverpool and Leeds. The divisions are bitter and the feud long-standing.

Athletics is on the periphery of all this, and yet for three years in the early 1950s there was no finer example in any field than the rivalry between the North and South and their two running heroes: the self-confessed up-and-coming "plodder" from Manchester, Walter Hesketh, and the thin, aesthetic "softie" from Surrey, Douglas Alastair Gordon Pirie. They had been born just two months or so apart – Hesketh on 30 October 1930 and Pirie on 10 February 1931 – and they were idols to their respective fans.

Pirie, ironically, was born in Leeds, with a Scottish cross-country international as a father, but brought up in Coulsdon, by the Surrey Downs, which was a short commuter ride into London. He went to a grammar school and before and after National Service worked in a bank. Hesketh was the more mature of the two, coming from working-class stock in Manchester, and was originally inspired by the comic-book hero, Wilson of The Wizard, and then by cross-country champions Jack Holden and Geoffrey Saunders when he saw them run in the National in 1946. This was a race in which he was too young to take part, though already at 15 a champion in his age group.

Hesketh had discovered that he could run by racing the tram the three miles home to Davyhulme to save the fare, resting whenever the tram stopped and then continuing on his way. This made him the fastest man in his club, Manchester AC, by the time he was 16 and then Northern and National youths' cross-country champion in 1948. In his first win he was battling with Jack Price, of East Cheshire Harriers, when someone told Price that there was a quarter-of-a-mile to go. Hesketh did not hear this, but both men sprinted, and when Price discovered that there was still three-quarters of a mile remaining he dropped out, and an amazed Hesketh kept going and won. At the National, at Graves Park, Sheffield, he won by 25 seconds. Pirie, incidentally, was 8th.

Hesketh, who was 5ft 10in (1.77m) tall and weighed just over 11st (70kg), was of stocky build, with powerful legs that made him almost unbeatable if there were hills on the course. He went into the Army for National Service and was 3rd in the National junior in 1949 to Geoff Saunders, who would be a future International Championship winner, and was a fellow Lancastrian from Bolton United Harriers. Hesketh suffered with several injuries that would have stopped a normal runner, but then at Aylesbury in 1950 he won the first of two National junior titles (Pirie 20th) before going on to succeed again at Richmond, in Yorkshire, in 1951, 55 seconds ahead of Pirie. He thus became the first man to complete a triple of the National titles in any of the age groups (and only one other man, David Black, has since repeated the feat).

While Hesketh was establishing a name for himself up North, and coming down to Aylesbury to show the "softies" how to run. Pirie was was making good progress himself, after helping his father to carry the Olympic torch on one stage of the road relay in 1948 and then seeing Zátopek run in the Games themselves, but still finishing behind Hesketh over the country and in age-group mile races on the track.

There were five races that brought the rivalry and the fans to battle, where the honour of both regions was at stake: the National junior cross-country of 1951 and the National senior of 1952, the AAA six miles and the match against France in 1951, and the AAA six miles of 1952 which would decide places in the Olympic team. Both sets of supporters thought their man was a certainty in all these races, and the South had an edge because nearly all of the athletics reporters for newspapers and magazines came from there and it was natural that they should back their man.

It was reasonable, too, that they should think that Pirie was certain to win. In the cross-country season of 1951, for example, Pirie had progressed so much that in the Inter-Counties race, which in those days was a stepping-stone to the National and International selection, he ran Dr Frank Aaron, the British six miles record-holder and the best cross-country runner in the land, very close, and he also won the Southern junior by two minutes. Pirie had been using Zátopek's training methods during his two years of RAF National Service, including wearing heavy military boots, and had a photo of the Czech champion over his bed like a film star.

Pirie was the favourite, but Hesketh finished almost a minute in front

Few except Hesketh and his Northern supporters thought that Pirie could lose in the National junior race, but he did so, and Hesketh infuriated the Southerners by shaking the hands of his fans and signing autographs in the finishing-tunnel before Pirie hove into sight. Even so, Hesketh got on well with Pirie but did not like the excuses he made when he was beaten. In the 1952 National senior race over a 10-mile course at Perry Barr, Birmingham, Hesketh was forced to answer a call of nature as they raced along, but caught his man and then stood for a moment at the top of the final hill before winning by 56 seconds. The first 10 were as follows:

1 Hesketh 55:32, 2 Pirie 56:28, 3 Fred Norris 56:42, 4 Jim Peters 56:50, 5 Frank Sando 56:50, 6 Eddie Bannon (Scotland) 57:00, 7 Charles Owens (Northern Ireland) 57:04, 8 Eddie Hardy 57:06, 9 Dick Adams 57:09, 10 Frank Aaron 57:25.

The two track races of 1951 involved nothing as dramatic as that, but in their last clash in 1952 the great rivals actually came to blows on the White City track and for a whole lap they fought and barged each other until the track referee, Walter Jewell, stepped into their path – by which time they were out in the third and fourth lanes – and told them that if they did not stop their wrangling they would both be disqualified

Walter Hesketh is now 72. He suffers from cancer, the after-effects of a stroke and a heart condition that could kill him at any moment. His working life has involved many jobs because he was often sacked for taking time off for running, and his c.v. would make a book in itself. Yet he still has the sparkle of old. He was a juggler in the Tommy Cooper mould and used to entertain his fellow-athletes on trips abroad. He can remember his athletics career with a clarity that belies his age, and when we talked in his home earlier this year he laughed as he recalled his contests with Pirie.

There is no doubt that he had far more natural talent than Pirie, but he lacked the concentration and determination that made the Southern "softie" a world record-holder, an Olympic Games and European Championships medallist, and a name that was known all over the world. Hesketh would not go on with his athletics career unless he gave it 100 per cent, but he lost interest after ill-health and not winning any more.

He recalled: "Our clashes were a bitter example of the rivalry between the North and the South in those days. There was no doubt that they considered we lived in an uncivilised part of the country. Those were the days when they always picked a Southerner over a Northerner if they were of equal ability – the University men over anyone else, and the Oxford and Cambridge men over all of us. It didn't happen with Pirie and me because I kept beating him, much to the annoyance of the Southerners and the press who always said he would beat me. I remember before the 1951 National junior that editor Jimmy Green wrote in 'Athletics Weekly' that 'I fully expect Pirie to beat Hesketh', but when I won by 55 seconds he admitted he was wrong and wrote, 'It's as fine a run as I have seen for many a year. He was in devastating form. Pirie no doubt feels a little disappointed, but it is no disgrace to be beaten by such a grand runner, and Gordon will give his rival a lot more trouble in the future than he did at Richmond. Hesketh ran his rival into the ground and I fully believe he would have won the Senior race' "

That senior event of 1951 was won by Dr Frank Aaron, who had been 4th in the 1950 European Championships 10,000 metres, and who ran Hesketh close in the Home international three weeks later. What others did not know was that Hesketh had run a six miles time-trial on the heavy Fallowfield track, in Manchester, a week before the National. Helped by David Coleman – then a promising member of the Manchester AC cross-country team and later BBC TV commentator – Hesketh ran 29:40 in a 30mph gale that blew the cinders off the track. The time was three seconds faster than Aaron's British record.

"Unpaid professionals ... we would have made real money"

It was after the junior National that year that Hesketh fell out with Pirie when the latter said that he had only lost because he had had flu. Hesketh recalled: "He always had an excuse, and I didn't like that. He was a bad loser. He was a great runner and I felt sorry for him because I reckoned that he would have been the first man to break four minutes for the mile if only he had concentrated on that distance.

"We were unpaid professionals in those days and our times were terrible by the times of today, but I only trained twice a week and raced on Saturdays, mainly in two-mile team events for the club. I didn't like travelling much, but I think that with the improved tracks, equipment, training methods, and the time to train we would have been just as good and we would have made real money. Our times on the track were not nearly as fast as those over the country. If you didn't go flat out from the start in cross-country and kept going you were left behind. On the track you usually only had to run fast enough to win".

In 1949 Hesketh had placed 3rd in the AAA Championships six miles, being knocked off the track by the Latvian-born winner, Valdu Lillakas, in the race to the tape while leading into the home straight and then being pipped on the line by Stan Cox. Lillakas won in 30:15.0 and Hesketh ran 30:19.2. Hesketh remembers: "Jack Crump ran over to make sure we were not going to protest. We didn't, but I think that cost me my place in the Empire Games team for New Zealand". In 1950 Hesketh was way ahead of Pirie in the athletics world, reducing the stage record in the Withington road relay, in Manchester, against the cream of the North from 17:03 to 16:27 and running 14:22 to finish just behind Aaron in the Northern three miles. He had to mix military service duties with limited running but was also Army champion at three miles.

For the track season of 1951 Hesketh had high hopes., but for the first time the Southern bean-pole got ahead early in the AAA Championships six miles and Hesketh misjudged the race and could not catch him. Pirie ran a British record 29:32.0, with Hesketh was 18 seconds behind. They were both selected for the match against France at the White City Stadium during the Bank Holiday weekend, Saturday 4 August and Monday 6 August. Having tried on their first GB vests in private, afraid of being accused of showing off, on the day they ran together until the announcer said that they were close to the British five miles record time of Alfred Shrubb from 1904 and Hesketh sprinted the last 100 yards to the mark to break the record in 24:28.4 and then kept going. Full of running, he raced away for a new British six miles record in the rain of 29:13.8, with Pirie nearly 20 seconds behind and complaining that Hesketh should have waited and they could have broken the five miles record together. The French pair were well beaten, and GB won the men's match by 115pts to 89 and the women's by 61 to 41 as among other winners were E. McDonald Bailey (100 and 220 yards), Arthur Wint (440 and 880 yards), Bill Nankeville (one mile) and both relay teams.

Hesketh and Pirie were both selected for the ill-fated tour of the Balkans when nearly everyone went down with stomach trouble. Hesketh was 3rd to Pirie at 10,000 metres against Yugoslavia (31:11.2 to 31:52.8, separated by a future International cross-country champion, Franjo Mihalic) and 3rd again in an incredibly slow 33:55.6 to Pirie's 32:28.5 against Turkey, but this was gallant running considering their illness which had struck so badly that Roy Beckett, who had beaten Chris Chataway by inches in the AAA three miles, had to run off the track after five laps of the 5000 metres. Away from the track Hesketh took the team's minds off their problems by his juggling act as he broke plates and saucers in a deliberately ham-fisted way.

Pirie and Hesketh meet again in the 1952 National

The last two of the great clashes between Hesketh and Pirie were in 1952. Prior to the National Cross-country Championships Pirie had been unbeatable, winning the Southern senior title by a minute, while Hesketh had been injured but had then recovered to win the Northern. Again the press was certain that Pirie would win the National in Birmingham but what they did not know was that in another of Hesketh's 10,000 metres time-trials the weekend before he had run 29:18, with David Coleman again cutting out the pace, which was not much slower than Zátopek's world record of 29:02.6, and this despite Hesketh suffering a virus infection.

Hesketh nearly missed the start of the National as the train on which he was travelling (and, in the process, winning £7 playing pontoon) was late, and he only had time to snatch a bread roll to eat as he ran for the bus. Pirie raced away from the 461 starters, but by the first mile Hesketh was marginally in the lead and the time was 4:18, which was fast for a mile in any circumstances in 1952. Hesketh vividly recalls the day:

"Pirie had decided to run the lot of us off our feet in the first mile to lay the foundation of a great win, and then this plodding Northern upstart storms past him to reach the mile marker first. I turned to look at him and smiled. He looked shocked and I could see his confidence draining away as the seed of doubt had been sown in his mind. I was bursting for the toilet because the queues were too big before the start, but Pirie was right behind me. At halfway I darted off the course and into the bushes. I then caught him up and told him I felt better now, but he kept trying to go away from me on the hills, and he should have known just how strong I was on the hills. I could beat anyone.

"I made my break three miles from home, halfway up the big hill. At the top someone shouted I was 30 yards clear, and as soon as I was off the gradient my strength and energy came flooding back and I was flying. I picked up a lead of about 600 yards and I coasted to the brow of the hill with about a mile to go. In sight of the large crowd several hundred metres away at the bottom I turned and looked back over the course to see where the rest of them had got to. I felt peace at the top of that hill, all alone with the hill, the cool refreshing breeze, and my thoughts. I had totally outclassed and eclipsed the best runners in the land to confirm my unofficial time-trial the week before, just over 10 seconds slower than Zátopek, and I would have beaten him that day in Birmingham. I thought of the Olympics just four months away, and at that moment I thought there was only Zátopek between me and the gold medal.

"There was still no other runner in sight. One of my supporters told me afterwards they thought that I'd killed Pirie and buried him and that I looked like the stag in Landseer's famous painting of the Monarch of the Glen, but I thought that I'd waited long enough and ran down to beat Pirie by 56 seconds. Inevitably he had an excuse, that he had strained his foot, and later I came across him being carried by his supporters, and I called across that it was too late for that. If they'd carried him up those big hills during the race he would have been in with a chance!"

Victory that day gave Hesketh five clear wins over Pirie in major cross-country races during their days in the various age groups, as follows:

1948: Youths - Hesketh 1st, Pirie 8th
1949: Junior - Hesketh 3rd, Pirie 12th
1950: Junior - Hesketh 1st, Pirie 20th
1951: Junior - Hesketh 1st, Pirie 2nd
1952: Senior - Hesketh 1st, Pirie 2nd

But then everything went wrong for Hesketh. He was 4th in the International Cross-Country Championships at Hamilton Park race-course, in Scotland, as Alain Mimoun led France to an easy win over England, 35pts to 64, but the virus from which Hesketh had been suffering turned to pneumonia. Against his wishes, his club wanted him to run in the prestigious Manchester-to-Blackpool road relay, and although he kept 3rd position on the penultimate stage, the illness was to end all his hopes and dreams of winning the Olympics. He knew he was not fit when he lined up for the AAA six miles and made a gallant attempt, but when Pirie started to come by ready to go away after three miles it was too much of an effort.

Hesketh recalled: "I'd tried to slow it down, but when he went by I grabbed him by the elbow and said, 'Where do you think you're going?' Astonished is not a word I often use, but he had that look on his face and he shrugged me off and banged me with his elbows. I was going at him as well, and we ran the whole lap fighting in the third and fourth lanes. He had lost interest in the race and we almost came to blows as went round. The referee, Walter Jewell, was waiting for us in the fourth lane looking like an angry Rottweiler and shouted that if there was any more of that we were both off. Then Pirie left me, followed by Frank Sando and Fred Norris, and I could have been 4th but I gave up. The Olympics was everything that I'd been working for. I was a 100 per cent trier and only a 100 per cent trier knows what it means to miss the Olympics".

This was the end of the Pirie-Hesketh rivalry, but it was not quite the end of Hesketh's injury-prone and exciting career. He missed almost all the 1953 cross-country season, and then Jack Crump picked him for an early-season trip to Morocco with Roger Bannister and Chris Chataway to make up for missing the Olympics. In his first 3000 metres race in Casablanca Hesketh fell and was trampled by the pack of 40 as they went over and round him, but he picked himself up, and to the roar of the crowd worked his way through until he reached the front. Despite grazed elbows and bleeding legs, he managed 3rd place behind the former Olympic 5000 metres champion, Gaston Reiff (8:40 2) in 8:57.0.

Opposite, top: Three Northerners lead the International Cross-Country Championships race of 1951 at Caerleon, in South Wales - left to right, Frank Aaron (2nd), Geoff Saunders (1st) and Walter Hesketh (4th). Hesketh had been selected after beating Gordon Pirie for the National junior title.

Opposite, bottom: One of Hesketh's numerous wins, at the East Lancashire junior event of 1950 - left to right, Jeff Eastham (3rd), Hesketh and Jack Price (2nd).
Photograph supplied by Neil Shuttleworth

Bannister later wrote of Hesketh: "He was the star of the tour. In his first race, accustomed to the freedom of the countryside, he was jostled and crashed headlong to the track. The crowd gasped as the other runners seemed to be trampling on him. He was yards behind as, streaming with blood, he looked furiously at the bunch of runners ahead. He climbed to his feet and courageously set off to catch them. Almost sprinting, he overtook them all before his anger died down. Although he did not win, the crowd were delighted with his spirit and courage.

"In all his subsequent races he was Morocco's hero, unmistakable as he ran, daubed with iodine from head to foot. At ceremonial banquets our team would be called on for some entertainment and Walter, a juggler by profession, was always happy to oblige, using oranges, plates, bottles and anything he could lay his hands on. With the Moroccans crying, 'Heeskeeth', his light-fingered dexterity followed the last course of every meal".

Jack Crump commented that Hesketh "has enough stamina and plenty of finishing speed but needs some fast lapping to put him right back where he belongs, a real rival to Pirie". Then in Brussels in June Hesketh ran away with a 10,000 metres race in the last lap, and Crump described his performance in glowing terms in "Athletics Weekly": "He produced a simply extraordinary finish. He went as if he'd been stung and the big crowd rose to him. He is getting back to his best form and he is a great fellow to have in the team".

It was not to be. The promise was not fulfilled. Hesketh's failure to go to the Olympics, his poor health and his lack of interest knocked the stuffing out of the Northerner, and 1953 was Pirie's year of years. Pirie was the best in the world, the king of all that he surveyed.

Hesketh was caught up in the flow. He won an early-season 10,000 metres in Brussels in 31:38.0 and ran a lifetime best three miles of 14:19.8 when finishing 4th in Pirie's wake in the Inter-Counties Championships. There was another personal best in the AAA six miles when he was 5th in 29:12.4 as Pirie set a world record of 28:19.4. Then Hesketh went on tour to Europe to run as second string to Frank Sando at 10,000 metres against Germany, where Pirie won at 5000 in 14:02.6 and also at 10,000 against Sweden in 29:17.2.

In the Germany-v-GB 10,000, Sando completely outclassed Hesketh and the two Germans, but when he had lapped them the real race began. The German, Eberlein, tried to stay with Sando as he lapped them and then Hesketh closed the gap before dropping back with cramp. He recalled: "We raced round the last lap until the German cracked, but in the last 100 metres he began to close up on me and I held on and knew that five metres from the tape I had it in the bag!"

The tour, his last, was notable for two very different matters. Hesketh overturned a canoe on a Swedish lake and was only just rescued from drowning by two of his team-mates and then he almost drowned Harold Abrahams in another lake by giving his boat a push and landing the distinguished hero of the 1924 Olympics, journalist, administrator and NUTS president, face first in the water. HMA was not amused.

Walter Hesketh's running career came to an end and he concluded our conversation by saying: "I never reached my potential – nowhere near. I was just a beginner scraping the barrel. I regret it now. Of course I do, but I had lost interest and did not have the power to force myself along. It's all in the mind, isn't it? Still, I remember all those scraps with Pirie. Great times. I often think of them".

Note: this article was first published in "Track Stats", Volume 40, No.3, August 2002. Walter Hesketh died on 15 June 2007, aged 76.

Only a mile from the finish – "Then I woke up in hospital, and there in the next bed was Jim"

In the spring of 1950 Stan Cox, Britain's top six-miler, decided to move up to the marathon because he thought he would not be quick enough at the age of 32 to defeat the up-and-coming youngsters. He was right: Frank Aaron, Walter Hesketh and Gordon Pirie were far faster than he was. Cox had a secret plan for the marathon that involved running 100 miles a week instead of his previous training of two or three runs of five or seven miles with his friends at Southgate Harriers. His secret weapon in his bid for Olympic glory was his plan to run in training at a speed almost as fast as he would run in the race itself, thereby attuning his body to accept that little bit extra on the day.

It was a clever move and one that succeeded beyond his wildest dreams. He became a wonderful marathon runner – but with a terrible twist to the tale. When he ran 2hr 21min 42sec to break the world record in the Poly marathon two years later he was only 2nd in the race. His old rival on the track and the man he could always beat, Jim Peters, of Essex Beagles, had also started training secretly for the marathon under the eagle eye of the 1924-28 Olympian, Johnny Johnston, who was 8th at 5000 metres in the latter Games, and was using the same methods that were to revolutionise the event.

No one had been more surprised than the two old friends when they lined up for the Finchley 20 miles road race in 1951 and tried to beat the old maestro, Jack Holden, who had won the British Empire and European marathon titles the year before. Holden saw them off on that occasion, but a few weeks later in the Polytechnic Harriers marathon Peters raced home and an injured Cox was 2nd, with Holden dropping out. The next year both Peters and Cox broke the world's best performance in the Poly and were Britain's greatest hopes for the Olympics in Helsinki. Two years later they were England's candidates for the Empire title in Vancouver. As we all know, both races were disasters and disappointments, caused by unforeseen events out of their control, but I will come to the story of those races in due course.

Stanley Ernest Walker Cox was born in Wood Green, Middlesex, on 15 July 1918, and was 5ft 7½in (1.71m), tall, weighing 9st 10lb (63kg). He had started running at school as a sprinter and continued with his club until a scouts' cross-country race in 1937 when he discovered that he was a natural-born distance-runner. He won county and regional age-group cross-country races and tried miling and a few two-mile races with some success. In 1939 he entered the AAA three miles just before his 21st birthday (the day he volunteered for the RAF on the eve of World War II) and in his first race over that distance was faster than Peter Ward's British record of 14:15.8 with 14:13.6 in 4th place. It was the best three-mile race ever seen in Britain as Jack Emery won in 14:08.0 from Ward, with Aubrey Reeve 3rd.

A few days later the novice was asked to be the pacemaker in Emery's two-mile record attempt in Manchester and did such a good job that he ran 9:08.0 behind Emery (9:03.4) and Ward, who were both inside Emery's old record of 9:07.6, with Cox just missing it. This performance brought Cox an invitation to the big Bank Holiday meeting at the White City to replace the injured Sydney Wooderson in the mile and he clocked 4:22.4 for a lifetime best, coming 5th to the ever-improving Dennis Pell. The two of them were in the Great Britain team which flew to Cologne for the eve-of-war match against Germany, and Pell combined the trip with his honeymoon, thus becoming the first British athlete allowed to take his wife with him to an away match. He ran a lifetime best to lose the 1500 metres by inches in 3:50.4. Cox, in his debut at

5000 metres, was last in 15:32.2.

Seven years later Cox was still in the GB team for the first post-war international in Paris against France where he came 3rd in 15:20.5. In between times he had kept his civilian occupation as a storeman in the RAF, spending over three years in the desert in Iraq and returning to Britain as a Sergeant and being posted to Felixstowe in Suffolk, to where he was to eventually retire in 1979. There he met his wife, Audrey, and did some running with the local Ipswich Harriers, winning the Eastern Counties cross-country for them and also winning and breaking the club record in a 4½ miles road race. This is a record which has lasted for 50 years.

During the war Cox went through France and Germany after the D-Day invasion and in 1945 he ended up as part of an elite squad of service athletes who did nothing else but train at the RAF track at Uxbridge. It paid dividends for him because he could live at home in North London and he became very fit for the track battles to come with his friend, Jim Peters. It was Peters who won the 1946 AAA track six miles and the 1947 10 miles while Stan stuck to the three miles and 5000 metres, finishing well in the Wooderson 1946 record AAA race. He also won a good battle at 5000 metres that year in Antwerp with the Belgian, Lucien Theys, after missing the start. The race was restarted and Cox set a lifetime best of 15:02.2. In addition, he ran for the AAA in representative matches.

In 1948 he moved up to six miles and won the AAA title from Peters (30:08.4 to 30:16.0) after a brief unofficial trip to Dublin to give the leading British Olympic hopes the chance of having a good meal away from the home rationing. Cox was first string for the Olympic 10,000 metres in London, but it was typical of those days that the only way he could compete was to take a day off work and lose a day's pay. With a wife and two young children, and being paid hourly by his then employers, the giant Standard Telephones & Cable (more of this later), that was as much as he could afford.

Seventh place in the Olympic 10,000 metres ... but did he run a lap too many?

In blazing heat the race was won by the astonishing Emil Zátopek in 29:59.6, lapping everyone once Viljo Heino, the former world record-holder from Finland, had stepped off the track – thereby causing considerable confusion amongst the lap-recorders. Cox finished 7th in exactly the same time as he had run the AAA six miles plus a minute, which matched the accepted form of conversion. However, he recalls: "Harold Abrahams insisted that I had run a lap too many. He said that the officials who were keeping the lap count were not concentrating on their job but on Zátopek. He said that I had run a lap too many because I did not get the bell when I should have done. He repeated it in his radio report, but there has never been any means of proving it one way or the other because there was no film. If he was right, I would have been 4th in a much faster time. Anyway, I was first Briton home and beat Jim. I could always beat him on the track but never on the road. He always had the edge there".

In 1949 Cox was still the top Briton at six miles, finishing 2nd to the Estonian refugee, Valdu Lillakas, in the AAA Championships, and with that behind him he hoped to go to Auckland for the 1950 British Empire Games, where he stood a very good chance of winning the gold. He said: "In those days the selectors sent you a letter in advance to make sure you could afford to go because you had to spend your own money and to get permission from your boss. I asked and a few days later someone from personnel came to see me and showed me a letter in a box-file that said 'as Mr Cox is a married man with responsibilities he should not want to go on such a venture'. The person took the letter away and that was it. I told a couple of friends in the press but they could not do anything without the letter and I could not get that. I went to personnel and asked what would happen if I did go and they said if I did there would be no job to come back to. I could not afford the trip so I missed it".

There was an interesting follow-up to this decision. He changed jobs, going first to a cash-register company and then becoming a salesman with a sports-goods company, and neither of these were jobs which he enjoyed much, but both employers gave him paid leave for the Olympics and Empire Games. Then in 1955 he ran in a two-mile team race for his club (he was always a great team man, racing well into the 1960s after retiring from top-class athletics in 1956) at the Standard Telephone & Cable sports and was greeted by the chairman, Sir Thomas Spencer, who asked how he was doing. Sir Thomas was astonished to learn that this international athlete no longer worked for the company and within a fortnight had him back. A week later Cox asked for time off to run in the Enschede marathon in Holland and was granted it with pay. He stayed with the same company, climbing the promotion ladder, getting involved early on in computers, and ending up as a computer systems manager.

Back to athletics: 1950 was the start of his secret long runs, which he once described as "commando training", increasing his weekly mileage from 20 to 100. He appeared in club races over the country and he ran through the winter until the Southern nine miles but not in the National. He also raced on the track and in road relays as always but not in the championships.

He had always found that running came naturally to him. It was never a bother and he was able to fit the extra 80 miles a week into his normal family life and still give priority to his wife and two daughters. He was coached on and off by the 1920 double Olympic gold-medallist, Albert Hill, and by the 1930 Empire three miles champion, Stan Tomlin, as well as the national newspaper journalist, Armour Milne, and Johnny Johnston, but mainly he coached himself in his marathon days.

Advice from a McWhirter twin, and the times improve

The training paid off in 1951 as he followed his 3rd place in the Finchley 20 with 2nd to Peters in the Poly, four minutes behind after pulling a muscle. He had the injury repaired so well at an athletes' clinic that it made his leg stronger, and he also benefited from a suggestion by the authoritative journalist, Norris McWhirter, that if he wore a lighter-weight shoe it would make him faster because of the thousands of times he lifted his feet over the marathon distance. He bought regular pairs of white thin-soled plimsolls for 9s 11d (just under 50 pence) and took seconds off his time.

In 1952 he started the year with the Mitcham 15 miles, which was an event he was to win four times, and he then faced Jim Peters again in the Poly. The two of them ran sensational times: 2:20:42.2 to 2:21:42 (Cox's best ever), with Geoff Iden five minutes behind. It was the first of Peters's four world bests and Cox was to be 2nd on three of those occasions. Peters's time in that first race was almost five minutes faster than the previous best set by Yun Bok Suh, of Korea, in the 1947 Boston marathon.

Cox recalls: "Our times had never been approached by anyone. We were the best in the world and when the times were queried the course was measured over four Sundays and found to be 800 yards over distance. We were the best in the world by far and favourites for the Olympic title". Even if they had known then that Zátopek was going to run the marathon after winning the 5000 and 10,000 metres it would not have bothered them, so confident were they.

Sadly, the circumstances leading up to the Helsinki marathon were all against the hopes of the British runners, as Cox ruefully recalls: "The selectors decided that, rather than go out with the rest of the team and have all that pressure because we were the top contenders, they would fly us out just four days before the race. We went in a rough old York aircraft, a wartime freight-carrier, with the team of cyclists. Jim and I, who were great friends and roomed together, had our luggage by our sides alongside one of the doors. As we took off I could see our labels flapping and spotted daylight through the door while we were airborne! We were eventually moved away, but the damage had been done and we both caught flu and collapsed because of this during the race.

"My troubles continued before the race. A Finnish doctor found my heart beats far too high 'due to pre-race tension' and said that I should not run. I found an American doctor, explained the situation, and he cleared me. Jim dropped out and I reached 20 miles and was in 6th place when I got cramp in my shoulders which spread down my leg and I collapsed. The doctor who was in the ambulance that picked me up was the one who examined me before the race. He said: 'You are Cox. I told you you should not run'."

Half-a-century later Cox still feels the sense of disappointment. When they returned to Britain he and Peters were examined by Harold Abrahams's distinguished doctor brother, Sir Adolphe, and by the Queen's surgeon, Sir Arthur Porritt, who had placed 3rd in the memorable Abrahams Olympic 100 metres of 1924. Cox said: "They wanted to find out the cause of our collapse. In the race my left arm had gone limp and then my left side became more or less paralysed and it reached my legs. I could not run any more and I collapsed in the road. They decided that the draught affected the left side of our bodies and caused the flu which came out 48 hours later and finished our chances".

Back in action after the Olympic disappointment, and more fast times to come

The setback stopped neither of them going on with their training and their shattering of world records. Cox, though still being advised by Johnny Johnston, who was also Peters's coach, followed his own ideas because he realised that in Johnston's eyes it was always Peters who took priority. Peters won the Mitcham 15 by two minutes and set a new world best of 2:18:40.2 in the 1953 Poly, with Cox unable to hold him and finishing 7½ minutes behind. Peters won the AAA race, which Cox missed because of a family holiday. The positions were the same as usual in the Enschede race in Holland: Peters breaking the record with 2:19:22 and Cox five minutes back.

Cox reflects: "It was always the same. He always had the edge over me. After that race Jack Crump, the British team manager, took us to lunch in Amsterdam as a reward for our efforts. Crump was there because British athletes going abroad always had to have a manager with them, and during the lunch he said he had a present for our wives as we had done so well. He produced two little carrier-bags from under the table and inside each was half a piece of Edam cheese worth a few pence! Compare that with what is happening today. You just think that if today's money had been around in my day I would have been a millionaire."

The 1954 season started well for Cox with wins in the Mitcham and Finchley road races, and then a great run in the Poly, though nearly six minutes behind as Peters went faster than ever with a time of 2:17:39.4. When the pair of them arrived in Vancouver for the Empire Games they discovered that their race was to be held in the blazing heat of the midday sun without any shade on the course, and so they repeatedly asked the organisers to move the start to a more sensible time.

Cox remembers: "We told them we'd be facing the hottest part of the day, but they wouldn't change it because it would interfere with the Bannister-v-Landy mile, which was the showpiece of the last day. We ran our normal race and hoped for the best, but we both had sunstroke and collapsed. I hit a telegraph pole and landed in a ditch a mile from the stadium and Jim was rolling around in a daze before they pulled him off the track. I woke up in hospital and there in the next bed was Jim. The Scotsman, Joe McGhee, had dropped out and was sitting by the roadside with his coach when he heard the news that both of us who had been a long way ahead

Stan Cox leads the great Zátopek in the 1952 Olympic marathon, but the roles were soon reversed. Cox and his GB team-mate, Jim Peters, dropped out, and Zätopek went on to win his third gold medal of the Games. Half-a-century later Cox still felt the sense of disappointment.

of him were out. So he got up and ran on to win. I've always thought that was not right because I'm sure his coach would have touched him at some time as they talked and that would have been the end of his race. But it's all a long time ago now". [*]

That was Jim Peters's last race – but not Stan Cox's. He believed that with his short stride and his never-say-die attitude that he still had some good racing in his legs. However, 1955 was not a good year for him as he pulled a muscle in the Poly and had to drop out, and then in the AAA race on a sunny 80°F day which was very reminiscent of his Canadian experience he was in the lead with his old rival, Geoff Iden, when he had an attack of cramp at 17 miles, and his advisers decided that no risk should be taken in the heat and pulled him out.

Cox kept training for the 1956 Olympics but missed the Poly because of illness. In the AAA championship event he gave Harry Hicks a tremendous race, coming through in the latter stages and getting within a minute of the Hampstead Harrier, and he thus thought that he stood a chance of going to Melbourne. It was not to be as the selectors took the first three in the Poly, all of whom failed in the Olympic race, while Cox went to the annual Kosice event in Czechoslovakia, where he fell heavily but picked himself up to finish 6th.

It is claimed that misfortunes come in threes, and Stan Cox's third mishap following the

---

[*] In justice to Joe McGhee, the winner of the 1954 Empire Games marathon, the press story that he had dropped out before resuming the race was untrue. In a letter to Peter Lovesey in 1980 he wrote: "At no time did I collapse. On one occasion only, I tripped momentarily on the kerb. Over the last four miles, indeed, I was engaged in a very active race, pulling away from the two South Africans Jackie Mekler and Johann Barnard."

Helsinki and Vancouver races occurred after he had been persuaded by an old friend and fellow-employee, Les Cohen, to take up officiating and did so as a javelin judge. Cox recalls the incident vividly.

"It was at Hurlingham and I was measuring the throws. I was just standing up after one measurement when 'Bang!'- a javelin went right into me, a quarter-of-an-inch to the side of my heart. The only thing that saved me was a blue plastic pen that was in my blazer pocket. The javelin hit the pen and went to the right instead of left into my heart, which would have killed me. It also diverted into a rib which stopped it, as otherwise it would have gone right through me. There was blood all over the place, but I didn't pass out. My wife and children were there and I was rushed to hospital and had my picture on the front of the evening newspapers.

"The young man whose javelin had hit me came and apologised and said that he would never throw again, but I told him that it was an accident and that he should carry on. One outcome was that they changed the rules to make sure that after a throw was measured no one else could throw until a signal was given".

The near-disaster did not stop Stan running and he continued at club level for some years, loving every minute of it. He regrets nothing, having had great races, made great friends, and mixed happily with Bannister, Chataway and the Oxbridge crowd in an era when you had to take your own soap, towels and shoe-cleaning materials to the Olympics because none were provided.

His last thought? "I don't think I could have run any faster, but obviously I would have done better if Jim hadn't been on the scene".

Stan Cox's personal best performances were 4:22.4 for the mile, 9:08.0 for two miles and 14:13.6 for three miles (all pre-World War II), 15:02.2 for 5000 metres, 29:53.2 for six miles, 31:08.4 (but probably faster) for 10,000 metres, and 2:21:42 for the marathon.

Note: this article was first published in "Track Stats", Volume 40, No.3, August 2002. Stan Cox died on 27 June 2012, aged 93.

A year before Bannister breaks four minutes, Stampfl finds someone else who "could run 3:55"

The "LAC News" was the magazine of the now defunct London Athletic Club, which had been founded in 1863 as Mincing Lane AC and had changed its name a year later. In 1948 a reporter wrote about a match at Camberley against the Royal Military Academy Sandhurst. "Right away let us record that the most promising young athlete we have seen for a long, long while was the Luton miler, D. Seaman, not yet 16 years old, who ran the mile in under 4:30. A Dalrymple discovery, this boy ran really well to finish very close to the winner in 4:28.8. Here are two names that will make news – if they are properly handled".

The winner of the race, Glover, of the RMA, never did go on to make news, but young Don Seaman, whose time was faster than either Sydney Wooderson or Roger Bannister at that age, most certainly did. The "Dalrymple" who had discovered him was Jock Dalrymple, an Olympic javelin representative whose son, Malcolm, was British record-holder in that event and competed in the 1948 Games. Both were LAC members.

Yet every circumstance was against Seaman becoming a champion miler. Born at Sawston, in Cambridgeshire, on 14 September 1932, his adult height of 6ft 4in (1.96m) was more suited to a quarter-miler and his stride of 9ft 6in (2.90m) was almost as long as that of the Jamaican 400 metres silver-medallist of 1948, Arthur Wint. Seaman had the most terrible trouble with his right Achilles tendon, and his career was put paid to prematurely by the ignorance and disbelief of an RAF physical training instructor about such an injury. Even so, in the three seasons that Seaman was active as a senior athlete, he had run a 1:52.6 half-mile relay stage and, much more impressively, a 4:08.0 mile behind Bannister's 4:05.2 in the 1953 AAA Championships to rank as 4th fastest Briton of the year.

Seaman became a world record-holder in the 4 x 1 mile relay that same year and would have been part of another British team that broke the world 4 x 1500 metres record at the end of the season but for his mother being taken seriously ill. Gordon Pirie, in his year of years, replaced Seaman to add one more record to his bag.

The renowned Austrian born Franz Stampfl, who coached Bannister, was so impressed by young Seaman's running that he predicted that he would run 3:55 for the mile, and that forecast was made the year before Bannister became the first man to break four minutes. Seaman did not believe Stampfl's assessment of him and thought only that 4:04 was well within his reach, but as he was no more than 21 at the time, and his best years were surely ahead of him, there is no reason why Stampfl should not have been proved right. Instead, Herb Elliott was the man who eventually beat 3:55 in 1958.

Above his bed as a youngster in the family home at Sawston and then at Luton, in Bedfordshire, to where they moved, Seaman had pinned a chart that contained three names on it – his own, Wooderson's and Bannister's – with the times which each had achieved from the age of 15 onwards. Already at only 11, Seaman had been 6ft (1.83m) tall, gangling and long-legged, and lacking co-ordination so that he was kept out of all sports.

More than half-a-century on, I went to see Don Seaman in the company of one of his old rivals, Doug Wilson, and at this point in the article I must declare an interest because my first out-of-school race was in the Cambridgeshire cross-country championships at Sawston in January of 1949. All I saw was the back of the enormously tall holder of the title as he hurtled off into the heavy fen countryside, and I finished 58 seconds behind him in 2nd place. A few weeks later I lined up with him again in the Eastern Counties youths event at Mildenhall, in Suffolk, and I finished well down, but poor Seaman twisted his ankle in the fern and bracken and dropped out.

The summer before, he had won the county 880/mile double in faster times than the senior champion after being spotted in a youth club cross-country race where he found that he could run – really run – with a reservoir of flowing natural talent. It has to be said that Cambridgeshire was a county short of top men, and among the few internationals were "Bonzo" Howland in the shot, Peter Ward in the three miles, and Malcolm Dalrymple.

Seaman repeated his county double in 1949, setting records in both races and again faster than the senior winners, and achieved another double in the junior match between Cambridgeshire, Norfolk and Suffolk in 2:03.4 and 4:33.6. By this time he had moved to Luton and was being advised by a former Sparkhill Harriers sprinter, Charles Foley, whose view, supported by other short-distance men, was that Seaman should train and race sparingly so that he did not burn himself out. Seaman later realised that this advice was wrong, and when he really blossomed in 1952 and 1953 he was self-coached, using a hilly bank in a park in Luton for speed-play interval training an hour every day, rather on the lines of what coach Percy Cerutty and Herb Elliott were to be doing in Australia at their training camp at Portsea.

AAA junior champion in 1950, and then a first venture into senior ranks

In 1950 Seaman, now aged 17, broke two minutes and 4:30 in the Cambridgeshire championships and he then went on to win the AAA junior mile at Port Sunlight, across the River Mersey from Liverpool, in 4:29.0 ahead of a future international cross-country runner, Ray Hatton, of Birchfield Harriers. What the newspaper cuttings don't show is that Seaman had also won his heat about 80 minutes earlier in 4:24.0. A week later he ran his first race at the White City, losing by two seconds at 880 yards to the up-and-coming Brian Hewson, who would become European 1500 metres champion eight years later.

By 1951 Seaman was racing against seniors for the first time, though still only 18, and in the Inter-Counties championships he took his personal best down to a fine 4:22.6, finishing 5th behind Roy Beckett, of Kent (winner over Chris Chataway in the AAA three miles that year), who ran 4:17.4, and Alan Parker, Len Eyre and Jack Ashby. It was young Seaman's first experience of the heavy use of elbows and even fists that was common practice in racing in those days by certain milers. He was to come across Eyre again the next year when he suffered the first of his two great disappointments in athletics.

Also during 1951 Seaman achieved his usual double for the county titles, but having won the LAC club mile championship in the two previous years he was weirdly told on this occasion that he was too young and was not allowed to run. He was allowed in the three miles but not as a competitor for the club, and having stayed on the shoulder of a leading steeplechaser, David Ross, he beat him in the straight. Seaman now recalls: "But they took away the tape as I went past him and hurriedly put it back again to his great embarrassment so that he could take the title!"

Seaman won his first representative mile for the AAA against Cambridge University on his local track at Fenner's (three laps to the mile) ahead of Charlie Walker, of Belgrave Harriers, in 4:21.2 and then took four seconds off that by winning the Southern mile by 25 yards in 4:17.2 from Gordon Pirie, but it was a race that brought disaster. Now a grandfather and the father of two sons who were both successful athletes – Nick, a county 400 metres champion, and Mark, a marathon man – Seaman describes the onset of his injury problems: "Because of my height, and where I was training, I was starting to get tender Achilles tendons, particularly the right one. The

Southern championships were held at Reading on a track of black cinders,and it had rained. Gordon made his move with 300 yards to go, and I took him, and as I went round the final bend there was a soft spot, a hole, and my right foot went under me and I was out for the season with Achilles trouble.

"I went to see a consultant orthopaedic surgeon, who was a wonderful Canadian called Plewes, at my local hospital. He strapped up my leg from my toes to my knee and told me I could not run or trot on it but should take up old-time dancing, which I did – quadrilles, all the dances – and it kept me remarkably fit. At the start of the next season, which was Olympic year, I was on the 'possibles' list, and Joe Binks, who I had met at Cambridge, asked me if I was fit enough to run in the British Games if he sent me an invitation. I told him I was". Binks, the former mile record-holder, was athletics correspondent for the "News of the World", who were sponsoring the meeting.

It was a great 1952 season for Seaman until the AAA Championships that were being used as a trial for the Olympics in Helsinki. He started by beating Hewson, 1:56.2 to 1:57.3, at 800 metres in the Leyton floodlit meeting, and he then won an 800 metres from Eyre by eight yards in 1:56.0 at Aylesford. In a star-studded 1500 metres at the British Games on 31 May, won by Bill Nankeville in 3:49.0, with the American Don Gehrmann 3rd, Seaman was 4th in a time of 3:52.0 which was a world best for a 19-year-old, improving his previous best by about seven seconds.

His return to the White City for the AAA mile three weeks later brought frustration. He was sure that he was good enough to get in the British team, but after a 4:16.2 heat it was not to be, as he recalls: "I was tucked into the kerb and tried to get out with Eyre outside me and he said, 'Stay where you are'. I used to make a long run for home, from about 600 yards, because I did not have a short kick. I had done that in the junior championships two years before, and I wanted to do it then, but Eyre made sure there was no way I was going to. He and one or two others used their elbows and fists in races. They were very rough".

Missing out on the Olympics but setting a world junior record

Although Seaman ran a lifetime best of 4:14.8, he was out of it, with Nankeville winning in 4:09.8 from John Landy (the future world mile record-holder from Australia), David Law, Len Eyre and Jack Brown. Among those behind Seaman were Peter Driver 8th, Doug Wilson 9th and former junior prodigy Derrick Burfitt 10th. "I was bitterly disappointed when I was not selected," Seaman remembers. "My times were better than Eyre's, but Jack Crump, the British Board secretary, told me I was too young and my time would come, but I said that I might not get another chance, and that's what happened. I was hoping they would take me as a travelling reserve or assistant, as they did with Bannister in 1948, but they did not". At the Helsinki Olympics Bannister was 4th in the 1500 metres final; Nankeville reached the semi-finals; Eyre went out in the first round.

Seaman's year went on with a 3:51.3 for 1500 metres in a triangular match – "He is one of Britain's coming stars", reported "Athletics Weekly" – and a close 2nd to Nankeville's 3:00.4 for ¾-mile at the Glasgow Rangers sports. In the scorching heat of Belgrade on 31 August, where he had to be woken up to get to the start line, he set a magnificent under-20 world record of 3:50.6 in beating Andrija Otenhajmer, conqueror of Bannister the previous year.

Seaman made his international debut in the match against France, finishing 2nd in 3:51.2 to Bannister's 3:49.0, and at the age of 19 was Britain's youngest ever full international at 1500 metres or the mile. His strangest race of the year was at the Cambridge August Bank Holiday sports, where he was invited to run in a short-limit handicap mile off scratch, with the handicaps based on him achieving 4:11.0, but when he got to the City football ground he discovered that it was a normal handicap race with runners given up to 190 yards start! "I ran 2:03 for the first half-mile but walked off the track with 300 yards to go because I wasn't reining in the front runners", Seaman recalls. "The race was won in under four minutes, and as I walked off I heard a man in the stand say, 'If that silly bugger had run the last two laps as fast as he ran the first two he would have won it'!"

In his last full season of 1953 Seaman took his mile time down by five seconds with a run in the AAA final behind Bannister which was as he liked it because the pace was so fast that the field was strung out and he could let his stride flow without interference from anyone else. He also ran an 880 yards in a medley relay at the White City in 1:52.6, showing just how good he could have been at that distance but for his belief that he did not have the speed for it. This was proved wrong when on tour later in the year he held Britain's leading 400 metres runner, Peter Fryer, comfortably over 300 metres.

A change of tactics brings his fastest ever mile against Bannister

Seaman had begun the 1953 season with a 3rd place to David Law's 1:54.5 in the AAA-v-Oxford University 880 yards and then had his usual win in the county 880. He ran a 4:13.4 mile behind Bannister's 4:09.4 at the British Games and 1500 metres in 3:53.8 for 3rd to the Belgian, Frans Herman, in Brussels. Following a 1:55.5 half-mile, Seaman ran a great 4:12.0 mile in Belfast, beating Victor Milligan, after a first lap in 57 seconds, and then took advice from the former British Empire three miles champion, Stan Tomlin, who said, "Go out and run it from the front. It will give you confidence". He did just that at the Kinnaird Trophy meeting, though Ralph Dunkley held on all the way and beat him, 4:11.8 to 4:13.6.

"But it did give me confidence", Seaman now says. "Stan said, 'Don't be disappointed. It's a start. You can't win them all'. By that time I realised that the previous advice I had been given was wrong, and my confidence grew as I planned my own training and was running more often and faster". After a heat in 4:17.8 at the AAA Championships came his lifetime best of 4:08.0 behind Bannister's Championship record 4:05.2, with Nankeville over two seconds further back. Seaman had hung on as the field had strung out with the Scotsman, Alex Breckenridge, who was back from the USA, setting the pace, but at the bell Bannister had shot away and Seaman took Nankeville 220 yards out.

In Antwerp Seaman was 3rd in 1:54.4 in a very bumpy 800 metres race and then 2nd to Chataway at a mile in the match with France, 4:12.4 to 4:13.2. He won for the AAA against the Combined Services in 4:14.9 and was 4th at 1500 metres against Germany in Berlin in 3:54.8 behind Werner Lueg's 3:51.6 and 3rd against Sweden in 3:49.5 – a world best for a 20-year-old – behind Sune Karlsson's 3:45.8. In another 1500 metres on the continent he was 3rd in 3:52.3 the Dane, Gunnar Nielsen, 3:49.4.

It was during the GB team's tour to Germany and Sweden that Seaman grew very friendly with Gordon Pirie and always thought that Pirie had left his best running on the training track, remembering that when Pirie could not train for seven days because of a cold he beat Vladimir Kuts and broke a world record. Another memory of that tour was of the two press-men who were so drunk on the air-flight from Berlin to Stockholm that they had to be given oxygen, and they then wrote their reports of the match against Sweden from a bar opposite the stadium, never attending the meeting!

In between all this activity Seaman ran as part of the British 4 x 1 mile relay team which broke the world record. Chataway kicked off with 4:11.8 and Nankeville ran 4:06.6, leaving Seaman 50 yards clear and having to make his own pace. He ran the opening half in 1:56.8 and finished with 4:15.0. Bannister ran 4:07.4 for a total time of 16:41.0 which was almost two seconds

Don Seaman leads from Rolf Lamers, Bill Nankeville and eventual winner and world record-holder Werner Lueg at 1500 metres against Germany in Berlin on 30 August 1953.

The World record 4 x 1 mile relay team, White City, 1952. Left to right – Chris Chataway, Don Seaman, Roger Bannister, Bill Nankeville.

inside the old record.

After the 1953 season Seaman continued training daily and was confident of a place in the teams for both the British Empire Games and European Championships the next year. He had completed his studies to be an engineer and he felt that he could run a mile in 4:04. When he nearly won an indoor 1000 metres against the French champion, Patrick El Mabrouk, on a 130-metre track in France's first indoor international meeting in January of 1954, everything looked on course. Despite the banking and bends which were so difficult for a man of his height, Seaman had forced himself into 2nd place behind the short-striding David Law and ahead of El Mabrouk.

In May he went into the Royal Air Force to begin his two years of National Service and was superbly fit and looking forward to a wonderful season after training every day through the winter from his Luton home, but his troubles began from the very start. His shoe size was 11½ but he was given size 12 boots that chaffed on his tendon for more than two months. Sydney Wooderson had also suffered foot trouble when he wore army boots during World War II and it was after initial training that he had his only mile defeat during war years.

Seaman related a sorry tale: "It got really bad when I went to the School of Physical Training. It was ridiculous, I couldn't do a forward roll or jump a box, and the NCO in charge did not believe that I had a problem. He made me run in two athletics meetings, inter-station and group, doing the double in an afternoon, and winning all four races in very slow time against no opposition. I could not train. I had to stop. It was very painful but I could not say anything because they didn't believe me.

"The NCO took an instant dislike to me and when he saw me walking he screamed at me to run. It was about the time that the cricketer, Colin Cowdrey, had been discharged with an injured toenail, and they thought I was trying to do the same thing. All they allowed was seven days 'excused boots'! Eventually I persuaded him that I had got a genuine condition, and it was arranged for me to see an expert, with the threat that if there was nothing wrong my life would not be worth living!" The problem turned out to be so severe that he was on crutches or in a wheelchair for seven months and was eventually discharged from the RAF after 18 months. He never raced again.

Even if he had wanted to compete, and it was very doubtful whether he would ever have been able to do so properly, and almost certainly not with the form he had in 1953, it would not have been possible. He started an engineering job with Esso and they made it clear to him that it was them or athletics, and not both. He stayed with Esso for 20 years and then set up his own property and office refurbishing company before retiring at the age of 70.

"I was bitterly disappointed by what happened in the RAF", Don Seaman reflects. "That NCO destroyed my athletics career and ruined my legs. I'm glad I ran before then. I would not like it now with the drugs and the money. I remember Harold Abrahams saying to me that athletics was going to go professional one of these days and that it would be the killing of it. I never thought that money would be about, but he was convinced, and he was right.

"Look at this silver caddy spoon. That's what I won at the meeting in Oslo one year. What would I get now?"

Note: this article was first published in "Track Stats", Volume 40, No.3, August 2002.

Sir Christopher Chataway, British Empire/Comonwealth Games Three miles gold-medallist & world record-holder

Outgrowing the ethos of effortless superiority. Then discovering the joy of running at 70

Everyone knows about Chris Chataway's vital role in the first sub-four-minute mile. This face-to-face interview deals with his other races.

On Sunday 27 May 1951 a 20-year-old ginger-haired Englishman lined up with two of the greatest of distance-runners – the reigning Olympic champion, Gaston Reiff, and Emil Zátopek's silver shadow, Alain Mimoun – for a 5000 metres race at the Stade Francais, in Paris. Chris Chataway saw no reason why he should not beat them. The young undergraduate from Oxford University had won the annual Inter-Varsity mile in 4:16.4 and then run a stunning two miles at the British Games, reducing his personal best by over 40 seconds to 9:03.8 against an international field.

He said: "I was in my first year at Oxford and had already adopted that effortless superiority we all had, where it was important that you were seen not to be too keen, and I was taken with it. Roger Bannister used to do it. The progress I made while I was there was as a result of a lot of races, and racing hard, and that was the only sensible training I did. Otherwise, training was ridiculously light. We followed the ethos of Jack Lovelock (whose Iffley Road track record of 4:12.0 Chataway had then recently equalled) of light training to retain freshness for races and not become stale and leave your best on the training track. It worked for him. Why not us?"

Four laps into his race with Reiff and Mimoun, Chataway realised that he was just not in the same class as his two experienced rivals. "I had been surprised by the amount I had improved, and I always seemed to be able to win and live the life I liked – lots of parties and that kind of thing. There came a time after about four laps when I could not stay anywhere near them. I finished a very bad 3rd (14:47.8 to Reiff's 14:30.4) and I was left way back. I came back from that pretty chastened. From then on I realised that you cannot be a good athlete and lead the same sort of life as your contemporaries".

It was more than chastening for the young Christopher John Chataway (born in Chelsea, London, on 31 January 1931), who was dubbed "The Red Fox of Oxford" because of his hair and his ability. He had iron in his soul and limbs and was desperately ambitious to be Olympic champion and best in the world. "Human ambition is just insatiable", he said as we talked in his London home. Since his athletic days he has gone on to be one of the "New Elizabethans" at the start of the Queen's reign, a Tory Government Minister, and chairman of major companies.

He took up running again in his 60s and loves it, training every day and competing in the occasional cross-country race for the Thames Hare & Hounds club. He retains great enthusiasm, laughs a lot as he reminisces, and if he regrets anything now it is not smoking. When breaking world records he rationed himself to seven a day and gave up in his 50s because his wife said she wanted him alive. He still dreams about smoking and found highly amusing the story of how an early post-World War II Oxford University athletics club president could not last the 12 laps of a three miles race without a quick drag before the bell!

Everyone knows how Chataway and his friend, Chris Brasher, paced Bannister to the first sub-four-minute mile. On the 50th anniversary, the bookshops were full of different tomes about how, why and where it was done. So it was a subject which we left alone in our conversation. For his career was far more than that, with four world records, the Empire three-miles title, an audacious challenge for gold in the 1952 Olympic 5000 metres, and the race where the unknown Vladimir Kuts ("I'd never heard of Kuts") ran away from him and Zátopek before Chataway gained revenge during what he described as the worst 15 minutes of his life in front of 40,000 fans at the White City. Then, finally, came the Olympic 5000 metres in Melbourne in 1956 when he knew he had every chance of winning, was determined and ready to do it, and suffered the oh-so-disappointing failure due to the most terrible stomach cramps that destroyed him with five laps to go.

Chris Chataway discovered that he could run distances better than anyone else at Sherborne School when he graduated at the age of 15 from the years of failure at 100 and 220 yards. In successive years, 1948 and 1949, he finished 3rd and then 2nd in distinguished fields in the Public Schools mile, beaten by two seconds in the latter year by Peter Robinson as he won with only one shoe in 4:25.2. Yet Chataway, the 5ft 9in (1.75m) tall captain of boxing from the West country who was self-taught with the aid of the first Achilles book of "Athletics" from the library (he was to contribute a chapter to the 1955 edition), was the only one from the bunch to find real fame.

He was commissioned in the Army. He said: "I improved tremendously. I would have a lot of very serious racing every so often for the Army and for Walton AC and the times came down a lot. I had nothing else to do during my National Service except run, and so I was very keen. I got a coach through the AAA. I never met him and we just corresponded. He had ideas from the 19th century – the Victorian days – saying I should hold sticks in each hand when training and telling me that I should not run too much but walk a lot. So solemnly in the evenings I would walk in the dark around the lanes of Oswestry where I was stationed". Chataway still managed 4:15.6 to win the 1950 Inter-Services mile at Uxbridge but now reckons he would have been a lot better if he had trained properly.

Three wins in the Inter-Varsity match and tougher training

He went straight from the services to Magdalen College, Oxford, where "sticks in the dark" became languid effortless superiority, and who was to say it was wrong? It produced Bannister and a string of other Oxbridge runners, although you get the clear impression that the real training was hidden from public view. Racing hard ("the only sensible training that I did") still gave Chataway three victories in the Oxford-v-Cambridge mile (with a best of 4:08.4), a planned tie in the three miles, and three wins in the Inter-Varsity cross-country. After that Paris defeat by Reiff, who was the best 5000 metres runner in the world in 1951 with 14:10.8, Chataway continued to mix with his friends, but as they swallowed seven or eight pints of beer he quietly made do with a couple of halves and started to train harder on his own.

It was no longer a case of putting in an appearance at Iffley Road to jog a couple of laps or do an uninspired time-trial. He meant business. "I got pretty serious. I got away with it at Oxford and I got into the international team. My two miles in 1951 was about 50 seconds better than my previous best, and that went really well. I remember it as the first time in a high-level race that I had been able to surge away from the field 220 yards from the end. I had decided that the three miles was my distance. I lacked the speed for the mile. I think my best ever half-mile was 1:52 and I never got inside 52 for a quarter. I just did not have very much speed."

Then came the first AAA three miles, and that started his pattern in being involved in inches finishes, winning once and losing twice unexpectedly. The now-forgotten Roy Beckett beat him in 1951 by inches in 14:02.6, but Chataway got his revenge on the tour of the Balkans when amongst a Great Britain team hit severely by stomach problems he remained illness-free and ran 5000 metres in 14:50.6 against Yugoslavia and 14:56.0 against Turkey before losing a planned dead-heat at 1500 metres against Greece with the 1950 Empire three miles champion, Len Eyre.

Chataway was then racing often against the other rising three-miling star, Gordon Pirie. "We were rivals, but I never really got to know him. I got to know his brother, Peter, better. He was a more sympathetic character. Gordon and I never had a harsh word, but we did not have a tremendous amount in common". With a very different outlook, apart from ambition, Pirie ground himself into the training-track and raced everywhere, while Chataway mixed running with his social life, picked his races over his best years carefully, and kept his obsession to himself.

Chataway could always beat Pirie over two miles and had little doubt that he could do the same over 5000 metres because he had more speed. Unfortunately, in 1953 when Pirie was "Cock of the world" Chataway was working furiously for his degree, and they only met once when an untrained Chataway finished 4th behind Pirie in the famous Emsley Carr mile in which Pirie, crab-like, beat Wes Santee, of the USA, in 4:06.8.

In 1952 Chataway had broken the Inter-Varsity mile record (4:10.2), had run an impressive 8:55.6 two miles, and then 13:59.0 to win the AAA three miles at the White City before going to the Helsinki Olympics. He qualified comfortably in his 5000 metres heat, chatting to Zátopek as he did so, and joined the other two Britons, Pirie and Alan Parker, in the final. Chataway said: "I was not trying for any other place in the final than 1st. I don't know if it seems presumptuous, as there was nothing in my record to let me have a chance, but I was really trying to win".

He went for it with bags of confidence and came very close to succeeding as he took off with 200 metres to go. "Looking back at it now, I ought to have gone later. I was very tired. I always put in my finishing effort at the start of the back straight. I ought to have waited for the final straight. I am sure I would have got a place. Instead, I went from 200 metres and I was tired coming round the bend. Zátopek (14:06.6) may have brushed me, but it did not matter. I hit my foot on the raised kerb and went crashing down, and then Mimoun and Schade went past and I picked myself up and jogged to the end (14:18.0). Pirie overtook me on the line for 4th. He had been 50-60 yards behind and did not realise what had happened."

Records all the way for Pirie, hard work for Chataway

For Pirie the next year was roses and records all the way. For Chataway it was hard work for his degree, which he crammed into six months without training, although he did run a 4:08.4 mile against Cambridge. He then went to the USA with the Oxbridge team, came back to win the mile for Great Britain against France (4:12.0), was a member of the 4 x 1 mile record-breaking team (16:41.0 with Bannister, Bill Nankeville and Don Seaman), and paced Bannister in a failed mile record attempt.

1954 was Chataway's best year. For a start the eccentric but brilliant Austrian coach, Franz Stampfl, came on the scene. Chataway, who was rather sniffy about coaches up to then, was to concede later: "What I know is that he would touch what you were doing with magic. By the time you'd listened to Franz you would be in no doubt that breaking the world record would be as good as painting the Mona Lisa. He just invested the whole thing with glamour and magic. He made certain that you could do it, and that it would be a disgrace if you didn't. If you missed a chance to break the record, how could you ever forgive yourself? All of this made a huge impression on me, and it must, I think, have made an impression on Roger, too".

In fact, it was like a boot up their backsides! For, talented as Bannister, Chataway and Brasher were, their training was too soft in the ever-increasing hot competitiveness of the world athletics bowl. Stampfl gave them what now is called a cutting edge that was to lead to the sub-four-minute mile, Chataway's world records, Bannister's Empire mile and European 1500 metres triumphs, and Brasher's Olympic steeplechase gold.

Once the sub-four-minute mile was out of the way – 40 years later Chataway ran on the Iffley Road track for the first time again in 5:48, with 400lb of tobacco and 7,000 bottles of wine to bridge the gap! – he had a go at the two miles record with Bannister and Brasher pacing him. In topped-up training he ran a 9:03.6 two-mile time-trial, 3 x 1 mile in 4:19, 10 x 440 yards in 63, and 6:33.2 for 1½ miles on a rain-soaked track which was faster than the world's best, and it all paid rich dividends. His two miles in 8:41.0 at the White City British Games on 7 June was just 0.6sec slower than Reiff s record, and that was mainly because the pacemakers could not take him far enough.

Then Chataway was part of the successful attempt by the Australian, John Landy, on the mile record on 21 June at Turku, 46 days after Oxford. They passed the ¾-mile together in 2:57.5 and then Landy went ahead to win in 3:58.0, with the Englishman timed in 4:04.2 (3:45.4 at 1500 metres). The AAA three miles brought a battle with the Midlands champion, Freddie Green, of Birchfield, who took Chataway on the crown of the last bend, and although Chataway fought back inch-by-inch it was to his amazement and disappointment that Green won. So close were they that both broke the world record with 13:32.2, just inside Hägg's 15-year-old previous best. In 3rd place was Nyandika Maiyoro, the first of the great Kenyans.

Chataway said: "It was a terrible shock, and the fact that it was a world record was no consolation whatsoever. By then my ambition in life grew. I just wanted to be 'Number One' in the world, and not to be even 'Number One' in England was a shock. The Empire Games in Vancouver was a very important race for me, to beat Freddie Green. It seemed that my finish had not been good enough against Beckett and then Green, and the only thing I don't know is how I lost to either of them. Then at the Empire Games I had a very good finish and won easily in 13:35.2 from Green with a 26.3 last furlong". Another of Britain's outstanding three milers of those days, Frank Sando, was 3rd in that race. Maiyoro was 4th. Pirie was absent through injury.

Guinness is good for him and for the McWhirters, too!

A boring but highly-paid job with the Guinness brewing company was of help to Chataway because it gave him much time to train and race. He had gone there after Oxford and shared a company house with the managing director, Sir Hugh Beaver, who later prepared the report for the Clean Air Act which was responsible for clearing London of its smog. "He said one day that he had got this idea that people would have this book in the pub to settle their arguments over the longest, highest, who won what. They would be able to look it up in this book, and it would be very good publicity for the firm. I said 'what a wonderful idea' and I knew just the people to do it. So the McWhirter twins were invited with me to lunch with the Board and they put on a bravura display. There was one little mishap – Ross said that there had never been an Irishman who had won a game in squash matches against England, and one Irish director said that he himself had. Anyway, the McWhirters got the job, and look where "The Guinness Book Of Records" is now!"

After the 1954 Empire Games three miles came the European Championships 5000 metres in Berne. "Having got my revenge on Green, I thought 'now I'm going to beat Zátopek', and that was all I was interested in. I beat him, but then there was this new Russian 100 yards in front of us. I had never heard of him, and I'm not sure that Zátopek had. I never gave it a thought as he went roaring off. It must have been after a long way, around nine laps, that it entered into my head that he was possibly going to finish. I don't think Zátopek had been beaten for a long time. He was invincible in big races. If you were keeping up with him, anyone out in front was a lunatic".

The "lunatic", Vladimir Kuts, stayed where he was and set a world record of 13:56.6 (with another world record of 13:27.8 for three miles on the way). Chataway was 2nd in 14:08.8 and

Zátopek 3rd in 14:10.2. No man ever ruined a big race like the Russian sailor, and it astonished everyone – not least the BBC commentator, Rex Alston, who just could not believe it and hardly mentioned Kuts at all until near the end. Chataway said: "It did not seem very funny at the time by listening to that commentary. Now it is".

That should have been the end of the season, and as part of his National Service commitments Chataway went to a training-camp on Salisbury Plain for a fortnight, where he drank and smoked to excess. "I really let my hair down, went to dinner after dinner – one of them finishing at 4am, by which time I had drunk a bottle of brandy. I was surprised that I felt perfectly all right. When I got home from the camp there was a letter saying that a match had been arranged between London and Moscow, and Kuts was due to run and would I like to? It was into September and the race was a month or so away. For a few hours I toyed with the idea of saying 'no, I have had a long season, and I have finished', but finally I decided to do it.

"I got back into training, and I remember that my mother had arranged to take a cottage at Studlands, near Poole, in Dorset, for my brothers and sister, and for us to go on holiday together for the first time. I had to do that, and I ran every day over the dunes, turning over in my mind the race I would run in which I would beat Kuts – it was always the same result. I got to the White City with just the knowledge of how terrible one would feel, and nonetheless one would still do everything to win. Mentally, the preparation was enormous. When I look at Haile Gebrselassie, he does not seem to be suffering like I did. The training was always too light, and I always trained more as a miler than a three-miler. I did not do enough stamina work and that race was certainly the most painful quarter-of-an-hour of my life".

Which makes you wonder what Chataway would have done if he had trained like the modern athletes, unless he had died of boredom first, because to me he was a superb racing-machine, not the product of miles a week of mind-sapping drudgery, which is essential for today's wonder champions.

The never-to-be-forgotten night under the White City floodlights

On the night of 13 October 1954 there were 40,000 people packed into the White City Stadium to see the floodlit match between London and Moscow, and top of the bill was the clash between undoubtedly the two best 5000 metres runners of all time. The publicity before was enormous.- "Thisaway, Thataway, He went Chataway" was one slogan, and the race was shown live on black-and-white television. I was living in Doncaster at the time, sharing a flat with two others, and we had a television so small you needed a telescope, but we could just see the race and we nearly broke the sofa as we leaped up and down in the closing stages, where our man won by a stride in the world-record time of 13:51.6 after Kuts went through three miles in a world-record 13:27.0 with Chataway a stride behind.

Chataway said: "I was not sure I was going to beat him, not sure at all. It was all right for the first four laps, and then he threw in these bursts that I had not come across before. No one ran like that. In theory I knew I would be able to haul him back if he established a lead. Really, in theory the correct response was to let him go and pull him back gradually, as these bursts were more tiring for him than for me. But I knew it was no option, and so I went with him. He went through one lap in 60-61 seconds when we were running around 66 seconds a lap, and there would be 50-to-100-yards bursts from the halfway mark and I was just holding on.

"The last lap I did not really feel I had experienced. It was 60-61 again and the last 200 metres inside 30 seconds. My oxygen deficit was horrendous. By the time I was entering the final straight, it was really like throwing oneself over the cliffs. My legs just had the capacity to accelerate despite the fact that my lungs were crying out for relief. I did not know I was going to win until I did win. I had almost given up in the final two laps. I felt I was deceiving myself by continuing to run at this pace and keeping with him. I thought I might last another 50 yards, and I did not really know I was winning, I was not actually thinking I was going to win until the last stride or two.

"Fifty years later I think it was a good thing to have done. I know that on that particular day and in that particular activity I could not have done any better. That was the limit, and you don't often get that feeling in life. I could not have gone any faster because the pacing was so uneven. There was nothing left".

Chataway's win brought him the first-ever BBC Television Sports Personality of the Year award ahead of Bannister. Chataway said: "A day or two later I was thinking to myself that I could hold every world record between 1500 and 5000 metres and I could go to the Olympics and win". There was to be nothing in 1955 to show that his thoughts were not feasible.

He ran his first and only sub-four-minute mile in 3:59.8 behind one of the great Hungarians, Lászlo Tábori, who clocked 3:59.0, and then set a fastest UK 2000 metres in 5:09.4, and won the Kinnaird Trophy three miles in 13:33.0 and the AAA three miles by over three seconds from Derek Ibbotson in 13:33.5. Chataway then wrote a letter to Ibbotson, who was doing his National Service in the RAF in Wiltshire, suggesting a plan that would defeat not only Kuts but the Germans as well in the two major international matches against Germany at the White City and then the Soviet Union in Moscow.

Two international-match wins but then defeat against Hungary

The idea of alternating laps worked very well. Against Germany Chataway amazed the crowd by going into the lead from the start, and then Ibbotson took over, and so they continued at a galloping pace until two laps from home, when Chataway went away to win in 13:23.2 (4:24, 8:54.8, and a 2:05 last half-mile) for a new world record, with Ibbotson nearly 20 seconds behind. In the Moscow match Kuts went for the 10,000 metres and did 29:08.2, which was the sixth fastest in history, and 200 metres ahead of Pirie and Ken Norris. That gave "Fox" an open goal and he ran a 25sec last 200 metres to win the 5000 metres in 14:12.0, with Ibbotson 3rd in 14:24.2. There was one blemish, and that was the match against Hungary where Chataway tried the double and was outclassed and outmanoeuvred by Tabori.

Chataway said: "The world record for which I trained properly was much easier and more comfortable than I expected. I tried the double against the Hungarians, and did not do terribly well, to harden me in case there was a semi-final or another heat at the Olympics. I meant to run hard over two days, but they were too good for me". Chataway did 4:04.6 for 3rd in the mile and 13:44.6 for 2nd at three miles, losing in a battle of tactics rather than speed but still beating Ibbotson and Sandor Iharos, the world record-holder.

As Chataway prepared for the Olympics he started a new career as the first newscaster for ITN, the news programme for the new commercial TV stations. He said: "It took one's nervous energy as well. After six months I moved to the BBC and Panorama, their main current affairs programme, and I was doing political interviews and weekly reports. I was also training hard under Stampfl and I really wanted my ambition. My sights were set on winning the Olympic 5000 metres and then finishing with athletics. At that time I had been caught up in something else. I was the 'Paxman' – the leading current BBC big political interviewer – as well as an athlete. I did things like the Tory party conference interviews before Suez. My first serious race in 1956 was the AAA three miles. I was reasonably pleased even though I lost by inches".

Right: Chris Chataway beats Vladimir Kuts in the unforgettable 5000 metres at the London-v-Moscow match of 13 October 1954. Chatway set a world record of 13:51.6.

Below: Chataway receiving first prize for winning the two miles at the British Games on 25 May 1953. Making the presentation is Mrs W. Emsley Carr, wife of the owner of the sponsoring "News of the World" Sunday newspaper. Facing the camera is Lord Burghley.

It was the same as in the races against Beckett and Green. This time it was Ibbotson who snatched victory on the line in 13:32.6. Chataway said: "I was training four or five times a week. I had a good two miles in July and won the 5000 metres against Hungary in 13:59.6. I really felt that I could go and win the 5000 metres in Melbourne and beat Ibbotson comfortably and also Iharos, who held the world record. I thought these two and Kuts were the ones to beat. I always thought I could beat Pirie because I had more speed".

Chataway finished his major political interviews before going out to Melbourne early for the Olympics with Brasher and staying with Stampfl until the Olympic Village opened. "I really thought I had a chance, but whether it was a bug I don't know, but after seven or eight laps when all was going well I was absolutely paralysed with stomach cramp. When it hit I slowed immediately. It was automatic. There was no conscious decision. Finishing was depressing and painful, and, I suppose, quite pointless. It just did not occur to me to drop out. I must by then have been programmed never to consider it as an option".

To say it was a disappointment is to understate his feelings. He fell back and saw Kuts take the crown in 13:39.6, with Pirie and Ibbotson the other two medallists in times which Chataway could run regularly. Afterwards he thought, wryly, that 'perhaps it was good for my soul'. Now, looking back, he says: "That was it. Disappointments are probably good for you". He never had a proper conversation with Kuts because neither spoke the other's language. "It was no more than a few pleasantries through an interpreter. The last time I saw him was at the Mexico Games and he was enormously fat – the effect, I guess, of drink, not drugs. I don't think there were any drugs for runners in those days, but Kuts did become an alcoholic and that, I suppose, was what killed him in 1975".

Chataway made sure that during his political and business life there was no room for such things. He was knighted in 1995 for his services to the aviation industry after being chairman of the Civil Aviation Authority. He loves running more than ever, which is surprising until he explained: "I liked the excitement and winning obviously. I liked discovering suddenly that I was good at something, and then getting better. But the major races were too painful to be enjoyed.

"I enjoy running more in my 70s than in my 20s. I have discovered the secret now. As soon as it begins to hurt, I go slower". And he smiled happily.

Note: this article was first published in "Track Stats", Volume 43, No.3, August 2005. Sir Christopher Chataway died on 10 January 2014, aged 82.

"You can always dream, but there was Zátopek ... and then there was the rest of us"

There are two ways of looking at the athletics career of Frank Dennis Sando, who was a champion who loved running across the country and filled in the time between the winter seasons by racing on the track. A cursory glance at his achievements would leave you thinking that he was the eternal runner-up – particularly to his arch rival, Douglas Alastair Gordon Pirie – in that silver era of distance-running in the 1950s.

Sando trailed behind the tall gaunt figure of the South London Harrier countless times over the country and on the track. Others, like Ken Norris and the late Peter Driver, also often beat Sando in their many great tussles, but if you check more carefully you will find that Sando's international record was excellent: silver and bronze at the British Empire Games over three and six miles; the first Briton and bronze behind Zátopek in the European Championships 10,000 metres; and 5th in the Olympic 10,000 metres after one of his shoes was torn off in the first lap. And he believes he might have finished much higher with it on!

His schoolboy ambition had been to run for England at cross-country, and he first achieved it as a junior in 1952 and then went on to win the International title twice and the National once. He was 9th on his first appearance in the International and always placed in the first four until 1960 when he finished 8th after injury. He was in the first six in the National for eight successive years. Pirie's best placing in the International was only 19th.

Sando always peaked for those two races, and if the weather was hot, as it was for the Internationals in Paris in 1953 and San Sebastian in 1955, it was a major bonus for the slightly-built and diffident man with the long raking stride. Born on 14 March 1931, he was just 54kg (8st 8lb) and 1.71m (5ft 7½in), and he found the real cold of winter an opponent with which it was hard to cope. His lack of self-confidence and of a killer instinct sometimes held him back when others took advantage, and he didn't realise just how good he was until a famous three-mile race at the British Games in 1952 when Pirie beat him, 13:44.8 to 13:48.0, with both of them smashing Sydney Wooderson's national record and becoming only the second and third Britons under 14 minutes.

By his achievement on that day Sando had reduced his three-mile time by 41 seconds in just a few weeks, and this was done mainly on 45 minutes' running five days a week. His training schedule remained much the same throughout his career, as he mixed in serious and fun racing, family commitments and hard studying. In the early days he worked for Aylesford Paper Mills, in Kent, and he ran for their club, among whose members was the international cross-country runner, Jack Charlesworth.

Sando would leave his work at West Malling at 5.20pm, catch the bus, be in his house 20 minutes later and out running five minutes after that – a mixture of steady runs, fast and slow fartlek on the road or on a cinder path. He would be back home for a meal at 6.30 with his wife, Sybil, before an evening of study for his professional exams. He joined club members for a longer run at weekends and raced for the club on the road and track or over the country most Saturdays for years.

Now, long retired from his job as a government chief statistician, Sando is a former president of the Kent AAA and organiser of the county cross-country championships which he won on countless occasions. It was at his home in Aylesford that he looked back on his running career of

50 or so years before.

It began at Maidstone Grammar School because he was too slight for rugby football and lacked eye-and-ball co-ordination for cricket. Instead, he had to run, and he discovered that not only did he like it but he was very good at it. He was school champion and record-holder in the mile (4:44) and after winning Kent cross-country titles in his age group and running well at youth and junior level in the National his breakthrough came in 1951 when he was 5th in the Inter-Counties cross-country behind Dr Frank Aaron and the up-and-coming Gordon Pirie. Sando greatly admired Aaron, who was three times National cross-country champion and was 4th in the 1950 European Championships 10,000 metres and British record-holder for six miles, and whose belief in "maximum efficiency with the minimum of effort" Sando closely followed.

Sando set an Army three miles record of 14:23.9 during his National Service, won the Inter-Services cross-country, and then followed Pirie home three times during the winter of 1952, with 7th in the Inter-Counties, 2nd in the Southern and 5th in the National. In the last of these races Pirie was beaten by the juggling policeman, Walter Hesketh, who was the first man to win three National cross-country titles and who also beat Aaron's British record for six miles but never fulfilled his early promise.

In the International that year Sando was 9th and was the second Englishman home behind Hesketh (4th), and by now he had left his first club, Maidstone Harriers, for the larger Aylesford Paper Mills club, though their track training was done round the edge of a cricket field until the groundsman expelled them to an area by the sewage works!

In the early summer of 1952 Sando won the Kent three miles in a record 14:09.8 and was 2nd in the Southern six miles to Andy Ferguson, of Highgate Harriers, 30:41.4 to 30:43.0. At the AAA Championships, Sando was much faster, 3rd in 29:00.6 behind Pirie's British record 28:55.6 and Fred Norris. Despite consistently high-class running Sando never was to win an AAA six miles title, finishing 2nd to Pirie in 1953, to Peter Driver in 1954 and to Ken Norris in 1955 and 1956. Injury kept him out in 1957 and by 1958 his studying and the arrival of his children (a son and daughter, and now two grandchildren) meant that he was losing interest in running.

Running was not the be-all and end-all of life – and track racing filled the summer gap

"I always preferred the country to the track", Sando recalls, "and my aim each year was to finish in the first six in the National and do very well in the International. Track running filled in the gaps between seasons. I never had the killer instinct which Pirie and others had. They would have been alright in today's running where the money is so good. The money might have attracted me, but I doubt it. To me running was fun and I enjoyed it very much indeed, but it was not the be-all and end-all of my life. I kept a balance of family, work and running, and a more relaxed view. I'm really glad that I ran then and not now.

"I really enjoyed running well and winning when I could. Today they say 'I don't want silver', but I don't understand that attitude. To make third place is an achievement. I was a bit shy, not gregarious, and I lacked that self-confidence which Pirie, for example, had. I also lacked a coach who would have said 'You're good' and would have been a shoulder to cry on, but that is in hindsight because I did not think I needed one at the time. Johnny Johnston – the man who coached Jim Peters – coached me by letter, and although I was very grateful to him I really think he confirmed what I was planning myself. He did get me into races I would not have run in.

"When others would go up and chat to Zátopek and the other stars I wouldn't. I'd say 'Hello' and 'Goodbye', and that was it. When I look back I think I might have gone a bit further if I'd had more killer spirit, but you can always dream. It would have been good to win an AAA title, but it didn't matter at the time. I liked it when I won and didn't like it when I ran badly and there was a post-mortem as to why, but by the next day it didn't matter.

"I didn't get fed up with coming 2nd. At the back of your mind when you were running in those days was that you knew you had to work and make a living. I accepted that with all the miles that he was running every day Pirie was going to be in front of me most of the time on the track, and that was a price you had to pay. The best runner of my days was without a doubt Zátopek. I just expected him to be out of my class. It's a bit like Roger Black and Michael Johnson. There was Zátopek ... and then there was the rest of us".

Killer instinct or not, Sando had a steely determination and would never give up. He discovered that all his stamina work on the road had given him a tremendous sprint finish, and among those who found this out were Ken Norris in a Southern three miles when Sando ran a lifetime best of 13:29.8 and the Hungarian, Szabó, and the German, Havenstein, in 5000 metres races at the White City. In each instance Sando won by inches.

He first showed just how good he was on his limited training at the 1952 Helsinki Olympics. After his shoe had come off in the first lap of the 10,000 metres he recalls that "I could have dropped out, but I thought that as I had got to the Olympics I might as well go on. It was the first time I'd beaten Pirie on the track, but when I finished 5th I didn't realise I was in front of him". Sando was just a stride behind the 4th-placed runner, Hannu Posti, of Finland, and finished 34 seconds behind Zátopek, who was in turn 15 seconds ahead of Alain Mimoun. Pirie was 7th and Fred Norris 8th.

Still the eternal runner-up – 2nd to Eyre, 2nd to Mihalic, 2nd to Pirie, 2nd to Driver

Over the country in 1953 Sando was 2nd in the Inter-Counties to the 1950 British Empire Games three miles champion, Len Eyre, 2nd again to Pirie in the Southern and the National (the latter by 67 seconds!), and 2nd to the Yugoslav, Franjo Mihalic, in the International, and thinks he should have beaten him. It was in this race that Pirie trailed in 19th. On the track Sando was 2nd once more to Pirie in the Inter-Counties three miles and won the Southern mile in 4:16.2 with a sub-60sec last lap (and in later years twice ran 4:08 in paced time-trials on grass). He was 2nd to Pirie in his world record-breaking AAA six miles, won the 10,000 metres against Germany when Pirie ran the 5000, and was 2nd to Pirie in the 10,000 metres against Sweden.

The 1954 cross-country achievements were as impressive as ever: 2nd to Pirie in the Southern, 3rd in the National to Pirie and Fred Norris, and 4th in the International behind Mimoun, Ken Norris and the mercurial Pat Ranger when Pirie did not start because of flu. This was the year of the Empire Games and European Championships, but after Sando had won the Inter-Counties six miles and then finished 2nd to Pirie in the three miles, the latter missed both these major meetings because of injury. In the AAA six miles Peter Driver's brilliant finish brought him home ahead of Sando.

In the Empire Games six miles the board showed that there were three laps to go as Driver and Sando pulled away from the field, and Sando felt ready to counter Driver's blistering finish, but when they came round the next time it was the last lap, emphasised by the bell ringing, and Sando knew his chance had gone. Driver went with 250 yards to go and although Sando never gave up he was still five yards down at the tape. Jim Peters was 3rd, and when Sando witnessed Peters's collapse and hospitalisation in the closing stages of the marathon a few days later he knew that marathon-racing was not for him.

Sando had also finished 3rd to Chris Chataway and Freddie Green in the three miles in Vancouver, with Driver 5th, and then ran what he considers to be his best race to take the bronze behind Zátopek and Kovács, of Hungary, in the European Championships 10,000 metres. Sando was 2nd early on but sensibly dropped back to Kovács and the German, Schade, as Zátopek pressed on relentlessly. By halfway the Czech was 100 yards ahead of Schade, who was clear of the rest, but towards the finish the Briton and the Hungarian went by and Kovács just got the better of the battle as the two of them finished in 29:27.6 and 29:28.8. Driver was 35 seconds down and lapped by the winner.

Despite the rivalry, Driver and Sando were great friends and roomed and trained together in Vancouver and Berne. Their friendship was to continue for some years and during 1971, when they were both working for the Civil Service, they met weekly for lunch. Sando remembers Driver telling him one week how well he was running. The following week he brought the dreadful news that he had cancer, and he died later the same year.

The early months of 1955 witnessed the usual build-up to a peak over the country, with Sando finishing 7th in the Southern, 6th in the National, and then gaining his first storming win in the International. On the track he set a personal best at three miles behind Derek Ibbotson at the Inter-Counties and won the six miles two days later. He was 2nd to Ken Norris in the AAA six miles on a sultry evening when Pirie miscounted the laps and dropped out. Sando was 3rd to Zátopek and Pirie in the match with Czechoslovakia (29:25.6, 29:54.0, 30:00.8), 2nd to Mimoun against France, and then ran in together with Ken Norris against Germany. He also ran a 14:11.2 for 5000 metres at one of the end-of-season White City meetings, placing 4th to Ilmari Taipale, of Finland.

Tendon trouble caused Sando to miss much of the 1956 cross-country season, but he still came back to finish 4th in the National and equal 2nd with Ken Norris in the International behind Mimoun. The track season began encouragingly with a win in 28:24.0 at the Inter-Counties six miles and then a lifetime best in the AAA race after a tremendous battle with Ken Norris. Sando had misjudged the pace and was 100 yards down with two laps to go but then put in such a fierce last half-mile that he would have caught the smooth-running Thames Valley Harrier if spectators had not warned Norris what was happening behind him. Norris held on by just six-tenths of a second in 28:13.6. Selected for the Melbourne Olympics, Sando continued his good form with a personal best winning 5000 metres of 14:10.6 at the White City and an 8:56.2 for two miles.

High hopes for the Olympics but too much training beforehand

His hopes were very high for the Olympic 10,000 metres, but it all went wrong. He finished 10th in the classic Kuts-v-Pirie contest in a bitterly disappointing 30:05.0 (Ken Norris 5th, Pirie 8th) and crossed the line with a huge blood blister on his heel. A fellow-athlete took him to the medical centre and promptly fainted when the doctor produced a needle and burst the blister, but there was another reason for Sando's showing that day.

"It was not the blister that caused me to run so badly", Sando recalls. "What had happened was that my employers offered to pay for me to fly out on my own and not with the main party. I didn't want to do that, but they insisted because it meant that someone else could go in my place. So I went out three weeks before the Games, and Pirie and I trained together. I always got on with him very well because if you gave as good as you got from him verbally he was fine! In training, though, I pushed him and he went faster and he pushed me and I went faster. The result was that I was over-trained and when it came to the race I never got going".

Sando came back home feeling a failure and determined to make amends. Despite tendon trouble he won his first National, coming through on the last lap in the mud of Parliament Hill Fields and running away from Driver and Ken Norris. He then took the International title equally comfortably, but the injury persisted and he missed most of the 1957 track season. Back in fine

Gordon Pirie leads Sando at the 1953 Southern cross-country championships.

form for the following winter he was 3rd in the Southern cross-country to the new star, Stan Eldon, and then 2nd in the National when Eldon missed the start and 3rd to Eldon in the International.

Sando then felt ready for the track season and his place in the line-up for the British Empire Games and European Championships, but he fell on the front steps when coming home for lunch one day and the ankle injury persisted. It stopped him racing on the track, but the softness of the country enabled him to finish 2nd in both the 1959 National and International to Fred Norris. In 1960 the injury and lack of training because of family commitments showed – but only a bit! He was 5th in the Southern cross-country, 9th in the National and 8th in the International, where he was England's third scorer after Basil Heatley and Fred Norris.

He did not race again seriously on the track and started the next cross-country season very late, hoping that the England selectors would take his past record into consideration, but his 22nd place in the National did not impress them and they did not break their iron rule of naming the first nine home in the team. Sando was disappointed and said he would make amends the next year. Because of other commitments that never happened.

Note: this article was first published in "Track Stats", Volume 39, No.3, September 2001. Frank Sando died on 12 October 2012, aged 81.

Imagine the newspaper headline – "Partially Disabled Ex-Serviceman Breaks World Record"!

More than 20 years after Freddie Green set a new world record for the three miles in an epic AAA Championships race with Chris Chataway he went to see his doctor in Australia because he was suffering from a tension neck-ache. The doctor asked the former Birchfield Harrier if he had ever experienced any trauma. He had done so. Towards the end of World War II he had volunteered to be a paratrooper because the RAF was over-subscribed with would-be bomber pilots. He was involved in a practice accident when the impact on landing knocked him unconscious and he chipped a couple of bones in his left ankle. He was in hospital for several weeks and emerged on crutches with his foot in plaster.

After completing military service Freddie Green (born 25 July 1926) took up running again with Birchfield Harriers in 1948. He had been discovered when ordered to set an example as a 17-year-old cadet sergeant in the Air Training Corps in 1944, and he had proved to be a natural, winning the ATC Midlands cross-country. He then ran the fastest stage in a road relay ahead of internationals Bobby Reid and Jack Holden, and won the Midlands junior mile and finished 2nd in a British Games youths' mile.

Green had given up athletics when he went in to the RAF, mainly because of the death of his coach, Jack Ashton, in a motor-cycle accident, and it was not until one of his fellow "Stagbearers" at Birchfield asked if he could coach him that he started again in 1948. From then until the end of 1953 Green improved considerably until he ranked just behind Chris Chataway and Gordon Pirie in that great era of British three-miling. Unlike his rivals, Green often had to race only against himself because he was far and away the best runner at the distance in the Midlands.

There were no more leg problems for him until 1953, when he increased his training to two hours a day straight after work in the production control department at the major Lucas car-component firm in Birmingham. Depending on whether he raced on a Saturday, he ran hard six or seven days a week under the watchful eye of his coach, who was Jack Emery, the former British record-holder at two and three miles and the International cross-country champion of 1938.

All this activity caused Green's left leg to stiffen and he had massage once or twice a week, but then after 32 races during the 1953 season, including international duty in the shadow of Pirie, he developed a swollen left ankle in October with serious discomfort that spread up to the left thigh. After treatment he began running again, only for the condition to return. A hospital doctor prescribed an arch support in his shoe and infra-red lamp treatment, while early in 1954 a physiotherapist specialising in sports injuries applied low electrical current treatment and the leg began to loosen up.

Green resumed training in March, and when the problem persisted he turned to another specialist. He recalls the occasion vividly: "He was not very forthcoming but did think I was suffering from 'pinched nerves' and advised me to give up athletics immediately! I returned to the physiotherapist, and Jack Emery and I met to make an important decision. The outcome was that if the treatment was successful I should go for short sharper training and revert to fartlek when necessary".

This he did, and he achieved his life's ambition to become world record-holder. He went on to win silver in the British Empire & Commonwealth Games three miles behind Chataway and ended his career in the European Championships 5000 metres when Vladimir Kuts ran away from the field. Green was still with the Russian sailor after five laps when he experienced a spasm in his left thigh and for the first and only time in his career he stepped off the track – and into full retirement.

Thus ended his hopes of running the 10,000 metres at the 1956 Melbourne Olympics, but he started a new life in Australia in 1957, taking up golf and getting down to a 14 handicap. Then came the neck-ache caused by working long hours installing a new computer system, and Green tells the tale thus: "When the doctor was told of my parachute accident he contacted the war veterans' department and arranged for x-rays of my spine. These revealed damage to the base and a quite marked narrowing of the cervical discs. I asked if this condition was related to my leg problem when running and was told that in all probability it was. Then came the verdict – no golf, no lifting of weighty objects, and most importantly no running or jogging. My doctor told me, 'You've been very fortunate. Don't push your luck!'

"He said that he would guide me through the application procedures for treatment as army medical records would need to be consulted. As I drove away I imagined a newspaper headline in 1954: 'PARTIALLY DISABLED EX-SERVICEMAN BREAKS WORLD RECORD'."

His condition is now under control, but he is classified as 50 per cent disabled and receives a war pension.

Club running over the country and on the road, and then the first track success

Freddie Green was a great runner, with his distinctive moustache, and could always be relied on to give that something extra to take his Birchfield club to victory – particularly in the two-mile track races and road relays round the Midlands in which he specialised. What follows is the story of his career, based on an account of it which he wrote specifically for "Track Stats".

His first successes came in 1949. He won the Kinnaird Trophy three miles in 14:36 from the Estonian refugee and AAA six miles champion of that year Valdu Lillakas, and ran the fastest stage in the London-to-Brighton road relay. Green was a master of this type of event, but even he could not match Alec Olney, who ran 23:04 to Green's 24:01 in the Thames Valley Harriers relay that season, though they did not actually race against each other, and Green took over with a two-minute lead. He also won the Midlands three miles and was to hold that title until his retirement five years later.

In 1950 he was 60th in the National cross-country and again was the fastest man in the London-to-Brighton but was a distant 2nd in the Kinnaird three miles, 60 yards adrift of Olney. Green also ran some fast two-mile times, including a close 2nd in an estimated 9:16 to Horace Ashenfelter, the future Olympic steeplechase champion from the USA, in a race in Glasgow, as well as 5th place in 9:21.2 behind Doug Wilson at the White City and a late-season 9:17.2 in Birmingham. Green's best performance was in the AAA three miles, where he stayed with the pace all the way with his familiar high-arm action and in a ding-dong last lap managed 5th in 14:14.6 (the fastest postwar time by a Midlander) as the Belgian cross-country expert, Lucien Theys, won in 14:09.0 from Olney.

In 1951 Green ran 14:36.4 to win the Midlands three miles and had a best time for the distance of 14:22.8 for 4th in the British Games at the White City on 11 August behind the 1948 double Olympic medallist from Holland, Willy Slijkhuis (14:00.8), Pirie and Alan Parker, also running 9:13.0 for two miles at the Birchfield meeting at Perry Barr two days later. However, he had not contested the AAA Championships because of a strained left knee. The following Olympic year was the last in which he followed the Emil Zátopek form of training, and he began by taking 19 seconds off the stage record in the London-to-Brighton and then winning the Midlands three miles in a record 14:07.4, but although he continued to run well all summer he could not match Chataway, Parker and Philip Morgan when they ran 13:59.6, 14:00.8 and 14:03.8 respectively at the AAA Championships on 21 June. Pirie, who had broken the British six miles record the night before, was selected for the Helsinki Olympic 5000 metres along with Chataway and Parker.

Writing in "Athletics Weekly", the editor, Jimmy Green, observed: "Green, expected by many Midlanders to give Chataway a hard race, ran with Parker in the lead for a good deal of the race, but when Morgan went in front with 1½ laps to go he could not hold the pace and dropped back". Green's time was a disappointing 14:09.8, but his other performances in his customarily heavy season included pre-AAA races of 6:41.1 for 1½ miles (just outside the British best and beating Pirie), an Irish all-comers' record four miles of 19:00.3 in Dublin, the Waddilove Trophy two miles by inches from Doug Wilson in 9:15.8, and several other wins, including one over Slijkhuis, and the Bournville mile (sponsored by the Birmingham chocolate-makers) for the third time in 4:16.0 ahead of lanky Don Seaman.

After the AAA Championships, Green continued to show the promise in his running that there was always more to come. There was something exciting about his action that caused shrewd followers of the sport to believe that he might one day break through on the track and match his efforts on the road. Green himself still considers that his ability to run better in the latter half of the track season came about because the demands of cross-country and road running into April gave him only eight weeks to be ready for the AAA race.

After the Olympics Green was 5th in 14:04.0 in the British Empire-v-USA three miles won surprisingly in 13:51.6 by the American, Charlie Capozzoli, but five days later it was Green who ran away from Capozzoli and his colleagues in a tactical winning 14:22.6. Green followed that with a 14:15.2 for the AAA v Combined Services, in which a young airman named Derek Ibbotson placed 3rd.

Another tough winter's work in Birchfield's colours, but at what cost?

A winner's team medal in finishing 21st and helping Birchfield to their first victory since 1937 at the National cross-country championships gave Green a good start to 1953, but his winter work-load provided another perfect example of running too often for his club over the country and on the road. He set the fastest stage by 43sec in the London-to-Brighton (20:51 for over four miles), and apart from that he took part in the National Business Houses road relay and cross-country championships for his Lucas employers, the Midlands seven-mile cross-country, plus club road-relay commitments in the Livingston, Wolverhampton, Bradford and Manchester-to-Blackpool events.

In the lead-up to the AAA Championships, Green won the Midlands three miles yet again in 14:15.0 and ran 14:17.2 in a match against Wales. He was 2nd to the 1948 Olympic 5000 metres champion, Gaston Reiff, with 8:17.4 for 3000 metres in Antwerp and ran a 9:03.2 two miles in Swansea and a 14:08.0 three miles in Dublin. He suffered two heavy defeats at two miles: 4th behind Chataway's record 8:49.6 at the May meeting at the White City, and 2nd, a long way behind Pirie (8:56.0 to 9:19.0) who was starting his year of years.

By the time that the AAA Championships took place Pirie was in sensational form. On the Friday evening he won the six miles in a world record 28:19.4 and then appeared again for the three miles the next day, as "Athletics Weekly" reported:

Freddie Green running on the outside against Curtis Stone (123) and Charles Capozzoli (83), both of the USA, at the post-Olympic British Games at the White City Stadium on 9 August 1952. Green went on to win this three-mile race in 14:22.6.

"A field of 30 turned out with the glorious Pirie in the rear at the first bend. Then he moved up and a group soon formed with him in the lead, then Eyre, Ken Norris and Green. By the mile, 4:23.6, Norris had dropped back and by halfway it was Pirie and Green with Eyre still close up. At two miles, 9:05, Eyre was weakening, but Green was still in close attendance of Pirie who was lapping steadily in 69sec. On the 10th lap Green made a couple of desperate attempts to pass, but Pirie would not give way and made still greater efforts to run his rival into the ground. At last Green could stand the pace no longer and had to let Pirie go. The last lap saw Pirie forcing the pace in gallant style to come home the winner in a championship best performance of 13:43.4."

Green set a personal best of 13:46.0, with Eyre well back in 14:02.0, and a fortnight later Green was under 14 minutes again in taking 2nd place to the Belgian, Frans Herman, in the British

Games. After that Green had another view of Pirie's back in the three miles against France at the White City (13:36.4 to 13:51.0) and then in the 5000 metres against Germany in Berlin when Pirie's attack on Gunder Hägg's world record only just failed and the Olympic bronze-medallist, Herbert Schade, was run off his legs and finished 3rd (Pirie 14:02.6, Green 14:27.2).

In the match with Sweden in Stockholm a few days later Pirie narrowly failed to beat Zátopek's world record at 10,000 metres with 29:17.2, and Green gained his first international-match win at 5000. The lead changed hands many times during the race before Green put in a very fast 55.5 last lap to win by more than two seconds from Bertil Albertsson. The season finished on a high note, with Green achieving his fastest ever times at the mile and two miles.

Yet another record for Pirie, and Green sets a personal best behind him

First, in the England-v-Holland match at the White City on 30 September, he ran 8:53.0 for two miles as Pirie's 8:47.4 established yet another British record after the two of them had been together through a 4:23.8 opening mile – no Slijkhuis, and no other "Flying Dutchman" on this occasion as the first of the visitors ran 9:22.4. Then at the Birchfield floodlit meeting three days later Green set a Midlands all-comers' mile record of 4:08.8 which beat the time of 4:12.0 set by Sydney Wooderson in the Bournville event in 1939. It was a fine race as Bill Nankeville and Ralph Dunkley (both world relay record-holders) battled it out with a future British Empire Games six miles champion, Peter Driver, until the last furlong when "along came Green with a terrific burst which saw him home".

At last, an enforced rest and a fresh start to the track season – with a secret ambition. Green's 32-race schedule, mixed with much training, led to the leg strain which at least had the benefit of forcing upon him a winter break of almost five months without running. So he started the 1954 track season fresh and with a special objective in mind. He tells the story as follows:

"I had a secret ambition which only Jack Emery knew about. I wanted the world record at three miles, and if I was selected for the Empire Games it would be a bonus. With continued physio support I set course for the AAA Championships with two three-mile wins for the AAA in Glasgow and in Wales in 14:21 and 14:28, an international 5000 metres in Saarbrücken in 14:47, a 4:17.6 in the Bournville mile and 4:11.6 to win the Inter-Counties, and a 1:57.6/4:17.7 local sports double".

He also finished 4th in 9:03.6 to Chataway's fine British two miles record of 8:41.0 at the White City in June, and he ran 9:02.8 at Darlington, won the Midlands three miles in 13:51.0, and did a two-mile club match in 8:56.0 three days before the AAA Championships. His racing schedule had been cut and his training was more selective and specific. He describes the day of the AAA three miles in graphic terms even almost half-a-century later:

"I awoke on Saturday 10 July deep in thought – positives and negatives. My leg felt okay. I came into the race with a 13:51 three miles and an 8:56 two-mile time-trial. I had my usual pre-race breakfast of poached egg on toast. I wore my Birchfield singlet, not my international one. At the track, Chataway was looking pretty serious and not his usual jovial self. At the gun the Kenyan, Maiyoro, who was the first of the great runners from that country, took off and proceeded to lay the foundations for a world record.

"The mile in 4:23.4 – fast but I was feeling OK. Chataway took over the lead just before the two miles, reached in 9:01.6. I was still feeling good. He stayed in the lead for two laps, but I sensed that he was slowing so I took over with two laps to go. I upped the pace a little and as we reached the bell I was clocked in 12:30.6. On a quick calculation a 61-second last lap would be close to the world record. I instinctively waved Chataway on, with my tactical sense telling me that I would rather be on his shoulder into the final straight. At 140 yards to go he wasn't going away, and so I prepared myself to sprint from the last bend. Then flat out and sensing Chris was on my left shoulder I went for it – and I had won!

"We recovered breath for a couple of minutes while waiting for the announcement. When it came the announcer sounded like one of the McWhirter twins and played to the crowd: 'Here is the result of the three miles AAA Championship. First, Fred Green, Birchfield Harriers, in a time that is a new English native, British national, British all-comers', European, Commonwealth and world record – 13 minutes 32.2 seconds'. The crowd erupted!"

Chataway was given the same time and was eager for revenge at the British Empire & Commonwealth Games in Vancouver, famous for the Bannister-v-Landy mile and the collapse of Jim Peters at the end of the marathon. Green recalls of the Games race: "I decided to run in the lead or front group to ensure a fast pace as a new world record was possible and to avoid any problems that can occur if you are in the pack. The Kenyan, Maiyoro, led with a lap to go, and I took the lead with 350 yards to go, but this time it was Chataway who was on my shoulder and he took off a furlong out, completing the last lap in 56sec. His time was 13:35.2, which was three seconds outside the world record and two seconds ahead of me in 2nd place".

In the European Championships in Berne, Green qualified comfortably in the heats, running in with his old rival, Frans Herman, of Belgium, in 14:42.8. Then, instead of the expected clash between Zátopek, Chataway, Green and the others in the final, the USSR's Vladimir Kuts ran away with the race. Green took the lead at the start, but after half-a-lap Kuts came roaring by, and the further the race progressed the further away he went to break the world record with 13:56.6, leaving Chataway and Zátopek (14:08.0 and 14:10.2) to have their own private battle after Green pulled out. "Kuts cleared out from the field," Green recalls, "and began his famous surge tactics – fast, slow, fast. I went after him, but after five laps I experienced a muscle spasm in my left thigh and for the first time in my career I stepped off the track. Even so, I was satisfied that I had accomplished what I had set out to do at the beginning of the year".

Freddie Green's retirement meant that he missed the showdown at the White City in October when Chataway ran himself to everlasting glory by beating Kuts by inches in a world record 13:51.6 for 5000 metres. After emigrating to Australia, Green and his wife brought up three daughters who all obtained university degrees and he won distinctions at a leading Melbourne business school and became a distribution manager before retiring to near Perth in Western Australia.

Note: My thanks to Ian Smith for putting me in touch with Freddie Green and to Freddie himself for all the information which he provided. This article was originally published in "Track Stats", Volume 39, No.3, September 2001. Freddie Green died on 17 July 2006, aged 79.

Jack Parker, European Championships 110 metres hurdles silver-medallist 1954

In Britain it was just his hobby, but for the Russians he was a "Master of Sport"

A funny thing happened to hurdler Jack Parker when he arrived in Berne for the 1954 European Championships. He had a room to himself, for the first time in his six-year international career. Usually he roomed with his fellow hurdler, Peter Hildreth, while they raced as the British pair in 15 head-on international matches between 1951 and 1956. Secondly, outside the window of his room and home for three nights was a track. And thirdly, there were hurdles on the track.

Jack said, "I arrived three days early and had two clear days before my first heat in the 110 metres hurdles. On each day I trained over hurdles twice a day and relaxed the rest of the time in splendid isolation, never going out. I squeaked by in my heat, coming 2nd in 14.7. I went and had a run over the hurdles before the semi-final and did 14.8, coming 3rd. There was another day before the final and again I polished my hurdling. In then final I got a good start and was ahead by the sixth hurdle. Then the Russian went by and I finished 2nd.

"It is an example of how important it is to have a facility like that. At the Helsinki and Melbourne Olympics I cannot remember going over a hurdle before my races. There was no practice track at either place and I never had such luxury as in Berne again. Having one shows the difference between going out and keeping an eye on it. It's like tennis – keeping your eye in. For a distance runner it does not make any difference, but for a hurdler it does. That was my experience".

The European final that year was one of the three races during his career that Parker felt pleased about. "They were", he reminisced in his country home on the Hampshire-Wiltshire border, "the only three races when I have finished content. I thought I could not have done better". The other two were his win against the Russians in Moscow in 1955 – his best year when he was unbeaten in Europe – in 14.4, for which he was named "Man of the Match" and honoured by the hosts with the award of "Russian Master of Sport, 2nd class", and his British National record equalling and English Native record of 14.3 for the 120 yards hurdles at the White City the same year.

He is silver-haired now but still erect and fit and plays tennis. He worked all his life as a civil engineer but became a civil servant at the end of his career when he was an under secretary, being Chief Highways Engineer in the Ministry of Transport until he retired aged 64. He is now 83 with three grandchildren, one of whom is a promising sprinter. Jack Parker ran in the 1952 and 1956 Olympics and also the 1954 Empire Games in Vancouver. He would have been at Iffley Road on 6 May that year when Bannister did his sub-four minute mile, but as he explained when invited to compete for the AAA against Oxford University he did not do Thursdays.

He only once broke his rule by taking an afternoon off to go to Fenners at Cambridge for an early evening race against Hildreth over 220 yards hurdles. The wrong-way-round three-laps-to-the-mile track and the early bend suited Parker perfectly and he won by 0.2 sec, equalling the British record in 24.0 just a few days after the pair of them had dead-heated at the Sward Trophy meeting over 120 yards hurdles.

For Parker, 6ft 2in (1.88m) and 98kg (15st 6lb) when racing, was a Saturday-only race man, a man for whom athletics was a hobby fitted in around his work. Internationals abroad meant using part of his holidays or leaving the office early on Friday afternoon and being back at his desk first thing Monday morning. In fact, because of work his hurdling career could have ended a year early after his brilliant 1955 season. He was just married and his firm sent him out to

Malawi for five months throughout the winter when he did barely any training at all. In the same way that Jerry Cornes came back to England after nearly two years working in Africa in 1936 without any running and still finished 6th behind Lovelock in the 1936 Olympic 1500 metres, so Parker returned in May of 1956.

And then he was asked to go and work in Hong Kong for three years, with the Olympics in Melbourne just six weeks away. His wife, Shirley, was pregnant with their first child – now a headmistress of a large London school – and he had been selected with Hildreth to go to Australia. He negotiated with the firm and they allowed him to go to Melbourne – as a stage to Hong Kong. His final race was his heat when he finished 4th in 14.8. "Even at my best I would not have done better than 4th in the final, but to be honest my mind was really on Hong Kong", he recalls.

Taking on the challenge of the Americans, but could they be beaten?

When he first began to show promise as a hurdler in 1950-51 Parker saw no reason why he should not beat the Americans. When he watched Harrison Dillard win at the 1952 Helsinki Olympics he knew he would never beat him, but he had hopes of beating the others until he eventually realised that they – and one or two more – were just that much faster than he was and that he would never breach the gap. He was 6th in his semi-final in Helsinki behind Jack Davis, the silver-medallist for the USA whom Donald Finlay once beat. Parker did, however, become the UK No.1, winning three AAA Championships, and formed a partnership with his friend, Hildreth that was extremely difficult to defeat.

Parker was also the only Briton to beat the incomparable Donald Finlay after World War II, in the pouring rain in Glasgow when Finlay hit a hurdle and they finished 3rd and 4th behind – inevitably – an American, Bill Fleming. Parker and Hildreth first ran together against France in 1951 and stayed as the automatic British selection until 1956 in Budapest. They finished with Parker leading 10 to 5 in their international matches together, with many of their races finishing inches apart, a common occurrence during the dozens of times they ran against each other. The photo of them side by side in the Southern championships in 1950 showed just how keenly they competed against each other and the rest, like Ray Barkway, who actually won this race with a foot covering all three. Barkway sadly died in a service flying accident in 1956.

Parker had one big advantage as a hurdler and one disadvantage. He had a natural stride pattern with which he never had any trouble, but he was also stiff round the hips. "It was incredible that I could do the times I did because I was so stiff. And I was not particularly fast", he explains. He won Surrey county titles at the sprints but never broke 10.0 for 100 yards and had a best of 22.8 for 220 yards.

Born in Richmond, Surrey, on 6 September 1927, Frederick John Parker (always known as "Jack"), he started sprinting at East Sheen Country School. His father, Fred, was a good sprinter in his day and impressed his young son by winning a veterans' race on holiday, finishing with a bigger winning margin than the handicap start he had been allowed. Jack took up hurdling as a side-line event when at Liverpool University. He won the University title with 18sec, plus a 25.2 220 hurdles win, in 1948. Team-mates and rivals in the Christie Sports (Liverpool, Manchester and Leeds Universities) included Olympians Harry Whittle, Joe Birrell and Alan Parker.

The next year Jack Parker's hurdling improved enough to win the Surrey title in 16.2, and by the end of the season – when he had met and lost to Finlay, then supreme at the age of 39, and Hildreth – he had taken another second off his time. That attracted the attention of the AAA and he joined others, including future Olympians such as Mark Pharaoh (4th in the discus at the 1956 Olympics) and long-jumpers Shirley Cawley and Roy Cruttenden, for coaching under John Le

Masurier. In 1950 he got down to 15.0 when losing by inches to Hildreth, the heir-apparent as Finlay was retiring at the end of the year, and was 4th in his first AAA final.

The next year Parker won four international vests and beat Hildreth for the first time when winning the AAA title in 14.8. He lost to him against France but won on the Balkan tour against Greece, losing to him against Turkey and Yugoslavia. He said, "That was the trip when everyone got the stomach virus. Against Greece it was ridiculous. Hammer-thrower Dr Ewan Douglas had to throw the javelin, and in that long stadium with marble seats he threw it into the stand, and it cluttered along the seats. There were squatters in the stadium, the first I had ever seen. Harry Whittle did the pole vault – 8 feet 6, I think – and Walter Hesketh shot off the track into the stands because of illness. In Istanbul Peter and I spent an evening looking at all the monuments and mosques. We were great friends, socialising as well as our racing, and we still keep in touch".

Parker was now catching Hildreth when they raced, tending to lose out early on and then coming through very fast at the end, and as the years moved on Parker was getting closer each time they met in highly competitive fights always right to the line. In the 1952 match against France, Parker ran a lifetime best of 14.6 to win and had hopes of reaching the final in Helsinki. He remembered, "We were like tourists at those Games, going round seeing the sights. It was like being on holiday. I went to a dinner given by the Russians which was very good". In the Games he reached the semi-final but then went out, and it was then that he realised just what the gap was between him and the Americans.

Knocked into the stands by one opponent

By 1953 he was consistently under 15sec and the regular choice with Hildreth for the 110 metres/120 yards hurdles. He said, "Against France I received such a heavy swipe from Ignace Heinrich, the Frenchman who had won the decathlon in the European Championships three years earlier, that he knocked me into the stands. I got him next time we ran. Then we went on the tour to Germany and Sweden and I won both from Peter". The next year he was AAA champion, just beating Hildreth, with both doing 14.7. As was becoming the custom in their races, Hildreth got away best and Parker had to fight over the last few hurdles to catch and just beat him.

Then came the two Championships, with the Empire Games in Vancouver first. Parker ran well in his heat to do 14.7 behind the Jamaican, Keith Gardner; but in the final very unusually he hit several hurdles and never got going to finish a disappointed 4th in 15.0, with his second string, Chris Higham, running the race of his life to win the silver in 14.9 behind Gardner. Parker said, "When I got back I went to the doctor with ear trouble. He had a look and found my ears were blocked with wax. They had been when I raced in Canada!" He was in the stadium for the Bannister-v-Landy mile and also the finish of the marathon where he reckons Jim Peters collapsed because of the 20-degree incline he had to descend coming into the arena in the heat, a step too much for an exhausted man.

On to Berne and his luxury lodgings and silver medal. "I was determined to beat the Russian, Bulanchik, next time I met him", he remembers. "I was ahead until the sixth hurdle. He must have been a beautiful hurdler like Finlay, and he went ahead between the sixth and seventh hurdle. I thought afterwards, 'Right, I'll beat you next time', but although I had two more races against the Russians he never appeared and I never saw him again".

Parker's mix of life was work in London and training in the winter just twice a week. He said, "I used to go to the Polytechnic gym in Regent Street on a Monday evening with Doug Wilson and others where there was an extremely aggressive trainer who really worked us very hard. I'm sure

Jack Parker competing in the 120 yards hurdles heats at the AAA Championships on 14 July 1956. He was 3rd in the final with a time of 14.6 seconds as his constant rival, Peter Hildreth, won the title from Eamonn Kinsella, of Ireland.

he did us a lot of good. Then we would have a quick run in the park after jogging and running on the spot in the gym. On Saturday mornings I would go to Motspur Park for a session with John Le Masurier over the hurdles, and we would run up a hill four or five times in Richmond Park. In the summer I tried to go over hurdles once a week to keep my eye in". His racing usually started with the Sward Trophy, then one or two major club matches for South London Harriers – "SLH had a very strong team in those days" – and the Inter-Counties, County championships, Kinnaird, Southern and AAA, and finally the internationals to end the season.

In nearly all the events he was running against Hildreth, and he started 1955 losing by inches in the Inter-Counties, both doing 14.8, and then beating him, 14.6 to 14.7, in the Kinnaird. Parker won the Southern by inches, but this time from Paul Vine (the man who finished ahead of Bannister at Oxford by coming last in the 120 yards hurdles, the event before the first sub-four-minute mile!), and then took the AAA in 14.6 from Opris of Rumania, doing the same time. Hildreth was a half-step behind in 14.7. "Athletics Weekly" reported: "The final was a great race and Opris looked all over the winner with two obstacles to go. But Parker pulled out one of those great fighting finishes for which he is so well known and caught his man almost on the line".

Five wins in five international matches

This was followed by five head-to-head internationals, and Parker won all five, with Hildreth 2nd in four and 3rd against Russia. The first match against West Germany was the best and the fastest win. Parker went away from the start for once and kept going superbly to win by half-a-second from Hildreth in 14.3 to equal Australian Ken Doubleday's British all-comers' record at 120 yards hurdles and break Donald Finlay's English Native record. Parker said, "Finlay was a delightful terrific chap and very courteous. After I had broken his record he sent me a letter which said that he was a little sad to have lost his record, but he congratulated me from the bottom of his heart".

Parker then did 14.4 against Hungary ("Parker seems to be getting those first few hurdles right now and was quickly in front and going strong," said "AW"), and it was left to Hildreth for once to almost catch him in the same time. In Bordeaux against France it was the same result and the same time of 14.7 in an inches finish, and then against the USSR Parker did 14.4 for the metric distance (120.3 yards) in Moscow (see above) and finally against Czechoslovakia in Prague he did 14.6, with Hildreth 0.6 behind.

Parker said, "I had spent most of my career catching Peter up, but that year I was on top. I thought that I would have got down to 14.1 or even 14, but that just would not have been anything against the Americans. I was ranked 8th in the world. I thought that at Melbourne I would have squeaked into the final and finished 4th or somewhere like that". But because of his work it was not to be. It was not until May of 1956 that he was back in the UK from Malawi, and he said, "I had done virtually no training for five months to keep fit, and it was absolutely remarkable I could run as fast as I did without winter training at all. It was a hobby for me, the last of the amateur era. I had three races where I ran as well as I could that year". And he was picked for the Olympics on the strength of those performances.

He beat Hildreth at the British Games twice. Neither won against better Europeans in the invitation race and Bob Shaw won the Inter-Counties, with the old gang 2nd and 3rd, and Parker did 14.7 to head the rankings. He won the Surrey county title in a record 14.9 and beat Hildreth by inches in the Kinnaird in 14.9, but the result was reversed in the Southern in 15.1. The AAA Championships was the final proof that the snap in his racing had gone as he finished 3rd behind Hildreth and Eamonn Kinsella, of Ireland, in 14.6, the winner doing 14.5. Parker and Hildreth fought it out against Czechoslovakia in a windy 14.3, with Hildreth just taking it on the line, and Parker did 14.7 a week later for the AAA against the Combined Services.

Then, when the team for the Olympic Games in Australia had just been announced, his company asked him to go to Hong Kong on a three-year posting to work at the airport. He said 'yes' but asked to delay it so he could run in Melbourne. His firm agreed and so he kept training. He lost by half-a-second in a match against his old rival on the Croydon track, and then the home highlight of the year, the match against the USSR, was cancelled at the last minute because Nina Ponomaryova, their discus champion, was involved in an allegation that she had stolen a hat from a London store. Instead Parker ran 14.7 against Hildreth in a Battle of Britain Trophy meeting and showed better form with 14.4 to finish well behind the Americans at a floodlit meeting at the White City. The world rankings that came out at the same time ended with 11 men doing 14.0 or faster – nine Americans and two Germans – and the USA's Olympic silver-medallist, Jack Davis, leading in 13.4.

In the home match against Hungary at the end of September Hildreth won by 0.1 in 14.4, but in the last race between the two at the White City in October Parker took it by the same margin in 14.5, with "AW" saying, "What a pity we shall not be seeing these two fighting it out in future meetings; so closely matched they have helped each other immensely and Hildreth is bound to miss his old colleague". In Melbourne they both went out in the first round. Parker travelled on to Hong Kong and Hildreth won many more races before retiring at the 1962 European Championships through back injury.

Parker said, "It was my last race, and with the best will in the world I did not really have my mind on track and field there. If I had kept on improving I would have had a chance of squeaking into the final, but I would not have been in the first three". He added, "Peter and I must have raced each other over a hundred times, the first being in an inter-university event when I was running for Christie. He beat me. I gradually caught up with him and then in 1955 got ahead. He went on after I had finished and did 14.3 too. We were great friends and great rivals".

Hildreth ran many 400 metres hurdles races, too. Parker did the event once or twice and was 3rd in the AAA Championships in 1951 in 55.2y (his best ever was 54.6y) but did not train for it and did not like it. He said, "For me athletics was always a hobby, but I enjoyed it very much. One of my main incentives was if I was beaten by a whisker and thought afterwards, 'If I had done that I would have won, I'll get him next time we race'. But after I was married to Shirley in 1955 I lost incentive.

"I am not interested now. It's all changed so much. In my day I had a canvas bag in which I had a track-suit, spikes, heavy starting-blocks, eight nails and a hammer to fix them, and I would lug it on a crowded trolley-car up to the White City and perform in front of crowds of 40,000 to 50,000 people. In return you got a plaque which was shoddy and worthless, perhaps a dinner afterwards, and no other reward, but we loved it. On one occasion Adidas turned up and handed out some running-shoes, just five pairs. I did not get one. Now it is all money and agents. I don't watch athletics because it is all about money. But they have such short careers and they have to live on it for the rest of their lives. I don't resent it, and nor am I opposed to it, as I never had the opportunity to be part of it".

Note: this article was first published in "Track Stats", Volume 49, No.1, April 2011.

Derek Johnson, Olympic Games 800 metres silver-medallist 1956

From the sprints to the steeplechase, the natural talent from East Ham that excelled in them all

On the afternoon of Saturday 14 September 1963 a 30-year-old computer management consultant left his Ladbroke Grove flat in West London and walked the mile or so to the White City Stadium. In the changing-room he put on his number and went out to line up for the invitation 800 metres before a crowd of 4,900, many of whom recognised him either by sight or by name. One minute fifty seconds later he crossed the line in a time that ranked high in the lists that year and would still almost get him into the British team 40 years later. In those days such a performance was nothing special, but the manner of doing it was.

His characteristic lovely running action had taken him past the bell in 53.5 seconds – much to his surprise – and it was only in the home straight that a British international, Tony Harris, led the charge past to leave the dark-haired 5 ft 9½in (1.76m) 10½st (66kg) figure in 4th place. The winner ran 1:49.4, which was much slower than the still-standing British record of 1:46.6 set in a titanic race in 1957 against the 6 ft 2in (1.88m) tall bull of an American, Tom Courtney, who had won the Olympic title the previous year.

By all normal standards Derek James Neville Johnson, the holder of that British record, should not have been there at all at the White City that day in 1963. In fact, by normal standards he should have died from tuberculosis four years before. During 1959 in Finland he had run a 4:05.0 mile and then the fastest British 1500 metres of the year (and the 10th fastest in the world) of 3:42.9. Incredibly, he had recovered from TB, had started training again for fun in the summer of 1963, and had done 1:53.2 in a club half-mile race. After his White City performance he really thought that he had a chance for the 1964 Olympics.

But Derek Johnson said sadly when we met at his London home almost 40 years later: "I thought I was mad, crazy, when I went to run in that race, but afterwards when I had improved three seconds I thought that if I had a good winter there were the Games in Tokyo. It was not to be because I got Achilles tendonitis and it wrecked me. In those days there was no cure. So I survived TB but went out because of tendonitis". It was a bitter blow – though not quite as bad as the TB which he had contracted at the peak of his brilliant career.

"I am not a believer, but I had this God-given gift", Johnson recalled. "I could sprint. I could handle any distance. I just had this natural talent". And how he used it! His range was top-class sprinting, steeplechasing and 400 metres hurdling; international 400 metres running; world-class 1500 metres and miling; and "Master Class" at 800 metres. His range was similar to that of Sydney Wooderson and Steve Ovett, but not quite as good because he lacked major talent at cross-country, although that might have been due to his illness.

He was Empire Games champion at 880 yards in 1954, 4th and 7th in the European Championships 800 metres in 1954 and 1958, and silver-medallist to Courtney in the legendary 1956 Melbourne Olympic 800 metres. He also won gold and silver in the Empire Games 4 x 440 and bronze in the 1956 Olympic 4 x 400. Tuberculosis was the worst of his problems, but he also suffered from tonsilitis, blackouts after heavy races, and a series of injuries, particularly in 1957 in Scandinavia when he ran in several races on summer nights that were some of the best seen in that era.

Of the onset of TB in 1959 he recalled: "I had just left Oxford University to continue my medical studies in London and went on the medical chest ward at the hospital in January 1959, where there was lot of TB flying around. I had won the Grafton Friendship Cup cross-country just before Christmas and I ran in the Essex championships and finished 7th. I expected to come in the top 20 to 30 in the Inter-Counties but instead was 98th. The following week I was laid up in bed, and I thought I had 'flu, but I'm pretty sure it was the primary infection."

He recovered but took no part in domestic competitions later that year, saving himself for the summer in Scandinavia where he ran the fastest 1500 metres and mile of his life but fell ill on the plane on his way back to Britain, and two weeks later he collapsed. "Obviously I was susceptible to TB and got caught", Johnson explains. "It was a very dramatic collapse. I was pole-axed and spent the next six weeks in bed. I finally managed to see the students' doctor, and he told me to go home and take an aspirin! Instead, I went to see another doctor who X-rayed me and 90 minutes after I had seen the 'go-home-and-take-an-aspirin' man I was wheeled back to see him on a stretcher. One lung was obliterated and the other two-thirds affected. Two more weeks and I would have had it."

He spent six months in a sanatorium in Surrey, gave up medicine and athletics, and took a job with a computer firm in Paris. Four years later, when he turned up for his White City race, Mel Watman, of "Athletics Weekly", wrote of the occasion: "Even if he never runs another race, Derek Johnson has proved when it comes to sheer guts there is not an athlete to surpass him". Johnson did, indeed, never run another track race, but if you want to see an example of his courage you can watch the recently-found film of the 1956 Olympic Games in which the 800 metres is shown in full. Watch him dart through the gap that Courtney and another American, Arnie Sowell, leave open for just a fraction of a second and see him race for the line 70 metres or so away and the superhuman effort by Courtney whose brute strength gets him home by the smallest of margins, 1:47.7 to 1:47.8. The victory ceremony had to be put back an hour because both Courtney and Johnson collapsed in the dressing-room.

Caught up in a melee in the fastest Championship 800 metres ever

Of the race Johnson says: "I was beaten fair and square and I have no complaints. People think it was my best race, but I don't. I would pick the 1954 European 800 metres that should have been mine, but instead I got into a melee at the first bend and I came out breathing hard. You don't normally feel your breathing until the last 300 metres or so. If I'd had a clear run round the first bend I would have won it". The outcome was that he placed 4th in a blanket finish that made it the fastest championship race up to that time, won by the Hungarian Lajos Szentgáli in 1:47.1 from Lucien DeMuynck, of Belgium (1:47.3), and Audun Boysen, of Norway, who was also to be the bronze-medallist in Melbourne (1:47.3). Johnson's 1:47.4 was the fastest ever by a Briton and took a second off Wooderson's then world record from 1938. In 5th place was the Belgian first string, Roger Moens, in 1:47.8. Five men under 1:48, and the next year Moens ran 1:45.7 to break Rudolf Harbig's 16-year-old world record.

Born in Chigwell, in Essex, on 5 January 1933, athletics had begun at a very early age for Derek Johnson when he and his cousins, then aged six or seven, used to practise starts with his uncle and it was obvious that young Derek was a natural. He had his first spikes when he was 10 and as a teenager ran for his school in a major Essex county competition and scored their only points by finishing 2nd at 100 yards. He was soon the best athlete at East Ham Grammar School and then in the whole of the country in his age-group, winning titles at the English Schools and AAA Junior Championships.

He was first spotted as a potential Olympic prospect at the age of 15 by the British team manager, Jack Crump, who saw him win the 880 in 2:01.2 at an Essex schools meeting – exceptional time at that age in those days – and then run a 52.2 440 an hour later. At 16 Johnson ran 50.6 in the All-England Schools meeting and broke 2min for the half-mile for the first time.

The next year he took the Schools 220 in 22.6 and then ran a 48.8 quarter-mile which was a sensation at the AAA Junior Championships. Crump wrote of Johnson's performance that "it was the most phenomenal of all" at that meeting and added: "It is, of course, impossible to say how this great little runner will shape when he is fully matured, but I never remember in all my life being so impressed with my first glimpse of a young athlete ... if ever there was a born champion, Derek Johnson qualifies for that place". Ironically, Johnson was to have long-standing battles with Crump in years to come.

By this time Johnson had been coached for a couple of years by "Legs" Lewis at the Fairbairn House Boys' Club, and later he was to be advised at Woodford Green Athletic Club by Ken Bone. With a background of winter cross-country and careful training, Johnson was ready for each summer season, though he now says: "I made two strategic mistakes in my career. After my first year at Oxford, when I finished 3rd to Ian Boyd (8th in the 1956 Olympic 1500 metres) in the cross-country match against Cambridge, I did not run cross-country again until the 1958-59 winter and then despite being infected by TB ran my fastest 1500 metres and mile. I think the fact I ran so well in the 1956 Olympic 800 metres was because I had been racing miles in the early season and I might well have gone for the 1500 metres if I'd not had such a disastrous race in the AAA mile" (there he was 5th in 4:10.8 after Ken Wood had produced one of his dazzling 55sec last laps to win in 4:06.8).

"Looking back – when it is easy – I know I would have been better at 1500 metres or even 5000 metres if I had kept racing cross-country in the winter. The other mistake was not leaving the 440 earlier. Although it was originally my best event, I was never good enough to win at international championship level, but I was good enough to enjoy it. I was a better relay runner and broke 46 seconds". It is an odd statistic in Johnson's career that his best 440 of 47.7 was set not in winning but in finishing 4th and failing to qualify in the heats at the 1958 Empire Games in Cardiff.

Rivalry with Brian Hewson ... and many other talented British half-milers

During 1951 Johnson had run 22.3 for 3rd place in the Southern senior 220, had retained his AAA junior 440 title in 49.1, beat the AAA junior 880 champion in an invitational race, and ran 1:55.4 behind Roy Morley and an unofficial sub-46 440 relay leg to put him on the Olympic "possibles" list. His junior opponent at the White City, when he won in 1:56.7, was Brian Hewson, who was to be one of the great 800 metres runners in Britain during Johnson's era. Hewson was 2nd to Johnson in the 1954 Empire 880, a finalist in the 1956 Olympic 1500 metres, 2nd to Herb Elliott in the 1958 Empire 880 and European 1500 metres champion that year.

There was plenty more British talent at half-miling in those years. John Parlett had won the Empire 880 and European 800 in 1950, with Roger Bannister 3rd in the latter event. Albert Webster was 5th in the 1952 Olympic 800. Mike Farrell was also 5th in the 1956 Olympic final. Mike Rawson won the European 800 in 1958. Added to them were Jim Paterson, of Scotland, together with Ron Henderson, from the north-east, and Ted Buswell, of Norfolk. All of them raced against each other regularly, never holding back, and the times reflected their ability which was much greater than our present crop in Great Britain at that distance.

Things did not go well for Johnson in the Olympic year of 1952. He had begun his two years' National Service and his times did not come down. He won the Army 440 and the Inter-Services in 50.4 and managed a 1:55.8 for 880 yards, but at the AAA Championships he could only do 49.3 for the 440 and went out in his heat and was not considered for the Games team. He then went out to Egypt to join his regiment, the East Surreys, as a 2nd Lieutenant and he missed all of the 1953 home season, although winning Army races in the Middle East. On his return and completion of service in the autumn he went up to Lincoln College, Oxford, to study medicine.

After his cross-country efforts he won the 440/880 double at the Oxford University sports and against Cambridge (49.8 and 1:53.1) early in 1954, and this gave the clue to the range of his abilities in the next few years, bettered possibly only by Wooderson and Ovett. Johnson was in the British ranking lists for every distance from 220 yards to two miles, and also for the 3000 metres steeplechase and 440 yards hurdles – and at the age of 50 he was to run 2:55.47 for 75th place in the Polytechnic Marathon.

He broke the Iffley Road ground record with 48.0 for 440 yards and also won the 220 in 22.4, but that was on 6 May 1954 and no one really noticed. But then he ran 1:50.2 to beat Hewson by over a second in the Inter-Counties, and people did notice. Johnson realised that the 880 was his best event, and this idea was reinforced when he was 2nd in the AAA 440 to the lanky 6ft 5in (1.93m) tall Peter Fryer. At the Empire Games in Vancouver Johnson won the 880 in 1:50.7 from Hewson (1:51.2) and anchored the England 4 x 440 relay team for his second gold medal. Back home he ran 47.9 to equal the English Native 440 record and picked up 12 yards on the USA's Josh Culbreath (3rd in the 1956 Olympic 400 metres hurdles) in a last-leg unofficial 45.8.

Anger directed at "incompetent" officialdom

Johnson's European Championships 800 metres has already been discussed in this article, but it was the 4 x 400 relay that caused his first clash with officialdom. This was the decade of the "Angry Young Men" – Osborne, Amis, Wain, Wilson and others – who were not actually angry but had been given that label by a journalist after Osborne's great play, "Look Back In Anger". Johnson, on the other hand, *was* angry, and the anger which started in Berne was to last through the decades as a founder-member of the International Athletes' Club following the events that almost caused a strike at the Melbourne Olympics. Johnson became a fierce opponent of the use of tobacco sponsorship in athletics and of the attempted Thatcher banning of the British team going to the 1980 Olympics. He also obtained a vast amount of money for the grass-roots of athletics in the South from the gate receipts of the Coca-Cola meetings (the last two of them organised with the aid of David Bedford) and helped set up medical insurance for athletes in pre-millionaire times.

The trouble with the European 4 x 400 in Berne was that the newly-passed rule that runners on the next leg lined up from the inside in the order in which the incoming runners were likely to finish was not used at the Championships. Instead, the old rule that you handed over in the lane order which had applied at the start of the race was still in force, and so Peter Fryer had to move out to lane eight across the Hungarian runner who was in lane two. Fryer clipped the Hungarian's foot and he fell. Johnson ran 46.2 to bring GB home for gold, but the team was disqualified.

Johnson says: "I thought that the fact that the officials were unable to argue the case properly on appeal showed their fundamental incompetence. To me, the management – Crump, Harold Abrahams and, at Melbourne, Les Truelove – were incompetent, just dreadful. Just a bunch of freeloading oafs". This is Johnson's point of view and there are some people who support it and others who do not. It is true that all three officials used their senior positions to write for the press and give their views while selecting and managing teams and that they would accompany individual athletes on overseas visits, as was the rule of the time.

In 1955 Johnson ran more than 60 races, including 18 at 800 metres or 880 yards, with an outstanding individual record. He did a 49.5/1:52.5 double against Cambridge, a 48.3/1:52.1 double at the British Games, and anchored the Oxford team with a 1:52.1 leg at 4 x 880 in the USA. He also ran 1:50.0 for Oxford against London University, another 48.3 against the US universities, 1:52.8 for 880 in the Kinnaird Trophy meeting, and 1:49.3 behind Audun Boysen at the White City.

He won his only AAA title in 1:52.4, leading all the way through a first lap in 54.1 but finishing very listless and tired. He followed this with the best 880 by a British athlete of 1:48.7, a stride ahead of Hewson in the match against Germany, beating Wooderson's record from 1938 by half-a-second, and then he anchored the winning 4 x 440 team. A few days later, at the Rangers' Sports in Glasgow in front of a huge crowd, he was involved in a great 880 race against Courtney and Hewson, coming 3rd in 1:49.7 as the other two ran 1:49.2 and 1:49.3.

Then he went down with tonsilitis which kept him out until the match with France in Bordeaux when he won at 800 metres in 1:49.8 but collapsed after anchoring the winning relay team. He had another collapse which was much more serious in the match against the Russians in Moscow, losing at 800 to Ivakin and Marichev (1:48.5, 1:48.7, 1:48.9) and then in a desperate finish beating the 1954 European 400 metres champion, Ardalion Ignatyev, by inches with a 46sec last leg in the 4 x 400.

Back in relay action and the Russian crowd suddenly falls silent

Derek recalls: "I took over from Mike Wheeler eight yards up on Ignatyev, but he had caught me by the home straight and I just got angry and thought, 'Sod it! I'm not going to lose'. We were side-by-side, but five metres before the tape the crowd went silent and I knew I had won. I collapsed and that put me in bed for three days. Then I had my tonsils out". This had also been the season in which Johnson had tried the mile for the first time after running a 3:00.8 ¾-mile time-trial the year before, and his first two attempts were 4:12.4 at Aldershot and 4:13.5 for Oxford against the AAA, doubling up with a 48.5 for 440 yards!

He did not race quite so much in Olympic year, but as president of OUAC he did a new double of 1:51.9/4:09.7 for the 880 and mile, was beaten by Rawson, 1:51.1 to 1:51.7, in the annual match against the AAA, and won the Universities Athletic Union and Kinnaird miles in 4:06.8 and 4:07.2 – the latter ahead of Peter Driver and Chris Brasher. After his disappointing 5th place in the AAA mile, Johnson went back to his first love of half-miling, although he ran 3:46.8 for 1500 metres in Sarpsborg, in Norway, in early August just a few days after chasing Boysen home at 800 metres in a personal best of 1:47.7 in Oslo.

Against Hungary in Budapest he was last in a blanket finish in 1:52.1, with Szentgáli winning in 1:51.9 and Rawson 3rd. A few days later Johnson turned the tables by beating the Hungarian by a stride at 880 yards in 1:49.2 but lost at 1000 metres to Roger Moens, 2:19.3 to 2:20.4. Then came the Melbourne Olympics and his silver medal at 800 metres and bronze at 4 x 400 with an unofficial time of 46.5 – and problems galore off the track.

For the first time there was almost a revolution by the bored British athletes. They were annoyed that they were not given any pocket-money and had to pay for their own laundry, and then officials exacerbated the situation by giving the athletes no more than two lapel-badges each. Johnson explains: "Lapel badges were the currency for social exchange and all athletes from different nations swapped them. We were not allowed any more. In fact, the management insisted there were no more. There were rumblings of discontent, but in the end they gave us some more. They had been hoarding them for themselves

"The management was a complete and utter disgrace. Athletes want to have status comparable to their peers, not to keep them inferior or superior but to keep them happy. The behaviour of the management made the team spirit poisonous and it was bound to infect everyone. By the time the Games were over, and the match between the British Empire and the USA was due, there was a team meeting and a strike was mentioned. The voting was eight to each view, and the chairman had the casting vote, but as we felt it was unfair to him we did not strike. But I and another athlete had a 'go slow' and I ran a 1:59 relay leg. Not a very nice thing to do, I know".

I believe that 1957 was Derek Johnson's best year (though he thinks 1954 was), and considering his injuries his performances were outstanding.

Without a cross-country background, he started with two indoor wins in Manchester followed by a mile victory in his final fourth year at Oxford in 4:09.0 against the old enemy. He failed to equal the record eight wins in Inter-Varsity matches by the 1924 Olympic 100 metres champion, Harold Abrahams, because of running the 440 only to secure maximum points and losing by inches to the Australian, Bob Solomon, in 49.3. Johnson ran his fastest mile of 4:05.0, losing to the 4:00.6 by Derek Ibbotson (who was to run a world record 3:57.2 later that summer) in the annual Oxford University-v-AAA match at Iffley Road, and then took the UAU title in 4:10.6 after placing 4th in the Sward Trophy 440 hurdles in 56.4. His best at that latter event had been 53.6 at Oxford the year before. Then at the Kinnaird Trophy meeting at Chiswick he tried yet another event.

Johnson explains: "I was down to run the 440 for my club, Woodford Green, but discovered when I arrived that I had not been entered because they thought I would be away. There was the steeplechase, and so for fun I thought I would have a go and run three or four laps. I had done the 440 hurdles and Eric Shirley (an Olympic steeplechase finalist the previous year) told me that you learned to do the water jump on the way round. After four laps I did another one, looked at the others and thought they were about to die, and as I didn't feel like that I thought I would finish. Eric was 40 yards up at the bell and I failed to catch him by two yards as he ran 9:14.2."

Meeting up with Courtney again and setting British records

Frequently popping over to the Continent for weekend races, Johnson ran 1:50.5 for 800 metres in Amsterdam and then at the White City met up again with Courtney, who had set a new 880 yards world record of 1:46.8 in Los Angeles in May. The result was the same as in Melbourne, the big man holding off his shorter rival in a great race in which Courtney ran 1:47.7 and Johnson set a British record 1:48.5 after a 53.9 first lap. They met again four days later at Manchester's White City in a 1000 metres race, but Courtney fell out with stomach trouble and Johnson, who had been watching him, found an enormous gap to make up and finished 3rd to Hewson (2:21.5) and Rawson (2:23.2).

Johnson had been running with a bandaged ankle, which was the result of falling over a track-side water-hose. His ankle had swelled up like a football and this caused him to miss six weeks, including the AAA Championships, but he then told the British Amateur Athletic Board that he was studying in Scandinavia and went out there for a feast of athletics that makes the mouth water even this far on in time. He and Courtney met four times, but the result was always the same. Johnson's injured ankle was made worse when he tripped on it, but it did not stop him running 800 metres in 1:52.5 and then 1:50.8 the next night behind the American's magnificent 1:46.0. The following night Johnson ran 400 metres in 48.8 to Courtney's 47.8. In his fourth race in four days he did 1:51.9, and then he set a British best of 1:46.9 in finishing 3rd in Oslo to Moens (1:46.0) and Courtney (1:46.2).

The next evening – for the hell of it! – he ran a mile in Stockholm in 4:11.2 ("Athletics Weekly" says "not racing seriously") and six days later he lost to Moens, 1:51.2 to 1:52.1, and then at the Oslo meeting two nights afterwards he ran a lifetime best 1:46.6, but again lost to the peerless Courtney's 1:45.8. To end his tour Johnson ran 1:49.4 and 1:49.1 on 11 and 12 August, and in the middle of all this he had flown back for the Glasgow Rangers meeting, where a crowd of 30,000 watched the cream of British half-miling fighting it out with the local man, Jim Paterson (who was to break 1:50 abroad the following week). Paterson took them through the bell in a suicidal 49.2, and in a charge up the home straight Mike Farrell just made it in 1:49.2, with Johnson, Hewson and Rawson following so close that the time-keepers could not separate them in 1:49.6.

After the superb air of Scandinavia Johnson was back on international-match duty but had to withdraw from the race against the Russians just before the start with a pulled muscle. He won from Farrell against Germany in 1:53.7 for 880 yards, lost to Rawson, 1:48.7 to 1:48.9, in Warsaw against Poland, and then did 1:52.1 to win for England against Poland. He finished his very busy season with 47.7 and 1:47.9 in Turku, a 21.8 for 220 yards on a straight track, and a 47.9 for 440 yards after another "local Derby" with Farrell, Rawson and Hewson in Manchester in which Farrell came out on top in 1:51.9, with Rawson running 1:52.3 and the others way out of it.

Johnson's last big season was in 1958. His normal training had consisted of a mix of early-season speedplay and then a lot of 300s with 15-minute gaps, but he did not train much that year because he had his final examinations at university coming up. He did 21.7 and 47.8 (behind John Wrighton and John Salisbury) for Oxford v AAA but little else, missing the AAA Championships. He was still selected for the Empire Games in Cardiff, where he went out in the second round with his lifetime personal best of 47.7 and ran a 47.5 leg for silver in the relay.

Dropped from the relay team – "Building for the future" Johnson was told

The European Championships followed in Stockholm and Johnson recalled: "I had no intention of running 800 metres, but then Herb Elliott beat Brian Hewson – we always got on well, and still do – and I thought I would run in the final trial and get selected, which I did. The selectors pushed Brian up to the 1500 metres, which I was very unhappy about because I thought he was clearly the best 800 metres runner we had. I thought it was grossly unfair of the selectors not to give an athlete his preference. Brian won the 1500 and Rawson won the 800. I was not fit, and I knew when at the last minute they increased the number of rounds from two to three that I would not make it. I had very stiff calves and came 7th in 1:49.2 to Mike's 1:47.8.

"Then, although there were five days in between, I was dropped from the 4 x 400 metres relay team. Truelove, the team manager, told me, 'We have got to build for the future', and as I was 25 at the time I remember saying, 'Les, the future has arrived'. We were clearly going to win the relay by a mile – which we did – but I thought they owed it to me after we had lost in the previous European final because of a disqualification. It was then that Truelove made his stupid remark, and after the Championships I wrote my 'peanuts' letter, saying that if you treat athletes like performing monkeys they should be grateful for the peanuts you throw them, and that I would not run for Britain again".

This led to the formation of the International Athletes' Club with Johnson as its first secretary and later chairman. The club did a great deal to improve the lot of athletes over the years, and he and David Bedford ("at first I thought he was brash, but we have got on marvellously") were at the forefront in many battles for rights. Johnson said, "What I did after I stopped running gave me more satisfaction, and particularly on the smoking issue because my father died of lung cancer, and in stopping the ban for the 1980 Olympics".

Hindsight is always a great comforter, but Derek Johnson does not need it. "I had a wonderful time", he said. "I enjoyed the trips and the teams and the companionship, and it was all due to having such a natural talent. That put me high in the ranking-lists in every event I tried, and I would have done even better if I had not gone down with TB. Today's athletics? I watch football – but unfortunately it's West Ham!"

Johnson's personal best performances were as follows: 100 yards 10.2, 220 yards 21.7, 440 yards 47.7 (45.9 unofficial relay leg), 800 metres 1:46.6, 880 yards 1:48.5, 1000 metres 2:20.4,

Derek Johnson winning from Brian Hewson at 880 yards in the Great Britain-v-Germany match at the White City on 1 August 1955. Johnson's time of 1:48.7 was the best ever by a British athlete, beating Sydney Wooderson's record from 17 years before.

1500 metres 3:42.9, 1 mile 4:05.0, 2 miles 9:15.0, 3000 metres steeplechase 9:16.8, 220 yards hurdles 25.4, 440 yards hurdles 53.6, Marathon 2:55:47 (aged 50).

Note: this article was first published in "Track Stats", Volume 42, No.1, February 2004. Derek Johnson died of leukaemia on 30 August 2004, aged 71.

Another hard night's work over the glue factory. Then stuck just centimetres away from a medal

Mark Pharaoh was born in Streatham, South London, on 18 July 1931. He studied at Manchester University, was a member of Walton AC, and joined the RAF in 1955 on a short-service commission until 1959, during which he was a Flight Lieutenant in airfield construction and maintenance. Returning to civilian life, he was a civil engineer, concerned with construction and consultancy.

Fifty years ago on the training field in Helsinki, the UK's finest discus prospect ever let fly and nearly hit the USSR No. 1, Otto Grigalka, on the head. Luckily the implement just missed. Then the 6ft 3½in (1.91m) tall 15-stone (95kg) hopeful went on to throw 45.24, which was 76cm short of the qualifying distance in the real competition at the 1952 Olympic Games. The Soviet athlete, as the eastern bloc made its first Olympic appearance, finished 6th.

Not being an over-emotional or excitable chap, Pharaoh went home from Helsinki happy for several reasons. He was improving his throwing. He had just finished university with a degree. He was starting work as a civil engineer; and he had celebrated his 21st birthday during the Games. The trip fitted in well with his adventure in athletics, which combined throwing the discus and the shot and seeing the world.

The opportunity to do so had come about when he and another boy at Manchester Grammar School were rummaging in a cupboard in the gym and came across an old discus and shot. Young Pharaoh, son of a former policeman who had been a Cumberland wrestling champion and a builder, was already large for his age and had outgrown the sprints and jumps. So the discus provided him with a new event, for which the head of biology, Alan Morgan, who was a former university thrower, taught Pharaoh the basic techniques. By the time that Pharaoh left school he had improved from 39ft 2in (11.93m) with the 12lb shot to 47ft (14.32m), thrown the discus 137ft 1in (41.78m), hurled the javelin 130ft (39.62m), and at 16 had done 17.4 for the 120 yards hurdles.

This was to lead to a successful throwing career in an event in which Great Britain had really been a non-starter internationally. George Robertson had been 6th of nine competitors with 25.20 in the Athens 1896 Games, and then George Mitchell, of the University of London, had been the only Briton to win at the AAA Championships in the inter-war period from 1920 to 1939 – and with a pathetic 110ft 3in (33.60m) in 1923. Mitchell threw so poorly in his one international appearance against France in 1923 that his performance was not recorded.

When young Pharaoh started competing, the British record was still held by David Young, a Scots policeman, with 153ft 8in (46.83m), set in Glasgow in 1938, and this was over 10ft better than the previous best of 142-10½ (43.55) by a perennial international, Douglas Bell. Until Pharaoh took over sole possession of the record in 1953 the mighty 6ft 7in (2.01m) Royal Marine shot putter, John Savidge, who was 6th in that event in the 1952 Olympics, and Scotsman Harry Duguid had moved it up to an unimpressive 155-3½ (47.33).

Pharaoh subsequently improved the record nine more times and added 22ft, taking it to a respectable 54.27 in his penultimate competition at the Melbourne Olympic Games of 1956, where he almost beat the third American, Des Koch, to stop a clean sweep (Koch's fifth-round throw was 13cm better). Pharaoh set a lifetime best and became the top European in the event, beating the next best by over six feet and leaving his regular UK rival and heir apparent, Gerry Carr, eight feet behind. Pharaoh is the only Briton in the modern era ever to finish in the top six in the men's discus at the Olympics or European championships. His near-victim of four years earlier, Grigalka, was 5th in Melbourne.

During his six years at the top of the British throwing ladder Pharaoh represented Britain 15 times in head-on discus and shot internationals, was in the 1954 European Championships and British Empire Games teams, and was AAA discus champion four times. It gave him the chance to fulfil his ambition to see the world, have a great time when athletics was not so serious as it is now, and take the opportunity to bow out at the top. He arranged an overseas posting in the RAF to the Middle East to change his lifestyle from the athletics adventure of seeing the world to living somewhere else in the world.

We talked about his career in his part-time home in Malvern under the hills that gave such inspiration to another local, Sir Edward Elgar. Pharaoh's other house is in La Manga, in Spain, where he was one-time caretaker of the enormous golf complex and international football teams' training ground, and he is still a very fit-looking man who continues to play golf.

Two matters were obvious. Firstly, he was not the most dedicated of athletes, but he worked hard all the same and took full advantage of the travel and fun opportunities by being an excellent discus thrower but reluctant shot putter in the early 1950s. Secondly, he only had one regret – that he could not have thrown the hammer competitively. When he did so whilst serving in the RAF, and was needed for six or seven events in an afternoon, he threw a British ranking 162ft 1in (49.40m) in 1956 without special training. He said: "If I had my time over again I would prefer hammer throwing to discus. A much more satisfying event because it lasts longer and has a nicer rhythm".

Picking up a discus at 16 – but definitely no weight-training!

When he first picked up and hurled the discus the expert advice was quite clear. Young throwers did not use senior implements, nor do any weight training, and nor – far worse – did they throw the hammer because it could affect the heart and cause strain. "Never heard of a case in my life", Pharaoh said laconically.

As a 16-year-old he won the Northern Counties junior discus with 133-0½ (40.54), and the next year he heard that there was an event called the Public Schools sports, held in London in April. He knew nothing of its history and that it had produced world-beaters like Godfrey Brown, Sydney Wooderson, Jack Emery, Dick Webster, Cyril Holmes, Dennis Pell and Alan Pennington, amongst a host of other internationals, but he recruited his friend, Bob Shaw, who in 1954 would be 3rd in the Empire Games 440 yards hurdles and 5th in the 1954 European Championships 400 metres hurdles, and another boy to enter a team. They came back with the trophy! Pharaoh won the discus and shot and Shaw was 3rd in the 120 yards hurdles, and their headmaster was delighted but advised that they should not let it go to their heads.

The next two years brought university, regional and national experience, with Pharaoh ever aware of the correlation between strength and distance. Weight training was frowned on as much as the use of senior implements, but he measured his improvement by the feel of the implement He recalls, "I knew that I should get strong so that the senior discus felt as light as the junior one and I could throw it as far. I knew I needed to build up strength, but it was not until I went to university that I did any weight training. The Director of PE at Manchester University was Roly Harper, who had competed in the 1932 Olympic 110 metres hurdles, and he befriended me and gave me a lot of advice. He was against the idea of any heavy weight training and was for all-round fitness and practice for the event. I knew I had to be stronger, knew I was not as strong as the Americans, the Continentals and the eastern Europeans. The question was how they got that strong. In those days there was no suspicion of drugs. It was only later that the question arose in eastern Europe. I did not hit the weights as heavily as other contemporaries were doing with the three Olympic lifts. I suppose eventually I was doing about 60 per cent of what, say, the world record-holder in the shot, Parry O'Brien, was doing in training. There was a big factor difference in sheer power".

Now Pharaoh realises that not doing a great deal of weight training did have one benefit. He has genetic arthritis which badly affected the bone structure of his right hand and he thinks it would have been far worse and would have come on far earlier if he had done the extra weight training. The weight training that he did do helped to advance his performance, although he thinks that most of his ever-improving distances came from natural body growth, training and "practice, practice, practice". This was one of the reasons that he quit at such a relatively early age.

He explained: "I got fed up with the event and could not face the grind of training. My main reason for going into athletics was to see the world, and I did. I had a lovely time, seeing places, banquets, meeting friends, and drinking Guinness was good for me! It was all fun with the head-to-head matches, going to places like Budapest and Moscow where we were feted because we were the first there after World War II. It was great. But the training put me off and I decided to leave when I was at the top. The one thing I did miss was the company in training. It was a very lonely existence. Training by myself was a bit soul-destroying. In the end I could not face another year of training on my own and knowing if I did not do it I would be past my sell-by date.

"I was not tempted by drugs at all. They did not exist except that some would take pep pills. One of the Swedes late in my career was supposed to be on steroids and the experts forecast a list of horrors that would happen to him, but he's still around! It's sheer speculation as to whether I would have taken them if they had been available". He went on: "Probably if I had been in competitive group training through the winter I might have progressed more rapidly and stayed on longer. When I left I suppose I could have speculated on what might have been, but I'm not that kind of person. It was over and I stepped away".

Lonely training in the middle of nowhere

But the loneliness of the winter training in a gym in the middle of nowhere got to him to such an extent that sometimes he could not face it and skipped it, and there is one graphic illustration of what training was like in those far-off days, when money did not come into the equation and athletics was a hobby, even at his level, that had to be fitted in with work. Pharaoh was in the RAF and stationed near Stratford-upon-Avon, and he recalled: "I had an old Matchless 350cc motorbike and three times a week I'd ride into nearby Warwick and train in a gym which was in a loft over a glue works".

Another international who used the same gym was boxer Randolph Turpin, who in 1951 had beaten the American, Sugar Ray Robinson, to become middleweight champion of the world and who was still British light-heavyweight champion. His brother and nephew, both handymen, also trained there, and Pharaoh recalled: "We nodded to each other as we trained in the same loft. Two of my friends came to give me encouragement and after the session with weights we would go and have a couple of pints before I rode the twenty minutes home".

The contrast with then and now is really incredible. Often Pharaoh was training on his own in a local school gym, or hurling out into the night the discus and shot that he regarded as brutal events that he never really enjoyed despite continuous championship and international selection.

However much he disliked it, he stuck at it, and the results were good. In 1951 he was over 150ft for the first time, was 4th and best-placed Briton in the AAA Championships (and 5th in the shot), and was selected – joy of joys – for his first overseas tour. This was the trip to the Balkans where nearly everyone in the team went down with stomach ailments. It did not bother Pharaoh unduly because he saw Belgrade, Istanbul and Athens and became the first Briton to win an international-match discus since 1931. He was also, for good measure, 10th in the AAA decathlon on his return.

Olympic year saw him getting his degree before winning the AAA title, then under-performing in the Olympics and seeing Paris when John Savidge, his friend and regular room-mate, beat him into 4th place in the international match against the French. In those days Savidge was No.1 in the shot with the young man No.2, and the roles were reversed in the discus. Pharaoh said of his Olympic debut: "I was young and taken to the Games to get experience. I was lucky because if it had been Australia I would not have been picked because of the expense. It was a blooding, seeing the Americans and Europeans, including the eastern crowd, for the first time. It was a lovely combination of athletics and seeing the world and gave me great motivation for the future.

"It was part of my big picture. I was not as motivated about the Olympics as some others are, but it was a new life for me, leaving university, starting my first job, celebrating my 21st birthday, and moving to London and getting proper training facilities". Those included a coach, John Le Masurier, who together with AAA chief coach Geoff Dyson was then taking the events in which Britain was far behind the world like shot, discus, steeplechase and pole vault, and with Savidge, Pharaoh, John Disley and Geoff Elliott, was shaking them into world-class. It was a successful partnership with them meeting every Saturday morning at Motspur Park.

Breaking the British record regularly on grass or cinders

The coach was in favour of weight training "done in solitude!" but, said Pharaoh, "I did not go into any particularly vigorous training, certainly not up to eastern European standards or those of British sprinters nowadays". Even so, his training added over 10ft to his best in 1953 when he started breaking the British record consistently on a variety of mainly grass and cinder circles rather than concrete and not caged as they are today. He was the first Briton over 160ft, throwing 161-1 (49.10). He retained his AAA crown, added the FISU (International University Sports Federation) students' discus and shot to his honours board, and threw against Germany and Sweden. In Stockholm he came from 3rd to 1st with his final throw to do the unthinkable against the Scandinavians.

By this time his competition diary was packed and so was all his free time. He was training hard throughout the week when he was not competing, and when he was it was fitted into work. The company for which he worked was close to the Walton club's track in Surrey, which was a help, and he would rush from work to get to evening meetings and fit even overseas internationals into the weekend. In 1954, for example, he competed in 22 events, including in the London area (AAA Championships 1st), Manchester, Hull, Oxford (where he broke the record but was overshadowed by the first sub-four-minute mile), Vancouver (for the Empire Games, where he was 3rd in the discus and 6th in the shot) and Berne (10th in the European Championships discus, 16th in the shot). This was an average year.

When he left his considerate employers to join the RAF he was involved with work on the M1 motorway and his boss said that he was owed three weeks' holiday. Pharaoh said he had used it. 'No', said his boss, that was for athletics and gave him three weeks' pay in lieu. In the RAF the competition grew more hectic because of service commitments and a new opponent in the up-and-coming Gerry Carr, who was to take over Pharaoh's mantle and record when he retired, but

1955 was the year when Pharaoh realised that his potential was far more than he thought. He let fly in an exhibition with 175-9 (53.57) in August at Motspur Park, to achieve his first 170ft-plus throw, as his British record stood at 166-9 (50.82). Then five weeks later he nearly did it in competition against the Czechs when finishing 3rd with 169-11 (51.79) during a season when he competed on 27 occasions, usually doing the shot/discus double, that included quick weekend trips to Moscow, Prague and Bordeaux.

He said: "It was a natural progression due to the national training scheme and training sessions while I was still physically developing. I was getting stronger and bigger and getting more and more practice and technique, improving all the time. I have no doubt in my own mind that if I had continued I would have continued to improve but I was getting fed up by then".

The training grew no less boring and lonely, and it was during 1955 that he decided enough was enough. At the end of the season he believed that one more year was all he could face and that he would retire after that, hopefully on a peak by reaching the final stages at the Olympics in December. He explained: "I knew that the only way I could get out of athletics was to get an overseas posting. I did not want to be a reluctant competitor because there is nothing worse in my view than going on past your sell-by date. Go out gracefully at the top".

Another AAA title, and then so close to an Olympic medal

And that is what he did. He obtained a posting to the Middle East and told British team manager Jack Crump, who expressed regret but accepted his decision to retire. The season, with 25 competitions, including three in Europe and two in Australia, became better and better. He retained his AAA title (his 4th win in five years), went over 170ft and 53m for the first official time with 174-0⅛ (53.04) in Prague in July, qualified in Melbourne as the 5th best, and improved his record to 178-0½ (54.27) in the final. That gave him his magnificent 4th place behind Al Oerter, who was achieving the first of his four Olympic wins. The world record-holder (at 59.28), Fortune Gordien, was 2nd and Des Koch 3rd.

Pharaoh said: "It was the motivation for the year. I had targets and achieved them in the sport. I went to the Olympics determined to do well but not seriously expecting to be battling it out with three Americans for the bronze medal. An interesting side-line on the psychology of athletics: at the training area I met Fanie du Plessis, an amiable Boer farmer, very good rugby player, Empire champion and a good friend. He had very powerful long arms. I greeted him like the long lost friend he was, but he was looking glum. I asked him why and he said that the Aussies had confiscated his biltong, the traditional chewing-meat like chewing tobacco that he regarded as a source of all his power. Once he had been deprived of it he was psychologically beaten from that moment. It shows how these little things can affect you".

Pharaoh was not affected by anything. He just hurled the discus further and further. "I had a wonderful ding-dong with the Americans, with everyone else way behind, and although I am not a highly emotional character I must have felt very satisfied. I am not one for looking back and thinking 'if only', but I was very happy with it". There was one more competition, an anti-climax, in the British Empire-v-USA match in Sydney, where he was 5th behind the Americans and du Plessis with a lacklustre 49.46.

He came home and could have changed his mind and cancelled the posting, but he had made his decision that the next adventure was living abroad, and although he threw the discus for four more years in RAF and minor events when the mood took him, with a best of 49.06 in 1958, he was not training, and squash, marriage, family and job took over. He said: "I went out on a lifetime high, though in hindsight it could have been marginally better. There is the thought 'what if I had carried on?' To continue you have to be motivated and I was not".

Mark Pharaoh winning the discus against Czechoslovakia at the White City on 6 August 1956. His 4th place in the Olympics that year was the best ever in that event by a Briton.

He left during an era when National Service in the armed forces brought through some outstanding juniors to world level, and athletics was a sport and fun. Looking back he said: "It was a good day when I discovered that discus and that shot implement in the back of that gym cupboard. It opened a new world of adventure for me, but now it's no longer a sport. It's a branch of show business. Money has come in. In my day athletics was a way of seeing the world. Nowadays it is a way of achieving a standard of living you couldn't otherwise anticipate.

"Sport has lost its ethos, and its ethics now are those of show business, and the two are the same. It has lost its fun, and once money takes over people will use any means at their disposal to achieve the best results. I think we are losing the battle with drugs. I think we have to go back and decide whether we are fighting drugs because those who take them are considered to be at an unfair advantage over those who choose not to, i.e. cheating, or are they being banned because they threaten the well-being of the user?''

Author's footnote: my thanks to Ian Tempest for letting me make use of his article, "Mark Pharaoh, Britain's Best Discus Thrower", in which Pharaoh's entire statistical career is mapped out in exact detail and which appeared in "Track Stats", Volume 32, No 1, April 1994.

Note: this article first appeared in "Track Stats", Volume 39, No.4, December 2001.

Derek Ibbotson, world record-holder One mile 1957

Four stages in the life of the "Four Minute Smiler", and he wouldn't have missed a day of it!

After Derek Ibbotson, as cheeky and chirpy a Yorkshireman as you will ever find, won the three miles event at the head-on match between Great Britain and Czechoslovakia over the August Bank Holiday weekend of 1956 in a very fast 13:28.2 he was approached by one of the organisers and asked if he would run a mile on the holiday Monday, two days later.

The official explained that Ibbo was a crowd-puller. Ibbo replied that he and his fiancée, Madeleine (née Wooller), herself an international, were taking her cousin from the USA on a sight-seeing trip round London and so he would not be able to run. But if by any chance, he suggested, there was an extra ticket for cousin Maureen to go to the dinner-and-dance at one of London's leading hotels after the meeting – Ibbo and fiancée already had their invitations as competitors – then he might just be able to race.

"I would have got £10,000 now," he joked when we talked recently. "But nowadays they don't get the fun we had then. They were fantastic days, friendly, competitive, and parties when the racing was over. Now they fly in, run, and off to the next meeting – loads of money but no fun". At that White City meeting of 50 years ago the extra invitation for cousin Maureen was produced, and the Yorkshireman not only ran but broke four minutes, equalling Roger Bannister's magical 3:59.4 of two years previously. Then, like Cinderella, they all went to the ball.

It was the start of the third of four stages in an athletics career that went from the late 1940s via world records to 1966 when he could still turn out 4:06 for the mile although he was barely training.

Stage One was as a boy on the Yorkshire moors chasing parachuting flares, and then getting his mother to make his first running-shorts from the parachute silk and winning lots of Yorkshire junior titles at the mile and over the country. He also finished 5th in the race that changed the face of British distance-running in 1952: the Inter-Counties three miles when Gordon Pirie beat Frank Sando in 13:44.8, smashing Sydney Wooderson's British record from 1946 by nine seconds and paving the way for a golden age. Ibbo did 14:06.8 and was also 2nd in the Northern event behind the third of Britain's Olympic trio of 5000 metres finalists, Alan Parker (the others being Pirie and Chris Chataway) but had to miss the AAA Championships because of exams and so lost the remote chance he had of making the team.

Stage Two came on 21 June 1955 when he was part of the field for a 2000 metres record attempt in Manchester by Pirie, who was then one of the top three distance-runners in the world. Ibbotson's early promise had been blunted by missing a year when he twisted his ankle badly in running to escape a coal fall in a mine, and then in 1954 he had done nothing of note until he joined the Royal Air Force for National Service and began to train properly. In the Manchester 2000 metres he threw any inhibitions to the wind, raced into the lead, ran his lifetime best mile of 4:08 en route, pushed Pirie to the line, and became a name.

He followed this with a series of wins and good performances, including 2nd to Chataway in the AAA three miles and winning his first international caps in head-on clashes, helping Chataway to set a world three-mile record of 13:23.2 against Germany. He had a good cross-country campaign which took him into the track season of the Olympic year of 1956, and at the Games in Melbourne he was 3rd to the USSR's Vladimir Kuts and Pirie in the 5000 metres. So on to the start of the Stage Three which ended with his world-record mile in 3:57.2 on 19 July 1957.

What came after was Stage Four and we talked about that and his career recently just after he had come back from a walk with his dog on the moors near his home in Huddersfield. He has shown that there is life after athletics, having in his later years coached three excellent milers with Longwood Harriers, by taking up squash and twice becoming Yorkshire veterans' champion at that sport because there was no veteran athletics in those days.

He recalled that following the Olympic bronze-medal success "I had a very good winter over the country and started 1957 with a 4:00.6 mile at Oxford, running away from Derek Johnson. After that I took everything before me. I went up to Glasgow and at 10a.m. in my hotel room my wife rang to say she had given birth to our first child, Christine, and like the modest young Yorkshireman I was I told her I planned to break the world mile record to celebrate the occasion. But it was over 80 degrees. I overtook the pacemaker after two laps and ran the rest on my own, but it was still the second fastest mile ever, 3:58.4.

The world record for the mile, and the beginning of a golden streak

"Soon after, on a Friday evening, July 19, I knew I could do it. The pacemaker was Mike Blagrove, who was just back from his honeymoon, but that did not stop him going through the half in a very quick 1:56. I knew then I could take the sting out of Ronnie Delany's sprint finish. I would have given him a good race in the Olympic 1500 metres which he won, but they picked Boyd, of Oxford, who I beat in the 3:59.4 1956 mile, because I was already in the 5k and they wanted him as captain, and I was miffed about that.

"Ronnie was boxed in, I heard later, and I beat him by 25 yards and was the world's fastest. And then I had a golden streak, winning everything, running three sub-four-minute miles in the year and only losing races at the end when I was tired. I ran 48 races that year. I loved to race. I won 37 of them and was placed in the first three in 47 of them. I had great ambitions to win the Olympics – I always thought Pirie and I could have done better if we had gone with Kuts when Chataway fell away in Melbourne – and to win European and Empire titles and to hold more records, including the 5k."

But then Stage Four of his career started. He explained: "Geoff Dyson, the leading coach, and other people told me to have a rest, take two or three months off, to recover from the hectic season I had. They said it would recharge my batteries. And for the first time ever I listened to other people and did what they said. It was a mistake, a major mistake, and a very costly one because when I started training I got a carbuncle on my neck because my system reneged, and so I missed three months' more training.

"By taking the time off and living the high rich life with parties and dinners, I let myself down. I did not train, and I should have done because I loved running and racing. If you don't do the training through the winter, you don't have the basis for the summer. By the time I made it back again about a year and a half had gone and I got down to quite good times. I missed out on the Rome Olympics in 1960 because of a calf muscle injury and nearly made it to Tokyo in 1964 but was just squeezed out in a trial race.

"But I never cut my times by two or three seconds, as I should have done, and the parade had gone by. Herb Elliott was on the scene by then running the times I should have been doing. I had missed a fantastic opportunity and it's the only regret I have. I should have been better and up there. But hindsight makes everyone a genius. C'est la vie."

He quickly realised how badly things had gone. He put on weight and when he ran in an autumn cross-country race in Belgium, where he had won a similar event the year before, he finished so far last (by two minutes) that they had to wait for him before they could start the junior race. In the 1958 Southern and National cross-country championships, where he had been 3rd in the Southern and 6th in the National in the winning South London Harriers team in 1957, he was 197th and 251st. He says now, "I had some success indoors and got into the Empire Games team and although I did some good times I was inconsistent. And that's how it went on."

In 1958 he had bests of 4:00.0 flat for the mile (behind Elliott at the White City), 8:47.6 for two miles and 13:46.6 for three miles, but he dropped out of the AAA three miles and finished 10th in the Empire Games at Cardiff in an unofficial 13:45 behind New Zealand's Murray Halberg before being in the British world-record-breaking 4 x 1 mile team, running his leg in 4:08.6. He still raced 44 times, winning 14 and being in the first three 32 times.

The magic was gone ... but it was not all gloom

It was a pattern he followed all his life through his love of running, and even when he was a champion and famous he would race as often as he could, accepting invitations in unlikely places for his status because he thought it was important to attract people to the sport. When he was at the top he was the Number One out of the great bowl of talent the UK had then and that the crowds loved most, the "Four Minute Smiler". But the magic – that extra ingredient that in cricket they call "fast focus" – had gone forever.

It was not all gloom. In 1959 he was 7th in the AAA three miles, ran for Britain against Poland and Finland, and had bests of 3:42.9 for 1500 metres, 4:03.1 for the mile, 8:00.0 for 3000 metres and 13:32.8 for three miles. He was slower in 1960 (and injured) but was still 4th in the AAA three miles, which was the event in which he had set a British record of 13:20.8 in 1957 after missing out on the mile title by dawdling in his heat.

In 1961 he was 4th in the AAA three miles and had a season's best of 13:33.6, plus 11th place in the National cross-country. He was also trying the indoor circuit, winning British titles and setting softish world records for the little-run two miles and three miles of 8:47.8 and 13:44.8. Once he ran 3:38 in a 1500 metres at Manchester, losing to Hewson but both running a lap short! He went to Perth, in Western Australia, for the Commonwealth Games in 1962, finishing 8th in the three miles in 13:44, and was 3rd in the AAA in 13:23.4 and had season's bests of 13:21.6, 8:41.4 for two miles and 4:03.6 for the mile – not bad for a "has been".

He had a big farewell at the White City at the end of 1964, but like Sinatra he was back and won the AAA indoor two miles and had bests of 8:42.6 and 13:51.6 the next year. In 1966 he was in the British club 4 x 1 mile relay with the three young milers he had been coaching. After athletics he took up squash, helping world champion Jonah Barrington to invent interval training for the game before Barrington went off with his wife. Then he moved into selling and became divisional manager for an international sports-goods company. After retirement he took up golf and now lives happily with his partner, his second wife having died tragically eight years ago. He has four daughters.

He remembers the old days with a great deal of affection and little regret even though he did not earn any money. He says, "I enjoyed it. I would have made a lot of money if I had been running now, but I had a fantastic time. There were trips everywhere and great friends and camaraderie and the parties and girls. When you went to warm up under the stands at the White City there were always 20 or 30 girls there, and they always invited you to a party, and of course being a red-blooded Yorkshire lad when I was single you didn't want to upset them by turning them down.

"Once in Moscow Brian Hewson and I were given a hotel suite each because we were world

The England team of Brian Hewson, Derek Ibbotson, Peter Clark and Mike Blagrove after setting a world record for the 4 x 1 mile relay against Finland at the White City on 27 September 1959.

record-holders. So we had a party and got all the men and girl athletes. They don't have that now. They go to the places, but they fly in and race and fly out again, and they don't have the head-on matches we used to when there was a chance of getting together and getting to know each other. What trips we had! Once in Finland we invited 20 nurses with matron's permission from a local hospital to our party and one of our blokes went off with the girl-friend of one of the Finnish athletes and did not come back for a few days. When I raced against the Finns the athlete knocked me off the track he was so angry!"

"I wouldn't have missed a day of it"

George Derek Ibbotson: born in Huddersfield, Yorkshire, 17 June 1932. 5ft 9½in (1.76m), 10st 6lb (66kg). Personal bests: 880 yards 1:52.2, 1500 metres 3:41.9, one mile 3:57.2, 2000 metres 5:12.8, 3000 metres 8:00.0, three miles 13:20.8, 5000 metres 13:54.4, six miles 28:52.0.

Note: this article was first published in "Track Stats", Volume 44, No.2, May 2006. Derek Ibbotson died on 23 February 2017, aged 84.

George Knight, world's fastest 10,000 metres runner in 1957
Building for the future four years away ... but the future came three years early

One of the most intriguing mysteries of track and field is how someone has a "year of years" out of the blue and then never matches it again. Sometimes it is because of drugs, and sometimes through a long build-up which is then ruined by injury in succeeding years.

Some have a great year like Jim Peters, the fastest marathon runner in the world from 1952 to 1954 who could never reproduce the times he achieved on the road from Windsor to Chiswick when he ran in Finland and Canada. Others are like Gordon Pirie, who reached a peak in 1953, when he was superb (and that is not an adjective I use often) but never did it again though injury or wrong timing – in 1956, in particular, when he was unbeatable in the summer, but it had all gone by the time of the Olympic Games in Melbourne in December; and in 1960, when his not quite so good form also vanished three weeks before the Games.

Everyone can come up with examples, and some might argue about Steve Cram, for instance, but none that I know is more fascinating than that of George Knight, of the Essex Beagles club. He was more than a good club runner in a team of good runners in the 1950s, such as Peters, Ted Baverstock, Eddie Sears, Dickie Douglas, Terry Learmouth, Bernie Hames and others, when Britain had a stockade of good distance runners.

Knight was born in Ilford, in Essex, on 12 March 1933 and was 19 when he lined up in the Inter-Counties championships three miles at the White City in Olympic year 1952, representing his county in a race that was to change British distance-running. He was 5ft 11½in tall (1.82m), weighed around 10st (63kg), and was known as a promising cross-country runner (8th in the Southern junior) and useful over three miles, with a best of 14:39.2 to win the county title. Just 13 minutes and 44.8 seconds after the gun in that Inter-Counties three miles, the tall and lanky Pirie had smashed Sydney Wooderson's 13:53.2 British best, with Frank Sando a few strides back in 13:48.0, and then in 4th place was Knight, with 14:04.4, which was later rounded down, and never satisfactorily explained why, to 14:14.8, still a considerable improvement.

That was Knight's best for the year and he was only 7th in the AAA Championships, although he had not trained like he did before his big breakthrough, and from then on he was watched as a man "who might do it". He nearly did but never quite enough – until 1957.

He did not race as often as some of his rivals. He was always happy to turn out for the club, and his long bouncing stride produced good but not sensational results, as others like Chris Chataway and Freddie Green, as well as Pirie, Sando, Fred and Ken Norris and Derek Ibbotson took the international places. In 1953 his best three miles was 14:19.0, and he also ran 9:05.6 for two miles. He was 6th in the Inter-Counties three miles that year, but did not make the rankings in 1954.

The next year was much better. He was 4th in the Inter-Counties in 14:14.2 and ran well over the country and on the road, ending the season with a win in the prestigious Rochester five miles road race. In the Olympic year of 1956 he ran even faster, with 13:54.4 in the Inter-Counties and 28:55.8 for 6th in the AAA six miles. He was 5th in the Southern cross-country and a very tired 10th in the National, probably because the nine miles was too long for him. On the road he ran fastest stages in the London-to-Brighton and Chelmsford relays and showed the kind of form that Freddie Green and Alec Olney did, when Olney was certainly seconds faster than he could ever manage on the track, as was Green until he became world record-holder at three miles.

Knight was the same, even without training.

The British all-time list at the end of 1956 showed Knight as 8th at six miles, but he was nowhere near good enough to make the Olympic team, and he was running over the country in Essex while Pirie and Ibbotson were winning medals in Australia behind Vladimir Kuts, of the USSR, at 5000 metres, and Pirie was giving the ex-sailor a fright for most of the way in the 10,000 metres before Vladimir pushed one time too many and the Briton had to let go with four laps left. The winning time was 28:45.6, and the best British time was 29:21.6 by Ken Norris in 5th place. Less than a year later Knight was to run the world's fastest 10,000 metres for the year.

What happened? George Knight told me about it recently, and he said that although the athletics world might have been surprised he was not. He had decided to deliberately train to be one of the stars at the 1960 Olympic Games, running daily throughout the summer and winter of 1956-57. Speaking in his home in Liverpool, he said: "During 1956 I decided to start training seriously for the 1960 Games. I had thought about the six miles and found that I was alright up to about four miles or so but fading after that, doing around 29 and a half minutes. Hugh Foord was running consistently good sixes at the time, and running against him I was losing it at four miles. I especially remember one at Enfield when I was with him at four miles and felt very good until that point.

"I was doing interval training with a clubmate, Dickie Douglas, who was faster and stronger than me, and I was always hanging on. I carried on during the winter training seriously and quite hard, and in 1957 I was doing 4 x 1½ miles in around 6:40, with a 500 or 600 yards jog in between at Mayesbrook Park in Dagenham, where I was living. My training went very well, too well. I thought it would take three years to get there, but unfortunately I came on in 1957 and then lost it completely really. It came on very quickly, and it was all too easy. There were personal things that took my time, and I lost it as easily as it came along. I never quite got the same feeling about training again".

Hard training throughout the winter – something was expected to happen

He had always loved running, and when he was 17, and his family had moved back from Newcastle, where they had gone while his father was at war (his mother was a Geordie), he joined Essex Beagles and was quickly spotted as someone with talent. He had tried for the big time before in 1952, when he did interval training daily until he got a stress fracture in February and did very little training until the Inter-Counties and Pirie's race. From the reservoir of fitness he had built during the winter he still had more than enough to run a lifetime's best and keep on for the rest of the season without training "until I ran out of steam".

In 1957 he expected some improvement but not what he got. A recently retired architect, Knight said: "I had done the work expecting something to happen, and I was not that surprised. I was surprised with the form early in the season, when I did not get what I had expected from the work that I had done. I don't think I consciously altered my stride – high and bounding – but I worked on creating a tempo in my mind when I was running. I tried to keep the tempo all the time, warming up, training and racing.

"In the match against France and Alain Mimoun, the contrast between his incredibly short stride and my time in the air was extreme, and I remember once in the last 200 of one race Peter Driver, the British Empire six miles gold-medallist of 1954, had picked up about four metres on me while I was in the air and before I could get a foot on the ground! I discussed this with people in the Beagles over a number of weeks – Bob Mortimer and Colin Young were two of them – and it was at this time that I started to adopt this tempo, with the aim of helping me to stay in touch with the ground. This probably resulted in a shortened stride, although by the time of the match against Poland that year, Dave Chapman, the steeplechaser, thought my stride was as long as ever but no longer in the air. All this was impression and conjecture, with no evidence to confirm what was happening or why".

At the start of 1957 Knight was 2nd in the Essex cross-country championships behind Alan Perkins, and then 38th in the Inter-Counties won by Ken Norris and 61st in the Southern, and did not run the National. He set new records for both the Ilford and Chingford road relays, but when he ran three miles for Essex on the track against the AAA in April in almost summer conditions he trailed off 4th in 14:20.8, almost 20 seconds behind clubmate Ted Baverstock.

Knight says: "I had worked through the previous summer and winter without really knowing how I would run on that hard training. I really anticipated doing something under 14 minutes and starting the season from there. Instead, I went out and did 14:20. I did know it was there waiting to go, no question, but it was a matter of being patient and relaxing, and allowing it to come through. I had no doubt it was there. Whenever I had put the work in, it always clicked in".

Personal bests for three miles and 5000 metres, but they go unnoticed

Less than a fortnight later he had improved to 13:55.2 behind Laurie Reed, who was one of the Pirie school at South London Harriers and ran 13:52.4 for a smooth win, with the tables turned on Baverstock, who did 14 minutes exactly. Then Knight ran a lifetime best of 13:51.4 to win the Essex title in record time and went even faster to win the Inter-Counties from the greatly improving Stan Eldon in 13:46.2. He had his first foreign trip and won a 5000 metres in Amsterdam at the Netherlands Olympic Day in 14:38.8 in extremely hot weather, where he was delighted to run the last 200 metres in 26sec. All these were respectable domestic times, but there was no comment in the press. Why should there be? Several others could do as well, and indeed had gone faster.

By the time that he lined up for the most open AAA six miles for years he was 2nd in the ranking lists at three miles behind Ibbotson but had not raced over the longer distance. He led at two miles in 9:22.4 from Ken Norris, Foord, Perkins and Eldon. Foord, a cross-country international, was ahead at three miles in 14:10, and then Eldon led at four miles in 19:06.4 and Perkins at five miles in 25:22, with the pack never splitting. Perkins led at the bell, only for Knight's giant strides to take him past to win by 20 yards in a personal best 28:50.4, followed by Eldon, Perkins, an unfit Norris, Foord and Gerry North 6th.

A week later Knight continued his excellent form at the London-v-New York meeting, highlighted by Ibbotson's world-record mile of 3:57.2, by beating Pirie, who was running very well at that time, in a fast two miles, 8:50.0 to 8:50.8, after Pirie had waited to kill him in the straight but could not get by. Knight reverted to his normal form a fortnight later when he met Mimoun at six miles in the match against France at the White City. Knight tried desperately to get away but was no match for the wily French master and Olympic marathon champion (plus a pouch full of silver medals), who ran away at 18 laps and eased ahead to win by 18 seconds in 29:22.2. Those who saw the old maestro do his lap of honour in his pinstripe suit in Paris during the World Championships four years ago will know what Mimoun was like – elegant.

Something happened between then and the match against the Russians and Kuts, the king of all he surveyed at 5000 and 10,000 metres. However you try to describe it, it can be put down to one thing: Knight's right training suddenly working like a new medical wonder cure. The British pair, Knight and Perkins (who was suffering from a cold), made no attempt to stay with the Russians as Zhukov led after a mile in 4:32 and Kuts went through two miles in 9:10, and then just before three miles (13:52.1), Knight left Perkins, seemed to somehow alter his bouncy stride, and within five laps was half-a-lap ahead of his team-mate. He put in a fast burst to catch

Zhukov, and for several laps they passed and re-passed each other in furious short bursts which took them nearer to the world record-holder. At 8000 metres Knight finally got away and proceeded to close the enormous gap that Kuts had opened; so much so that he finished only 13 seconds behind as the Russian ran 29:13.2 for a new British all-comers' record and the fastest time in the world for the year – so far.

The experts went away wondering (a) what had got into Knight, and (b) what would have happened if he had not allowed that enormous gap to open in the early stages. A fortnight later, against Poland in Warsaw, in front of a 75,000 crowd, Knight showed what would have happened by racing away from Stanislaw Ozog and Jerzy Chromik by over a minute as he lapped in 68/69 all the way to win in the world's fastest time of the year, 29:06.4, which was better than Pyotr Bolotnikov's 29:09.9 when he unexpectedly beat Kuts by 0.2 in Moscow the week before. It was over 10 seconds faster than Pirie's British best and a complete shock in the athletics world.

Knight says: "It was a bit of a dream. It was just one of those races that happen to you naturally and you feel good. When I was training inconsistently, I tended to have a very good run out of the blue. Poland was just one of those runs, but on the back of what I had done. It felt like a dream. It was very easy, and I felt I could have run a lot faster, even though I was completely on my own. When you train hard, you build up a lot of residual tiredness, and it is not until you start to race and ease up on the training that the power starts to come through".

More successes to come against international opposition on the track

To prove it was no fluke, he did it again a week later – a slightly slower but extremely confident and easy 29:16.2, beating Pirie, who had won the 5000 the day before in 14:20.2, by over 30 seconds. Knight simply ran away from the start and no one ever looked like staying with him. He was not finished for the season, because a few days later at the White City he won the 5000 metres in a lifetime best 13:57.6 after a tremendous last-lap battle with Chromik and a final sprint that not only won the race but the match for England against Poland.

And still there was more to come. A week afterwards he outsprinted Frank Sando and Hugh Foord at the Brighton floodlit meeting in a 13:48.6 three miles, and then at the Glasgow floodlit meeting he did the same to the Pole, Zdzislaw Krzyszkowiak, in masterly fashion in 13:38.7 after a furious race with Ozog, Al Lawrence of Australia, and Ian Binnie, who set a Scottish record in 4th place in 13:51.2. Krzyszkowiak went on to win the 5000/10,000 double and Chromik the steeplechase at the European Championships the next year, while the former was also to become Olympic steeplechase champion in 1960.

Knight finished his 1957 season by losing narrowly at 5000 metres to the German, Heinz Laufer, in Cologne, 14:10.2 to 14:10.4. Knight remembers: "I led all the way feeling quite good, with Laufer sitting on my shoulder. The finish was very fast, with us locked within a quarter of a stride for the last 150 metres. Laufer, although at the end of his career, was a fast finisher and he acknowledged surprise at how difficult it was to get past me". In the autumn Knight ran the fastest stage three for his club in the London-to-Brighton relay (40 seconds faster than anyone else over 5½ miles) and was also fastest in the Chelmsford relay.

His heading of the world list for the year did not merit much publicity. People just did not seem to appreciate what he had done. This was the Kuts era, as he had beaten Pirie's world 5000 metres record with 13:35.0 in October, and unknown British runners were not supposed to come out of the woodwork. No one really took in just how much Knight had improved (well over a minute); not even the "Master", Roberto Quercetani, who did not comment on it at all in his book, "A World History of Long Distance Running". Perhaps it was because George Knight came and went so quickly – as quickly as he ran. He never did anything remotely approaching his 1957 level again.

Whilst some of the Europeans he had beaten went on to Olympic and world-record heights – the Poles, in particular – Knight never again ran like he did on the tracks of London, Warsaw and Hanover. The man who ranked 7th in the world at 5000 metres and top of the class at 10,000 metres in 1957 went back to being a good club and district runner. Why?

Knight explains: "I think I thought I would just go on and on and get better and better. But I moved to Kent and there was nowhere to train – no decent surface or street-lighting. So I could not do a proper run without the danger of being injured. It was not training for club level, little knows championship running. I did not back up my running for the beginning of 1958, and I won the 1958 Inter-Counties cross-country after very little work throughout the winter. I did not feel fed up about stopping my training. Running was the only thing in my life, but at the time I found it was just an activity in its place.

"I had moved from being a plumber into an architect's office, which then led to training and becoming an architect, and then it was partly because I found it difficult to cope with the pressure and tension I was getting. Suddenly, from just enjoying running I was the centre of attention, and I could not handle it very well. People's attitude had changed. Lots of people wanted to know you and had a less than charitable sort of response. It was just a different world. So I eased back on the running when I felt like it, only going out two or three times a week.

"I was bitterly disappointed in 1958 that it was not the year I had hoped for. I would not have liked a coach to tell me what to do. Things were not like they are now with psychological information. We were on our own. We flew by the seat of our pants".

Continuing running in 1958 but a shadow of what he was before

Knight had best times of 9:01.0, 13:44.7 and 29:21.4 in 1958 but was a shadow of the man of the season before. In 1959 it was the same, placing well over the country and running 13:42.6 for three miles at Leyton and 13:44.0 in the Essex championships. He ran a faster three miles in 1960 of 13:39.4, but by then everyone else was even faster, and his best time the next year of 13:53.4, when he was 3rd at Leyton, is the last occasion that he made the British rankings.

He ran for his club regularly, but that magic mix that made him outstanding had vanished as it had come – not that he did not try. His love of running made him twice hit the hard-training road to reach the top, and he showed his ability again on a stage in the London-to-Brighton relay when he raced away – "I was flying" – and then when a new record and a big leap up the field for the Beagles seemed on he tore a ligament in the arch of his foot which took months to heal. That was the end of that attempt.

The other time was much more serious. He was leading an eight-mile road race in 1961 at Thurrock, in Essex, by half-a-mile when he collapsed. "At the time I was probably as fit as I had been at any time since 1957", he recalls. "I woke up in hospital and could not remember a thing. It was pretty frightening and left me with a depression that went on for nine months, and it was three years before I began to feel completely recovered". He still went back to running, and he has no regrets because he had that great year, and he adds, "I had more than that. I had lots of runs that I got so much pleasure from, staggering runs, and it was always exciting".

He now lives with his wife, Pat, in Liverpool, and for the last four years he has been running once a week after a gap of 20 years. He also races once a year in the same Liverpool five kilometres road event and has a best time so far of 28:26. It never goes away.

George Knight running in a road relay on 11 October 1952. Such events – including, most notably, the London-to-Brighton relay, pictured here – were a major feature of the British domestic athletics calendar in the 1950s. As can be seen, the traffic behind Knight, led by the motor-coach carrying his Essex Beagles club supporters, was sparse in those days. Eventually, as the roads became more densely filled, relays were forced off.

Note: this article was first published in "Track Stats", Volume 45, No.3, August 2007.

Suzanne Allday, British Empire/Commonwealth Games Discus gold-medallist 1958

Competing against the mighty Russians, wondering whether her turn will ever come

Winning a major title is the pinnacle of any athlete's career. You are a country's number one for over a decade and yet you are dwarfed by the mighty Russians and eastern Europeans. You suspect they might be aided by drugs but can never prove it, and you suspect, too, that they are not totally feminine. So, however hard you try, you wonder whether even with more strength and better technique your turn will ever come.

So it was for Suzanne Allday, 5ft 9½in (1.77m) tall and weighing just over 13 stones (82kg), when she stepped into the discus circle for her final throw, and the final throw of the whole competition of the women's discus in the Commonwealth Games at Cardiff Arms Park on 26 July 1958. The day had already started well when her husband, Peter, a one-time UK record-holder, had finished 3rd in the hammer, a great performance by a man who weighed only 11 stones (70kg). So Suzanne, who had achieved her furthest-ever throw with 156ft 6in (47.70m) a few weeks earlier, was determined to give of her very best.

The Official Report of the Games said: "There was a quiet tenseness as Suzanne prepared for her last throw. In complete silence she stepped into the circle just as the wind blew up with increased force. She waited, an age it seemed, for the wind to abate. She changed her stance once and started again. Then came a lull; Suzanne turned with a smooth and strong acceleration, the discus sped from her hand, a winner all the way – a most dramatic win with the last throw of the competition". Her discus landed 150ft 7½in (45.90m) away, 60 centimetres further than Jennifer Thompson, of New Zealand, with the shot-put winner, Valerie Sloper, also from the All Blacks, 3rd. Sloper had beaten Suzanne by 1.10 metres seven days earlier for the shot title.

The Report did not tell all the story of that day. Suzanne filled me in with the details at her home in Lancing, near Brighton, in Sussex, recently. She is still tall and erect at 75 and looks younger, and she is three stone less than she was at the peak of her career which ended in 1964 when she had twins, a boy and girl. She recalls the details of the Games clearly:

"The New Zealand girl was leading, and I had one last throw. It was a silly little thing, but I changed out of my training-shoes and put on my sand-shoes, the ones I wore on the beach. I changed them because I thought I could go faster in the circle. They did not have spikes. I always had a problem fearing that my feet might slip. My father, who was my coach from the very start when I was just a teenager because I injured my ankle long jumping and changed to the discus and shot, had made me shoes with one central spike. I had a pair with a spike on the left shoe only so I did not slip when turning, but I put that to one side and used the others. I knew I had won as the discus left my hand. It was the greatest moment of my athletics life and made all the going without worthwhile".

And there was plenty of that in the career story of the girl from the Brighton area who was always modest and diffident but was also very successful, coming 5th in the 1958 European Championships shot-put in Stockholm and competing in three Olympics, although never matching her best home performances in them. She says: "I think it was because the competitions went on for so long. I have often wondered why it happened but still cannot put my finger on it, although I think it was because the length of time they took which can make a difference".

For the record in 1952, as Suzanne Farmer, she was 15th with 37.96, and it was at these Games that she met husband Peter, who was 21st in the hammer, and they married on Boxing Day 1953. In 1956 she did 41.45 but did not qualify, having done 154ft 4½in (47.05) at home. In 1960 she did even worse with 41.12, having done 148-11 (45.38) before the Games.

She did better in the Empire and then Commonwealth Games. In 1954 she was 2nd in the discus with 131-3½ (40.02) and 6th in the shot and javelin (the latter because she was told they needed points for the competing nations' table) and she managed 92-10 (28.20) for an event she almost never competed in. Four years later, as we have seen, she won the discus and was 2nd in the shot. In the European Championships in those same years she was 10th and 15th in the discus and way below her home best. But in 1958 her 5th place in the shot is still the best ever result by a British woman in these championships. Ahead of her was the lady who had so often beaten her, Tamara Press, of the USSR, but by less than a metre, 15.54 to 14.66, because Press was beaten, too, this time by the mighty Marianne Werner, of Germany.

Suzanne was delighted with her result. It was a just return for many years of sacrifice that she and her then husband had undergone to get as far as they had. For some time they had worked nights so they could train during the day, and they had worked all hours in the winter so they could take the summer off and train at least twice a day. She had many kinds of different jobs, including sewing in a hessian-sack plant – the worst she recalls – and cooking for 100 night workers in a factory. "And it was all worthwhile", she says. "We had fun and enjoyed every minute of the sport".

Starting with the long jump, but she was just too good to last

But back to the beginning. She was one of four children, the second of three girls from a sporting family born on 26 November 1934 in Shoreham, near Brighton. Her father was a cyclist and boxer and her mother a swimmer. She says, "I started at 10 or 11, and I wish they did now for my grand-daughter, but they don't. I was always encouraged at school and at home. I did PE and then athletics, high and long jump and the relay and ran in the house matches". She was so good at the long jump that she became a Southern Counties champion in her age group. Then came disaster.

"I became so proficient at hitting the board in the long jump that I damaged my right ankle and had it bandaged. I suppose I was about 14 or 15. I would have continued to aggravate it if I had continued jumping. So I took up discus, and because of that I took up shot putting as well, as they went together, and loved both of them". She even added the javelin, winning the inaugural Sussex championships. "I liked throwing the discus. When you throw it you get more of a sensation of how well you have done the moment you release it. The amount of power you get in gives you that feeling of 'Yes!' much more than the long jump. My father was my coach. He did a study of throwing the discus so he could coach me. Even when my husband was overseeing it, my dad, who was a fantastic man, a marine engineer, was still there".

She went on: "Let me tell you about his understanding of how a coach should go about things. Once I said I did not want to go training and he said, 'You must'. I said, 'No, I don't want to'." So her father made her get into the car, took her to the recreation ground where they trained at night near Brighton, under the lighting from a nearby factory, and made her get the discus out, do some exercises and have one throw, and then he announced that training was over.

She explained, "He made me realise you should always go training even if you did not want to. I was happy because I could go home and he was happy because he had shown me how to do it. Another time down at the rec a policeman came up and asked me what we were doing. We told him. He asked, 'What are you training for? Think you are going to the Olympics?'. Then he laughed and went on. I don't know what he thought four or five months later when he saw I was going to the Olympics in Helsinki."

This was the start of her career and domination in British women's discus-throwing for over a decade, sometimes throwing 10 feet more than her nearest rival in the year's ranking-list.

After winning three All-England Schools titles (her brother, John, won a discus title, too) in a row, she won seven Women's AAA titles and 11 Southern Counties titles between 1951 and 1964 and represented GB in 35 internationals. She set her first UK record aged 17, with 132-5½ (40.37), and in 10 instalments took it to her lifetime best in 1958 at 156-6 (47.70). At the same time she set eight UK shot-put records, taking her best up to 49-9¾ (15.18) over eight years. She also won seven WAAA titles outdoors and two indoors. When she retired the world records were 18.55 and 59.29 by Tamara Press, of the USSR.

From the start her father made her concentrate on technique: "He was very decisive about it, saying that if you started with a slow turn and got the technique right you could then speed up". Her first bid for championship honours was at the WAAA in 1950, aged 15. She remembers, "I went to the circle with my own discus and an official said, 'Sorry, you cannot use that'. I put mine down and used one of theirs and could not perform at all. I just could not get a decent throw in. The reason was it was the wrong weight. We discovered later that mine was the intermediate men's discus which I bought locally and it was heavier than the women's one. When I tried throwing the lighter discus I needed a different technique. When I competed in the Sussex championships a few weeks later, I had learnt how to throw it and won with a longer throw than the winner of the WAAA!"

"Are you ready, Miss Farmer?" She was, and she won again

"I did not know the regulations. My dad had a look and discovered I could throw my own discus, and so he made me learn all the rules. When I was 17 and competing in the All-England Schools, they told me again I could not use my own implement. I called for the field events referee, gave the 10-shilling note you had to pay in those days to query such a rule, and she told me I was right and gave me my money back. But that caused another problem. In the qualifying round everyone was called by a number. After I had got my ruling, they said, 'Are you ready, Miss Farmer?' and I told them I should be called by my number just like the others. I have always hated being singled out like that"

As she improved so her trips abroad started: "It was all fine. We girls always got on well. There was never any bad feeling or animosity. We would travel to the venue, compete, have the social evening, and then come back. It was lovely and I enjoyed every minute of it".

After her marriage to Peter they lived only for athletics, and she was successful, first selection for both events from 1952 until 1963. She said: "At one stage, in order to be able to train more and harder, we took on night work so we could train during the day. It did not work out very well. We worked through the winter and saved every penny so we could stop work and train and compete through the summer.

"We had a caravan at Portslade, near Brighton, and I would cycle in to do a 12-hour night-shift as cook at a factory. I used to bargain with the greengrocer to try and get something that cost a shilling for two pence less, we were so hard up. We were that tight on money. I had to literally watch every penny. I did not mind. To me the challenge was the thing. We gave up an awful lot for athletics, but it was worth it. I had a lot of enjoyment, a lot of fun, and a lot of hard work. But as my father said, 'You only get what you work for'. We worked to do well in the major championships, even taking a year out to train to reach a higher level".

On one occasion she was beaten by Mary Peters, then an up-and-coming star who went on to

Left: Even husbands and wives were kept apart at the 1956 Olympics. Suzanne and Peter Allday meet up with a wire-mesh fence between them.

Right: No one else in sight as Suzanne wins the Women's AAA title earlier that year.

win the Olympic pentathlon in Munich in 1972, and Suzanne's father said, "I'm pleased. Now perhaps you'll train a little bit harder". She said: "It was his idea to say that to spur me on. And it did."

During her career Suzanne trained regularly with her husband, who was one of the first members of the Hammer Circle, and so it was inevitable that his wife would try the event, too: "I asked if I could join the Circle, and Dennis Cullum said I could if I threw over 140 feet and I thought, 'Yes, I'm going to do it'. I was using the men's 16lb hammer, not the 4kg women's one they use now. I was good at it and threw well over 140. My best measured throw then, back in 1953 or 1954, was 148 feet (45 metres). I told Dennis this, and he said, 'Sorry, you cannot join, it is for men only'. Having worked so hard to get in I never managed to get accepted and that upset me. I reckon I could have thrown well over 50 metres with a women's hammer. I enjoyed it, and that was the whole point of it."

That would have made her world class when the hammer became a national event in the 1990s. But what would the Russians have done? They were always the bane of her life, and whenever she came up against them, like Tamara Press or Nina Ponomaryova (of the hats), she knew she was going to lose: "It never worried me. I went into the competition knowing they were going to beat me unless something drastic happened. I went in wanting to improve my best performance, and if I did that I was successful. It was all about that."

Sometimes the winning margin was as much as 40 feet, a long way: "We did not know definitely if others were on drugs. They were bigger with a better technique. One of them was like a bear and used to give me bear-hugs. It never occurred to me that she was a man. She was just a very very big lady, but she did not come out of Russia once they had the sex checks. We were very friendly, but they were just so much better. I did not do weight-training as such, but did the hammer-throwing which was a form of it". The strength she gained was formidable; so much so that she beat the arm-wrestling champion of Loughborough, Robbie Brightwell, three times in a row!

Stand-off at the White City: Tamara said, "If Suzanne doesn't throw, I won't either"

When the authorities brought in sex checks, Suzanne had to go to her doctor, who she knew well and who laughed as he wrote out her certificate. She said, "Some of the Russians did not come out again. Tamara Press did. At the London-v-Moscow match I was in the parade, and immediately after it the discus started. I said I wanted to warm up and they said there was not time. I said that if I could not warm up I would not compete. Tamara saw that I was upset and asked what was wrong and I told her. She went over to the officials and said that if I did not throw she would not throw. They gave me half-an-hour to warm up!"

She went on several tours to Eastern Europe during the Cold War and remembers one visit to Hungary which upset her: "We were eating in the dining-room and there were people outside watching us eat through the window. It was too upsetting for me, knowing what we had and they had nothing. I did not go in again". Then there was the time in Poland when she and some of the other girls put together a bag of make-up because the women who looked after them had none: "You would have thought we had given them the Royal Mint, they were so grateful. It is not until you come across things like that that you realise how lucky you are. I gave one girl a sweater and she wanted to give me something in return – but she had not got anything.

"You learn so much when you travel. In Moscow four of us British girls were in a lift in the hotel and two Russian men were in it, too, and obviously talking about us. So when we got out I said, 'Thank you' in Russian, one of the only two phrases I knew. They thought we had understood all they had said and were very embarrassed. And there was the time in Helsinki at the Olympics when I had been out and came back what I thought was a bit late. But there was no one in my room nor the one next door, and after creeping down the corridor like a naughty schoolgirl – I was only 17 — I found they had all gone out. It was at those games that Arthur Wint came over to me and told me to relax and just do my best. McDonald Bailey said the same, both encouraging me like that. It was nice".

1958 was Suzanne's peak year. The extra training that she and Peter did had paid off, and he finished 9th in the 1956 Olympics, 5th in the Empire Games in 1954 and 3rd in 1958, but after that they did not have the time to train so hard. He became a teacher and she the matron at a boys' boarding-school in Norfolk, she cycling the 100 miles-plus back to her parents' home in the Brighton area on a Friday night, and then the 50-plus miles into London to compete for Spartan Ladies on Saturday, and back to Norfolk that night. She said: "There were no expenses in those days. Eventually we got a motor-bike, and once when we set off for Sussex it started snowing after 10 miles. So riding pillion I put both feet on then ground to act as a three point for the bike and kept them on the ground until we got there."

From the school, the Alldays moved in the early 1960s to Timsbury Manor in a remote part of Hampshire. The plan was for it to become a centre of excellence for athletics, but it never really worked. Peter and Suzanne ran it, and their training fell away and thus their performances. In Suzanne's last year Rosemary Payne and Mary Peters arrived on the scene to take her titles away. And then she became pregnant with the twins, who both weighed over 7lb at birth, and she stopped training so it would not interfere with her pregnancy. For 13 years she did very little in athletics. She wanted to coach, but there were too many exams to pass and too much paper-work over insurance, and there was the family to bring up. But in 1977 her daughter, Karen, was in the Sussex championships as a 13-year-old throwing the discus and suggested to her mother that she should compete.

Without any training Suzanne's technique stood her in such good stead that she won with such good throws in both discus and shot that she ended up in the top 12 in the British ranking-lists for 1977, 25 years after setting a British record of 43.28 at the same meeting. She threw 42.90 with a shot put of 12.22, while daughter Karen was 2nd in both junior events. Suzanne has not competed since, although she occasionally gives advice at the local school. She and Peter were divorced after 25 years of marriage. She and her second husband, Ray, have been together for 30 years.

Suzanne concludes: "I think I was a lucky one because I competed at the time when it was all fun as well as being a sport. Now money has come into it. And drugs. I remember once when I was warming up and one of the top Russians came over and said, 'Suzanne, your left foot is too close. You move it and you will throw further'. I did move the foot and I did throw further. You don't do that now. It's money, and they don't want you to go further". She added: "It is not happening in schools any more. It's all egg-and-spoon and three-legged races. They are not taking up the sport like they should. You learn so much from it. It's not just technique but general behaviour. I would like to get involved more but they make it so difficult."

One final thing: she still smokes just as she did when competing, sometimes having a cigarette between throws at the White City.

Note: this article was first published in "Track Stats", Volume 48, No.1, March 2010.

Peter Hildreth, European Championships bronze-medallist 110 metres hurdles 1950

"Never a superstar, just a good international", but still making the headlines at the age of 80

On 14 September 1958 Peter Hildreth lined up for the start of the 110 metres hurdles for Great Britain against France. It was a very special occasion during his year of years in an international career that stretched over 12 years for this was the same track, Colombes Stadium, where 34 years earlier his father, William, had competed for India in the 1924 "Chariots of Fire" Olympic Games.

His father, who was born and worked in India, had been selected for the 100 metres and 200 metres. He had set an Indian 220 yards record of 22.2 on a 300-yard grass track in Calcutta and the record stood for over 20 years. In his first round heat of the Olympic 100 metres, for which the gold medal was won, as we all know, by Harold Abrahams, Hildreth finished a poor 4th to a Hungarian, Lajos Kurunczy, who did 11.4 (HMA ran 10.6 in the final). In the 200 metres Hildreth started, ran a few strides, and then pulled out, injured from his previous efforts. Even so, says Peter, now aged 82; "It was a great moment to realise I was running on the same track as him". He has the certificate given to all competitors in the 1924 Games hanging framed on his bedroom wall in his home in Famham, Surrey, though his father's Christian name is wrongly given as "Wilf".

In his race at Colombes, Peter ran 14.3 to win by 0.2 from his second string, Vic Matthews, in a match that GB took 124-88. It was the fourth occasion on which Hildreth ran that British record-equalling time in 1958. It was held by his hero, Donald Finlay, who Peter considers the greatest British hurdler. He modelled himself on Finlay's style as he improved year after year, self-coached and extremely determined.

Finlay won bronze in the 1932 Los Angeles Olympics, silver in Berlin in 1936, and the European championship in 1938. He rose from Aircraft Apprentice to Air Commodore in the RAF, was a Battle of Britain hero, shooting down four Germans and winning medals, and then returned to almost his same standards of athletics achievement after World War II. He took the oath for the athletes at the 1948 Olympic Games, tripped while leading in his heat, but came back to beat the world's fastest man, Dick Attlesey, in 1949 and finished 4th to end his career in the 1950 Empire Games hurdles in 14.7 in New Zealand. He also played football for Tottenham Hotspur, long jumped well over 22ft, and would have been a leading decathlete had he had the chance. Some hero to follow!

That international, towards the end of a very long career, which was curtailed due to back trouble when he was 36, was one of 28 in which Peter Hildreth took part between 1950 and 1960 and included a 14.4/52.9 120 yards hurdles/440 yards hurdles double against Czechoslovakia in 1956. He also competed in the Olympics of 1952, 1956 and 1960, reaching the semi-final in Helsinki, and in the British Empire Games once in 1958 when he was 5th in 14.4, and was selected for four European championships, 1950-54-58-62. The first of those European appearances was in Brussels and was his international debut. He had come up the hard way, progressing from a schoolboy champion at Ratcliffe College, near Leicester, through National Service in the RAF, and then on to Downing College, Cambridge, where he got a history degree. He won both the high hurdles and 220 yards low hurdles against Oxford and was secretary of the Cambridge University Athletics Club when Chris Brasher was President in 1951.

The weather was awful for the 1951 Inter-Varsity match in March with fog swirling around.

Hildreth said: "Harold Abrahams was doing the commentary for BBC radio from the box high up in the stand on the opposite side of the track at the White City. They always had the hurdles as the first event because the track was lopsided. They could not hold the event in the home straight. So by having it on the back straight they could set up the hurdles before the meeting started, and when the race was over they could take them away. Harold said that the fog was so bad he could not see the race, but he told me afterwards that he had said my name a couple or three times because I was the favourite and he was very relieved when I won".

Hildreth's first race at the White City had been in 1948, representing Bedfordshire in the 120 yards hurdles (he had won the county championship in 18.1), but he was eliminated. He went away determined that it would not happen again. The reason for representing Bedfordshire was that his parents came back to England so that Peter would be born here (in Bedford, 8 July 1928) and not have to face any problems that a non-British born passport-holder might have.

His family had been in India for years and a relative had been there during the time of the Indian Mutiny. Hildreth first learned to hurdle at school there during World War II, liked it, and set his mind on becoming good at it. He won the AAA title in 1950 for the first time, beating his great rival, Jack Parker, who was slightly older (born 6 September 1927). In 15 international matches between 1951 and 1956 they shared 13 victories (Parker nine, Hildreth four) and 12 2nd places (Parker two, Hildreth 10). They raced week in and week out for years and there was little between them, Parker doing 14.3 in 1955 and Hildreth doing it every year between 1957 and 1960 after his rival had retired. Parker was 2nd in the European Championships in 1954; Hildreth was 3rd in 1950 and 4th in 1958.

Hildreth-v-Parker – a rivalry renewed in at least 80 races

Hildreth, whose club was Polytechnic Harriers, said, "We got along fine and often roomed together. But athletics is not a very sociable sport. We were very evenly matched and I enjoyed racing against him. We ran as hard as we could against each other – and we must have raced against each other well over 80 times, easily – and accepted the result. We travelled all over the world together". Parker was a member of South London Harriers and represented Britain 18 times.

Hildreth, 6ft (1.83m) tall and weighing 10½ stone (66kg), reached the final in the 1950 European Championships in Brussels with a 15.0 heat and was drawn in the outside lane. The favourite was Yevgeniy Bulanchik, of the USSR, who had beaten him in the heat in 14.8, but he finished last and Hildreth a delighted 3rd behind André-Jacques Marie of France, who won in 14.6. Years later, when Hildreth was athletics reporter for the "Sunday Telegraph" (a job he had for 30 years), he met the Italian, Albano Albanese, who had finished 4th a stride behind him. Hildreth remembered, "It was at a coaching conference in Canada and he asked me if I knew how I managed to finish 3rd, and I said 'No, you tell me'. The Russian was in the next lane to him, and Albanese said that he had stuck his right arm out at every flight so Bulanchik could not get past. Bulanchik won the title in 1954 and clearly would have won it in 1950 but could not because he was kept back".

In 1954 Hildreth, who was then 0.3 seconds faster, was eliminated in 14.7 in the semi-final, and Bulanchik won the final in 14.4, with Parker 2nd in 14.6. Four years on and Hildreth made headlines because one British journalist claimed that a photo-finish picture showed him 3rd and the man given the bronze medal was not in the photo at all. Hildreth said, "It wasn't true. The man had the photo of the semi-final in which the bronze medal winner was not running". Hildreth had high hopes for the European Championships again in 1962 but was injured and did not start, which was a sad way to end his career.

He said, "I was never a superstar, just a good international. I tried to imitate Donald Finlay, improving every year, and that's what happened".

He first raced against Parker in 1949, when he beat him and had a best time of 15.0 in his last race of the year, winning the freshman's trials at Cambridge. The next year he ran at least 27 races, improving to 14.8 and finishing 3rd in the ranking-lists to Finlay and Parker. He won the AAA title in 15.2, was 3rd in Brussels, won the Kinnaird, and beat Parker every time out.

In 1951 they clashed in regular inches finishes, but Parker won at the AAA, 14.8 to 14.9. Olympics year saw them meet nine times, with Hildreth winning six and partnering Parker in all three international meets. Hildreth got his best time down to 14.4 to equal the British record when losing the AAA title to Australian Ray Weinberg but was completely outclassed at Helsinki, finishing last in his semi-final in 14.9, having done 14.7 in his heat.

By this time he was working as a hospital administrator. He said, "I'd get up in the morning, catch the train from Richmond, where I lived, to London Bridge, where I worked, and then back home in the evening; then a two-mile cycle ride to the track at Chiswick where I trained three times a week. Like Finlay I steadily improved over the years rather than any big breakthrough". He said that he had three weeks' holiday every year, or 15 working days, and the trips to the international meetings took at least 10 days: "Each year I had practically no holiday at all. I did not complain about it because it was something I wanted to do. But if you were an amateur – and we most definitely were – you had to come home and earn a living". Later as a journalist and also working as a commentator for BBC radio he went all over the world.

Another Olympics in prospect, but first comes a "Cinderella" record

In 1953 he won the AAA again in 14.6 and tied with Parker to the top of the rankings, although he did the time in yards and Parker in metres (110 metres = 120.3 yards), but there was still only inches between them. The next year they swapped titles, with Parker winning the AAA, and while Hildreth stayed at home for the birth of his son the South London Harrier went to Vancouver for the Empire Games to finish 4th and see the Bannister-v-Landy mile. Hildreth had already seen a four-minute-mile, and it was the first, because his 220 yards hurdles race was the previous event before Bannister's historic performance at Iffley Road on 6 May 1954. Hildreth was putting his track-suit on as they went past him on the back straight three times.

1955 was another typical year, with Hildreth and Parker racing each other week in, week out; first the Inter-Counties, then the Kinnaird, then the Southern and the AAAs before the international tours and matches. Parker won the AAAs in 14.6, with Hildreth 3rd a tenth of a second behind, and then in the match against Hungary they both clocked 14.4, with Parker just winning. Parker did the same time again versus the USSR and topped the rankings with a lifetime best of 14.3. Hildreth had the consolation of setting a European record 23.3 for the 220 yards hurdles on a straight track at Imber Court. It stood for a very long time because, he joked, it is a Cinderella event run very rarely.

The next year, with the Olympic Games in Melbourne in December, was their last year in constant enjoyable battle because Parker retired at the end of it. They met at least 10 times, with Hildreth winning six to his rival's four. Hildreth won the AAA in 14.5, with Parker a tenth behind, and then against Hungary they had a ding-dong that ended with Parker just getting in front on the line, both recording 14.4. But Parker was ahead of Hildreth in equalling Finlay's 14.3 British record. He did it against Germany, with the Poly Harrier half-a-second behind him, the largest gap ever between them. The long long season finally ended in Melbourne when the two great British hurdlers came up against the real class of the Americans and others and were eliminated in their heats.

Peter Hildreth at White City. The 120 yards hurdles was usually run on the back straight there. The event couldn't fit into the home straight due to the track's lop-sided dimensions!

In 1957 the Irishman, Eamonn Kinsella, beat Hildreth for the AAA title, both clocking 14.7, but the Englishman finally managed 14.3m in a blanket finish against West Germany, and then came his best year, 1958. He had a slow start, not breaking 14.7 until the Kinnaird (and finishing 3rd in 16.3 at the Sward Trophy, his first race), and then running 14.5 behind Empire Games champion-to-be Keith Gardner, of Jamaica. Hildreth was 5th in those Games with 14.5, did the same time for the AAA v Combined Services, and then against France ran 14.3 – and kept on doing it. He said, "It was undoubtedly my best year. It just clicked and I hurdled beautifully".

He did 14.3 four times, in Paris, Oslo, Hanover and Gothenburg, winning only in France but losing to the very best elsewhere. He also managed that 4th place in the European Championships in 14.4. All the years of hard work paid off, giving him deep satisfaction, and after that he was never so good again and back injuries interfered with his racing programme. In 1959 he did 14.3 on the suspect three-laps-to-a-mile track at Cambridge, won the Inter-Counties, and then got progressively worse, finishing 6th in the AAAs.

He did 14.3 at Welwyn Garden City in 1960, was 4th in the AAA, and went out in the first round of the Rome Olympics. He did not compete in the AAA in 1961 and injury kept him out most of the season, but in 1962 he was the first Englishman in the AAA with 14.7, which made him No.1 choice for the European Championships. In the British Games just before the team left, he won in 14.5 (described as "the ancient warrior" by "Athletics Weekly") and then had a wind-assisted 14.3, but his back gave way before his heat in Belgrade and he did not start. His long service to Britain was over, with best marks of 14.3, 24.0 for 220 hurdles, and 52.9 for the 440 hurdles, which was an event he ran rarely because he did not like training for it.

During his career press coverage of athletics was about facts, not the more colourful version today with plenty of quotes from winners, losers and others. Some time ago Hildreth commented that after Bannister broke the four-minute-mile he was not quoted in any newspaper. Hildreth's only real headlines of his own making came two years ago when he caused a minor furore by running up the down escalator in his local store, where he meets friends for a coffee most mornings. For good measure he travelled by bus to nearby Guildford and did the same thing in a multi-store. He then met a local newspaper reporter whose offices are near his home and told him, and it not only made headlines in that publication but also in the national papers, leading to a feature article or two as well.

Hildreth explained, "I wanted to celebrate my 80th birthday by doing something different. When I was young and quite fit, I often used to run up the escalators on the Piccadilly line underground stations, and that was very hard work. I decided to do it against the escalator in Elphick's store because it was more interesting. And all I got for my trouble was to be banned from the store. When they saw the publicity, however, they were delighted, and I was allowed back in. I've never had such publicity in my life. I even made the cover of the magazine, 'The Oldie', as one of their personalities of the year."

But he has had other publicity, not as big but persistent, over his fight against the use of drugs in athletics. He said, "I did not know about it when I was competing. I heard rumours in the early 1960s. I even heard of an Australian who built himself up on steroids and became a shot-putter instead. The thing is that steroids were not banned until the 1970s, but we know they were definitely in place in the 1950s, first in Russia, then in the USA, and then everywhere. At the elite end of athletics you could not afford to be without them. The use of them helped to be the monster which is here today."

He believes that many top athletes have to take them to beat the old standards and win the golds at Olympic Games. Every day he goes to the public library to read the papers to gather more for his dossiers which he hopes one day to publish, and he has collected together details which are circumstantial but not proveable.

Note: this article was first published in "Track Stats", Volume 48, No.3, September 2010. Peter Hildreth died 25 February 2011, aged 82.

Ian Thompson, Commonwealth Games and European Championships marathon gold-medallist 1974

Road-running's revelation of 40 years ago, still training hard, still ambitious, still seeking the "magic in that stride"

Old marathon runners don't fade away. They simply look to the next challenge. And for Ian Thompson, who celebrated his 65th birthday on 16 October last year, that means racing as a veteran. He is not as fit as he would like to be and wants to get back to 40 miles a week in training to give the current veteran champions more of a race. He does not think he can beat them on his present fitness, but he is ambitious, as befits a man who counted up a few years back that he had competed in 84 marathons.

I (with the assistance of the "Track Stats" Editor and Andy Milroy and others) found 52. Ian adds quite a few on top of those, particularly when he was working for the Thomas Cook's agency and travelling round the world, and also when he was promoted by a coffee company for whom he ran several in the mid-1980s. "I did eight in a year", he says. "No great performances, but I never really ran well after that. There's a lesson in that, if you do too many marathons!"

Of the 52 marathons in my total he won 19 of them. In the added 32 he won quite a few more. 84 marathons? That's over 2,100 miles of racing on the roads. You must be mad to do so! "I am mad", Thompson confesses in his attractive renovated Victorian cottage home in Devizes, in Wiltshire. "My wife, Margaret, is as mad as me". They both still train and race. She is not as fit as she would like to be because of arthritic conditions. They have three daughters – the eldest is a three-hour marathon runner – and two grandchildren. The kind of dedicated life they lead is typified by the fact that when Margaret broke down at 15 miles on a training run and rang Ian to come and fetch her, she had reached 16 miles by the time he got there.

Ian trains daily at lunch-time, working in information technology for the Ministry of Defence on Salisbury Plain. Nearby is Box Hill, from where Arthur Newton started his 100-mile runs to London many many years ago, and Ian says, "I train up it as it is near work. It's a bloody long hill, and when Newton got to the top he had another 99 miles to go. The London-to-Brighton run was the special run of my life. I did it after the disappointment of Moscow and the 1980 Olympics. I ran two marathons in 2:32 back-to-back, even-paced in faster miles than I can run now. I ran in the London-to-Brighton because of the history of the event as I've always been a sucker for the old romantic history thing. It felt right all the way. I felt good doing it and won it convincingly I was trying something new and found I was quite good at that and wished there was a whole lot more of those races, but there were not many around in those days. I regret not going to the Comrades Marathon and running in that. But there was apartheid". South Africa was one of the few countries, apart from those in South America, where he did not race. Otherwise, you name it, he ran there.

There was no money in those days, the 1970s and 1980s, except for expenses. There were some bizarre prizes like a live chicken which he gave to a woman in the Italian crowd and an enormous haunch of ham which he (now a vegetarian) and his wife lived off for two years. During his main competitive period from 1973 to 1986-87 his favourite places were New York, Tokyo, Paris and New Zealand. He competed there regularly and ran fast times. But none of those ever compared to his first international race – and only his second marathon – at the 1974 Commonwealth Games in Christchurch, New Zealand, where he ran 2:09:12. He remembers: "I felt very easy and relaxed and I knew I was going to win from the start. There was more than normal confidence". He still has the red shoes he was given by Ron Hill and in one of which he wore through a hole because of the way his foot landed.

It is not his best race, however. That was at the European Championships later that same year in Rome. This was the fourth in the wonderful first five races, all of which he won with a magic in his stride and an ability that then went away and never came back. Of this second title he says, "There was more pressure in the sense that I was the favourite. There was that expectation. I suppose the whole environment of Rome made it a bit special. I overcame the heat and everything else. It was a special win."

He has always loved running, and it is a love affair that is as strong today as it was when as a little boy he started timing himself running to and from primary school. Ron Clarke inspired Ian when he saw him run sub-13 minutes for three miles at the White City back in the 1960s, and Ian wanted to be a 5000 and 10,000 metres champion, but a best time of 3:51 for 1500 metres was never going to make him one. Instead, he took part in the 1973 AAA marathon to make up the team numbers for his club, Luton United AC, and ran away with the race. Of his training he says, "David Bedford was running 100 miles a week to race 10k. So I did. It clicked with the marathon. The competition to run and train for, plus my own physiology, suited better to the longer distance". He trained twice every day for the 10 years when he was at the top, and now he says, "I train six days a week with the occasional rest day. I'm not a Ron Hill who insists on going out every day."

Maybe going too far in training, always at the limit

So where did the magic that made him "King of the Marathon World" go – and where did it come from? The answer is probably from the training he had done. It was not hereditary. "It was so easy in those first few races", he remembers, "and then it was more normal. I did not have the consistency I would have liked. And looking back, I wonder if I over-trained, going that little bit too far and not having the balance I had in the early days". And that, he thinks, may have been the cause of all the coughs and colds and viruses he got throughout his career – and even now: "The big thing that blighted my career was virus infections through over-training, getting run-down, coughs and colds. The body was always at the limit and I was pushing myself too hard".

In 1976, when he was one of the three best marathon-runners in the world, he contracted a virus in the week before the AAA trial for the Montreal Olympics, and the selectors had decided on the American 1-2-3 system for the team. He says, "I was over-trained, run-down and lethargic. I struggled through and finished 7th. I was the best runner around, but they picked the first three and that was that". The three selected Britons came nowhere at the Games and were never going to do so on the evidence of their personal bests. They ran five minutes and more worse than at the trial. Again over-training, Ian thinks, was the cause of his failure in the 1980 Olympic marathon. He won the trial race and all looked well for him to give Waldemar Cierpinski, the East German holder, a good race. But "it was a disappointment. I was over-trained and got a virus and was not well. I felt rubbish. Nowadays you would be checked out. In those days you were very much on your own".

And he thinks that the whole build-up to those 1980 Moscow Games had an impact – the political rows going on, the boycott by the Americans, and the fact of the public not wholly being behind the British team. None of the British marathon trio finished for various reasons.

Not that it put him off. He was back racing within weeks and has continued ever since. He says,

For drama, few moments can equal the marathon winner entering the stadium. Here Ian Thompson does so at the Commonwealth Games at Christchurch in 1974.

"I love running. If I don't run I feel twitchy and feel cheated. Getting away from the computer at lunchtime is a real stress-buster. I think one of the reasons I have kept injury free is that I don't do any exercises. My wife goes to classes and she is the one who gets injured. I start very slowly and don't get running properly until a mile or so. I think being gentle with your body is the thing when it is not used to exercise".

This attitude will continue to help in the future because of his ambitions in the veteran class. He explains, "I don't race much now. I run in long cross-country races locally – they are like fell races but over chalk not granite – and occasionally road races, but I get frustrated that I cannot do the marathon now. What I would like to do as a veteran is get up to 50 miles a week and get down to 40 minutes for the 10k. I know they are doing 33 minutes, but I think I can get down to 40".

He always enjoyed marathon racing even when running badly, and it was not a personal thing either. He says, 'You are not competing against each other but against the distance. When you are racing conscious thinking is not there. You push the chatter in the brain to one side and you run on automatic and just let it flow. It is not until the fatigue comes through that you start having to think about it. I never felt a marathon was going to be painful or something I did not want to do. I never went in dreading it or that it was going to be very hard. It was always a good experience". And for future marathon runners he gives these tips: "Relax. Don't fight it. Let it come naturally. Don't force yourself into racing and training and be more understanding with your body".

One thing he is sure of is that there will be a two-hour marathon: "Ten years ago I would have said 'no', but now it is possible. When I won in Christchurch 40 years ago I was doing 4:50 a mile. Now they are doing 4:40-ish. Now you have a whole population running. In my day there was just a handful. There is a much bigger proportion of elite athletes. Given the course and the weather are right, I can see it happening. All it needs is an almost world record 10k four times and then the bit at the finish".

Note: this article was first published in "Track Stats", Volume 52, No.3, October 2014 as part I of a two-part series. David Thurlow then examined Ian Thompson's career in more detail in "Track Stats", Volume 52, No.4, December 2014.

At last, after half-a-century!
The long-awaited meeting with the legend

At least 50 years before I ever met him, David Thurlow's name had a place of legend secured firmly in my mind. I'd had the greatest good fortune to be employed for a few weeks during school holidays in the 1950s as a general assistant at the incomparable McWhirter twins' monthly magazine, "Athletics World". Their office was incongruously set among the lawyers' chambers in the Inner Temple in London, where we were assailed on every side by chaps in immaculate pin-stripe suits, striding purposefully off to decide someone's court-room fate, bulging brief-cases under their arms.

I have to admit that I didn't contribute much of any consequence to the McWhirters' publication, though my bye-line is occasionally to be found, thanks to their generosity. As it was, listening to the astonishingly erudite and wide-ranging conversations which Ross and Norris McWhirter conducted between themselves – often after some curious tale had been spotted at the foot of a newspaper column – was an education in itself. Their chortles of glee at discovering some hitherto unsuspected "superlative", whether it concerned athletics, angling, astronomy, aviation, or any other conceivable subject from "a" to "z", was always a delight to share, if only vicariously.

Either in print at Inner Temple or in discussion there, the name "David Thurlow" would keep cropping up – and always voiced in the most respectful tones. This man Thurlow was clearly among the elite of athletics enthusiasts, and I wanted to find out more about him. I knew nothing of anyone calling themselves "track NUTS" in those days, and this was hardly surprising because the organisation which was to carry that apt name was not formed until 1958, a year after Her Majesty had annoyingly required my services for two years of RAF store-room tedium. This was relieved only by inter-station cross-country every Wednesday afternoon at two of the more obscure rural retreats to which we boys-in-blue were despatched. Compton Bassett and Watton – I wish never to see their likes again.

For some years after that era of my exile, David and I pursued our various journalistic ventures the length and the breadth of the country, on behalf of both regional and national newspapers, with never a chanced crossing of paths along the way. So it was only eventually in 2002 that we at last met up at the launching in Manchester of my book about the Commonwealth Games, and from there a most rewarding friendship has developed. Munich and Gothenburg for the European Championships were a couple of prolonged excursions which we shared along the way, and this was the sort of athletics companionship that I certainly cherish most, and I'm sure that David shares that sentiment.

Maybe it's old-fashioned – well, actually, it is old-fashioned – but neither of us feel the need for frenzied stadium broadcasters bawling relentlessly at us. Nor do we require a Bolt or a Farah always on show to be convinced that we are having as much fun as these microphone martinets demand of us. Make a noise!!! Hug your neighbour!!! Wave your flag!!! Ugh!!! No, thank you very much!!! David and I are made of sterner stuff than this.

Apart, too, from those lovely, interminable chats about the merits of Wooderson and Lovelock, Nurmi and Clarke, Pirie and Viren deep into the night over a few glasses of the vineyards' finest, David has made a much wider-reaching contribution to the preservation of athletics history.

When I took over control of the NUTS quarterly journal, "Track Stats", in April of 1995, the previous editor had – for reasons best known to himself – used up every single remaining article in the files. This presumably left him with the satisfactory feeling of having gone out on a high note with a bumper issue as his legacy. Surprised, and somewhat aggrieved, I found myself starting from scratch, but help was in sight.

David began a series of articles which have been the bed-rock of the journal ever since. Most important of all, he has gone out and re-discovered athletes from the 1920s onwards. Of particular note among them are such as Jim Alford, Jack Braughton, Alec Burns, Arthur Collyer, John Disley, Peter Hildreth, Jack Holden, Derek Johnson, Bill Land, Sir Arthur Marshall, Crew Stoneley, Stuart Townend, Doug Wilson, Sydney Wooderson – all of whose voices are now sadly stilled. The prevailing theme, repeated time and again by these elderly ex-athletes in response to David's astute questioning – was that sport was great fun in their far-off athletic youth.

No doubt it was, though there are also frequent references in a resentful tone to the social divide between the Oxford and Cambridge University athletes and the working-class members of Great Britain teams in the 1930s. Very little is said by any of David's interviewees of the advance of under-developed countries in athletics over the last half-century or so, but then that trend would have been outside the direct experience of almost all of them – the oldest of the ex-internationals who David met was already 77 years of age by the time of the 1980 Olympics!

That staunchly amateur era of British athletics before and after World War II seems almost unimaginable in 2017, and full credit is due to David for recording so many vivid first-hand impressions of it whilst there was still the opportunity to do so. Now that rampant commercialism is, sadly, the driving-force of international athletics, it is marvelously refreshing to be reminded that there was once a front-rank British sprinter whose first wins of note were achieved against a future Bishop and a consultant surgeon and who promptly retired after winning an Olympic silver medal to play cricket instead. Not a likely recurrence in 2017 – times were indeed very different then.

Spurred by David's words, cinders flicking at their heels, these ghosts of the track run forever.

Bob Phillips, May 2017.

David Thurlow in 2017

Index of names

The interviews in this book were first published in Track Stats, the quarterly journal of the National Union of Track Statisticians. The publication is still going strong in its 55th year, featuring a mixture of statistics, book reviews, in-depth historical research and comment on the athletics of today. Full lists of contents and details of how to subscribe, and how to join the NUTS, may be found on the NUTS web-site at www.nuts.org.uk.

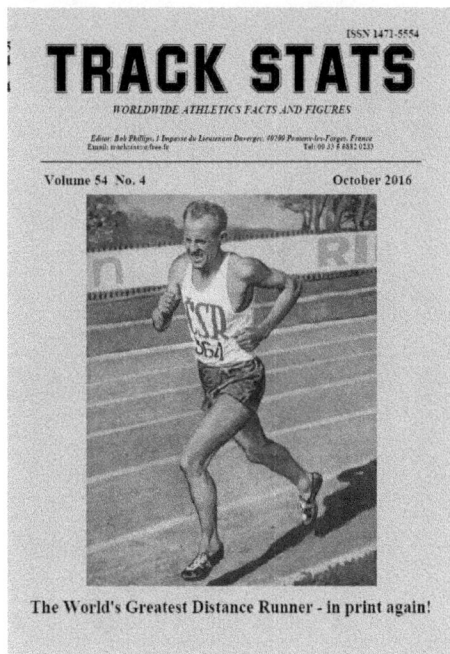

ISSN 1471-5554

TRACK STATS

WORLDWIDE ATHLETICS FACTS AND FIGURES

Editor: Bob Phillips, 1 Impasse du Lieutenant Duverger, 76190 Pommereux-les-Forges, France
Email: trackstats@free.fr   Tel: 00 33 5 8882 0233

Volume 54 No. 4   October 2016

The World's Greatest Distance Runner - in print again!

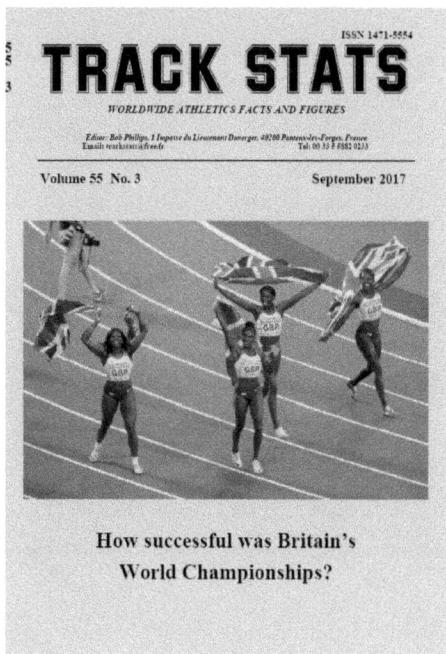

ISSN 1471-5554

TRACK STATS

WORLDWIDE ATHLETICS FACTS AND FIGURES

Editor: Bob Phillips, 1 Impasse du Lieutenant Duverger, 76190 Pommereux-les-Forges, France
Email: trackstats@free.fr   Tel: 00 33 5 8882 0233

Volume 55 No. 3   September 2017

How successful was Britain's
World Championships?

The NUTS is also publishing a series of historical and statistical books about British athletics, many covering a single event from the earliest days to the present. Recent titles include:

No. 17 - **British Athletics 1866-80** by Peter Lovesey and Keith Morbey
No. 16 - **Walks** by John Powell and Peter Matthews
No. 15 - **Heptathlon and Pentathlon** by Stuart Mazdon
No. 14 - **Decathlon** by Alan Lindop
No. 13 - **Hammer** by Ian Tempest

For full details of these and earlier titles, see the NUTS web-site, nuts.org.uk.

www.ingramcontent.com/pod-product-compliance
Lightning Source LLC
Chambersburg PA
CBHW070346090426
42733CB00009B/1310